BUREAUCRATIC POLITICS
AND ADMINISTRATION IN CHILE

Bureaucratic
Politics
and
Administration
in Chile

PETER S. CLEAVES

University of California Press

Berkeley, Los Angeles, London

University of California Press
Berkeley and Los Angeles, California

University of California Press, Ltd.
London, England

Copyright © 1974, by
The Regents of the University of California

ISBN 0-520-02448-6
Library of Congress Catalog Card Number: 73-76111
Designed by Jim Mennick
Printed in the United States of America

To Dorothy

CONTENTS

TABLES

FIGURES

PREFACE

Many students of comparative politics maintain ambivalent attitudes toward the subdiscipline of public administration. On the one hand, bureaucracy is commonly believed to be a very boring subject for analysis. The idea of administrators filling out forms, issuing contracts, and attending staff meetings does not fire the imagination as does an aggressive trade union movement, an elaborate political party system, a guerrilla uprising in the hinterland, or rapid agrarian reform. On the other hand, the most casual observer cannot avoid recognizing that almost all attempts to make a nation more productive and equitable are filtered through, or depend on, the bureaucracy. Thus public administrators cannot be ignored in any strategy for industrialization, social development, or structural upheaval.

In the past, scholarly contributions to understanding bureaucracy in low-income countries have sprung from either optimistic or pessimistic assumptions. The optimistic approach stresses the instrumental role played by national bureaucracy in the development of the country: In the absence of relative equality of power among competing groups in the society, of a progress ethic, or of sufficient economic and industrial infrastructure, bureaucracy is the only institution capable of leading the country toward developmental ends. In my opinion, much of the literature on development administration has been ethnocentric and lacking in conceptual and semantic precision.

A second approach to public administration in Third World countries has focused on the bureaucrats themselves, their values, motives, and behavior. This more pessimistic current of literature places an onerous burden of responsibility on the ethical epiderm of the individual, while neglecting significant structural factors in the administrative setting. Such a line of reasoning usually begins by noting the bureaucracy's malfunctioning, whether due to corruption, failure to make courageous decisions, empire-building, redundancy, or any of a series of other malaises. Since bureaucracy is typically made up of native-born administrators, the search for the root causes of bureaucratic deficiencies begins and sometimes ends with observations on the socialization process of the men holding administrative posts. Often, by severely exaggerating the true explanatory worth of these social variables, analyses of this type can explain almost anything their authors wish about in-country administrative behavior.

The present study of administrative processes in Chile leans away from both a generalized developmental approach and the gamesmanship of predicting behavior from imputed psychological variables. The concepts most frequently used here have more specific empirical referents than do those of either of these schools. *Bureaucracy* refers to the aggregation of state ministries, agencies, and public enterprises formally considered within executive jurisdiction. *Administrative processes* are routine and frequent bureaucratic activities that monitor, guide, or control interaction between two or more organizational entities, or between relevant publics and units of government. An array of *actors, groups, and organizations* have identifiable *goals* inside of or in association with public bureaucracy, and they have at their disposal *resources* to attempt to further their aims. If the goals of two or more groups are partially reinforcing, they may join in a *coalition* of more or less temporary duration. Whether inside or outside a coalition, actors devise *strategies* and adopt *tactics* to reach their goals. These maneuvers are more or less rational in terms of the way political resources are managed.

In my approach to this research, I first chose a number of ongoing processes that characterize bureaucracy: budgeting, planning, organizational reform, coordination, and client relations. The three chapters on budgeting and short-term planning examine these processes in the administration as a whole. However, limitations of time and finances prevented a thorough examination of reform, coordination, and client relations throughout the Chilean public and private sectors. Accordingly, for the latter half of the research I identified certain target institutions which interested me personally, were accessible for interviewing, and seemed to lend themselves to a political analysis of their activities: the ministries of Housing and Public Works, the large building contractors, and shantytown dwellers.

Via preliminary interviews and published and unpublished sources, and from my own knowledge of Chile, I listed the major issues and crises associated with these five processes in the different agencies, especially from 1964 to 1970. I then conducted open-ended interviews from one to three hours long with many of the major actors. These 150 interviews represent the empirical base of this research and provoked many comments on Chilean administration. In assembling these data in chapter form, I have attempted to double- and triple-check the facts as put forth and to insure that the final product is as fair and accurate a picture as possible of what transpired. In many chapters I have adopted the position of an armchair advocate, overtly speculating on the implications of the research for the responsibilities of leadership, induced administrative change, and greater public service to society.

The timing of my research contributed in practical terms to the study's methodology, and theoretically to its conclusions. I began my interviews in Chile the day after the election of Salvador Allende. This meant that many high-level administrators from the previous regime of Eduardo Frei received me as private citizens, or at least liberated from the code of prudent silence imposed by the responsibilities of office. At the same time, their memory of the events of the previous six years was still quite fresh. In addition, it was feasible to compare notes on the Allende regime until its overthrow, with the problems faced by Frei, and to develop propositions applicable to Chilean bureaucracy under two different governing philosophies. As this book goes to press, Chile's military rulers have initiated a wave of repression which promises to alter the past roles of the political parties and Congress, and reduce the scope of democratic choice at least over the short term. The descriptive sections of this research thus serve as a baseline study of Chilean bureaucracy before the political system entered into this authoritarian period; however, my desire has been to keep the focus on comparative bureaucracy, not on Chile.

In a certain sense I have prevailed upon the patience and goodwill of Chilean acquaintances to derive generalities from their experience to apply to other cases. For their kindness and help I am deeply grateful. In return I hope that they, and other students of Chile and Latin America, will find much in this book valuable for a historical understanding of Chilean bureaucracy, and for devising specific strategies for bureaucratic change. An earlier draft of this manuscript is in the libraries of the National Planning Office (ODEPLAN) and the Interdisciplinary Center for Urban and Regional Development (CIDU) of the Catholic University of Chile.

This research was funded by the Henry L. and Grace Doherty Fellowship Committee for 1970–71, and the Fulbright-Hays Fellowship program for 1971–72. Some of my observations on the budget were generated during my participation in a project headed by Aaron Wildavsky and Naomi Caiden, *Planning and Budgeting in Low-Income Countries,* sponsored by the Twentieth Century Fund. While in Chile, I received assistance from the Convenio Universidad de Chile–Universidad de California. Colleagues at the University of California at Berkeley—Warren F. Ilchman, Robert L. Ayres, and Francis Violich—encouraged me and provided helpful comments throughout the research and writing of this work. Giorgio Alberti, Lois Athey, Jorge Cauas, César Díaz-Muñoz, Clifford Kaufman, Gustavo Levy, Federico Lorca, Martin Scurrah, and Eugenio Yrarrázaval read portions of the text, corrected errors, and suggested modifications prior to the final draft. Juan Armijo and Katherine Hewitt generously helped type earlier drafts of the work. My wife, Dorothy Barcham Cleaves, continually offered moral support and intellectual stimulation, and gladly removed some of the excess verbosity from the text.

Without the collaboration of these persons and institutions, and of the informants who granted me time from their busy schedules, this research would not have been completed. I express my thanks to all of them and willingly credit them with much that is worthwhile in this book. Unable to incorporate all of their suggestions and observations, however, I must accept responsibility for the final product.

P. S. C.

Lima, Peru
September, 1973

LIST OF ACRONYMS

A.I.D.   Agency for International Development
CAP   Pacific Steel Company (*Compañía de Acero del Pacífico*)
CCAP   Central Savings and Loan Fund (*Caja Central de Ahorros y Préstamos*)
CCC   Chilean Construction Chamber (*Cámara Chilena de la Construcción*)
CIDU   Interdisciplinary Center for Urban and Regional Development at Chile's Catholic University (*Centro Interdisciplinario de Desarrollo Urbano y Regional*)
CORA   Agrarian Reform Corporation (*Corporación de la Reforma Agraria*)
CORFO   Development Corporation (*Corporación de Fomento de la Producción*)
CORHABIT   Corporation for Housing Services (*Corporación de Servicios Habitacionales*)
CORMU   Urban Renewal Corporation (*Corporación de Mejoramiento Urbano*)
CORVI   Housing Corporation (*Corporación de la Vivienda*)
COU   Urban Works Corporation (*Corporación de Obras Urbanas*)
DIRINCO   Industrial and Commercial Agency (*Dirección de Industria y Comercio*)
ECLA   Economic Commission for Latin America, United Nations (*Comisión Económica para la América Latina, CEPAL*)
ENAMI   National Mining Company (*Empresa Nacional de Minería*)

ENAP   National Petroleum Company (*Empresa Nacional de Petróleo*)

ENDESA   National Electricity Company (*Empresa Nacional de Electricidad, S.A.*)

ENOS   National Sanitary Works Company (*Empresa Nacional de Obras Sanitarias*)

F.V.A.S.   Housing and Social Assistance Foundation (*Fundación de Vivienda y Asistencia Social*)

INDAP   Institute for Agricultural Development (*Instituto de Desarrollo Agropecuario*)

INSORA   Institute of Administration, University of Chile (*Instituto de Administración, Universidad de Chile*)

MINVU   Ministry of Housing and Urbanism (*Ministerio de la Vivienda y Urbanismo*)

M.I.R.   Leftist Revolutionary Movement (*Movimiento de la Izquierda Revolucionaria*)

ODEPLAN   National Planning Office (*Oficina de Planificación Nacional de la Presidencia de la República*)

PAP   Popular Savings Plan (*Plan Nacional de Ahorro Popular*)

SINAP   National Savings and Loan System (*Sistema Nacional de Ahorros y Préstamos*)

1

ADMINISTRATIVE THEORY
AND THE POLITICAL SETTING
OF CHILEAN BUREAUCRACY

Alternative instruments for political action, organization, and diffusion exist in Chile. Among these are party structures, labor unions, mass media, the armed forces, peak interest associations, and even small paramilitary and indoctrination groups. Newly elected regimes, however, have usually chosen to implement their policies through the public bureaucracy.[1] One reason for this delegation of responsibility is that Chilean presidents have had little difficulty gaining bureaucracy's allegiance. Almost all middle and upper administrative posts are spoils of the new government. Though protected from summary dismissal and salary cuts, the displaced administrators from the previous regime are delegated minor tasks in which they lose almost all influence. Their experience is not tapped; they are in a position neither to initiate policy nor to sabotage it, if such were their intention. When the ruling group is unified, the objectives of the regime can be dictated to the bureaucracy with very little slippage.

Even reliable public officials, however, cannot be pointed down the road to goal achievement and expected to arrive by self-guidance and good intentions alone. Administrative subcultures permeating all complex organizations result in skewed resource flows and displaced goals at every level of authority.

This fact lies behind two very important questions about bureaucracy.

[1] In the three years of its mandate, the Allende regime depended somewhat more heavily than its predecessors on the unions, parties, and paramilitary groups to make headway on its political program (especially the expropriation of large industries and extension of agrarian reform). Simultaneously, however, pertinent public agencies attempted to consolidate the gains achieved by vanguard elements of the Unidad Popular.

First, what elements internal to an organization explain administrative behavior? Second, what is the relationship between changes in an agency's setting and its internal operations? This book, treating these inquiries as central themes, examines how organizations can be controlled, reinforced, or enervated for the implementation or thwarting of public policy. It proceeds from a consideration of generic features of organization to a series of case studies that generate propositions with comparative applicability. These case studies show that Chilean public agencies compete over scarce resources and often take advantage of supportive outside groups to maintain or increase their operating capacity. The strategies and tactics employed by clients and public agencies to gain an upper hand in bureaucracy and to mitigate the power of competitors have demonstrable effects on administrative processes such as budgeting, planning, coordination, and reform. They also have connotations for executive behavior, goal mutation, and organizational productivity.

The theoretical construct used in this book assumes that all organizations share at least three common features: resources, goals, and environment. *Resources* are elements of power valued for their exchangeability in the satisfaction of perceived wants. Organizational *goals* describe a future state of affairs denoting material objects or tangible services. Often overall institutional goals are not easily distinguished from inwardly oriented objectives (e.g., personal welfare, job security), which induce cooperation from the organizational members, and other functional ends (e.g., efficiency, effectiveness) important for maintenance and survival.[2]

Environment refers to those entities with their own resources and goals which operate outside the boundaries of the organization under study. Organizations are most sensitive to the activities of reference groups or clients in their *task* or immediate environment who exchange resources with the organization in function of their perceived interests. In addition, cyclical or sudden events in the organization's *contextual* or general environment may alter the availability of resources to both clients and the organization, fundamentally changing the nature of their interaction.

ADMINISTRATIVE THEORY

This book owes a heavy intellectual debt to a number of well-known treatises on general organizational theory. These authors and

[2] Lawrence B. Mohr has usefully summarized the relevant literature in "The Concept of Organizational Goal." He views organizational goals as multiple rather than unitary, empirical rather than imputed, and dichotomized into outwardly and inwardly oriented, or "transitive" (functional) and "reflexive" (institutional), categories.

their work are discussed in greater detail below. An equally important influence, however, has been the inability of much comparative administrative theory to answer basic questions on Chilean bureaucracy satisfactorily. I have found it necessary to reject two of the most common approaches to comparative administration because of their lack of explanatory power and their apparent biases. The "detrimental values" school attributes bureaucratic rigidity and conservatism to the bureaucrat's socialization within a particular cultural milieu, which implies that poor countries pretty much deserve the bureaucracy with which they are plagued, because bureaucratic values mirror those of society as a whole. Alternatively, the writings on development administration decry the technical incapacity of something arbitrarily called "development administration" to reach the unspecified but presumably desirable goals of development. To place this book in perspective, therefore, this first chapter reviews several propositions purporting to explain individual behavior in bureaucracy and bureaucracy's relation to Third World societies. Contrasting these efforts with the concepts, and their empirical referents, employed in subsequent chapters makes my approach more explicit and introduces a certain amount of background information on Chilean bureaucracy.

The "Previous Socialization" *Theory*

A number of writers have used cultural and class values to describe less laudatory aspects of non-Anglo-Saxon bureaucracy. Lucian Pye's perspective on the Burmese bureaucrats, for example, stems from his observation that they suffered from three serious shortcomings in administering the government's polity: ambivalence over the nature and forms of progress and modernization; profound confusion over the difference between ritual and rationality in administrative operations; and, most important, a fundamental, all-pervasive lack of communication within the bureaucracy.[3] During his inquiry into Burmese personality, Pye discerned two Oriental cultural traits that served as foundations for much of his analysis: the Burmese was highly motivated by the contradictory social forces of *awza* and *an-ah-deh*.[4] *Awza*—similar to power, influence, and prestige—led the male to try to aggrandize himself in relation to his peers. Concurrently, the Burmese was severely restrained in his outward aggressiveness by *an-ah-deh*, probably best translated as selflessness, or generosity and meekness before his fellow human beings.

If in the Burmese administration there was a search for status, crippling lack of communication, poor coordination, exaggerated corruption,

---

[3] Lucian W. Pye, *Politics, Personality, and Nation-Building: Burma's Search for Identity*, p. 213.
[4] Pye, pp. 146–150.

form without substance, and an obsession with personal popularity and career mobility, *awza* was probably at fault. If at the same time there was insecurity, fear of face-to-face relations, intention without deeds, indecision, suspicion and mistrust, inconsequential actions, ritualism, loneliness, and fatalism, *an-ah-deh* was to blame.[5] These values were not necessarily mutually exclusive, and many of the problems of the Burmese bureaucrat issued from the fact that these driving forces had to be reconciled, no matter how painful the internalization process.

Though he discusses structural constraints, Fred Riggs also prefers to explain administrative behavior through value patterns prevalent in Third World society.[6] For Riggs, overlapping, fossilization, and attenuation in bureaucracy result from the fact that administrators are subjected to contradictory social forces. They are inextricably caught in the ambiguity of more modern (diffracted) and traditional (fused) value orientations. Incapable of coping with the movement toward modernity, they reflect a curious duality in their behavior, resulting in an epidemic of characteristics typical of "prismatic" or transitional bureaucracy: attainment rather than achievement, "clects" (a combination of sects and cliques), selectivism, polyfunctionalism, formalism, nonenforcement, double-talk, administrative prodigality, nepotism, and normlessness.

One problem with this approach is that any administrative pattern imaginable can be attributed to one of these two value strains. The authors were remiss in not indicating why *awza* and *an-ah-deh,* or fusion and "prismatism," did not motivate behavior highly appropriate for a goal-oriented bureaucracy. The former might have spawned decisiveness, perseverance, bold decision-making, courage in the face of attack, experimentation, and emphasis on personal excellence; while the latter might have increased the frequency of honest, generous, and modestly confident bureaucrats in public administration. Each author selected the most detrimental manifestations of each tendency in describing his subjects, which leads one to question the validity or desirability of this approach for replicable research.

Their attempt was reminiscent of early psychosociological attempts to explain why the Hispanic American "race" was incapable of keeping up with Northern Europe and the United States during the nineteenth century. For many writers the answer lay in the pathological mixture of the

[5] Pye made the critical assumption that because these bureaucrats who were confused, ritualistic, and noncommunicative were also Burmese, these characteristics could be traced to the local socialization process. There was not a corresponding attempt to determine if being Burmese was a sufficient or even a necessary condition for these characteristics to predominate in bureaucracy.

[6] Fred Riggs, *Administration in Developing Countries: The Theory of Prismatic Society.*

bad traits of both Indian and Spaniard after the conquest. The intention and method of one of these authors, Carlos Octavio Bunge in *Nuestra América,* were very similar to those of Lucian Pye:

The practical objective of this work is to describe, with all of its vices and peculiarities, the political life of the Hispanic American peoples. In order to understand it, I must first penetrate the collective psychology that engenders it.[7]

Bunge deduced that the colonial Spaniard was ritualistic, conformist, arrogant, indolent, and discordant. He intermarried with the Indian, who was fatalistic, passive, and vengeful. The unfortunate cultural progeny was a Latin American oriented toward laziness, sadness, and arrogance.[8] The concrete manifestations of this mixture were "creole laziness" (*pereza criolla*)—responsible for an absence of activity, discipline, method, and work hygiene—and "creole fibbing" (*mentira criolla*)—a morbid tendency to exaggerate and a total lack of precision. Perhaps overly infatuated with his schema, Bunge could not resist lambasting fellow Latin Americans for their "psychological disharmony," "degenerate semi-sterility," "disregard for the law," "lack of a moral sense," and tendencies toward envy, literary sophistication, inconstancy, melancholy, and napoleonism. In this case, *caudillismo* (tyranny) was a direct outcome of *pereza criolla*. In a situation of social laziness, it was only natural that the most active and venal should rise to the top.

From a different angle, but still dealing in values, James Petras attempted to explain bureaucratic output in Chile by the social background of the bureaucracy's administrative elites.[9] Basing his observations on a large-scale survey carried out in 1965, he concluded that: (1) Chilean bureaucrats were not oriented toward "development"; (2) the lower-class members of the Chilean bureaucracy were more likely to hold modern and progressive attitudes; and (3) the upper reaches of the administration tended to be characterized by uniquely conservative postures toward social change—all of which could be explained through the bureaucrat's social background. The administrator's position

on issues tends to be related to the social stratum into which he was born. The bureaucracy may be organized rationally . . . but social background still determines attitudes.[10]

---

[7] Carlos Octavio Bunge, *Nuestra América*, p. 51. The first edition was published in 1903. See also works by Agustín Alvarez and José Ingenieros.
[8] It is remarkable how widespread this interpretation has been in Chile, among all strata of society.
[9] James Petras, *Politics and Social Forces in Chilean Development*.
[10] Petras, p. 290.

Substantiation of this argument depended on the existence of significantly different attitudes toward social change among the upper and lower members of the bureaucracy. The data presented, however, were hardly apodictic; despite differences in class and hierarchy, orientations within bureaucratic subgroups were remarkably similar, as Table 1 indicates. If the administrative elite were self-interested, so were the service and unskilled personnel; if the professionals and technicians saw the best hope for the country in a traditional liberal education, so did the office workers; if the semiprofessionals were severely harmed by runaway inflation, the same could be said for the technical assistants.

Petras mentioned two agencies in the Chilean bureaucracy which were actively pursuing innovative goals at the time he conducted his research. To substantiate his argument, he contrasted the preferences of the administrative elites with the performance of the Agrarian Reform Corporation (CORA) and the Institute for Agricultural Development (INDAP).

Thus, the reforms supported by the elite for the campesinos are not the structural reforms advocated by CORA or INDAP (the government's agrarian-reform agencies) but incremental changes pursued by Radical-party governments.[11]

The admission that upper-middle-class administrators in CORA and INDAP used their organization for change makes it difficult for the author to sustain his thesis that class background is a predominant influence on the orientation of Chilean public agencies. Indeed, Petras' study suggests that many administrative characteristics are determined more by vertical than by horizontal factors. That is, competition between agencies is often a more important indicator of bureaucracy's impact on society than are the relations between superiors and subordinates in separate administrative entities.

Petras jumped all the way from manifest class values to organizational output (development-oriented administrative behavior) in one move. Pye and Riggs made a quantum leap in their analyses from esoteric cultural and religious values to bureaucratic behavior, completely skipping over or minimizing the structural factors affecting career uncertainty, the rewards for indecision, the disincentives for individualism, the fear of censure, and the obligatory conformity to administrative routine. If Pye and Riggs explained everything through their own brands of *yin* and *yang*, they may have explained very little. Bureaucratic apathy, indecisiveness, torpor, a desire for status accrual, poor communication and coordination, extensive formalism, cynicism, and general wariness of

---

[11] Petras, p. 292.

TABLE 1. COMMITMENT TO SOCIAL CHANGE: HIGH-PRIORITY RATING
OF ISSUES AMONG STRATA OF BUREAUCRACY
(*In percent*)

	Issues					
Strata of Bureaucracy	Education	*Agrarian Reform*	*Copper Reform*	*Full Employ-ment*	Housing	Inflation
Administrative Elite	45	2	0	9	0	39
Professionals and Technicians	45	2	11	11	3	28
Semiprofessionals	39	6	8	10	1	36
Office Workers	48	1	8	7	1	34
Technical Assistants	44	3	2	11	5	35
Service and Unskilled	46	3	5	16	3	25
Bureaucracy as a Whole	44	3	7	11	3	32

SOURCE: James Petras, *Politics and Social Forces in Chilean Development*, p. 333.

other administrative units are hardly unique to Third World bureaucracy. There is little in these analyses which proves that cultural or class values are the most important, or even one of the more plausible, explanations of why bureaucrats act the way they do.

The "Development Administration" Approach

Works imputing behavioral propensities to administrators on the basis of criteria enthetic to bureaucracy have provided few links between culture (or class), personality, role, role-set, and bureaucratic structure, precisely because they have not considered individual inducements within the organizational context. The "development administrative" literature, an alternative approach to studying comparative bureaucracy, has been deficient in defining bureaucratic goals and administrative structure and assaying their effect on the fulfillment of social ends.[12]

In studies of development administration, the principal independent

[12] See, for example, Ferrel Heady and Sybil L. Stokes (eds.), *Papers in Comparative Public Administration*; Martin Kriesberg (ed.), *Public Administration in Developing Countries*; Dwight Waldo (ed.), *Temporal Dimensions of Development Administration*; James Heaphey (ed.), *Spatial Dimensions of Development Administration*; Edward W. Weidner (ed.), *Development Administration in Asia*.

variable is the activity and output of administration, while the dependent variable is development itself.[13] Operationalizing these variables for research has proved almost impossible, for two reasons. First, the approach transforms administration into a general concept called "development administration," which tends to remove bureaucratic units from an empirical base and infer to them standard goals that often do not withstand close scrutiny. Second, this approach does not treat development as a concept, but as a concrete fact. The vulgarization of "development" conjures up the impression that everyone knows exactly what the term means. But that is hardly the case.[14] Even though academicians have con-

---

[13] What is meant by *development administration* can be culled from several quotes on the subject. "Development administration in government refers to the processes of guiding an organization toward the achievement of progressive political, economic, and social objectives that are authoritatively determined in one manner or another." "Development can be described as a concerted effort in various interrelated fields leading toward high forms of social and economic life." Its administration is a "continuous process of formulating, reformulating, and implementing a set of related plans, programs, operations, activities, and undertakings directed at realizing stated developmental ends in a prescribed time sequence by optimal means." "It is necessary to modernize parliaments, to make the executive versatile, to shake the bureaucrats out of their routine, to revamp the tax and budget systems, to mobilize all moral, intellectual, and economic forces in an effort to attain projected goals. All this poses a challenge to public administration. Up to now we have given attention to planning for development, but very little to the administration of development."

"The study of development administration can help to identify the conditions under which a maximum rate of development is sought and the conditions under which it has been attained." "As a part of the policy sciences, the end-object of such research would be to relate different administrative roles, practices, organizational arrangements, and procedures to the maximizing of development objectives. Interest in personnel, budgeting, and O and M would be confined to a study of the manner in which these aspects of administration contribute to or negate development. In research terms, the ultimate dependent variable would be the development goals themselves." The student of "development administration can help discover which [developmental goals] under what circumstances seem to lead most fully to the achievement of development objectives." In order, these quotes are by Edward W. Weidner in Heady and Stokes, *Papers* (p. 98); Aryeh Attir (p. 79), Donald Stone (pp. 54–55), and Guillermo Nannetti (p. 2) in Kriesberg, *Public Administration*; and Weidner (pp. 99, 103, and 99–100) in Heady and Stokes.

[14] John Gunnell has pointed out that a considerable step lies between the definitions of development and its operationalization for scientific research: "It is unlikely that we shall succeed in clarifying our ideas about development administration until we arrive at a more meaningful concept or theoretical definition of development." He adds that in discussion of development, "there is often either an immediate redefinition in terms of another concept such as 'modernization,' 'industrialization,' 'Westernization,' 'self-sustained growth,' 'structural differentiation,' and/or a shift to a consideration of the requisite conditions, causes, goals, or impact of development. Although this *may* be quite relevant, development in the end seems to connote much, whereas its denotation is vague and its defining characteristics tend to remain unspecified." Gunnell, "Development, Social Change, and Time," in Dwight Waldo (ed.), *Temporal Dimensions,* pp. 48–49.

sumed reams describing, subdividing, categorizing, and then reconciling the different components of development (such as economic growth, mobilization, and institutionalization), the nature of the concept remains as controversial and varied as before.[15] The use of such indefinite concepts in both the independent and dependent variables may mean that no proposition can ever be put forth linking "development administration" with "development" in any meaningful way.[16]

It is precisely this vagueness that enables national elites to use the term "development" to disguise the true extent of their commitment to innovation. Even when leadership declares that certain parts of the bureaucracy have been elected to carry out policies connoting far-reaching change, the battle is only half won. What is often not visible is the continual wrestling match between the chosen agencies and other bureaucratic units over very scarce resources. The aims of the traditional units of government may not be patently "anti-developmentalist," but because of the nature of complex bureaucracy, some overt or covert conflicts are inevitable. Semantic aspects of the competition need never refer to change or social justice. Discussion usually revolves around more technical items, such as the quality of essential services, the return on investment, fiscal equilibrium, full employment, or monetary stability.[17]

The relative productivity of bureaucratic units is ultimately a function of their access to resources, and their resource base in part is an outcome of bureaucratic politics. When technical discussion over fiscal equilibrium, full employment, or monetary stability evolves into politics,

[15] I feel that the concept of development is not very useful for conducting in-depth research on specific bureaucracies, since bureaucracy apart from the nature of its goals does little or nothing different when it contributes to development from when it does not. Usually it serves little purpose to consider a bureaucracy in the abstract, as an integral whole acting on society as a single force. Rather, it is more appropriate to conceive of it as divided in goals, resources, and skills, and having a variable impact depending on its field of activity and institutional coherence. Compare with Charles Perrow, *Organizational Analysis: A Sociological View*, p. vii.

[16] "Development administration" as first introduced in the literature is employed here as an example of the type of systems-level theorizing that relates to neither resources nor structure, and only vaguely to purposes. This approach has now mutated into a new form with greater conceptual rigor and policy implications. See Joseph Eaton (ed.), *Institution Building and Development: From Concepts to Application*, especially the contribution by Milton Esman. While "institution-building" emphasizes purposeful administrative behavior and resource management, its theoretical relevancy is unnecessarily weakened by deliberate ignoring of the effects of violence on administration, or coercion on society—which, though distasteful subjects, give considerable insight into administrative behavior in a turbulent environment.

[17] James Q. Wilson has pointed out that "of all the groups interested in bureaucracy, those concerned with fiscal integrity usually play the winning hand." Wilson, "The Bureaucratic Problem," in Alan A. Altshuler (ed.), *The Politics of the Federal Bureaucracy*, p. 28.

the agency attempting to implement innovative policies tends to be at a disadvantage. It is usually newer, less allied with powerful clients in the political community, often staffed by younger personnel—and, most important, dealing in areas of social action where the marginal utility of investment is difficult to measure in economic terms. If it has little money, few qualified personnel, and stringent legislation, and is abandoned by political leadership when it requests cooperation or runs into trouble in the outside world, its impact cannot be very great. Likewise, if traditional agencies are financially solvent and have consistent political support, prestige inside and outside of government, and wide legal latitude, they are more likely to respond to and reinforce special interests or social purposes consistent with their organizational goals. While the concept of "development administration" is too soft a tool for analytical precision, it is quite probable that "administration for *non*developmental ends" is a fair description of the majority of public bureaucracies.

How did agencies within Chilean bureaucracy rank in terms of these criteria? Figure 1 tentatively distributes the most important public organizations in the Chilean government according to the amount of political support they enjoyed during the 1960's and whether their institutional goals denoted social change. The figure indicates that within Chilean bureaucracy many of the *less* innovative units tended to profit from greater political backing. A majority of the agencies called "innovative" clustered together in a condition of low general support.

At least two observations can be made concerning Figure 1. First, despite the disadvantages of change-oriented agencies, Chilean bureaucracy on the whole during this period should not be considered stagnant. Agriculture, Housing, and Education affected large segments of the population and acted as aggressive change agents in the society, not to mention the less dramatic contributions of Health, Planning, and the other agencies not receiving such consistent support.

Second, it is impossible to ignore the interrelationships of individual agencies in the study of comparative administration. For instance, one of the more common ways for an organization to consolidate its operating influence within a sector is to be classified as a *decentralized agency*. In Chile, these organizations were also known as semi-fiscal, autonomous corporations, or state industries. Decentralized agencies profited from direct authority links to the president of the country; they usually had a large percentage of guaranteed revenue; they were liberated from sending their regulatory decrees to the General Comptroller's office for prior approval; they could change their organizational chart and number of personnel without going through Congress; and they could set their

FIGURE 1.   THE POTENTIAL INNOVATIVE IMPACT OF CHILEAN
BUREAUCRACY

	Less Innovative Goals	More Innovative Goals
More Political Resources	Finance 1 Interior Public Works National Defense Mines General Comptroller	2 Agriculture Housing Education
Fewer Political Resources	Lands and 3 Colonization Foreign Relations Justice	4 Health Labor Planning Economy

salary scales above the levels in the centralized portion of government. Decentralized agencies, and those centralized agencies preferring autonomous status, claimed that they need to carry out their functions with extensive institutional "agility" to respond more quickly to changes in their environments and to perform their functions with fewer bureaucratic hindrances.

The more influential agencies in Chilean bureaucracy are identified by the criterion of political support for their activities, often reflected in their decentralized status. The rule of thumb is that decentralized agencies in high-priority sectors are considerably more influential than their centralized counterparts in low-priority ministries. This rule leads to an ordinal power scale which, though not perfectly consistent throughout government, is helpful in predicting the outcome of internal bureaucratic competition. The organizations with the most favorable configuration of resources during the period studied are the decentralized agencies in boxes 1 and 2 in Figure 1 (such as the Central Bank, INDAP, and CORA). They are followed by the decentralized agencies in boxes 3 and 4 and centralized agencies in boxes 1 and 2 (such as the Development

Corporation, CORFO, the National Health Service, and Public Works).[18] Finally, the least favored are the centralized agencies in boxes 3 and 4 (such as the Department of Prisons, Indigenous Affairs, and the Labor Arbitration Board).

The concepts of "development administration" have not been useful in focusing attention on factors such as these which appear to be crucial for estimating the impact of bureaucracy on society.

POLITICAL ECONOMY AND PUBLIC ADMINISTRATION

In my opinion, the two approaches to comparative administration examined above do not hold the prospect of either contributing to integrated and comprehensive theory or serving as guides for policy implementation. Class and value differences between and within bureaucracies may contribute so little to explaining administrative behavior that analysts might do well to lump them together with other unexplained and unmeasured factors in the error term of some hypothetical equation. Moreover, variations in bureaucracy's relationship with society from country to country appear to be differences more of degree than of kind.[19] One might argue that Riggsian neoterisms derived from observations in Asia are useful for describing the "disintegration" of Anglo-Saxon administration.[20] I am convinced, however, that a more promising strategy is to refine and build on the wealth of concepts and insights in classical North American and European administrative theory to study bureaucracy everywhere.

[18] With the arrival of the Allende regime, the ministry of Economy gained new stature vis-a-vis Finance, because of the prestige of the minister and the key role Economy played in the expropriation of large industries. As a result, one could say that Economy (and CORFO) then moved up to box 2 while Finance (and the Central Bank) fell to box 3.

[19] This idea is consistent with a quote by Charles Parrish: "It is hoped that this divorcing of organizational concepts and political development theory may be beneficial and may, if pursued, provide a greater understanding of the similarity of the problems presented by organizations in society, whether that society is a rich, industrialized one such as the United States, or a relatively poor, industrializing one such as Chile." Parrish, "Bureaucracy, Democracy, and Development: Some Considerations Based on the Chilean Case," last page.

[20] In arguing "that the work accomplished by Riggs and others is at this point in time of great practical relevance to the conditions of American political-administrative life," Kenneth Jowitt referred to the fact that "many of the phenomena which supposedly characterize underdeveloped or backward states are currently visible in 'postindustrial,' 'end of ideology' America." He felt that the "form" of Riggs' theory is appropriate for generating a conceptual breakthrough necessary for raising consciousness and highlighting the political, cultural, and ideological variables in decision-making settings. Jowitt, "Comment: The Relevance of Comparative Public Administration," in Frank Marini (ed.), *Toward a New Publc Administration: The Minnowbrook Perspective*, pp. 250–260.

What follows is not an exhaustive review of classical organizational theory.[21] The main purpose of the exercise is to identify and characterize the concepts most commonly used in this study of Chilean bureaucracy, such as *resources, structure, hierarchy, goals, tactical exchange,* and *environment.* Except for the concept of contextual environment, the reader will find few empirical referents specific to the Chilean case in the next few pages. Nevertheless, he should keep these concepts in mind for the sake of clarifying the subsequent empirical chapters concerning inter-organizational competition over the Chilean budget, short-term planning, administrative reform, and certain types of client relations. The development of this construct continues in Chapter 9 with a number of propositions summarizing the work as a whole.

An emphasis on resources and strategies places this research in a more general body of literature called *political economy.* Charles Anderson, who has written extensively on Latin America, notes one of the important principles of the new political economy when he states that every "government, after all, has a finite quantity of resources at its disposal. Its capacity to effect change cannot be greater than the resources available to the society of which it is a part." [22] Warren Ilchman and Norman Uphoff have developed a model which makes political economy especially relevant to the study of Third World Countries.

Each regime is differentially endowed with a supply of resources. Combined in policies, resources are the means by which a regime induces or coerces compliance in order to implement its objectives for the policy. Policies of different regimes can be compared over time and among countries on the basis of the comparative efficiency of different combinations of resources. These resources, and their currencies, used or withheld, constitute the regime's factors of political production.[23]

Authors using the political economy approach have tended to emphasize the relationships between political leadership and the various organ-

---

[21] The eclectic discussion of these authors cannot do justice to their arguments. Their contribution even to the approach used here goes much beyond that recorded explicitly on the following pages, and I refer the reader to the original works.

[22] Charles W. Anderson, *Politics and Economic Change in Latin America,* p. 4. See also R. L. Curry, Jr., and L. L. Wade, *A Theory of Political Exchange: Economic Reasoning in Political Analysis.*

[23] Warren F. Ilchman and Norman T. Uphoff, *The Political Economy of Change,* p. 32. Mayer N. Zald has attempted to apply political economy to the study of bureaucracy in his "Political Economy: A Framework for Comparative Analysis," in Zald (ed.), *Power in Organizations,* pp. 221–261. Zald joined with Gary L. Wamsley in "The Political Economy of Public Organizations." Also see Jerry L. Weaver, "Bureaucracy during a Period of Social Change: The Guatemalan Case"; Gary W. Wynia, *Politics and Planners: Economic Development Policy in Central America;* and Oscar Oszlak, *Diagnóstico de la Administración Pública Uruguaya.*

ized sectors of the society. One of these sectors is public administration itself, which can facilitate or frustrate the government's ultimate aims. However, there is no implied restriction within political economy making complex bureaucracy a consistent and unified whole. Competition among bureaucratic units comes to the fore throughout the process of policy-making and in the subsidizing and implementation of programs. In the quotes above, substituting the words "group" or "agency" for "government" and "regime" helps relate political economy to bureaucratic politics among and within agencies, between agencies and political leadership, between clients and agencies, and between relevant publics and political leadership, through bureaucracy.

Inducements and Resources

Chester Barnard's main concern in his book *The Functions of the Executive* was with the inducements for individuals to join and cooperate in organizations. He identified two characteristics of persons which were similar to organizational attributes: the individual's *powers* in the situation, and his *determination* or volition within the limits set by his powers.[24] Barnard joined questions of power and purpose throughout his discussion of incentives and inducements to cooperation. He noted that above a subsistence level, the "opportunities for distinction, prestige, personal power, and the attainment of dominating position are much more important than material rewards in the development of all sorts of organizations. . . ." [25] The "economy of incentives," or the calculation of the "precise combination of incentives and of persuasion that will be both effective and feasible, is a matter of great delicacy." [26]

Herbert Simon was more explicit than Barnard in recognizing the crucial role of resources as primary, though not irreducible, elements of organization. Simon treated authority as a tool which in strategic combination with other resources can achieve compliance-related aims, such as permitting coordination of activity and securing information in making decisions.[27] Information too is a marketable resource which often serves personal and group interests. It

tends to be transmitted upward in the organization only if (1) its transmission will not have unpleasant consequences for the transmitter, or (2) the superior will hear of it anyway from other channels, and it is better to tell him first, or (3) it is information that the superior needs in his dealings with his own superiors, and he will be displeased if he is caught without it. . . .

---

[24] Chester I. Barnard, *The Functions of the Executive,* p. 39.
[25] Barnard, p. 145.
[26] Barnard, p. 158.
[27] Herbert A. Simon, *Administrative Behavior,* p. 126.

There is a converse problem that arises when a superior [uses] his exclusive possession of information as a means of maintaining his authority over the subordinate.[28]

One of the advantages of political economy is that it differentiates resources into manageable forms; viewing them as factors of production relates them to societal goals or purposes. In bureaucratic studies, groups and individuals inside and outside of the organization have resources that define their power capabilities. For Ilchman and Uphoff, the resources of the regime (or leadership) have counterparts in the various sectors (or agencies).[29]

Regime Resources	Sector Resources
Authority	Legitimacy
Economic goods and services	Economic goods and services
Coercion	Violence
Information	Information
Status	Status

Organizations contain different combinations of resources which, when managed and quantified, constitute their power capability in the environment.[30]

This juxtaposition is helpful in clarifying Barnard's concept of authority. He believes "the decision as to whether an order has authority or not lies with the person to whom it is addressed, and does not reside in persons of authority or those who issue these orders." [31] This use of the term "authority" turns out to be inconsistent when an order is accepted by some and not by others. Also, one may agree that rightful authorities exist in certain domains, but still not follow orders (e.g., *"Obedezco pero no cumplo"*). Accordingly, this treatment of authority differs from Barnard's by distinguishing between the resources of those who *emit* orders and those who *submit* to them. Within bureaucracy,

---

[28] Simon, p. 163. Given the widespread use of confidential files, the need to smooth over personal relations among employees, and the benefits accruing from timely rather than precipitous announcements, Simon's contention that withholding of information is symptomatic of an "incompetent and insecure executive" seems to me too harsh.

[29] Ilchman and Uphoff, *Political Economy*, p. 58. The conceptual distinction between regime and sector resources can be used to analyze interaction within the regime, so long as there is a formal hierarchy present. Upper-level bureaucrats generally use the equivalent of regime resources in managing their subordinates, while those low in the hierarchy utilize the equivalent of sector resources in dealing with their superiors.

[30] Amitai Etzioni drew an intriguing construct from this basic idea in *A Comparative Analysis of Complex Organizations.*

[31] Barnard, *Functions*, p. 163.

authority involves the right to issue directives that change the conduct of persons formally subjected to them. To the extent that this right is legitimated by relevant groups, the weight of *effective authority* approaches the scope of formal authority. Legitimacy connotes acceptance and support. Subordinates can accord or deny legitimacy to authority positions, their occupants, or the decisions they emit. Regular refusals to comply usually constitute a *de facto* denial of legitimacy to the superior position, which does not automatically negate formal authority but certainly reduces its effective weight.

In most situations the amount of legitimacy flowing up the hierarchy exceeds the amount of authority flowing downward, because superiors generally use other inducements or sanctions to secure continued compliance from subordinates. As we will learn later, even when Chilean planners have had access to formal authority, their inability to mobilize complementary political resources helps explain their difficulties in monitoring and guiding programs in the public bureaucracy.

Resource Exchange

Extremely important to this analysis is the idea of resource exchange, conceived to be at the core of bureaucratic dynamics and a clue to the form of organizational structure. Peter M. Blau, in *Exchange and Power in Social Life,* identified two conditions necessary for human behavior to lead to social change: "It must be oriented towards ends that can only be achieved through interaction with other persons, and it must seek to adapt means to further the achievement of these ends." [32] "Exchange processes, then, give rise to differentiation of power." [33] Persons and organizations sometimes aspire to and successfully do monopolize certain resources or exchange channels by which they establish a hegemonic advantage.[34] Regardless of the level of power concentration, resource flow is seldom unidirectional; subordinate agents both contribute and receive, although in some cases a closed market may cheapen their resources considerably.[35]

Blau's concept of social exchange was limited to actions "contingent on rewarding reactions from others (that cease when these actions are not forthcoming)." [36] The principle is that "one person does another a favor, and while there is a general expectation of some future return, its

---

[32] Peter M. Blau, *Exchange and Power in Social Life,* p. 4.
[33] Blau, p. 39.
[34] Karl Wittfogel, *Oriental Despotism: A Comparative Study in Total Power.*
[35] See Riggs, *Administration,* pp. 105–116, for a discussion of this phenomenon.
[36] Blau, p. 6.

exact nature is definitely *not* stipulated in advance." [37] The constricted parameters of the construct compelled Blau to exclude *economic exchange* and *physical coercion* from the gamut of social transactions he considered.[38] Much of Blau's analysis, therefore, is not directly relevant to bureaucracy, because of the prevalence of economic inducements and coercion in policy-making.[39]

Though William Foote Whyte was not specific in labeling major resource flows in bureaucracy, he went a step further than Blau in developing a particular nomenclature for exchange theory. In a two-actor figure based on his extensive observations of people working in cooperative arrangements, Whyte paid close attention to rewards, punishments, sequence, and duration.[40]

In Whyte's term, Blau was discussing positive exchange (a favor or service with indefinite reciprocal obligations). Whyte also considered trading (voluntary exchange in which resources are always different and explicit); joint payoff (similar rewards and penalties apply to each actor, and these rewards-penalties are provided by individuals, groups, or organizations outside of the immediate joint-payoff situation); competitive zero-sumness, negative exchange, and open conflict (each uses his resources to damage the other); and bargaining. (See Figure 2.) The reader will later recognize that some client relations between bureaucracy and private interest groups in Chile were typical of *joint payoff,* and that budgetary transactions were characterized by *trading* and *competitive zero-sumness.* Presidential style in managing the Chilean bureaucracy has often been based on *positive exchange,* whereas certain political actors, such as poor residents of urban areas, have sometimes found *open conflict* a suitable means for obtaining short-term benefits from the public sector.

[37] Blau, p. 93.

[38] Blau, pp. 94, 91.

[39] Pye (pp. 165–166) recognized that violence sometimes impinges on bureaucracy, yet his discussion of that fact seems to lack empathy. "The enthusiasm of the administrators in describing the violent ways of the politicians reflected their need . . . to justify their own inabilities to act more effectively. They felt that by accepting the prevalence of violence they explained fully why rational administration programs are impossible in Burma. . . . Thus the administrator can attribute his feelings of insecurity, inadequacy, and hesitation in action to the fact that he lives in an environment in which physical danger is a realistic threat. . . ." Even if *an-ah-deh* were as powerful an independent variable as Pye suggests, it is difficult to imagine a bureaucracy in which the good possibility of violent physical harm would not have a sobering effect on the attitudes of the bureaucrats.

[40] William F. Whyte, *Organizational Behavior: Theory and Application,* pp. 148 ff.

FIGURE 2.   A NOMENCLATURE FOR SEVEN EXCHANGE SITUATIONS

Type	Net Value Balances For A	For B	Temporal Forms
1. Positive Exchange	+	+	Alternating
2. Trading	+	+	Simultaneous
3. Joint Payoff	+	+	Simultaneous, continuing
4. Competitive Zero-Sum	(a) +	−	Simultaneous
	(b) −	−	
5. Negative Exchange	−	−	Alternating
6. Open Conflict	(a) −	−	Simultaneous, continuing
	(b) +	−	
7. Bargaining (usually combination of above types)	(a) −	−	Simultaneous, continuing
	(b) +	−	
	(c) +	+	

SOURCE: Modified slightly from William F. Whyte, *Organizational Behavior*, p. 149.

Individual, Group, and Organizational Goals

Michel Crozier, in his study *The Bureaucratic Phenomenon,* presumed that human agents take advantage of all means to further their own privileges.[41] He discovered within organizational units variable combinations and quantities of resources which, when transacted, tended to further and protect the interests of those in possession of them, sometimes with deleterious effects on the organization as a whole. For example, Crozier observed that predictability of behavior decreased each unit's bargaining power—which, contrarily, could subsequently be restored by withholding resources critical for fulfilling organizational functions or the ambitions of competing groups. Within the limits imposed by cultural codes, each actor strove to control the conditions of resource exchange, either to create uncertainty for others or decrease it for himself.[42] Crozier's observations on the control of uncertainty appear to be generally applicable to organizational transactions in Chilean bureaucracy—for example, in the period studied, during the budgetary cycle. By monitoring the flow of information and economic resources, different actors in the budgetary process attempted to manage uncertainty at key points for the furtherance of their institutional objectives.

Simon realized that in pyramidal organizations, groups at different

[41] Michel Crozier, *The Bureaucratic Phenomenon,* p. 194.
[42] Crozier, pp. 161–167.

levels in the hierarchy tend to have different orienting principles. If Crozier's low-level administrators are concerned about their working conditions, Simon's executives reflect on value questions and alternative ways to transmit decisional premises or operating norms downward through several levels of intermediate supervisors until they reach the technical core.[43] While the productivity of the organization may depend on the effectiveness of the technical core, the success of the executives generally depends on the fate of the organization in the environment. Combining Simon and Crozier, one would expect persons at various locations in bureaucracy to employ different strategies and resources for goal-oriented action. This observation helps explain the behavior of groups at different hierarchical levels who are attempting to resist administrative reform, as in the Chilean housing sector in 1965.

In *Organizations in Action,* James Thompson rejected an abstract reification ("group mind") of organizational goals, nor was he convinced that they represent the accumulated interests of group members. He preferred to view them as an imagined state of affairs (i.e., the unit's range of products, services rendered, or populations served) that can be attained or approached through organizational activity.[44] Political economy would emphasize that organizational goals have resource and productivity components, because movement toward future states implies a recombination of external and internal elements of power. In determining who defines organizational goals, Thompson suggested locating the unit's dominant coalition and examining its preferences in terms of quality, quantity, and beneficiaries of output. "In this view, organizational goals are established by individuals—but interdependent individuals who collectively have sufficient control of organizational resources to commit them in certain directions and withhold them from others." [45]

When the ideological makeup of the dominant coalition changes, the chances are that many organizational goals in bureaucracy will be modified, although the nature of such modifications has to be determined empirically in each case. For example, while the Chilean Budget Bureau has traditionally had goals connoting a restrictive fiscal policy, the agency's behavior has varied over the years, even within the same presidential period, due to changes in the composition or outlook of leadership in the ministry of Finance. The chapters on the Chilean Economic Committee reveal ways in which the preferences of the dominant coali-

[43] Simon, *Administrative Behavior*, pp. 11–16, *passim.*
[44] James D. Thompson, *Organizations in Action*, pp. 26, 127.
[45] Thompson, p. 128. See also Mohr, "The Concept of Organizational Goal."

tion in an important decision-making body can affect national economic and social policy.

Environment

In developing a sociological theory of the firm, Barnard speculated on the significance of transactions up to and including those assuring the continued existence of the unit, which "depends on the maintenance of an equilibrium of complex character in a continuously fluctuating environment of physical, biological, and social materials, elements, and forces, [and] which calls for readjustment of processes internal to the organization." [46] In some instances the maintenance of this equilibrium is critical for the survival of the organization; normally, transactions across organizational boundaries consist of routine resource exchanges oriented more or less rationally toward achieving organizational goals and adapting to new contingencies.

Thompson refers repeatedly to the organization's *task environment,* which is relevant or potentially relevant to goal-setting and goal attainment and normally consists of clients, suppliers, competitors, regulatory groups, and their activities.[47] Philip Selznick, in *TVA and the Grass Roots,* devotes the majority of his analysis to the TVA's relationship with its task environment, noting that an

organization in action must deal primarily with those who are immediately and directly affected by its intervention. In order to endure, it cannot depend only or even primarily upon the diffuse support of elements not directly involved in its work; its administrative leadership must find support among local institutions, and develop smooth working relationships with them.[48]

Selznick discovered that formal and informal cooptation (essentially, the sharing of authority with outside actors) deflected the TVA's goals in ways quite contrary to those intended by its founders.[49] Although Selznick emphasized cooptation, it is evident that this is only one of many ways that organizations seek to adapt and survive, given constraints in their task environment. Thus in times of stress, Chilean agencies have displayed signs of nonenforcement and even capitulation.

Eric Trist states that it is necessary to distinguish between

the immediate, operational or task environment and the more remote, general or contextual environment. The task environment consists of all organizations, groups and people with whom the organization has specific relations,

---

[46] Barnard, *Functions,* p. 6.
[47] Thompson, pp. 27 ff.
[48] Philip Selznick, *TVA and the Grass Roots,* p. 20.
[49] Selznick, pp. 12–16.

on both the input and output sides, even though it may not be aware of their complete range. The contextual environment consists of the relations which the entities included in the task environment have to each other and to other systems not directly entering the world of the organization's own transactions. Events in the contextual environment may at any time obtrude into this world, constructively or destructively, predictably or unpredictably.[50]

This book on Chilean bureaucracy during the 1960's, when dealing with environmental influences, will concentrate almost exclusively on the task environment of the various agencies studied. From the vantage point of the individual units, the contextual environment (consisting of the configuration of purposes backed by resources in national and international society) is rather insignificant for its day-to-day operations. In times of turbulence, revolution, or natural disaster, however, the task environment may actually disappear in its old form, leaving the agency vulnerably exposed to a completely unfamiliar set of clamorous demands and power capabilities. Likewise, as Trist hints, cyclical tides of expectations and resource combinations in the society-at-large, though not directly related to organizational output, can alter the task environment in significant ways, obliging the unit to adjust its activity and perhaps modify its goals.

This last comment will become somewhat clearer in the next section, which provides more specific empirical referents for the concept of contextual environment and introduces a number of constraints impinging on the operation of Chilean bureaucratic units.

THE GENERAL ENVIRONMENT
OF CHILEAN BUREAUCRACY

In Chile, the possibilities for administration tend to rise and fall with the fate of leadership. Generally, if leadership is articulate, receives continuing support from society, and can gain acceptance for its programs and compliance with the sacrifices it asks, the potential of bureaucracy is outstanding. On the other hand, it is evident that a regime lacking in status and authority cannot provide much assistance to a public administration carrying out unpopular programs.

Over the past few decades, popular support of a Chilean government has tended to vary with its time in office. According to the 1925 Constitution, Chilean presidents cannot succeed themselves, an important consideration in explaining and predicting the intensity of ideological debate, demands for government action, recourse to coercion and

[50] Eric L. Trist, "Key Aspects of Environmental Relations," p. 44.

violence, and the steadily declining electoral support characterizing the six-year presidential term of office. These patterns have been important components of the contextual environment of Chilean bureaucracy, and converged dramatically in the coup d'état overthrowing the regime of Salvador Allende.

In the year before inauguration, presidential candidates have prepared their electoral strategies with none of the advantages of office. They usually have held no nominal authority post, have had little knowledge of the workings or possibilities of bureaucracy, and have not had access to the official forces of coercion (though supporters often used violence). Campaign platforms were notable for their intentions—contained in ideological statements appealing to specific publics—which often did not pay heed to the limits of governmental action. Charles Anderson has gone so far as to explain the high incidence of ideology in Latin American politics by the lack of accurate information available: "Policy formation is apt to be an activity of guesswork, of high risk, in which the capacity to anticipate consequences of proposed actions . . . is most restricted." [51] One might agree that before the election the typical party candidate in Chile has not known enough about "the character of the problem he confronts to make a choice on the basis of the situation itself." [52] Indeed, many campaign speeches, permeated with hints of far-reaching programs, have represented little more than a bluff in terms of predicting what really could be accomplished after assuming office.

While the executive and his top administrators have lacked adequate information at the commencement of the regime, they have enjoyed considerable esteem and legitimacy. Parliamentary or municipal elections held within a year after inauguration have tended to reveal strong sentiment in favor of the president's party or coalition, reflecting the electorate's desire to give the new executive a chance to get started. This support traditionally has meant that the regime's authority roles were accepted and it had little need to resort to coercion.

For the past twenty years, the Chilean president has always faced a paradoxical situation at the beginning of his term. While he enjoyed new authority, and much legitimacy and status, his store of practical knowledge was very low. When he could have performed most decisively to implement the ideological aspects of his program, he knew least exactly how to do so. One typical act, however, was to increase the economic base of his regime by altering the tax structure or the monetary

[51] Anderson, *Politics and Economic Change,* p. 116.
[52] Anderson, p. 135.

policy.[53] This timely foresight insured that he would have adequate finances to underwrite his projects later on, when they were in the takeoff stage. Over the short term, these extra resources were used to expand, with the aid of career bureaucrats, the more palatable programs of the previous government.

During the normal six-year period of office, most of these power factors changed either in value or quantity. First, information increased rapidly as the executive and his advisors learned more about the machinery of government, what had been done, and what could realistically be accomplished. Ideological statements by public officials usually became fewer and farther between, and technical argumentation characterized the voice of government. Second, support of the regime by the voting public declined steadily. The political honeymoon is rather short in Chile, and the populace soon abandoned its propensity to back the president simply because he was president. The vote became more particularistic and vengeful, indicating either that the government had not done everything that it said it would, or that a good part of the public wanted more, or less, than it did when the regime entered office.

With the decline of support for the incumbents, the stature of opposition groups was enhanced. Their eyes to the next election, claimants for authority re-injected ideology into the political scene. Again, these continued references may have reflected poor information-gathering capacity, but these groups also attempted to mold the definition of national purposes and create the impression that they had the will and capacity to fulfill them. The way in which the regime gained some of its support added to the level of ideological debate. One of the realities faced by recent Chilean governments has been that certain accommodations must be made with groups which, according to principle, should be totally ostracized. Unwilling to start from zero in implementing programs, regimes have worked with these elements and sometimes even solicited their backing. Government's tacit or overt decision to tolerate, cooperate, and sometimes even share authority has been an important prerequisite for achieving many of its goals within the short span of six years. However, these contacts and accords gave added impetus to the attacks of the opposition. They often led to factionalism within the ruling groups, when purposeful cooptation was conspicuous treason to the ideals of the party or coalition members.[54]

[53] Sergio Molina, the former Finance minister, referred to this juncture in his economic review of the Frei period, *El Proceso de Cambio en Chile*, p. 69.
[54] Robert L. Ayres commented on the "social-coalition-disintegration thesis" in his "Electoral Constraints and 'the Chilean Way' to Socialism." Michelle Proud analyzed the divisions in the Allende government, based on an unofficial working

At some point, usually near the middle of the presidential term, the "learning" and "legitimacy" curves crossed each other, marking a critical juncture in the style of government. Though the regime's technical capacity may have been optimal for implementing fundamentally sound, innovative policies, the citizenry was less in a mood to let it do so. Typical results have been an increase in the incidence of violence and coercion and an attempt by the regime to consolidate its gains without risking repudiation by dissatisfied sectors of society.[55] At this writing the complex of events surrounding Allende's overthrow has yet to be analyzed, but it is instructive to note that it occurred precisely at the midpoint of the presidential period. His immediate predecessors faced somewhat similar crises after three years in office (Chapter 4 describes Frei's predicament at this juncture) and usually responded by adopting a cautious political style, trading blows intermittently with the opposition until the next presidential campaign.

The sixth year of normal Chilean presidencies has tended to be an administrative fiasco, with programs completely subjected to electoral considerations, increased inflation due to the regime's incapacity and unwillingness to hold the line, general exasperation of the citizenry with the whole political process, and leadership trying somehow to maintain equilibrium without upsetting the presidential aspirations of its preferred candidate. In the past, however, the excitement and anticipation on election eve have dispelled lingering doubts over the ultimate value of the Chilean political system, and inauguration of the new president began the cycle anew.

Four Recent Regimes

These observations on the relationship between government and the political community can be partially substantiated with available data on four recent regimes governing from 1952 to 1973. Although differing widely in style, ideology, programs, and personalities, all of these leaders had comparable opportunities, and their bureaucracies had to cope with a similar political environment during their tenures.

The first of these trends was an increase, and then a decline, in electoral support after the first year in office. Figure 3 shows that the presi-

paper prepared by one of the Unidad Popular's minor political groupings, the MAPU, in "Continued Uncertainty in the Wake of Chilean Elections," *Peruvian Times*, March 16, 1973, pp. 6–7, 18. Allende's attempt to bolster his regime by placing military men in cabinet posts was anathema to purist elements in the Unidad Popular.

[55] David Apter treated information and coercion in *The Politics of Modernization*, p. 40 and *passim*.

FIGURE 3.   DECLINING ELECTORAL SUPPORT FOR CHILEAN PRESIDENTS
DURING THEIR REGIMES, 1952–1973

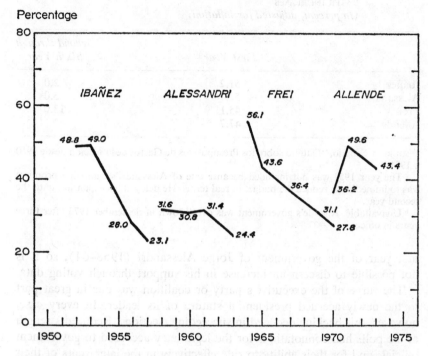

SOURCE: Election Registry Office; also, *La Nación* (Santiago) of May 1, 1953 (p. 11),
May 4, 1953 (p. 5), and April 7, 1956 (p. 5).

NOTE: Among groups supporting the Ibáñez regime were Agrarian Labor, Popular
Socialist, People's Democratic, Labor, National Christian, Doctrinaire Radical, National Independent Union, National Ibañist Movement, National People's Movement,
Feminine Progressive, Chilean Feminine, National Agrarian, and Independent Ibañist.
Because electoral data were never officially compiled for the 1956 municipal election,
the percentage figure represents the number of councilmen elected. Supporting groups
for Alessandri were the Liberal and Conservative parties; for Frei, the Christian Democratic party; for Allende, the Socialist, Communist, Radical, Social Democratic, and
Popular Socialist parties.

dent's collectivity tended to do better at the polls in the first year than
it did later on. The governments of Carlos Ibáñez (1952–58), Salvador
Allende, and the Christian Democratic party of Eduardo Frei improved
their electoral positions immediately after inauguration. Frei (1964–70)
received a disproportionate percentage of the presidential vote in what
was essentially a two man race, a rarity for Chile. The next year his
Christian Democratic party increased its number of votes by 100 percent over the 1963 congressional returns. No elections were held in the

TABLE 2.   INCREASES IN THE GOVERNMENT'S BUDGET AT THE BEGIN-
NING OF FOUR REGIMES (1953, 1960, 1965, 1971) COMPARED WITH
LATER INCREASES
(*In percent, adjusted for inflation*)

	First Year	Second through Sixth Year
Ibáñez	51.2	2.0
Alessandri	52.7[a]	5.0[a]
Frei	45.1	13.0
Allende	47.7	[b]

SOURCE: Senado, "Estudio sobre los Presupuestos de Gastos de la Nación desde 1950 a 1971."

[a] The year 1959 was not included because one of Alessandri's campaign promises was to immediately reduce the budget in real terms. He delayed his expansion until the second year.

[b] Unavailable. Allende's government was overthrown in September 1973 after three years in office.

first year of the government of Jorge Alessandri (1958–64), so it is not possible to discern an increase in his support through voting data.

The surge of the executive's party or coalition was due in great part to the newly accrued presidential stature of its leader. In every case, however, this backing declined in succeeding elections. Reduced strength at the polls had connotations for the legitimacy accorded to government officials and for their ability to rule effectively in the later years of their term.

Two possible indicators of the regime's authority vis-a-vis the political community are its ability to increase its economic capability and to hold the line against inflation.[56] Chilean governments have tended to be much more successful in these areas at the beginning of their terms of office than later on. First, soon after inauguration, they have convinced the public and Congress of the advisability of new taxes or expansionary monetary policies for increased government spending. Table 2 shows the remarkable differences between real budgetary increases early in the regime and the average of those increases subsequently.[57] For example, Ibáñez's first budget was 51.2 percent higher than the previous year's, but the average increase for the five succeeding years was only 2 percent. Similar patterns prevailed in the Alessandri and Frei regimes, and

[56] See Albert Hirschman's analysis of Chilean inflation in *Journeys Toward Progress*, pp. 129–223.

[57] See also the research of Steven W. Sinding, *Political Participation, Public Expenditures, and Economic Growth in Chile.*

Allende continued the trend by receiving congressional approval for a much larger budget soon after his election.

It was suggested above that the regime's effective authority tends to decline over time. Virtually all Chilean presidents commit themselves to reducing inflation. Success in this area entails taking a hard line on price increases and strike petitions. Figure 4 reveals that the Alessandri, Frei, and Allende governments sharply reduced inflation in the initial years of their regimes; later, however, the ability of the first two to hold the index steady declined gradually, meaning in part that powerful sectors of the economy ignored government directives in setting prices

FIGURE 4. VARIABLE RATES OF INFLATION DURING CHILEAN PRESI-
DENTIAL REGIMES
(*In percent*)

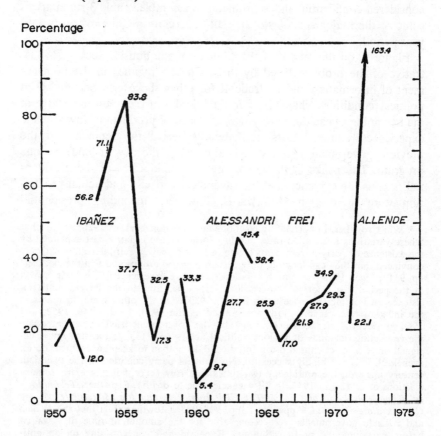

SOURCE: National Office of Statistics and Census.

and demanding wage increases. The Ibáñez data do not fit this pattern so well, but Ibáñez and his three immediate successors left power with inflation proceeding at a faster rate than at the lowest point in their regime.[58]

Though the correlation is not perfect, the incidence of violent challenges to the government increases as legitimacy is withdrawn, either because of the clumsy performance of the regime in power or, more commonly, because of the incapacity of authorities to respond to "exaggerated" sectoral demands in the society without resorting to coercion. From the Ibáñez to the Allende regimes, violence and police repression seemed to follow two patterns: violent confrontations occurred earlier in the regime, and they reoccurred more frequently, especially under Allende. Unfortunately, complete statistics on injuries and deaths of protesters in encounters with *carabineros* (the national police force) are considered confidential and are difficult to assemble. Table 3 summarizes some of the major acts of violence and coercion in Chile over a twenty year period.

Figure 5, on the output of the Chilean public housing sector, is illustrative of the problem faced by three Chilean regimes in the management of information and its tradeoff for other short-term benefits when political conditions change. After an initial spurt of housing starts at the beginning of each term of office, the pace of production slowed while experienced administrators permanently buried the remnants of the previous government's policy and adjusted to the new regime's unique program. The peaks in the curves near the midpoints of the presidential periods are evidence that both technical capacity and actual production were quite high. Afterwards, however, impending presidential

[58] Win Crowther, in correlating elections and inflation back to 1926, argues that "these variations in inflation rates and in allocations are in large part explained by the existence of party governments acting in their perceived self-interest, mistakenly convinced that they can 'pay off' only certain political groups and win the election" (p. 911). Since 1938 "six-month inflation rates have experienced their least growth in the period just prior to Congressional elections," due to the government's insistence on holding the price index firm (p. 920). On the other hand, increases in the inflation rate became more pronounced as the 1932, 1942, 1946, 1952, and 1964 presidential elections drew near and the government tried to accommodate the conflicting demands of various political actors (p. 913). If the strategy is designed more to elect chosen presidential candidates than to keep government on an even keel, it is not highly successful. No political party coalition in the twentieth century has won the presidency two times in a row (except in the extraordinary elections of 1942 and 1946, to fill vacancies due to death). Crowther, *Technological Change as Political Choice: The Civil Engineers and the Modernizers of the Chilean State Railroad*, Appendix I, pp. 908–955. Crowther feels that the Ibáñez and Allende governments were remarkable for the amount of time they waited before curtailing the post-election payoff period and concentrating on an anti-inflation drive. See also Rolf Lüders, *A Monetary History of Chile, 1925–1958.*

TABLE 3. MULTIPLE DEATHS DURING POLITICAL UPHEAVAL IN CHILE, 1952–1973

Year	President	Year of Regime	Deaths	Event
1957	Ibáñez	5th	8	Anti-inflation protest
1962	Alessandri	4th	6	Shantytown riot
1966	Frei	2nd	8	Miner's strike
1967	Frei	3rd	5	Wage demonstration
1969	Frei	5th	10	Urban land invasion
1970	Frei	6th	2	Student strike
1972	Allende	2nd	2	Shantytown revolt
1972	Allende	2nd	5	Shopkeepers' and transport strike (curfew violations)
1973	Allende	3rd	22	Barracks revolt
1973	Allende	3rd	Unknown number	Overthrow by military coup d'état

SOURCE: Biblioteca del Congreso, Fichero de Artículos de Diarios, "Hechos de Sangre." Also, "Reseña de Represión Policial, 1850–1970," *El Siglo*, Aug. 20, 1970, p. 11; *El Mercurio*, 1971–1973.

NOTE: Other deaths occurred in acts of political upheaval during this period; the table summarizes those that resulted in more than one known death.

elections sabotaged the sector's output. Housing began to lose financial resources at least two years in advance of the presidential election—representing the approximate length of time between the initiation of construction and the occupation of a house by its owner. Politicians felt that if they could not give the keys to the heads of households until after the elections, the allegiance of their vote was problematic. It is important to remember, however, that after the production peaks, the officials in the housing agencies would have been capable of maintaining, and even improving, the level of their output had financial resources been forthcoming. But with the election looming on the horizon, this capacity was squandered. The years 1964 and 1970 saw grossly reduced numbers of housing starts—one-fourth of Alessandri's peak period, and less than one-sixth in the case of Frei.

Resource Patterns and Ideology

Until 1973, Chile proved to be one of the most stable countries in the Western Hemisphere. But surface stability did not preclude considerable alterations in each regime's power relationship with society, as the preceding analysis has shown. It could be argued that some of the patterns described in this section were recognized as the facts of political life in Chile and, until Allende's downfall, actually constituted and contributed to the nation's political maturity. With such a high degree of cross-identification between upper echelons of administration and government leadership, however, the constraints posed by power mutations were crippling to important sections of the bureaucracy. In addition to housing production, there are numerous ways of describing how changes in bureaucracy's political environment upset standardized administrative procedures. Some aspects of this phenomenon will be examined more thoroughly later on with regard to short-term planning (Chapter 4) and the servicing of lower-class clienteles (Chapter 8).

The concept of contextual environment implies not only resource

FIGURE 5. FLUCTUATING ADMINISTRATIVE OUTPUT IN THE HOUSING SECTOR, 1959–1972
(Thousands of units initiated by public housing agencies)

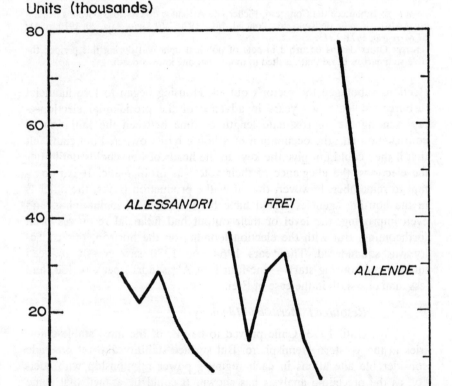

FIGURE 5. (*Continued*)

Year	Total Units	Year	Total Units
1953	5,735[a]	1963	11,988
1954	6,244[a]	1964	6,938
1955	6,969[a]	1965	37,514
1956	7,800[a]	1966	13,433
1957	6,857[a]	1967	28,285
1958	6,160[a]	1968	32,730
1959	28,946	1969	14,460
1960	22,080	1970	5,914
1961	25,060	1971	79,327
1962	17,615	1972	30,692

SOURCE: MINVU, *Política Habitacional del Gobierno Popular: Programa* 72, pp. 22, 45. Also MINVU Statistics department.

[a] Prior to 1959, housing starts are not broken down between the private and public sectors.

flows but also the parochial and overlapping goals of social actors. The preceding paragraphs have somewhat neglected the purposes, ambitions, and ends extant in Chilean society. A description of political party ideologies with their policy connotations would be a possible shortcut to that task. Past regimes have asked bureaucracy to regulate the economy (Alessandri) or provide a broad range of social services (Frei). With the Allende regime, the public sector played an even greater role in sponsoring welfare programs and managing the country's factors of production. The Unidad Popular's attempts to move toward a quasi-socialistic state appealed to large segments of public opinion which agreed that the philosophy of private enterprise and individual initiative was no longer suitable for eliminating gross differences between classes inside of the country, or for improving the nation's standing in the world economic community.

Unfortunately, discussion of all the different schemes for income redistribution, and of utopian organizations (such as communism, communitarianism, classical liberalism, trotskyism, democracy, and anarchism) and their most forceful spokesmen (the Communist, Christian Democratic, National, Socialist, and Radical parties, and the M.I.R., respectively), would take us far afield and not necessarily improve upon the available literature.[59]

[59] For example, Kalman H. Silvert, *Chile: Yesterday and Today*; Peter G. Snow, "The Political Party Spectrum in Chile"; Ernst Halperin, *Nationalism and Communism in Chile*; James Petras, *Chilean Christian Democracy: Politics and Social Forces*; Federico G. Gil, *El Sistema Político de Chile*. More recently, Sergio Onafre

Moreover, such an exercise might engender the impression that these ideologies do indeed encompass the precise desires of large sectors of Chilean society. The attrition of popular support for Chilean presidents, graphically presented in Figure 3, is one indicator that, though political sophistication is high in Chile, written and expounded ideology has little more than a transitory hold on any but the most dedicated activists in each political party. The high level of politicization and fluidity of individual wants and public purposes make Chile an interesting case for generating propositions on bureaucratic behavior with wider theoretical significance.

CONCLUSIONS

Comparative administrative theory has tended to focus either on the individual bureaucrat, his values, orientation, and deficiencies, or on higher-level abstractions (development, development administration) with few empirical referents. One of the advantages of concepts used here is that they help join organizational behavior to concrete problems in a way that enhances the ability of administrative elites (and, when necessary, counterelites) to utilize organization theory for purposeful action.

First, the book deals with intermediate-size organizations containing individuals (with their values and personal idiosyncrasies) and groups (with their own internal structure and goals). These organizations make up a larger system (many such organizations plus their interrelationships). The focus is not on the individual or on whole societies, but on two- and three-unit organizational sets. Agency A interacts with agency B and group C, with an outcome X. Groups D and E impinge on organization F in order to change productivity trends from Y to Z.[60]

Second, the main concepts are few in number and lack highly symbolic connotations. At the research site the observer can assign empirical referents to "resources," "purposes," and "environment." The concepts

Jarpa, *Creo en Chile*; Jaime Castillo Velasco, *Las Fuentes de la Democracia Cristiana*; Claudio Orrego V., *Empezar de Nuevo: Chile, después de la Unidad Popular*; Volodia Teitelboim, *El Oficio Ciudadano*; Julio César Jobet, *El Partido Socialista de Chile*; Clodomiro Almeyda, *Sociologismo Ideologismo en la Teoría Revolucionaria*; and *El M.I.R.*

[60] For examinations of politics intervening in administrative processes, see Aaron Wildavsky, *The Politics of the Budgetary Process*; Gordon Tullock, *The Politics of Bureaucracy*; Gerald Caiden, *Administrative Reform*; John Friedmann, *Venezuela, From Doctrine to Dialogue*.

themselves, however, always imply a wider range of variables than those present in any single research situation, and they are only metaphors for what organizations actually accumulate and transform, attempt to achieve and confront as external constraints.

Third, these case studies are policy-oriented. They skirt a fine line between political science as discipline and political science as action. The theoretical problem (that of explaining administrative behavior) originates in the discipline, while the research findings (means of controlling and penetrating bureaucratic units) suggest applications in experimental and real-life situations.[61] As Abraham Kaplan points out, discipline and action join ultimately for scientific ends, because "relating the inquiry to practice has the advantages of providing anchorage for our abstractions, and data and tests for our hypotheses." [62]

Fourth, the elaboration of this construct depends not only on additional substantiation of the propositions presented here, but also on deductive and inductive reasoning to complete the paradigm. While the book contains little about the behavior of individuals in organizations, or the relation between interorganizational activity for system survival, it presumes that basic tenets pertaining to resources, goals, and environment will be appropriate for explaining and predicting behavior at "lower" and "higher" levels of inquiry.[63]

Resource exchange as an analogy for political activity and the effect of power fragmentation on administrative processes underlie this work on the Chilean bureaucracy. Though political economy aids in the understanding and description of power, it still does not provide the tools for measuring it. The previous section attempted to substantiate power cycles in Chilean presidential regimes by means of voting returns, budgetary data, inflation figures, and number of casualties in civil disorders. For many, these indicators would be unsatisfactory substitutes

[61] James S. Coleman, "Policy Research"; also see Yehezkel Dror, *Public Policymaking Reexamined,* pp. 3–11; and Austin Ranney, "The Study of Policy Content: A Framework for Choice," in Ranney (ed.), *Political Science and Public Policy,* pp. 3–21.
[62] Abraham Kaplan, *The Conduct of Inquiry: Methodology for Behavioral Science,* p. 399.
[63] That is, bureaucrats with ambitions (*goals*) and variable personal qualifications (*resources*) operate within a role set (*environment*). Similarly, administrative units carry out specific tasks (*goals*) with legal and budgetary support (*resources*) in interaction with particular reference groups (*environment*). The bureaucracy pursues multiple objectives (*goals*) with a whole range of power capabilities (*resources*) in dealing with constraints posed by society (*environment*). This statement by no means denies the likelihood of emergent or recessive properties as one moves from one level to another.

for legitimacy, economic capability, authority, coercion, and violence. The adequacy of any such fit always depends on the rigor of the critic and the degrees of freedom he concedes to the analyst. Though it may be granted that some of these are not bad measures for the resources indicated, other critical variables such as status and information flow almost defy measurement.

For Ilchman and Uphoff, in an aggregate sense, "power is measured by the incidence or degree of compliance with public policies and group demands." [64] Unfortunately, simple compliance or noncompliance is only a rough measure of power. The existence of compliance does not necessarily reveal how much power has actually been employed for the acceptance of the public policy or group demand. And when noncompliance exists, the statesman or the sector have no immediate way of knowing how many more resources need to be invested, and in what combination, to reach a state of acceptance. As a matter of fact, it is precisely these quandaries in making objective measurements of power which often lead to what Ilchman and Uphoff call the "political bankruptcy" of the regime.

In addition to their effect on ultimate compliance, these resources must also have a value in relation to each other. Here the problems are compounded, since the value of the resource in any single exchange between two parties is basically a subjective determination, influenced by situational factors as well as broader market conditions. The value of resources such as status, violence, legitimacy, and coercion also varies from culture to culture, and era to era, according to the expectations of the society. The propensity of citizens to use violence as a tool to prod government, for example, is probably higher in Chile than in Sweden, but lower than in many other Third World countries.

It should not be assumed that moving from the macro to the micro level of analysis necessarily makes these measurement problems simpler. Indeed, the concepts of authority, legitimacy, and compliance become even more elusive within bureaucracy. There are few statistics for particular agencies as satisfactory as the data in the tables and figures used in this chapter. I would simply point out that the current limitations of the method are recognized, and I have tried to work within them. The problem is not a new one nor, as Francis Rourke points out, one likely to be resolved tomorrow.

While the various factors which help to shape differentials in agency power can thus be sorted out, there is no easy way in which the effectiveness of one source of power can be weighted against another. No common unit of

[64] Ilchman and Uphoff, *Political Economy,* p. 33.

measurement exists for making such comparisons. This is a familiar problem which arises in connection with all efforts to measure power, influence, or authority. . . . In any case, a single agency may draw power from several different sources, and there is no way of telling how much of an agency's success should be attributed to [each].[65]

[65] Francis E. Rourke, *Politics, Bureaucracy, and Public Policy*, p. 64.

2

BUREAUCRATIC STRATEGIES
IN FORMATION AND EXECUTION
OF THE BUDGET

Many of the budgeting practices described in this chapter prevail in other countries besides Chile. Incorrect estimates of cash flow, global cuts and amplifications, poor programming, incrementalism, and skewed spending habits are characteristic of financial affairs in the most disorganized to the most organized of modern states. Their nature is attributable less to traditional value structures, bureaucratic incompetence, or even political instability, than to systematically definable elements in public bureaucracy itself.[1]

The novelty of this exposition is to treat these behavioral tendencies as bureaucratic strategies reacting to certain independent factors. None of these strategies develops capriciously or is inescapably permanent; they are all the predictable outcome of a series of assumptions on the meaning of the budgetary process, and of a particular way in which resources are distributed in the public sector.[2] The argument presented

---

[1] This analysis follows the lead of pioneering contributions to budgetary theory by Aaron Wildavsky, Anthony Downs, and John Crecine. See Aaron Wildavsky, *The Politics of the Budgetary Process*; Anthony Downs, *Inside Bureaucracy*; John P. Crecine, *Governmental Problem-Solving: A Computer Simulation of Municipal Budgeting*.

[2] Except to the extent that they are observably present in budgetary decisions, this analysis will not consider inorganic environmental factors (e.g., population density, education levels, property ownership) that have been correlated with expenditure levels in United States state and local governments. See, for example, Harvey E. Brazer, *City Expenditures in the United States*; Glen W. Fisher, "Interstate Variation in State and Local Expenditures"; Otto A. Davis and George H. Haines, Jr., "A Political Approach to a Theory of Public Expenditures: The Case of Municipalities."

here contends that incrementalism, for example, disappears when budgetary assumptions shift in certain directions.[3] The usual approach is to hypothesize that incrementalism is an inherent and unremedial characteristic of the budget which persists under all "normal" circumstances.[4]

The budgetary process offers a convenient starting point for observing the specific effects of power fragmentation on administration. All government agencies participate in budget-making, because they need financial resources to survive. In Chile as in most other Latin American countries, where central planning is still at a level of incipient development, the budgetary process is the one central mechanism extending procedures into all of the ministries, agencies, autonomous corporations, and state industries in the public sector. Despite their technologies, their position in the bureaucratic hierarchy, the degree of uncertainty in their environments, or their centralized or decentralized status, these organizations must compete with one another to receive adequate funding for their programs.

An initiation to Chilean budgetary practices can prove to be conceptually confounding. (See the appendix for a full description of the formal aspects of this cycle.) The budgetary law ostensibly gives the Finance ministry the authority to distribute all allocations, yet Congress intervenes to provide special taxes for individual agencies. Though the budget is legislated with considerable fanfare in the month of December, the allocation of funds in major amounts continues throughout the year. Despite strenuous efforts at programming, budget execution is marked by a multitude of transfers between current and capital accounts, between agencies, and between ministries. Quite aptly Aaron Wildavsky and Naomi Caiden have termed these tendencies "repetitive budgeting." [5] Intermittent overestimates and underestimates of revenues are part of the game, as are bogus accounts, civil service strikes, and recourse to international loans. Though the majority of agencies trudge along without causing special problems, some appear to be particularly ruthless in their pursuit of more resources for their operations, obliging the Finance minister to reach into his bag of tricks and perform a sleight-of-hand to accommodate them.

[3] This is not the same as advocating a comprehensive approach simply because it would give much greater opportunities for far-reaching and more coordinated action. See Arthur Smithies, *The Budgetary Process in the United States.*
[4] See Otto A. Davis, M. A. H. Dempster, and Aaron Wildavsky, "A Theory of the Budgetary Process"; Aaron Wildavsky and Arthur Hammond, "Comprehensive versus Incremental Budgeting in the Department of Agriculture."
[5] Naomi Caiden and Aaron Wildavsky, *Planning and Budgeting in Poor Countries.*

In this chapter I will lay out various theoretical and empirical parameters for comprehension of the Chilean budget, and will concentrate on simplifying the roles and projecting the behavior of the principal entities involved in this administrative process. I will argue that the Finance ministry has a near monopoly over one kind of resource—economic and financial subsidies—while the agencies in the public sector maintain a near monopoly over another kind of resource—information. This assumption reduces the budgetary process to a transaction between two kinds of organizations dealing in two types of resources, and helps construct a typology that contemplates four idealized exchange situations. Not all of these are mutually advantageous for both the Finance ministry and the agencies, a fact that lies at the core of budgetary dynamics. The agencies pursue strategic lines of action which favor them in their dealings with Finance. The Budget Bureau works to neutralize sectoral strategies while it tries to negotiate the budget under conditions furthering its best interests. The substantive strategies of the different public organizations are the dependent variables discussed extensively in the latter part of this chapter.

PAROCHIAL ASSUMPTIONS AND
RESOURCE MONOPOLIES

Figure 6 is a simplified means of asserting that in most administrative systems the organizations at the two poles of the budgetary hierarchy display a reinforcing opposition between goal definitions and resources. The word "budget" has quite different connotations for the Budget Bureau, on the one hand, and the agencies, on the other. Their contrary interpretations of the same process are quite consistent with their respective objectives in the bureaucracy and their perceived interests in the political community at large.

The Budget Bureau's job is to collect revenues, balance accounts, and supervise the distribution of public funds. For it (and its mother organization, the Finance ministry), the budgetary process is a unique opportunity to prevent the ambitions of parochial agencies from bankrupting the state. The Finance ministry measures its accomplishments by pegging agency expenditures at a level somewhat consistent with program needs but, more importantly, leaving the central treasury in healthy financial shape. The Budget Bureau is not charged with issuing more marriage licenses, arresting more delinquents, educating more pupils, or building more houses. These major preoccupations of indi-

FIGURE 6. DIRECTIONAL FLOWS OF ECONOMIC RESOURCES AND INFOR-
MATION IN THE BUDGETARY PROCESS

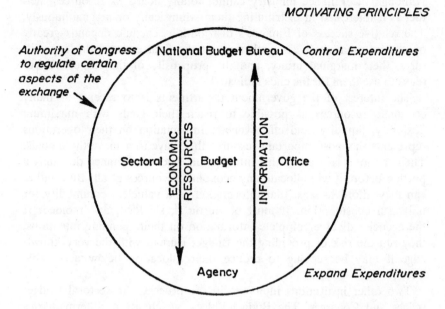

vidual agencies are only the secondary concerns of the national budget officials.[6]

It is not difficult to appreciate why most agencies' motives are singularly expansionary. Increased allocations mean greater organizational flexibility. More money represents more negotiating power inside and outside the public administration. Higher achievement levels, more organizational prestige, dependency relationships with a wider array of clients and supportive groups, and higher morale in the departments can all be associated with significant increases in the agency's budget. Until the day when public organizations adopt more altruistic attitudes, this ordering of preferences will remain standard. Agencies will fight for more funds whether or not they have a clear idea of how this money will be used.

Access to different types of resources reinforces the cleavage between the agencies and the Budget Bureau. The Finance ministry controls tax collection in the country, prints new money through the Central Bank, grants credits through the State Bank, and allocates resources through

[6] Compare with the standard working assumptions of the departments and the mayors in Crecine's *Governmental Problem-Solving*.

the Budget Bureau. Government agencies are dependent on one or more
of the branches of the Finance ministry to sustain their operations.
Although the Finance ministry cannot totally hoard its resources, neither is it interested in distributing them whimsically or magnanimously.
The relative success of Finance's distribution schedule depends greatly
on the information it can gather about the final ends of the expenditures, their marginal utility, and the propensity of the respective bureaus to use them for the ends indicated.

The interest of the government departments is to receive as many
economic resources as possible to reach their goals with maximum
flexibility, liquidity, and effectiveness. Information on their operations
represents the most important resource they have to achieve these goals.
They cannot hoard all of this information, because Finance demands a
portion before it will allocate any economic resources at all. But neither
can they afford to treat that information as a valueless commodity for
universal consumption. It must be nurtured, shielded, and molded. If
the agencies divulge complete information on their spending intentions,
they run the risk of providing the Budget Bureau with the very knowledge it may be seeking to reduce their allocation below acceptable
levels.

Two other institutions intervene in the process, the sectoral Budget
offices and Congress. The Budget offices, which act as intermediaries
between the agency and the Budget Bureau, are not considered neutral
actors. Agencies often distort or withhold complete information from
them because of their responsibility for dividing up resources within the
sector. The national Budget Bureau does not often confide in its sectoral colleagues, because of their authority links to the ministries. Congress, as one of the supreme powers of the nation, has the right to
control the flow of both informational and economic resources and
indicate the degree of monopoly that each institution in the budgetary
hierarchy can maintain over the two principal resources. In regulating
the flow of information, the budgetary law instructs each agency to provide the Finance ministry with all information pertinent to formulation
of the budget.[7] However, there is no way that laws can oblige the
agency to provide information escaping its own cognizance, or attest to
the accuracy of the information provided.

Congress' more outstanding intervention is the manner in which it has
helped guarantee financial resources to decentralized agencies through
earmarked funds, special taxes, and legal dispensations to sell services.

---

[7] Article 5 of Ministerio de Hacienda, *Ley Orgánica de Presupuestos.*

From 1964 to 1967, the revenues that actually passed through the National Treasury represented only 50 percent of the total handled by the Chilean state. On the average, 63.9 percent of the income of the decentralized agencies and state industries came directly from independent sources.[8] This fragmentation has helped break the monopoly of the Finance minister over the allocation of resources, even though he must still formally approve all budgets in the public sector.

In summary, Finance has financial resources, wants information from the agencies, and wants Congress to use its authority to facilitate the gathering of that information. The agencies have information, want funds from the Finance ministry, and want Congress to use its authority either to increase their subsidies or to give them access to autonomous funds. The ministerial Budget offices start out with neither information nor financial resources, but are besieged by Finance for the former and by the agencies for the latter. Generally, each unit is jealous of its inherent prerogatives and strives to extend those prerogatives whenever feasible.

TRADING SITUATIONS

When bureaucratic actors are motivated to deprive one another of precisely those resources the other wishes to retain, their interaction evolves into a dynamic administrative process characterized by a series of resource tradeoffs at variable rates of exchange. Most of these transactions are structured in competitive zero-sum, trading, and positive-negative exchange terms, and are seldom elevated to a conscious level of bargaining.[9] Figure 7 illustrates four idealized budgetary exchange situations between information and economic subsidy, whereby each resource, in relation to its counterpart, is either free-flowing and cheap (+) or restricted and expensive (−).

Brief reflection on the figure reveals that the conditions of Box I, in which both information and economic subsidy are cheap, are difficult to simulate. State revenues are never sufficient to subsidize all public programs. Full access to accurate information is improbable for several reasons, one of which is information's inherent elusiveness. An agency's impact on society, no matter how such relevance is measured, cannot always be translated into informational units easily passed from observer

[8] Ministerio de Hacienda, *Balance Consolidado del Sector Público de Chile, 1964–1967*, p. 68.
[9] See William F. Whyte, *Organizational Behavior,* pp. 148 ff.

FIGURE 7. RESOURCE FLOWS AND EXCHANGE SITUATIONS IN THE
BUDGETARY PROCESS

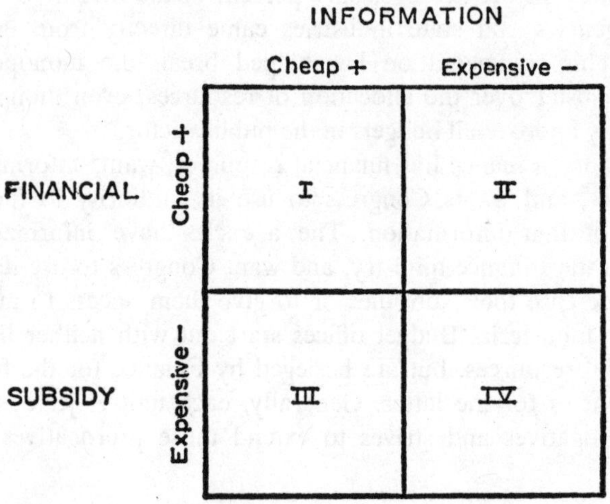

INFORMATION

Cheap +   Expensive −

I	II
III	IV

(rows labeled) FINANCIAL — Cheap + ; SUBSIDY — Expensive −

to recipient. Moreover, quite understandable political reasons, to be described below, restrict information flow within the bureaucracy.

More common exchange situations are represented by Boxes II, III,
and IV. Box II, preferred by the agencies, describes a market in which
they can procure all the funds they feel they might use over the coming
year without having to justify each expenditure to a minute degree.
Finance prefers to foster transactions in Box III, where it can learn
everything pertinent about the individual agencies without committing
financial resources in advance. In Box IV, the prevalent situation, both
resources are withheld, bringing a high incidence of uncertainty to both
Finance and the agencies and hindering the coordination of sufficient,
though not exaggerated, levels of resources to reach basic objectives.

To draw from this scheme more fully: Finance is interested in creating
a budgetary situation connoting favorable terms of trade for economic
subsidies in relation to other resources, notably information. The general
strategies used by Finance to achieve this end attempt to: (a) maintain
the high value of economic resources; (b) extract information at the
least possible cost; and (c) protect its vulnerability when full information
is not forthcoming. Strategies a and b tend to move the budgetary market
more nearly into the conditions of Box III. Strategy c is a response to the
unfavorable characteristics of Boxes II and IV.

The Finance ministry in Chile tries to preserve the value of its economic resources through several *tactics:*

- taking a hard line on inflation;
- adopting a very restrictive position on petitions for increased expenditures; and
- estimating its revenue low, to force the agencies to keep their projected expenditures under an artificial limit.

It attempts to increase its store of information by:

- structuring its organization to allow the greatest facility in learning about agencies in the public sector;
- promoting the program budget; and
- delaying promulgation of the definitive budget (*oficio final*) until the last possible moment.

Finance protects itself against poor information by:

- allocating money on a global basis;
- letting incremental increases be the standard rule of operation; and
- participating in repetitive budgeting throughout the year.

During the budgetary process, the general interests of the agencies are to create favorable terms for information in relation to other resources, especially financial subsidy. Their *strategies* are to: (a) maintain a high value for accurate information, (b) extract financial resources from Finance at the least possible cost, and (c) protect themselves against the uncertainty of a deficient flow of financial subsidy. Strategies a and b are designed to move the budgetary market more nearly into the conditions of Box II, while strategy c is a reaction to the unfavorable characteristics of Boxes III and IV.

Agency *tactics* to increase the symbolic value of accurate information are:

- resisting the program budget, and
- filling the arena with inaccurate or extraneous information that misleads the Finance ministry in determining their needs.

Agencies tend to increase their chances for extracting more funds from the Budget Bureau by:

- presenting their requests in exaggerated fashion to convince Finance of their high priority;
- underestimating expenses and overestimating revenues, which leads to budgetary *faits accomplis* that require extraordinary funding from the Finance ministry; and

• spending rapidly at the end of the year to insure that no excess remains.

The principal tactic agencies use to protect themselves against receiving inadequate allocations from the Finance ministry is to arrange for autonomous sources of money, through special taxes and earmarked funds.

FINANCE ATTEMPTS TO MAINTAIN THE VALUE
OF ECONOMIC RESOURCES

Fighting Inflation

Inflation is one of the major enemies of the Chilean Finance ministry. As the value of the national currency declines, the relative power of Finance's monopoly over economic resources declines as well. In a year of persistent inflation, the money spent at the end of the year has considerably less purchasing power in certain categories of the budget (nonpersonal goods and services, real capital investment) than it did at the beginning. Since state income in Chile does not increase at a rate even with the inflation, each unit of revenue that Finance collects during the year is worth less than when it was originally budgeted.

For example, if the inflation rate were 2 percent per month in relation to prices of the previous year, the money spent in the month of December would be worth only 78 percent of that spent in January. The real value of the total allocation to the public sector would be only 87.3 percent of the amount passed by Congress the previous December. Each agency's budget would be automatically cut by 12.7 percent in real terms by the time the budget year ended. Taking a hypothetical budget of 300, this deterioration can be illustrated as in Table 4. Inflation rates over a twelve-year period of Chile's history are included in Table 5, showing that within this period the average rate of inflation was considerably higher than the rate used in the example.

What does persistent inflation mean in practical terms? Certainly it causes difficulties for the individual agencies, but these difficulties are compounded for the Budget Bureau. The inflation rate, an unknown datum at the beginning of the year, cannot be programmed into agency allocations. As the agencies' purchasing power diminishes, their capacity to achieve their goals is seriously impaired. Not content to let their financial base slip away without a fight, they attempt to recover lost ground by making heavy demands on Finance to supplement their allocations, especially during the second semester.

The undeniable fact that the budgetary figures are artificial because

TABLE 4. THE EFFECT OF INFLATION ON AGENCY BUDGETS

Month	J	F	M	A	M	J	J	A	S	O	N	D	Total
Scheduled Nominal Payments	20	20	20	20	20	20	30	30	30	30	30	30	300.0
Progressive Inflation (percent)	0	2	4	6	8	10	12	14	16	18	20	22	22
Real Payments	20.0	19.6	19.2	18.8	18.4	18.0	26.4	25.8	25.2	24.6	24.0	23.4	263.4

NOTE: Finance generally decrees 40 percent of the allocation in the first semester, and 60 percent in the second semester.

TABLE 5.   TWELVE YEARS OF INFLATION IN CHILE
(*In percent*)

	1962	1963	1964	1965	1966	1967	1968	1969	1970	1971	1972	1973
Inflation	27.7	45.4	38.4	25.9	17.0	21.9	27.9	29.3	34.9	22.1	163.4	528.0

SOURCE: Government price statistics, compiled by the National Office of Statistics and Census.

of inflation leads to allegations from the agencies that these same figures are artificial on other grounds as well—such as that Finance did not allocate them enough in the first place. The realization that no budgetary item is secure means that Finance has greater difficulty taking a hard line against those agencies that want to build more miles of highway, more houses, or more sanitary works, or expropriate more farms, despite the projections of the original budget law. When the Budget Bureau gives in to the requests of the ministries to compensate for inflation, it often must resort to deficit financing, which simply aggravates the inflationary spiral.

The Restrictive Position

Finance's method to help prevent inflation and counteract some of the expansionary pretensions of agencies is to be extremely restrictive in the allocation of supplementary funds. Because client pressures for increased services often undermine this policy, Finance looks for additional institutional support to maintain its restrictive line. Its relative success in this domain will be examined more thoroughly in the following two chapters, which include a discussion of the Economic Committee, a high-level policy-making body. For the moment it can be said that the Budget Bureau in Chile has succeeded in establishing the hard-nosed reputation that it will always take time to listen to plaintive cries for more funds, lend a sympathetic ear, but very rarely deliver the goods.

The Budget Bureau is forever pushing the agencies to reveal the minimum budgetary allowance with which they could survive over the coming year, including remunerations, the barest of operating expenses, and those capital projects that are absolutely undeniable because they have already begun, or carry heavy political commitments. By inducing an agency to perform the same functions with an allocation of 90, whereas previously it had been receiving 100, the national budgeters achieve two goals. First, they increase the value of the 90 by approximately 11 percent in terms of marginal utility. Second, they retain access to the remaining 10, which can be redistributed at their own discretion. A restrictive position also responds to the Budget Bureau's prejudice that most agencies are inherently inefficient, and that cutting funds will help improve their "administrative capacity."

Underestimating Revenues

One method used by Finance to complement a restrictive position is to underestimate its revenues for the budget year, and then require the bureaus in the public sector to formulate their individual budgets in line with the reduced figure.

The process of underestimating is not carried out by arriving first at an accurate projection and then cutting it by a safe amount. The department of Programming and Global Statistics first makes separate estimates on each revenue source. Given the uncertainties of the real levels of economic activity many months hence, these estimates are never exact. But they can be ordered from the most optimistic to the most pessimistic. In formulating its estimate of total revenues, the Budget Bureau selects in each case a figure that is very close to the most pessimistic.

In the 1968 copper account, for example, the department of Programming and Global Statistics predicted that the average price of copper for the year would be somewhere between 45 and 57 cents (in U.S. money) per pound. Each price between the two extremes would have resulted in a different level of state revenue. The Budget Bureau was almost positive that the price would not be as low as 45 cents, yet it calculated the state's income on that figure. (The actual price was 56.28 cents.) The same procedure occurs perennially in other accounts, such as the sales tax, customs duties, and luxury taxes. Conservative figures for every category are added up to give the total estimated revenue for the next year. This total revenue is then divided up among the sectors in terms of ceilings (*cifras topes*) with which the agencies must formulate their draft budgets. Naturally, unless the year turns out to be an economic disaster, the total revenue estimates are low, the ceilings are artificially depressed, and the budgets proposed by the agencies are unwarrantedly diminutive. But the Budget Bureau hopes that, by being diminutive, they represent a facsimile of the skeleton budget of the sector. Table 6 illustrates the tendency of Finance to underestimate its revenues for the year.[10]

Finance's fight against inflation, its restrictive posture on allocational requests, and its tendency to underestimate revenues are efforts to protect the value of the resource it controls—money. If it could slow infla-

---

[10] The years 1969 and 1970 were difficult ones for the Chilean economy, and the Budget Bureau did not anticipate the seriousness of the situation in time to underestimate the revenues sufficiently. When income fell short of even the most pessimistic figures, Finance cut the budgets of those ministries with the least political clout.

TABLE 6. ESTIMATED AND REAL REVENUES IN THE CENTRALIZED PUBLIC
SECTOR, 1961–1973
(*In millions of escudos only, excluding dollar revenues*)

Year	Estimated Revenue	Real Revenue	Percentage Difference
1961	794.5	932.8	+17.4
1962	1,006.3	1,105.0	+ 9.8
1963	1,299.4	1,398.7	+ 7.6
1964	1,770.8	2,022.3	+14.2
1965	2,817.4	3,423.5	+21.5
1966	4,174.7	5,460.5	+30.7
1967	5,426.2	6,275.9	+15.6
1968	7,408.7	8,792.5	+18.7
1969	12,720.0	12,058.6	− 5.2
1970	18,926.0	18,588.0	− 1.8
1971	28,614.2	31,814.4	+10.1
1972	39,120.2	62,056.0[a]	+37.0
1973	131,292.7	[b]	[b]

SOURCE: Ministerio de Hacienda, *Ley de Presupuesto*, 1961–1973; Contraloría General de la República, *Memoria*, 1962–1971. Also, Budget Bureau statistics.
[a] Estimated by the Budget Bureau Statistics department.
[b] Unavailable.

tion, it could deflate the arguments of agencies continually in need of new funds. When it restricts supplementary allocations and makes agencies cut below artificial ceilings, it is attempting to induce the agencies to squeeze a high degree of marginal utility out of the money that is allocated. With these tactics, the Finance ministry hopes to forge a trading situation that is much more favorable from its perspective of controlling the overall deficit.

FINANCE ATTEMPTS TO EXTRACT INFORMATION AT LEAST COST

Structural Reorganization

As the pattern of public expenditures has become more complex, administrative reform in the Chilean Budget Bureau has been consistently geared toward facilitating the compilation of useful information on the spending habits of governmental units. Before 1964, Finance was incapable of gathering more than a crude appreciation of the real needs of the agencies and their capacity to carry out programs. A small number of analysts were responsible for either the current or the capital account in each sector, but never for both. In ministries such as Education and Interior, few difficulties arose, since these sectors had no capital account of any dimension. But the arrangement was partially responsible for the endemic lack of control in other sectors, such as Public Works, in which significant portions of the total budget were concentrated in both current and capital expenditures. During these years Finance was pretty much dependent on the ministries and decentralized agencies to balance their own accounts. The results were often "accidental" miscalculations of sectoral requirements during critical periods of the year, and last-minute interventions by the Central Bank to print up money, saving the agency from its financial crisis.

After 1964, the Budget Bureau began to alter its organizational chart to build a defense against sectorally induced emergencies. It absorbed a department of Economic Studies from the Central Bank to help estimate total revenues and program sectoral allocations. No longer were separate personnel working on each ministry with little communication between them, but individual analysts were assigned to each agency or sector. These analysts were responsible for keeping abreast of every financial aspect of the sector's activity, integrating the current and capital accounts to diminish the number of contingencies, and encouraging the agencies to adopt more rational programming techniques.

In 1971 the Budget Bureau went through a further reorganization designed to place more emphasis on the execution of the budget than on its formulation, in an effort to prevent spending overruns. The operations department was divided into seven sub-units to review expenditure tendencies in the different realms of the government apparatus. In general, one analyst oversaw each of the seventeen major governmental bodies, and additional personnel covered some of the larger decentralized agencies and state industries, such as the National Health Service, the national airlines (LAN-Chile), and the national railroads (Ferrocarriles del Estado). Figure 8 presents the organizational chart of the operations department, which demonstrates its functional specialization for information-gathering.

In 1972 the Budget Bureau employed data-processing equipment (IBM model 1401) located in the National Treasury to trace the expenditure patterns of the individual governmental units. This mechanical information-collector helped reduce uncertainty by providing up-to-date readings of agencies' expenditures in each budgetary item. The information was oriented toward: (1) preparing statistics on global demands of the public sector; (2) helping the Treasury manage the cash position of the government; (3) analyzing the pace, destiny, and composition of public expenditures; and (4) providing necessary background for the

FIGURE 8.   SECTORAL DIVISIONS IN THE BUDGET BUREAU'S OPERATIONS
DEPARTMENT

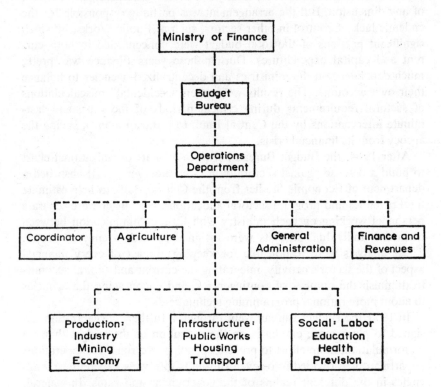

SOURCE: Ministerio de Hacienda, "Proyecto de Reorganización de la Dirección de
Presupuestos, Descripción de las Funciones de los Departamentos y Divisiones de la
Subdirección de Presupuestos."

analysis of transfers and other budgetary modifications.[11] Through these
techniques Finance hoped to mitigate the agencies' tendencies to spend
indiscriminately at certain points in the year, and apply compensatory
sanctions when such practices were detected.

The evolution of structures and practices in the Budget Bureau has
been directed toward increasing its access to information on the agencies'
capacity to execute programs and the marginal utility of the funds they
spend. However, several obstacles still had to be overcome to achieve
complete success. In the first place, the IBM program contained slots
only for disbursements of those items included in the national budget law.

[11] Gustavo G. Santa Ana, "El Sistema Mecanizado para el Control de la Ejecución del Presupuesto por Programas del Sector Fiscal."

The budget passed by Congress omitted the individual allocations of all the semi-autonomous agencies and state enterprises, which spent about 50 percent of governmental income each year. Nor had a method been devised to record the commitments and orders made early in the budget year by agencies promising creditors that they would be paid out of funds decreed later on. The total amount of these bills represented a floating debt often exceeding the agency's full allocation. While it was easy to record on IBM cards the amounts of money the agency actually spent, Finance had to recur to more subtle or coercive means to oblige the agency to give a running account of how many goods and services it had ordered from the private sector.

The intention of appointing an analyst to each sector was to assign financial experts to the budgetary affairs of specific agencies in order to further the restrictive orientation of the Finance ministry. But in the Chilean case, oftentimes the ministry or the autonomous agency "captures" its respective analyst.[12] After the analysts have been working on the same account for a period of time, they become intimately acquainted with the ministry's activities and develop positive exchange relations with those persons charged with promoting the organization's budgetary requests. The analysts are continually subjected to personal pressures to argue the sector's case favorably before the minister of Finance. Often the analyst empathizes as much or more with the need for more generous financing for his sector than with his job of searching for that extra margin to be dispersed to other priorities. The capture is complete when the analyst is actually hired away from the Budget Bureau by the agency or ministry with which he has been dealing. The prospects for *pantouflage* (skipping from one organization to the other) can influence the attitudes of the analysts toward their job, impeding information flow at the very heart of the Finance ministry.

Program Budget

Finance's most ambitious attempt to cheapen the value of information is through implementation of the planning-programming-budgeting system, or PPBS. Under PPBS, a program's unit of production is described and quantified in terms such as houses built, families settled on expropriated farm lands, students matriculated, and tonnage of freight moved.[13] Differing amounts of human resources, capital outlay, and current expenditures, organized over time and filtered through the agency's infrastructure, are combined to achieve measurable levels of program

[12] Interview material.
[13] Joint Economic Committee, *The Planning-Programming-Budgeting System: Progress and Potentials.*

output.[14] The composition of the inputs is tightly monitored in order to control the cost and magnitude of the output. With PPBS, political leadership can theoretically list its goals on one side of a ledger sheet, and the real cost of achieving them on the other side, and proceed to match preferences with the resources available. The bureaucracy's full acceptance of the program budget would give the government a tremendous tool to orient public sector activities toward national priorities.

Notwithstanding, there are many criticisms of the technique, most of which boil down to the problem of gathering and organizing the tremendous amount of information required for the system to operate with complete success. For example, it is contended that the difficulties in quantifying organizational functions, the vast areas of ignorance on the unit's activities, the obstacles to developing a common language to transmit the information that exists, and the lack of time to integrate and coordinate these data into a relatively inflexible budget document, all dictate against fulfilling the conditions of PPBS. These arguments against the feasibility of program-budgeting, however, are little more than academic when they emphasize the abstract weaknesses in the concept without judging how much information is necessary for the system to operate with partial success, or the relative preferability of a deficient program-budgeting system to no program-budgeting system at all. The evidence shows that the concept is sufficiently sound to convince bureaucracy after bureaucracy to attempt to implement it.

This system was first introduced in the Chilean public sector in 1960 by the National Health Service, a decentralized agency. In 1967 Finance began to extend it throughout the public bureaucracy. Gradually the forms on which the agencies submitted their budgets corresponded to the PPBS model. The Budget Bureau also issued a comprehensive manual on the system, *Methodological Bases of Budgetary Reform,* which relied heavily on United Nations publications and emphasized the technical advantages of programming.[15]

Finance has attempted to proselytize the agencies through an ideology of a budgetary technology accepted in international circles, but so far has met only partial success. Substitution of the traditional routine with the appurtenances of the program budget has been slow, because of the fundamental changes involved and the resistance of the administrators in the public sector. Congress has not passed the basic legislation officially changing the old system into the program budget. There has been no ultimatum from the political leaders of the country obliging adminis-

[14] David Nevick (ed.), *Program Budgeting*; Fremond J. Lyden and Ernest G. Miller, *Planning Programming Budgeting.*
[15] Ministerio de Hacienda, *Bases Metodológicas de la Reforma Presupuestaria.*

trators lower on the hierarchy to accept PPBS. This resistance to the program budget by the agencies will be examined in more detail below. Nonetheless, spurred by the obvious advantages the system connotes for managing the country's fiscal policies, the Budget Bureau continues to encourage its implementation.

The Oficio Final

Partially because Finance lacks the full advantages of the program budget, it uses the promise of increased allocations to extract additional information from the agencies before the budget is definitely submitted to Congress. Since the regime has made very few of the relevant political and economic decisions by September 1, the budget originally presented to Congress represents little more than a repetition of the previous year's allocation plus its modifications. The revenue figures are quite conservative compared to what the Budget Bureau really expects them to be, and pending allocational problems have yet to be resolved.

Beginning in September, the Budget Bureau starts working on a final draft of the budget called the *oficio final*. Very near the end of the fiscal year (usually in the second half of December), the president sends a communiqué to Congress proposing modifications in both the revenue and expenditure side of the budget and substituting the oficio final for the draft submitted in September. The oficio final, reflecting the government's latest political decisions, usually equals the budget that begins the next year. The extent to which the oficio final can differ from the document initially submitted to Congress is shown in Table 7.

During the months of September, October, and November, the Budget Bureau is involved in fervent discussions with the sectors in an attempt to reconcile their stated with their real needs, and the capacity of the government to finance them. Most discussion revolves around each agency's Expansion List, or those projects requiring funds over and above the ceilings originally issued in April. In the course of these proceedings the position of Finance remains very restrictive. The burden is on the individual agencies to submit new reports and graphs proving their financial requirements. The Budget Bureau expects that by suffering an excruciating number of visits to argue their case, the agencies will reveal tidbits of information extremely useful for deflating their budgetary pretensions.

Although Finance insists that information should be passed with no impediments or distortions from the operating departments to the Budget Bureau, this does not mean that it freely divulges privileged information to the sectors. Finance's secretiveness is most accentuated when it tries to maintain reserves to cover for contingencies in the activities of im-

TABLE 7. CHANGES IN THE DRAFT BUDGET IN SELECTED ACCOUNTS FROM EARLY SEPTEMBER TO LATE DECEMBER
(*In millions of escudos and millions of dollars*)

Year	Account	September Draft		Officio Final		Official Budget		Percent Diff. From Sept. to Dec.	
		Escudos	U.S. $	Escudos	U.S. $	Escudos	U.S. $	Escudos	U.S. $
A. Total Government									
1967	Current	4,083.7	68.0	4,258.4	69.6	4,258.0	69.6	4.3	2.4
	Capital	1,752.5	85.3	1,766.9	87.9	1,766.4	87.9	.8	3.0
1968	Current	4,691.5	77.7	5,578.3	31.6	5,578.3	81.7	18.9	−8.8
	Capital	2,251.4	59.3	2,311.0	58.1	2,311.0	58.1	2.6	−2.0
1969	Current	7,634.3	85.2	8,028.8	85.2	8,022.9	85.2	5.1	0.0
	Capital	3,205.8	102.3	3,315.3	103.7	3,313.9	102.3	3.1	1.4
1972	Current	25,431.3	118.0	28,781.9	125.5	28,565.7	126.4	12.3	7.1
	Capital	8,946.6	134.1	10,338.3	137.4	9,017.9	137.3	.1	2.5
1973	Current	48,046.0	156.2	98,661.0	156.1	97,740.3	156.0	103.4	0.0
	Capital	28,370.5	151.2	38,489.2	133.8	33,552.4	130.8	18.3	−13.5
B. Agriculture									
1968	Current	170.8	—	194.2	—	194.2	.1	13.7	—
	Capital	264.9	—	289.6	—	289.6	.4	9.3	—
1969	Current	229.9	—	245.0	—	245.0	—	6.6	—
	Capital	278.2	—	344.3	—	344.3	—	23.7	—
1972	Current	1,213.6	.1	1,701.4	.1	1,701.4	.1	40.2	0.0
	Capital	1,789.5	—	1,136.6	—	1,086.6	—	−39.3	—
1973	Current	2,973.0	.1	3,466.3	.1	3,055.7	.1	2.8	0.0
	Capital	3,168.2	—	4,257.7	—	2,154.3	—	−32.0	—
C. Education									
1968	Current	1,151.6	1.0	1,183.5	1.1	1,183.5	1.1	2.8	15.5
	Capital	196.3	.3	227.7	1.2	227.7	1.2	16.2	300.0
1969	Current	1,561.1	1.3	1,657.5	1.2	1,657.5	1.2	6.2	−6.1
	Capital	110.3	1.0	136.1	1.0	136.1	1.0	23.5	23.4
1972	Current	5,963.2	.2	6,565.6	.1	6,553.1	.1	9.9	−50.0
	Capital	95.8	.3	614.1	.3	614.1	.3	541.0	0.0
1973	Current	11,598.6	.1	14,499.8	.1	14,374.0	.1	23.9	0.0
	Capital	2,051.5	.3	2,918.1	.3	2,918.1	.3	42.2	0.0

SOURCES: Cámara de Diputados, Legislación Ordinaria, *Sesion 41a* (*31 August, 1966*), 4714–6; Cámara, Extraordinaria, *Sesion 24a* (*26 December, 1967*), 2034–6; Cámara, Ordinaria, *Sesion 41a* (*5 September, 1967*), 3383–5; Cámara, Ordinaria, *Sesion 30a* (*3 September, 1968*), 3065–8; Senado, *Sesion 25a* (*18 December, 1968*), 1286–8; Ministerio de Hacienda, *Cálculo de Entradas de la Nación Correspondientes al Año 1972, 1973* (Santiago: Dirección de Presupuestos, 1971, 1972), Folletos 119 and 121; *ibid.*, *Oficio Final N° 2164* (December 21, 1971), mimeo; *ibid.*, *Oficio Final N° 3318* (December 18, 1972), mimeo; *ibid.*, *Ley de Presupuesto 1967–1969, 1972–1973*.

NOTE: These figures pertain to the centralized ministries. Data were not obtained for the 1970 and 1971 budgets. Dashes mean "zero."

portant agencies. In preparing the 1970 budget, for instance, an analyst noticed that the ministry of Health had not included the costs of equipping a new hospital due for completion near the end of the budget year. The Budget chief felt intuitively that Urban Services was going to require a greater sum than originally estimated by the ministry of Housing and Urbanism. The Finance minister observed that the number of bridges and roads built by Public Works would turn out to be more than the number requested in the budget.[16] In general, central budgetary officials make mental notes of these pending problems and discuss them in staff meetings, but the question marks they represent are not communicated to the respective sectors. By submitting its Expansion List, the agency is in essence informing the analyst of those particular expenses that are truly most probable. The analyst rarely inquires about the other items on his own list, since the ministerial Budget office would immediately add them into the draft budget, transforming them from "possible expenses" to "certain expenses."

The Budget Bureau's ambiguous attitude toward the free flow of information is not unexpected, given its motivation to protect its bargaining position. Until information is made available to it, Finance has no reason to pass information naively to the agencies. By withholding knowledge in this manner it is able to hoard a portion of its financial resources over the short term and help extract additional information from the agencies. An unavoidable side effect of these practices is to make the budget passed in December a conglomeration of concealed information, hidden resources, and artificial accounts.

FINANCE ATTEMPTS TO COUNTERACT
RESTRICTED INFORMATION

Global Allocations

One of the conventional tactics used by the Finance ministry to protect itself from poor information is to allocate on a global basis. Through the budgetary cycle, Finance routinely swings from a global position to a finite examination of the sector's requirements, and then back to a global allocation. First, the step of setting limits in April is an exercise in macro economics. When the ceilings are sent out, the budget is perfectly balanced. This ceiling implies no obligations as to the specific projects included within its limits. The presumption is that the agencies will respond by providing two sorts of data: those expenses that

[16] Interview material.

are ostensibly the basic requirements of the organization and which fall within the ceiling, and those expenses that facilitate the agency's reaching its goals, included in the Expansion List. Second, this information is scrutinized by the budget analysts, who evaluate the priority of the items on the Expansion List and report to the budget chief on the total allocation being requested. Third, at the end of the process, once the definitive budget for all the sectors has been decided, the agencies retain considerable independence in dividing their allocations as they see fit. There is widespread recognition that in the final analysis, the Finance ministry is interested in the *global* amounts that each sector receives and not necessarily how this money is going to be used.

In a diagram similar to the one in Figure 6, it would be possible to correlate higher levels in the Chilean budgetary hierarchy with a scale of decreasing interest with program content and increasing preoccupation with the size of the total allocation. The representative of the individual agency has fairly complete information on his desired expenditures for the next year, but is incapable of comparing his requested allocation with those of other governmental units, or of empathizing with the norm of a balanced budget. The ministerial Budget office, whose data on the expansion projects of the sector are less exhaustive than those of the specific agencies, is concerned with increasing the global allocation of the sector as a whole.

The Budget Bureau analysts, located in the middle of the process, receive information from two sources. From above come political and economic decisions from the head of the Budget Bureau and the Finance minister on the global limits for each sector. The analysts' task is to cut and slice projects on paper until that global limit is reached. The Finance minister is juggling all the numbers for the public sector, not just those of the individual agency. Naturally he wants the budget to represent to some degree the political priorities of the government, but he has little time to be impressed with the tangible benefits of specific projects in school-building, health facilities, or sanitary works construction. His predominant concern is to whittle down the magnitude of the deficit, and devise a way to finance it.

Once the final ceilings have been proclaimed in the December budget law, the agencies have a renewed opportunity to divide their allocation among the different items. While the apparent objective of this procedure is to make the budget a more realistic document, given last-minute contingencies, the final ordering often changes the priorities the agency had been pushing in negotiations with Finance. To illustrate, the original March ceiling for hypothetical Sector A was 900. Given the sector's spending request of 1100, the Finance minister decided between March and September that the maximum could be raised to 950. After an exhaustive, definitive examination of the sector's programs between September and December, the analyst in the Budget Bureau arrived at a formula allowing Sector A to include several of its most important projects in the budget at a cost of 953. Under this scheme, a very impressive new project X, costing 35, and two old projects, costing 12 and 15 respectively, were included in the budget. Because of the analyst's positive testimony on the presumed importance of project X, the Finance minister acceded to the 953 figure for the oficio final. However, once the budget law was passed, and no more discussion or bargaining on the ceiling was allowed, the agency had the freedom to divide this 953 among its projects in the manner it deemed advisable. For the purposes of the budget that began the year, the agency decided that it really was not too interested in project X, reduced its quota to only 5, and spread the remaining 30 among projects Y and Z. The heavy emphasis on project X was simply a convenient means to increase the total allocation.

The fact that information, progressively more capsulated and general, is passed upward, while global allocations are sent downward, places the Budget Bureau analysts at a relay point between the two. In order to have their ceilings raised at all, the sectors have to present convincing arguments to the analysts, who sift through them to provide the minister of Finance with cues that help set the global limits on the sectors' allocations. The analysts' supposed function is to cover every possible angle in forging an informal limit to the sectors' spending. But in the brief span from December to January, the substance of much of this information can become null and void as the agencies rethink the most effective way to divide their total allocation. The information gathered by the analysts during the period of budgetary formation is treated like many gadgets of the modern world—it is disposable.

When the lack of information makes their job totally impossible, however, the analysts in the Budget Bureau also deal in global figures. After Finance receives the draft budget on June 30, the personnel in the Budget Bureau obviously cannot quantify and verify every account submitted. They have two norms to orient their attitude toward the spending request: the degree to which the request goes over the ceiling, and the agency's reputation for cooperation and for skilled budget-making.

There is no legal dictum preventing the agency from submitting a draft budget exceeding the ceiling by unusually large amounts. Nor do all agencies always make sincere efforts to provide the Budget Bureau with even the minimal amount of information solicited. When an agency submits inflated figures for grandiose plans for expansion, Finance immediately asks why no political indication preceded the budgetary request. In the case of agrarian reform, for example, after the Christian Democratic government came to power in 1964, the budget for the ministry of Agriculture was obviously going to rise significantly. The political agitation around the issue was sufficient to expect large requests from that sector.[17] But if an agency is programmed to continue working at more or less the same level of output, a gross exaggeration in the spending requisition unsettles the analysts and makes them rather impatient. They do not place the request aside and review it as time permits. Nor do they go through the step of petitioning more background information. Rather they call up the offending ministerial Budget office and tell it that the draft budget is completely unacceptable and that the request is being cut arbitrarily to the ceiling first indicated.

Global allocational decisions are the response to requisitions that vastly exceed the *cifras topes*. If the original maximum of 100 is returned by the agency blown up to 250 (not an uncommon occurrence), the presumption is that a serious study is not worth the effort. On the other hand, a projected budget falling somewhere near the ceiling first proposed by Finance profits from an entirely different set of working assumptions. A draft budget of 120 on the basis of a ceiling of 100, considered fairly reasonable by the personnel in the Budget Bureau, prompts a very sympathetic study in return. The Budget Bureau tends to be impressed that the agency has used a methodology to arrive at this figure, most likely studied the full program connotations of the projected allocation, and really tried to hold expenses down. If the agency wants only an additional 20, it probably knows where the 20 is going and what program goals it will serve.[18] If the agency requests 250, the conclusion is that the budget was prepared hastily and irresponsibly and the best way to handle it is to cut it, period. Under these standards, the agency requesting 120 has a far better chance of winning the full 120 at this stage of the process than the overambitious agency has of receiving anything above 100.

Incrementalism

Perhaps the most widely discussed hedge against the lack of information used by practically all allocating agencies is budgetary incrementalism.[19] The basic precepts of incrementalism are (1) the agency

---

[17] Interview material.
[18] The National Defense ministry has been especially adept at this practice. Its programs are anatomized down to the amount of protein consumed by each trooper. The magnitude of this information, and the competence with which it is organized, leave very little margin for the analyst to cut.
[19] See Davis et al., "A Theory of the Budgetary Process."

performed more or less satisfactorily in the previous budgetary period; (2) there is not enough time or technical skill to make a comprehensive examination of the agency's total budget; so (3) any changes in this year's budget need not be more than marginal. If Year 1 proved to be fairly routine with no breakdowns, the budget for Year 2 should not differ very much. If hospital care continues at about the same level, if secondary-school students are coming from the same social class, and if no new services are extended to the indigenous population, and so on, there is no compelling reason why sudden shifts are necessary. Practically speaking, incrementalism boils down to an analysis of all *changes* in the current allocational request and a benign affection for recurrent expenditures.

Usually incrementalism is interpreted as pro-status quo, with only the most innocuous modifications built into its operations. In the Chilean case these change elements are not very dynamic. In the educational sector, the Budget Bureau allows personnel increases equal to the increase in projected matriculation. If school attendance rises by 4 percent, it is expected that remunerations will rise by 4 percent as well. Analysts have data stretching back for many years showing that all noncapital expenditures in the National Health Service have risen at a level of 5 percent per year. Accordingly, all increases of 5 percent are ignored; only when the request is higher does Finance become curious about the purpose of the funds.

Of course, it is difficult to determine whether the consistent tendency dictates the rule of thumb, or the rule of thumb has dictated the consistent tendency. The arbitrariness of these mechanisms points to the Budget Bureau's ignorance of what constitutes the marginal utility of activity in the sectors. When information is lacking, the easiest solution is to increase budgetary allocations according to some scale that is measurable and convenient. In the education budget, there is an enormous difference in the amount of knowledge needed to make an allocational decision on the basis of, on the one hand, levels of new school enrollment and, on the other, the relative benefit of all funds spent on existing or potential programs in education.[20] Incrementalism becomes entrenched when ritualistic conservativism and stand-patness become the basic assumptions of the budgetary process.

Budgetary incrementalism need not be a faithful harbinger of administrative incrementalism. Innovative, fundamental changes can occur in governmental programs without showing up in the total figures of the

[20] Aaron Wildavsky discusses the problems of complexity in *The Politics of the Budgetary Process*, pp. 8–16.

agency's budget. Through a change in the subject matter and daily academic routine, it is possible for the educational experience to be completely overhauled with no corresponding increase or decrease in the budget. Yet while revenues are tightly limited, the state does not have the means to hire 60 percent more teachers or simulate a boarding-school environment for all children from poor families. Nor can the government consider a massive hospital construction program or pro-vide every urban shantytown dweller (*poblador*) with a house of his own.

The frequent recourse to incrementalism is a function of both poor information and the onerous limitations of state revenues. The Budget Bureau practices incrementalism because it does not know the marginal utility of the scarce funds it distributes. If its store of resources were to increase dramatically, as they tend to do in Chile at the beginning of each presidential period, the emphasis on marginal utility would not be so obsessive and Finance could distribute them more freely. When resources (in the case of budgets, either information or money) are not in such short supply, one can expect incrementalism to decrease.

Repetitive Budgeting

Another protective device used by Finance against the vicis-situdes of poor information is to delay assigning funds for agency use until the visible need is so evident that it cannot be denied—even if that moment does not arrive until the last quarter. Repetitive budget-ing is essentially a series of increases in sectoral allocations during the fiscal year.[21] Finance sets the stage for repetitive budgeting when it subscribes to a budget law that lowers starting allocations to a level unrealistically oppressive for some sectors. The extra income entering the public treasury during the year represents a perpetual margin of liquidity for Finance which, as unprogrammed contingencies come to the fore, it can allocate based on the very latest information.

The observation that the final budget, including modifications, has little to do with the budget passed by Congress leads to the question: Which budget is the real budget? The answer is not confined to these two choices, however, since the amount of money that the agencies actually spend can be interpreted as a more accurate indicator of the organization's impact on the society.[22] Different stages in repetitive budgeting are documented in Table 8.

The most satisfactory way to determine which stage represents the

[21] James W. Wilkie documents repetitive budgeting in Mexico from 1869 to 1963. See *The Mexican Revolution: Federal Expenditures and Social Change since 1910.*
[22] This is Wilkie's interpretation in his analysis.

TABLE 8.   REPETITIVE BUDGETING AND THE GROWTH OF PUBLIC EX-
PENDITURES, 1961–1973
(*In millions of escudos only, excluding dollar expenditures*)

Year	Budget Law	Index	With Supplements	Index	Final Expenditures	Index
A. Total Centralized Government (*Capital Account*)						
1961	285.5	100	285.7	100	227.1	80
1962	328.4	100	328.3	100	282.9	86
1963	440.7	100	474.7	107	414.5	94
1964	555.9	100	657.2	118	700.5	126
1965	993.7	100	1,457.7	151	1,303.8	131
1966	1,582.9	100	2,291.4	145	2,210.2	140
1967	1,766.4	100	2,498.0	141	2,016.6	114
1968	2,311.0	100	3,261.7	141	2,954.1	128
1969	3,313.9	100	4,062.5	123	3,720.3	112
1970	4,053.0	100	4,860.8	120	4,753.3	117
1971	7,808.1	100	11,208.6	144	8,598.6	110
1972	9,017.9	100	11,792.4	131	11,516.1	129
1973	33,552.4	100	63,552.4[a]	189	[b]	
B. Education (*Current Account*)						
1961	147.9	100	152.1	103	132.8	90
1962	166.3	100	183.7	110	164.1	99
1963	203.6	100	226.6	111	211.1	104
1964	264.3	100	347.6	132	336.3	127
1965	397.6	100	511.6	128	496.8	125
1966	581.9	100	727.6	125	705.3	121
1967	786.9	100	933.9	118	900.6	114
1968	1,183.5	100	1,432.0	121	1,362.4	115
1969	1,657.5	100	2,242.3	135	2,146.2	129
1970	2,707.4	100	3,690.8	136	3,496.8	124
1971	4,254.9	100	5,766.3	136	5,955.7	140
1972	6,553.1	100	12,381.8	189	11,933.5	182
1973	14,374.0	100	22,459.8[a]	151	[b]	
C. Public Works (*Capital Accuont*)						
1961	45.2	100	47.7	105	43.5	
1962	59.2	100	68.8	116	63.8	97
1963	129.3	100	172.6	133	170.3	107
1964	269.1	100	315.1	117	294.4	132
1965	363.6	100	497.0	136	440.7	109
1966	435.9	100	586.3	134	586.3	121
1967	473.2	100	612.8	129	570.0	134
1968	662.8	100	759.5	115	751.1	120
1969	807.4	100	1,135.5	140	1,135.1	113
1970	1,519.9	100	1,823.4	120	1,817.0	140
1971	2,027.6	100	2,052.8	101	2,027.8	119
1972	3,017.5	100	4,325.9	144	3,926.2	100
1973	10,392.0	100	18,892.0[a]	182	[b]	125

TABLE 8.   *(Continued)*

Year	Budget Law	In-dex	With Supple-ments	In-dex	Final Expend-itures	In-dex
		D. Agriculture (Capital Account)				
1961	1.4	100	1.4	100	0.2	14
1962	4.8	100	4.8	100	2.1	44
1963	32.6	100	32.6	100	9.3	28
1964	20.5	100	24.9	121	22.6	110
1965	55.5	100	135.8	244	69.7	125
1966	127.7	100	127.8	100	121.0	95
1967	209.7	100	210.6	101	174.7	83
1968	289.6	100	289.8	100	237.4	82
1969	344.3	100	391.4	113	375.6	109
1970	533.6	100	534.4	100	529.2	99
1971	1,354.1	100	1,354.1	100	1,053.7	78
1972	1,086.6	100	1,086.6	100	1,130.5	104
1973	2,154.3	100	4,007.4[a]	186	[b]	

SOURCE: Contraloría General de la República, *Memoria*, 1962–1972. Also, Budget Bureau statistics, 1973.

[a] Estimated by the Budget Bureau Statistics department.

[b] Unavailable.

"real" budget is to refer to the administrative forces behind each step and then associate the nature of those forces with a subjective definition of the budget. The allocations in the budget law represent the overall priorities of the highest government leaders. After they locate the margin in the budget, the president, his most trusted advisors, and the Finance ministry consciously expand some accounts more quickly than others. The budget law emerges after the only intensive attempt to program new directions in the pattern of public spending. However, the budget reigning at the end of the year, after all the modifications have taken place, is a function of twelve months of agency strategies to receive more funds. Not counting natural disasters or gross miscalculation, the amount of increase is a measure either of political influence inside the bureaucracy or of clever maneuvering by the agencies to outwit the Finance ministry. Finally, the column "final expenditures" tends to indicate the administrative capacity of the respective organization. If it succeeds in augmenting but not spending its allocation, the bureau's political skill evidently outran its administrative skill. Either it overestimated the cost of achieving certain goals or simply did not have the initiative to put the available money to use.

The four sections of Table 8 reveal an instructive pattern of increasing repetitive budgeting after 1964, when the Christian Democratic government began extensive programs in social reform and economic development. Since repetitive budgeting is a result of uncertainty and lack of information, its incidence *should* increase as the use of public expenditures becomes more dynamic and innovative. Combining this observation with others in this section, incrementalism and repetitive budgeting should be negatively correlated as levels of public expenditures increase. Chapter 4 will contain further observations on these variables.

Let us now move from the Finance ministry to agencies attempting to negotiate their budgets under the terms of Box II in Figure 7.

AGENCY ATTEMPTS TO MAINTAIN THE VALUE OF INFORMATION

Resisting Program Budget

No doubt the program budget is the most challenging administrative technique proffered to Chilean public agencies over the past decade. At first glance, full cooperation appears to be in an agency's best interests. By arranging the budget by means of programs, the agency's administrators can gain a clearer idea of the real investment in each area of activity, and help determine whether that investment is commensurate with its internal priorities. The use of quantifiable output units, even though they can never be precisely determined, provides a continuous method of checking the organization's current effectiveness. Knowledge of the approximate cost of achieving each unit of output under various environmental conditions can facilitate the distribution of funds and personnel among the departments and regional subsidiaries. In times of induced expansion or reduction, agency officials can calculate relatively accurately the specific formula of inputs to achieve the planned outcome. By participating in PPBS, an agency can gain access to systematically arranged information to manipulate its activities with the least experimentation, either in its regular operations or in times of crisis.

Important clues to the problems of program budgeting come from the invectives of central functionaries who dismiss intransigent bureaucrats hesitant to pass along information, the key to program budgeting, as anachronistic, recalcitrant, obstructionalist, lazy, senile, or even stupid. Only the most elliptical argument can identify PPBS with one of the agency's principal aims: an increase in its allocation. Officials at the sectoral level are not blind to the fact that the state does not have the capacity to finance *every* unit of government in a manner commensurate with its internal priorities. Nor is there a guarantee that Finance will provide adequate subsidies needed by *any* one *particular* agency to carry out its programs. Since budgeting decisions are always passed downward and programming information must be fed upward, there are real dangers for every level in providing too much information to superiors. The level above can use this information to expand the required output with the same input, to change the priorities under which the subordinate unit was operating—or, most dangerous, to "cut the fat." Agencies often interpret Finance's emphasis on PPBS as a smokescreen for its manifest concern with control over public expenditures.

If subtle resistance to the program budget is not altogether a calculated attempt to restrict information flow, at least it is an outcrop of a centrally sponsored policy that induces little cooperation from lower levels in the budgetary hierarchy.[23] While there are considerable advantages for each level to have access to information from the lower units, there is little incentive to send this information upward in undistorted fashion.[24] The program budget runs into most difficulty at the

[23] A long-time participant in the Chilean Budget Bureau writes: "The implantation of a system of program budgeting has led to a simple modification of the procedures formalizing the relations between the Budget Bureau and the ministries, agencies, and other entities at that level. . . . The program budget has not obtained the active adhesion of the middle-level administrator. Since it is only a scheme for transferring information, it becomes only one more duty on top of all the rest that pop up in his daily activity. In sum, the development of the Chilean budgetary system has been primarily a super-structural phenomenon interesting the top of the administrative hierarchy only very partially, and has experienced very weak penetration in the bases of the institutions." Darío Pavez, "Alcances sobre el Desarrollo de las Técnicas Presupuestarias," pp. 14–15.
[24] Pavez (p. 13) astutely points out that "If we remember that normally bureaucracy looks upon all changes in its procedures in terms of their effect on status, security, control, etc., we will have to accept that this resistance is doubly vigorous when there is an attempt to bring discipline to the handling of financial resources, and establish mechanisms that openly evaluate how well they are being managed. The bureaucrat who has exclusive authorization over budgetary administration controls an appreciable command and negotiating power that is difficult for him to give up." Moshe Shani found that "PPBS was inferior to conventional budgeting in mobilizing resources both from the central budgetary department and from the legislature. As soon as operating departments felt that their ability in obtaining resources was largely dependent on the bargaining and negotiation that shaped the conventional budget 'rules of the game,' their motivation in engaging in PPBS weakened. This was because the use of PPBS was costly in resources and organizational effort, whilst the direct benefits derived from PPBS appeared insignificant." Shani concludes that "PPBS should be viewed not as a substitute for the conventional budget but as a system aimed primarily at meeting the informational

points of interaction between the agencies and the ministerial Budget office, and between the sectoral Budget offices and the Budget Bureau in the Finance ministry (see Figure 6).

Once the sector has received its ceiling from the Finance ministry, the ministerial Budget office becomes engaged in a running battle with the different agencies in the sector to define their basic needs for the coming year. The appropriate step at this stage in the formation of the program budget is for all the officials involved to meet and exchange ideas on the projects in preparation. The ranking administrators from the agencies and the ministerial Budget office should sit around a conference table and arrive as nearly as possible at an optimal use of the funds allocated. The meeting would aim at integrating the programs already in progress and resolving any emergent conflicts or inconsistencies. All trimming and redistribution of funds among programs would occur at this meeting.

The experience of these meetings shows, however, that agency officials cannot conceptualize interlocking programs, but only greater and greater resources. Each agency head arrives with his samples and statistics, all of dubious validity in the eyes of the other participants, to demonstrate his agency's exclusive necessities. These statistics are seldom mutually consistent, and only serve to distend the discussion. In cases where the different functions of the agencies are technically independent (e.g., in education, primary, secondary and university teaching do not really overlap), structural walls between the agencies serve further to reduce the necessity for substantive communication.[25]

What is supposed to be a refined process to formulate a standard conception of the agencies' necessities soon reduces to bureaucratic politics. The agencies view their goals mainly in terms of asking for sufficient amounts of money to parallel or surpass the ceilings imposed by Finance, even at the expense of their sister organizations. Almost by definition, the heads of the agencies cannot reach a satisfactory agreement, and these meetings result in a highly imprecise statement of the sector's policy goals.[26]

---

needs of top management." Shani, *Administrative Considerations in a Planning-Programming-Budgeting System: The Case of the New York State Education Department.*

[25] Pavez (p. 9) observed that not all of the problems with the program budget in Chile could be attributed to agency apathy and resistance; another problem was determining the standard units of output. Many bureaus in the public sector originally were quite specialized, but then had a multitude of other functions added on. This has made them conglomerations of departments, divisions, and sections, all of which work with much functional independence.

[26] Interview material.

The ministerial Budget office does not usually compensate for the lack of cooperation of the agencies when it sends the combined request upward to the Budget Bureau. Since the organizational loyalty of a Budget office is to its sectoral ministry, not the Finance ministry, it does not cut extraneous or outlandish items from the Expansion Lists submitted. In addition, its dedication to the norms of the program budget are reduced because it recognizes that the *cifra tope* imposed by Finance is hardly sufficient to cover the bare necessities of the ministry. Finance may peg budgetary increases due to inflation, for example, at 20 percent, when the ministerial Budget office can prove categorically that operating costs have risen by at least twice that figure. The ministerial Budget office receives the impression that the more it cooperates with the Finance ministry, the more it is going to fall behind other sectors.

Though the material at its disposal is fairly consistent from year to year, the manner in which Finance wants it presented changes regularly. Filling out statistical tables requires considerable time, and reasonable delays can transform into purposeful evasion. When Finance asks for clarifications on program estimates, the Budget office is handicapped in providing a satisfactory answer by a lack of cooperation from the agencies, lack of time to reply, and lack of experience in the manifold aspects of the program budget. But also there are few inducements to work diligently to obtain the information. It is difficult for the Budget office to sympathize with Finance's request to set goals and reach them through the program budget when it feels that the resources allocated are both insufficient and artificially reduced to prevent the sector from doing so.

Distorting Information

The presumptions of Box II in Figure 7 are that Finance is precommitted to provide the agency with adequate resources to fulfill its functions, but that the agency somehow obscures complete information on the real costs of its operations. If Finance does not have accurate information on the efficiency of expenditures, it has no way to judge the minimum amount of subsidy necessary for the agency to reach its goals and the marginal utility of the money spent. By manipulating information, the ministerial Budget office can pretend to provide pertinent data when the true situation is quite the contrary. It can attempt to take advantage of the fact that well-presented allocation requests are often accepted, while those that are poorly laid out are automatically rejected.

In its 1971 proposal, an agency wanting 100 new electric typewriters to replace manual models pointed out that: (1) its current machines were very old; (2) the amount of money *estimated* for up-keep would pay for new machines in three years; (3) considerable working time was lost because of the condition of the machines; and (4) plans were under way to establish a typing center to process the work in a more rational manner. The real situation was that the agency had 35 perfectly good machines sitting on the shelf not being used, and it eventually used the money for other purposes.[27] Whereas with more accurate information the Budget Bureau could have refused this request, by distorting reality the sectoral organization transformed central surveillance into ineffective "remote" control.

A discussion of the Chilean Agrarian Reform Corporation (CORA) instructs on the dangers of informational backlash when the agency in Box II of Figure 7 operates in a more straightforward manner and allows unknowns to be cleared up. In 1964, the unprecedented nature of the agrarian reform effort and the very unstable task environment in which it worked severely hampered the gathering of accurate information. The novelty and magnitude of CORA's tasks made the true cost of many facets of the program almost impossible to determine in advance.[28] The dates when important enabling legislation would be passed by Congress, the level of production after the *latifundios* (large estates) were expropriated, the costs of supplying the agricultural cooperatives with adequate working capital, the exact number of *campesinos* (peasants) who would become the responsibility of the state, the new personnel requirements of the agency—all were mysteries when CORA began its operations in earnest.

Once these elements began to crystallize, however, there was little means of determining their consistency. One of the latent functions of the agency was the complete disruption of its own task environment by fomenting rapid change in the countryside. In its early history, the more CORA upset patterned agricultural relationships, the more successful it judged its performance. The agitated state of the agricultural sector precluded estimating stable cost and performance indicators on any conventional scale.

While the agrarian reform movement had the highest political priority, CORA's percentage of the national budget increased almost five-fold (see Table 9). From 1964 to 1969 it was generally conceded that the Budget Bureau did not care about calculating the lowest cost of placing a campesino family on a land reform settlement (*asentamiento*).

[27] Interview material.
[28] Other effects of rapid growth are summarized in Downs, *Inside Bureaucracy*, pp. 9–13, 248.

TABLE 9.   FINANCE SUBSIDIES TO THE AGRICULTURAL SECTOR, MINISTRY
OF AGRICULTURE, AND CORA, AS A PERCENTAGE OF ALL CENTRAL
EXPENDITURES, 1964–1969
(In millions of escudos each year)

Year	Total Central Expenditures		Agricultural Sector		Ministry of Agriculture		CORA	
	Escudos	%	Escudos	%	Escudos	%	Escudos	%
1964	2,378.3	100	117.6	4.9	63.9	2.7	13.0	.5
1965	3,991.7	100	231.1	5.8	127.2	3.2	34.4	.9
1966	5,693.3	100	337.9	5.9	226.9	3.9	77.4	1.4
1967	6,884.3	100	446.6	6.5	323.8	4.7	134.4	2.0
1968	9,692.4	100	635.8	6.6	439.2	4.5	181.4	1.9
1969	13,109.7	100	887.2	6.8	666.1	5.1	312.3	2.4

SOURCES: Corporación de la Reforma Agraria, *Balance Presupuestario del Año 1969*;
Ministerio de Hacienda, *Exposición sobre el Estado de la Hacienda Pública*, 1969.

Finance was predisposed to allocate CORA almost everything it requested, despite the fact that neither CORA nor the Budget Bureau had any idea of the marginal utility of the investment.

During this period CORA was unable to spend its full budget. The perpetual margin meant that personnel nearer the technical core of the agency had little reason to fear that their funds would or could be reduced to a point of depriving them of their customary degree of flexibility. This widespread perception assisted CORA's budgetary-accounting office to gather statistics on the costs of expropriating and working latifundios. By 1968, CORA had devised a fairly accurate program budget.

Despite the past priority of its activities, CORA soon learned that there were good reasons for not treating this program information as a free commodity that could be handed to Finance with little fear of retaliation. Indeed in 1968, using CORA's program budget as a source of valuable information, Finance tried to force the agency to operate more efficiently, resulting in an intense political struggle which caused the regime considerable embarrassment.[29] Although CORA had profited from several years of "most-favored-agency" status, this attempted cutback proved that its interests over the long term were the same as those of any low-priority unit in the central government: negotiate the budget under conditions whereby it controlled the information, not Finance.

This example, like others, tends to demonstrate that the immutable

[29] See Chapter 4 for the outcome of this struggle.

characteristic of the budgetary process is not that information is inherently unmanageable; great quantities of data can be processed and stored with the aid of technology. Rather, truly useful information is distinguished not by its quantity but by its quality, and practical considerations dictate against treating it as a free commodity.[30]

AGENCY ATTEMPTS TO EXTRACT SUBSIDIES
AT LEAST COST

High Priority

As in the case of CORA, most governments distribute money more freely to programs that must show quick results, are crucial prerequisites for longer-range political goals, or represent basic new directions in the polity. Agencies attempt to combine low information flow to Finance with high-priority status in defining a favorable budgetary market. Since the Budget Bureau may believe that the organization's current allocation is perfectly adequate to accomplish policy objectives, the simple acceptance that a particular agency is a key component of the government's political program is not sufficient cause for the agency's allocation to be increased. When they argue that their activities have the highest intrinsic importance, the agencies are saying: "You should not worry about the financial utility of investments in our activities. Money spent on us is not wasted. On the contrary, only in this way can we be effective and serve the national interest."

An agency's desire to gain an important increase in its allocation follows a standard pattern. When Finance sends the ceiling out in March, the aggressive agency treats it with relative disdain, if not disbelief.[31] It may ignore the directives and return a complete budget vastly exceeding the ceiling, with no separate Expansion List. Or it may include so large an Expansion List that it is impossible for the analyst in the Budget Bureau to make sense of it. It may use more subtle techniques, such as placing lower-priority items within the ceiling—continuance of a program at full capacity, for instance, even

---

[30] Thus my emphasis is quite different from that of Downs, who says (p. 248) that there is "an enormous disparity between the complexity of bureau operations and the limited information-absorbing capacity of any individual or small group. This disparity lies at the heart of the budgeting process."

[31] Ira Sharkansky, in *The Politics of Taxes and Spending*, finds that the assertive agencies tend to do better than their more passive rivals. In Chile, allocational increases have been determined more by political considerations external to the formal budgetary process than by the amount the agency's request exceeds previous spending levels, though the two factors are often related.

though it could easily be cut back—while delegating an absolutely indispensable item, such as the amortization on an international loan, to the Expansion List. When an agency places its pet projects before the repayment of international loans, it is trying to raise the symbolic importance of its activities above the financial reputation of the state.

Whereas most agencies are eventually forced to compromise with the Budget Bureau, those that perform important social functions (e.g., building houses, reducing unemployment, spreading revolution) are a bit more persistent when Finance refuses to allocate them everything they request. The most powerful executing agencies in the Chilean public sector—such as the Housing Corporation (CORVI), the General Public Works Agency, and CORA—seem to follow distinctive steps in their efforts to have the budget raised. The first is to make exaggerated requests of the Budget Bureau in submitting their draft budgets. These draft budgets imply sufficient financial resources to achieve a wide range of agency goals at a relatively low marginal utility. The second is for the head of the agency to go directly to the president of the country to argue his case. This technique appears most feasible when the official is a close personal friend of the president or when the social manifestations of a restriction on the budget will predictably impair the political aims of the government.

If these two probes do not result in a favorable resolution of the request, a third alternative is for the agency to loosen its dependence on the Finance ministry and seek financing completely outside of the closed political-economic system. When Felipe Herrera, a Chilean, was president of the Inter-American Development Bank (B.I.D.), agency heads often went to Washington, D.C., to present their case for expansion. Qualifying for B.I.D., World Bank, A.I.D., and other international loans often proves a successful way to cheapen Finance's resources still further, by making them inconsequential for some large-scale budgetary negotiations.

Poor Programming

The pursuance of increased economic subsidy does not cease with the signing of the budget law. During execution of the budget, agencies employ tactics to increase their allocation and administrative flexibility. These methods can be listed more or less in the chronological order in which they occur: underestimate revenue from the agency's independent sources of income; exhaust the allocation in important categories early in the year; transfer money from one budgetary item to another; solicit supplements on the basis of higher state revenue; and spend money rapidly at the end of the year, in order not to risk having it reabsorbed by the National Treasury. Not all agencies are able to participate in each of these tactics. The most common are the transfer in the second semester, the periodic supplement, and the tendency to spend heavily in the last quarter. Those agencies with independent financing, recognized political and social missions, or large capital projects can engage in overestimating revenues, underestimating costs, and budgetary *faits accomplis*.

To what degree is poor programming either a result of the agency's self-interested strategy to increase its allocation or a function of random environmental influences that disrupt the agency's actions? Generally, Finance maintains that much of the state's financial difficulty is attributable to overambitious organizations using every trick in the book to expand their allocations. On the other hand, the individual agency prefers to represent itself as an unfortunate victim of circumstances, forced into an unorthodox role by elements beyond its control.

Most agencies put forth suitable explanations of why their behavior takes unusual directions—quite frequently, that irresistible political pressures necessitate camouflage of some aspects of their activities. In Frei's CORA, for example, money lent to farm cooperatives before harvest was theoretically to be repaid the following year. These repayments had to be included in CORA's budget, even though there was little possibility that the fledgling cooperatives would actually be able to repay the loans in their entirety.[32] Though the CORA officials expected to recover only about 80 percent of the loans, they could not reveal that deficit in the projected budget, since their political opponents would have had a field day trumpeting the state's losing proposition in agrarian reform. Nonetheless, the practice ultimately worked to the detriment of the Finance ministry. The incentive to spend the full allocation persisted at the local level of CORA, despite the knowledge in the upper echelons that the revenue side of the budget was artificially inflated.

The Budget Bureau casts a suspicious eye on the General Public Works agency, but officials there portray themselves as helplessly beset by a series of debilitating constraints completely undermining their efforts at accurate programming. First are the usual pitfalls in the execution of capital projects, from the hesitancy of contractors to submit bids, to natural disasters and the collapse of works half completed. Second, the political nature of Public Works in garnering electoral support disrupts the normal unfolding of the yearly operating plan. In reviewing the Public Works budget, Congress passes a multitude of amendments representing pork-barrel legislation for regional consump-

[32] See Richard Meyer, *Debt Repayment Capacity of the Chilean Agrarian Reform Beneficiaries.*

tion. The minister of Public Works often travels throughout the country promising projects that have been long-time points of contention between the local citizenry and the central government. And the president likes to make a political impact during his occasional official tours, committing additional projects without necessarily checking their feasibility with the engineers and budget officials in the General Public Works agency.

The list of Public Works projects becomes longer and longer, but no commensurate financing is voluntarily offered by the Budget Bureau to cover the unprogrammed expenses. While the agency sees itself continually losing ground in its struggle to cover expenses within the strictures of the original budget, Finance questions the degree to which it is sincerely attempting to manage its fiscal position and eliminate spending overruns. The image in Finance is that Public Works has a predilection for using these outside pressures to arrange *faits accomplis* requiring the Budget Bureau to take responsibility for their consequences. Chapter 7 will examine in more detail the specific types of relations between Public Works and private contractors leading to this accusation.

Those agencies with sources of income independent of their subventions from the National Treasury can *overestimate* these revenues for strategic purposes. This income may come from special taxes, tolls, service charges for particular agency functions, repayments of loans, investment in the agency's sinking fund, or the sale of goods and property. Some agencies also obtain outside financing through credits from national and international banking institutions. The extent to which these independent finances can be overestimated is illustrated in the case of the Agrarian Reform Corporation: Section A of Table 10 represents CORA's estimated and real income in the capital account from 1965 to 1969, while Section B shows the degree to which the agency obtained the loans it had originally projected. On only two occasions did the agency underestimate its independent revenues.

Certain advantages accrue from a deliberate overestimate of this independent income. The agency can almost completely circumvent Finance's restrictive position during formation of the budget between March and December, giving it a clear advantage over other bureaus that desperately try to stretch their *cifra tope* to cover a reduced number of programs. The agency can set the size of its budget at virtually the figure it wishes by adding in "expected" independent revenues. The expenditures side of the ledger can proceed at full speed, even though the revenue side is forever behind. Orders can be made, services contracted, and purchases completed with the knowledge that most of the bills will not have to be paid until later in the year.

TABLE 10. OVERESTIMATING INDEPENDENT REVENUE IN CORA
(*In millions of escudos*)

A. General Revenue

Year	Estimated Revenue[a]	Real Revenue[a]	Percent Over-estimate
1965	3,648,000	1,801,546	102
1966	9,649,000	14,514,760	b
1967	78,690,000	57,323,248	36
1968	226,010,000	135,223,452	67
1969	317,154,000	285,854,664	10

B. In-Country Credits

Year	Estimated Credits	Real Credits	Percent Over-estimate
1965	14,663	2,599,074	b
1966	5,000,000	4,256,634	17
1967	48,000,000	26,493,494	81
1968	134,600,000	64,232,692	109
1969	237,600,000	162,639,792	101

SOURCE: Corporación de la Reforma Agraria, *Balance Presupuestario del Año 1969*.
[a] Refers to loan recoveries, bond issues, and sales of stock, and excludes central government subsidies.
[b] Underestimate.

The agency profits first from committing the full allocation in the budget, even though the budget was based on artificial revenue estimates. It profits a second time by being freed of responsibility when these bills fall due. This effective pardon stems from the fact that the agency's funding from independent sources, whether specific income or credit, can be considered a constant. During the year, the repayment of loans, special taxes, and services charges proceeds at a rate difficult for the agency to alter. It can estimate its total income within certain bounds, but it can do little to insure that revenues will reach the most optimistic calculations. The special taxes are fixed by law; service charges depend on the demand for its products or services in the society; it cannot suddenly sell all of its fixed property. Likewise, although the agency may hope to receive important credits from banking sources when it makes up its budget in March, progress in this domain depends very much on the cost of credit, its availability, and the lenders' conception of what constitutes a fair risk.

On the other hand, the agency views the subsidy provided by the central treasury as a variable amount because under certain conditions it can rise. The Finance ministry may gain access to supplemental economic resources by taking advantage of "unexpectedly high" tax revenues (see Table 6), by cutting allocations in other sectors, or simply by printing up new money. This disposable income is opportunely available in a way not typical of independent funds. If an agency miscalculates its revenues and begins to run a deficit, it can hardly expect private banking sources to be frantic about the urgency of the situation. Nor is it likely that those who indirectly contribute to the agency's welfare by paying special taxes will volunteer to increase their allotment. Those private citizens or public bureaus owing the agency money are not apt to rescue it through sudden cancellation of their debts. International lending organizations are not in the business of bailing out state agencies that find themselves in tight financial straits in the middle of the year. In sum, the most likely fountain of new revenue in a crisis situation is the central government itself.

Could not the agency achieve the same result by underestimating the amount of independent revenue and then use the flow of extra money for its programs? This practice would be preferable for the Finance ministry, because no deficit in the agency's operations would ever result. But if a particular eventuality might be advantageous to the Finance ministry, it is almost certain *not* to be in the best interests of the agency. If the agency underestimates its revenues, its original budget is correspondingly smaller and its revenues tend to run higher than its programmed expenditures. The Chilean Budget Bureau is continually checking the cash position of public organisms with large sources of independent funds. When those funds are higher than expected, the Budget Bureau slows down the release of subsidies from the National Treasury in order to keep its budget balanced. The agency would have a difficult time spending the extra funds that materialized, since the Budget Bureau would pounce on them to distribute the money as it felt best.

Under the current rules of the game, an agency encounters less resistance when it solicits supplementary funds to carry out an *existing* budget than it does when it seeks the approval of a new and more generous budget, regardless of whether it has the funds to cover the excess. An agency that had *overestimated* its independent revenues to formulate the original budget could very well be the beneficiary of surplus revenues suddenly appearing in the ledgers of another agency that had initially *underestimated* its independent funds.

The ministries of Public Works and Housing profit from a special dispensation allowing them to undertake long-term capital projects through the mechanism of *deferred payment,* by which they can pay private companies from following years' budgets. Projects eventually costing millions of dollars enter into the budget in accounts of one escudo, while the contractors begin work with credits from private banking sources. Deferred payment responds to the fact that many Public Works endeavors take several years to complete; the procedure also provides convenient opportunities for several of the agencies' reference groups. Elected representatives in Congress are able to have some of their pork-barrel legislation implemented; the contractors are making money; the credit market is stimulated; and unemployment is absorbed.

Projects begun on a deferred payment basis, however, often transform into budgetary *faits accomplis.* Contractors usually initiate construction with a verbal agreement that officials in Public Works will make a supreme effort to pay some of the costs of the project during the current fiscal year. Because the agency's budget is already in deficit, very seldom are they able to deliver on the promise. When credit sources dry up, the builder has little choice but to slow down the pace of work at the work site, which creates unemployment and presents the regime with the visible embarrassment of a half-finished project.

Other agencies lacking the legal facility of deferred payment often provoke their own brands of fiscal crises. The national railroads accept bill after bill during the year, with no funds in the budget to cover the debts, and ask the Budget Bureau to play the role of Daddy Warbucks in the last quarter. The Maritime agency refuses to dispose of six old ships, even though Finance just provided it with six new ships to take their place. The result is that in the first quarter the maintenance costs of the old vessels exhaust the total allowance for the new ships as well. CORA designs its budget in a lopsided fashion, allocating too much money to expropriation of farmlands and not enough to physical infrastructure in buildings, equipment, and storage facilities. To correct the situation CORA requisitions supplements, which are granted. But then the agency uses these supplements primarily to expropriate more farmland and not to correct the lag by making the farms productive agricultural units. All these practices lead to built-in deficits in the agencies' operations which act as continual leverage for more funds.

Spending the Maximum

Agencies try not to leave money in their accounts after December 31, since it cannot be used for new purchases. If an agency perennially fails to spend its full budget, its negotiating position is weakened and Finance is less tolerant of requests for larger allocations in subsequent periods. Accordingly, if any slack exists at all, operating departments try to protect their financial reputation by transferring excess monies from surplus to deficit accounts and accelerating their overall spending. Purchases and service agreements proceed at a vertiginous rate, even if such spending goes for items with little or no relationship to the agency's official functions. The purpose is to dissipate the impression that the agency never needed the money in the first place.

Expenditures are often heaviest in the last month of the budget year, when agencies inch their spending up to cover the residue in the different line items. Figure 9 reveals that even though CORA spent approximately 25 percent of its capital budget in December 1969, the effort still fell somewhat short of completely exhausting the allocation.

AGENCY ATTEMPTS TO SECURE INDEPENDENT FUNDS

The previous exposition may give the impression that, collectively, agencies have the upper hand in Chilean budgetary negotia-

FIGURE 9.   CORA'S EXPENDITURES IN THE LAST QUARTER, 1969

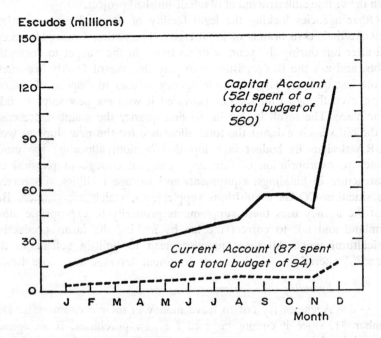

SOURCE: CORA, *Balance Presupuesterio del Año 1969.*

tions. The individual agency, however, is continually in a vulnerable position vis-à-vis Finance, since Finance always retains the option of refusing supplements and cutting off funds. The tenuousness of the situation leads the agency to try to guarantee its financial future by obtaining independent sources of funding. The largest source of autonomous funds comes from the economic interaction of the government unit (decentralized agency, state industry) with the public. This income can come from fees, utility tariffs, and investment in sinking funds for specific purposes. Another source of independent funding is through earmarked taxes and special accounts.

The tendency of Congress to set up special accounts scatters the ultimate designation of collected taxes in Chile to individual agencies, schools, universities, regional development organizations, municipalities, national commissions, charitable organizations, and activities within a ministry. Usually the congressmen do not act autonomously in proposing such legislation; the unit in need of such funds actively solicits this type of backing and performs the requisite research to determine how much the tax will provide.

In 1968, for example, the civil servants in the subministry of Transport went on strike for higher salaries. The Finance ministry made an issue of not granting their request with general revenues, so Transport had to locate alternate sources of funding. It hit upon the idea of charging all bus owners a fee to have their vehicles undergo the annual safety checkup; previously this examination had been performed without charge. As the strike became more detrimental for the regime's prestige, Congress passed the special law giving Transport this additional source of independent financing. The funds were sufficient to allow a pay raise of 100 percent for the personnel in the subministry. The means proved so successful that officials there began thinking about charging the same fee to truck owners. In this case they hoped to rouse support for the measure not through a strike, but by pointing out that Transport would need only two-thirds of the forthcoming truck revenue, and that the Finance ministry and Congress could distribute the other third as they wished.[33]

Earmarked funds and special accounts have detrimental effects on the solvency of the central government. First, a circular effect of reinforcing arguments induces government organizations to seek an increased percentage of their budget in independent funds. Every agency that solicits autonomous financing does so on the premise that with autonomous financing its economic situation will be more liquid, or at

[33] Interview material.

worse, no less solvent than it was with central subsidies. If the global amount of revenues available during any one period is conceived as fixed, increasing the liquidity in decentralized treasuries can only reduce it in the National Treasury. In this situation, the autonomous agencies become better payers of their financial obligations while the central state becomes worse. When central government has trouble meeting its payment schedule, additional reasons exist to give a guaranteed flow of funds to important public services.[34]

Second, many of these smaller special accounts have little chance of fully subsidizing the programs they are supposed to benefit. A law obliging all pharmaceutical supply factories to donate a portion of their total sales to the construction of hospitals in Renca and Barrancas, two poorer municipalities, provided only forty thousand escudos in 1969, while each hospital entailed construction costs of two million escudos. Because of this gap in financing, the Finance ministry resisted approving work on the hospitals as long as possible.[35] The more the construction was postponed, the more vehement became the denunciations of the congressman who sponsored the original law. Eventually in 1970, when the pressure became too great, the Budget Bureau had to start building the hospitals at its own expense, bearing the brunt not only of construction but also of the upkeep and personnel costs.

To break out of the orbit of the Finance ministry, the agencies attempt to have as large a percentage of their budgets as possible subsidized by independent sources. If an agency can be assured that 50 percent of its budget is guaranteed before it starts planning its expenditures (as in the case of CORVI), its uncertainty about the relative generosity of the Finance ministry is correspondingly reduced. Once it obtains these funds, it tends to consider their use as an inviolable privilege, and its incentive to provide full information on its operations to the Budget Bureau is correspondingly lower.

These ideas are summarized in Figure 10. Substantiating evidence is that state industries needing little help from Finance provide only the scantiest information to the Budget Bureau on the efficiency of their operations. Although their subsidy may be equivalent to the entire budget of a centralized agency, the fact that this money represents only a small fraction of their total revenues induces them to inveigh against the Budget Bureau when they have to provide more than a half-page resumé justifying the request.

[34] Interview material.
[35] Interview material.

FIGURE 10. GUARANTEED INCOME AND INFORMATION FLOW TO THE FINANCE MINISTRY

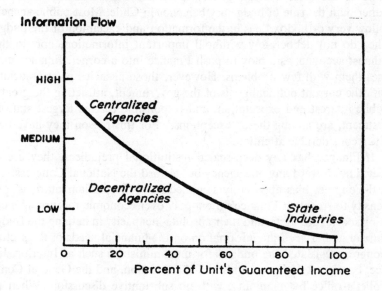

CONCLUSIONS

Does the previous discussion portray a Machiavellian Chilean bureaucracy in which every unit is desperately trying to outfox the competition in a never-ending series of strategic ruses, reversals, and sabotages? If an organization were perpetually under siege, as Finance has been described above, it might be expected to display low morale, high bureaucratization, and defensive attitudes toward its principal reference groups. But the administrative esprit de corps inside the Budget Bureau is very high, and the relationships between Finance and the sectors are not considerably strained. Despite Finance's tremendous responsibilities and functional specialization, very little formal hierarchy characterizes the Budget Bureau's internal activities. Personnel feel free to talk directly with the Budget chief or the Finance minister with little deference to protocol, and sometimes even without arranging a previous appointment. Analysts in the Budget Bureau are usually on a first-name basis with budgetary officials in the sectors, with whom conversation is continual and generally low-keyed.

This relaxed atmosphere and lack of acrimony are partly due to the fact that the rules of the budgetary game are well-known and accepted by all the principal participants, who expect that their counterparts will try to tip the pending balance in their own favor. It could also be argued that some of the more esoteric strategies discussed here are the exception rather than the rule of budgetary behavior in Chile. Most public agencies follow very orthodox lines in the formation and execution of the budget. They do not deliberately withhold important information, nor do they exhaust accounts as a ploy to push Finance into a corner. Finance manages them with few problems. However, those agencies most associated with the current political goals of the government, attracting the greatest public interest and expectation, and responsible for the largest state investment, are among these "exceptions." For this reason they have been given considerable attention.

If Finance has any deep-seated institutional prejudices, they are directed not toward any one agency but toward the National Congress. The anti-Congress bias apparently stemmed from the parliamentarians' propensity to fragment Finance's monopoly over economic resources by creating special accounts, and their absolute incapacity in helping the Budget Bureau gather accurate information on the financial needs of the sectors. Congress legislated the budgets for most ministries such as Interior, Justice, Foreign Relations, Lands and Colonization, and the General Comptroller's office by unanimity, with no substantive discussion. When the congressional secretary opened debate on the Public Works budget, however, the blustery spectacle commenced. The congressmen thrust roads, bridges, waterways, irrigation, and construction projects into the budget at a dazzling rate, with no concern for their programming or financing. Once an opposition senator or deputy succeeded in including some project for the benefit of his constituency, he sent a telegram to the district delineating what he had done in its behalf. Though the president vetoed almost all of these legislative initiatives, the opposition representatives did not try to override them, because it gave them a convenient issue with which to cudgel the government among their constituency. Sometimes however, in order to build political compromises on more substantive issues, the president had to allow an occasional amendment to stand, virtually obliging the Public Works agency to begin work on the project. The fiscal mismanagement resulting from the congressmen's airy intervention accounted for Finance's general exasperation with the legislative body.

These congressional actions, and those that establish earmarked taxes and special sinking funds, tend to move budgetary decision-making from the conditions of Box III in Figure 7, where Finance has the advantage, to those of Boxes II and IV, where important public agencies are able to withhold information, extract additional resources, and protect themselves against the uncertainty of insufficient funds. It is important to recognize that roles in the budgetary process, as described here, depend very much on bureaucratic goals and the distribution of different resources between the Budget Bureau and the various agencies. This chapter has explained agency behavior in terms of strategic responses to a resource imbalance in bureaucracy. The next two chapters will examine the efforts of the state, represented in this case by the high-level Economic Committee, to use short-term planning as a means of bringing some of these units under better control.

3

COALITION FORMATION
FOR SHORT-TERM PLANNING
IN THE ECONOMIC COMMITTEE

Since 1964, a high-level planning commission has arbitrated economic disputes among important public agencies in the Chilean bureaucracy. Born as a coordinating body for short-term policy-making under the Christian Democratic regime, the Economic Committee (*Comité Económico*) continued to play a major role in the government of Salvador Allende.[1] Although its meetings are rarely mentioned in the press and the general population is unaware of the Committee's existence, its sessions bring together several of the country's most influential political and administrative personages to sort out priorities and arrive at decisions relating to employment, inflation, trade, the balance of payments, and the budget. Permanent members are the president of the country, the ministers of Economy, Finance, and Agriculture, the vice-president of the Development Corporation (CORFO), the presidents of the State and Central Banks, and the head of the National Planning Office (ODEPLAN).[2]

[1] The custom from 1964 to 1970 was to hold meetings once a week on Monday afternoons in the cabinet room of the ministry of Finance. During more hectic periods of the year (e.g., the formulation of the Annual Operating Plan), the Committee met two or three times a week. When lunch was to be served, the session was transferred to the executive suites of the Central Bank; when the president attended, the group congregated in the government palace (La Moneda).

[2] The ministers of Labor and Mining were full members but did not participate on a regular basis. When the Committee treated sectoral issues, the head of the respective agency or ministry was invited to present his point of view. Other steady participants were the head of the Budget Bureau, the president's personal economic advisor, and the Committee's executive secretary. The president participated in approximately half the meetings, when the Committee was to make definitive decisions on important matters. Other sessions consisted of formal work sessions in which less significant decisions were made.

Policy-making in the Economic Committee is affected by factors both endogenous and exogenous to public bureaucracy; discussion of the latter will be postponed until the next chapter. Here we will treat the Economic Committee as a hermetic decision-making group, relatively shielded from the larger social and ideological forces around it. Indeed, the Committee was originally conceived as a "think-tank," fed by heavy infusions of specialized know-how and characterized by collegial relations among the participants. In 1964, conditions were propitious for operationalizing such concepts into a successful planning commission. The Christian Democrats believed that their regime was a technocratic aristarchy; it was true that all the permanent members of the Committee were highly qualified professionals in their respective spheres. Their common party affiliation, their allegiance to the president, and their high regard for rationality should have eliminated almost all points of contention. In addition, they were riding the wave of the government's extraordinarily large popular vote in the 1964 elections, which promised to pave the way for the easy application of the Committee's decision-rules in the society-at-large.

One inherent factor persistently penetrating the Committee sessions, however, was the permanent members' affiliation with important state agencies. If the Economic Committee had not existed, these same institutions would occasionally have conflicted over alternative policy choices during execution of the regime's programs. In the Economic Committee, however, they were supposed to detach themselves from organizational interests and make short-term economic planning their main preoccupation. Though the various members of the Committee were genuinely committed to elevating the discussion above parochial concerns, the planning approaches preferred were closely related to their institutional goals. Also, when presenting their positions, they had difficulty in speaking louder than their organizational power base permitted.[3]

This chapter will analyze the Committee's decision-making style from 1964 to 1970.[4] This period witnessed competition within the Economic Committee over the definition and scope of development planning. Institutions with different operating norms and policy goals tended to

---

[3] Amitai Etzioni suggests that decision-making is "not just a process of information-collection, calculation, and the expression of commitments, but also a process of the mobilization and use of assets (resources)." Etzioni, *The Active Society,* pp. 304, 301–303.

[4] There are practically no public data sources for the activities of the Economic Committee. These two chapters are based almost exclusively on interviews with ex-members of the Committee, conducted in December 1970, soon after their last session as a governing group. See, however, the book by Sergio Molina S., *El Proceso de Cambio en Chile.*

cluster in two informal coalitions, one of which was more "development-oriented" than the other. The president deemphasized divisions in outlook and sources of influence to encourage his advisors to discuss major issues in an artificial atmosphere of power equality. Nonetheless, the developmentalist group was unable to gain the president's backing on a wide series of policies, and the hegemony of the restrictive group was decisive in defining the planning methodology adopted. The level at which these men worked meant that the stakes were rather high: the reward for the victors was the right to set the tone for a whole style of government.[5]

SHORT-TERM PLANNING AND CONFLICT RESOLUTION

The basic functions of the Economic Committee were to assist the president in the formation of short-term economic policy, and to provide the machinery for the resolution of economic conflicts arising in the public sector. The planning function both predominated and preceded the conflict-resolution function in the Committee's month-to-month calendar. The Economic Committee first set forth the basic norms of the short-term plan and then tried to conform the behavior of the public and private sectors to those norms.

The Annual Operating Plan

The first order of business for the Economic Committee was the preparation of the Annual Operating Plan (*Plan Operativo Anual*),

[5] In essence, Frei implicitly attempted to use the Economic Committee as the forum for multiple-advocacy decision-making similar to that described by Alexander L. George in "The Case for Multiple Advocacy in Making Foreign Policy." In that article, George set out three major conditions for multiple advocacy to result in "better" decisions (p. 759):

First, no major maldistribution of the following resources can prevail among the various actors: power, weight, influence; competence relevant to the policy issues; information relevant to the policy problem; analytical resources; and bargaining and persuasion skills. Second, the president must participate in organizational policy-making in order to monitor and regulate the workings of multiple advocacy. Third, there must be time for adequate debate and give-and-take.

Data gathered for this chapter tend to show that the first of George's major premises was conspicuously absent in the Chilean Economic Committee, where "multiple advocacy" often reduced to bureaucratic politics and the president consistently aligned himself with that group which, for reasons to be examined below in detail, appeared to provide the most "rational" advice. See also Richard E. Neustadt, *Presidential Power: The Politics of Leadership*; Keith C. Clark and Lawrence J. Legere (eds.), *The President and the Management of National Security*; N. R. F. Maier, *Problem-Solving Discussions and Conferences: Leadership Methods and Skills*; Richard F. Fenno, Jr., *The President's Cabinet*; and Graham T. Allison, *Essence of Decision: Explaining the Cuban Missile Crisis*.

which delineated the government's economic policy for the following year. The annual plan dealt with the salary adjustment to cover the rise in the cost of living, the levels of credit to both the private and public sector, projected prices for agricultural products, the composition and level of durable and perishable imports, the monetary policy of the Central Bank, and financing of the budgetary deficit.

The Economic Committee began considering the Annual Operating Plan in July of the year preceding its implementation. Each of three member institutions (the Central Bank, the Finance ministry, and ODEPLAN) prepared separate reports covering the full range of subjects in the plan. Practically all committee sessions during July and August were dedicated to merging the three points of view into one set of guidelines. Never more than a series of memoranda, equations, and graphs with which the Committee worked internally, the Annual Operating Plan was not published as a separate document. But its principal intentions were outlined to Congress by the minister of Finance in November.

In November 1969, for example, Finance Minister Andrés Zaldívar began his talk on a partisan note. He complained that the social values of the Chilean people were oriented toward consumption, not toward savings and investment. He criticized politicians who continually pandered to the masses by offering more and more, with no discussion of the requisite investment necessary for the future of the country. The minister underlined the 1968 drought, a lower level of new savings, and exorbitant salary increases as factors impairing the economic health of the country. While the seriousness of the drought was impossible to foresee, he blamed the detrimental savings rate and the exaggerated salary increases on the political opposition, which had refused to collaborate with the regime on a series of important economic measures.[6]

With this introduction, Zaldívar discussed the concrete fiscal, tax, monetary, foreign trade, and credit policies that the Economic Committee planned to apply in the coming year. He pointed out that the cost of living had risen by less than 30 percent in 1969 and predicted that inflation would be kept under 30 percent again in 1970. He read off the expenditures in the public sector: major increases in investment would be concentrated in agriculture and industry. Only 6 percent of fiscal expenditures would be financed with internal and external credits. He listed the real increases in tax revenues and credits from the Central Bank, briefly described the balance of payments and foreign debt pic-

---

[6] Ministerio de Hacienda, *Exposición sobre el Estado de la Hacienda Pública,* 1969.

tures, and then indicated that the increase in the Gross National Product would be in the range of 6 percent for the year 1970.[7]

After the first of January, the committee members reviewed the short-term plan monthly to compare its projections with the current situation. The problems arising in the implementation stage often escaped easy solution because they involved conforming reality to a plan written several months earlier. The Committee's typical procedure was to conform the plan to reality by making minor adjustments in its expectations and predictions and identifying those variables that could be manipulated to keep the economy on a controlled course.

For example, a new projected growth rate would cause predictable variations in the level and composition of imports. The foreign reserve situation might deteriorate, necessitating a modification in the exchange rate for the dollar. If the demand for hard currency rose significantly, the number of dollars that travelers could export might be reduced. Fluctuations in the stocks of hard currency and the price of imports would affect the level of inflation, requiring an updated monetary policy from the Central Bank. With the change in monetary policy, it might be necessary to delay the payment of certain debts to the private sector. This move would have appreciable consequences for the size of the floating debt, the pace of economic activity, and the demand for business credits on the private banking system. To counterbalance an undesirable contraction in the economy, the Committee would review the state of budgetary allocations to high-investment agencies. An expansionary fiscal policy might then serve more immediate goals, such as halting a strike or increasing credit in the rural areas.

Choices Affecting the Private Sector

Although this group was called the Economic Committee, its activities had both social and political connotations. The prevalence of the state in the Chilean economy meant that these decisions set important parameters for economic behavior in the private sector. The members of the Committee could not avoid being the arbiters between those favored by the Annual Operating Plan and those whose interests were ignored or impaired.

The Committee made very few decisions which did not have ramifications among the working population. Committee members felt that any short-term strategy not taking into account the probable reactions of organized labor was unrealistic.[8] The inflationary spiral naturally

[7] Ministerio de Hacienda, *Exposición,* 1969.
[8] Interview material.

reduced the real value of the workers' earnings. But efforts to stabilize the inflation usually had detrimental effects on the progressive income gains of the union members. The authorization of high-quality imports that consumers preferred to the local product could raise unemployment. A preferential distribution of state credits to labor-intensive enterprises would reduce unemployment, but the policy might not represent the best way to build industrial infrastructure.

Decisions made behind closed doors in Committee sessions often affected critical social issues of the Chilean countryside. Keeping agricultural prices steady was an effective means to brake inflation. Contrarily, the lot of the *campesinos,* especially those working on *asentamientos,* could be improved only by increasing farm prices with minimum lag and in direct proportion to increases in the costs of production. Committee decisions determined the allocation of both budgetary and credit resources to CORA. Without sufficient budgetary resources and timely credits during the year, the rhythm of CORA's expropriations and technical assistance programs would decelerate, undermining the manifest political goals of the Agrarian Reform program.

When authorizing budgetary supplements, the Committee faced a continual quandary between fulfilling social goals, such as increased educational or health facilities, and economic goals, such as mining and industrial investment that would increase the productive capacity of the country. Even when it committed itself to social goals, the element of choice was not absent. A decision to increase the capital budget of the ministry of Public Works by 5 percent, to reduce unemployment, was a choice in favor of the large contractors and the most marginal workers, and to the detriment of a wider segment of the lower class which would profit from alternative programming of the resources, such as for medical clinics in newly urbanized areas.

Choices Affecting the Public Sector

In modern governmental structures, most issues affecting the society as a whole are the specific concern of some agency of public bureaucracy. The previous chapter discussed the ways that certain agencies in Chile try to increase their operating capacity by augmenting their economic resources. These agencies apply pressure at strategic points in the administrative hierarchy, sometimes at the level of the president himself, to obtain all the money necessary to perform as well as they can. The responsibility for developing the short-term plan, plus President Frei's desire to be buffered from some of these pressures, converted the Economic Committee into a clearinghouse for the innumerable disagreements over economic matters arising among the institutions in the public sector. The most important of these conflicts derived from credit and remuneration questions, spending overruns in the capital account, and the size of the external debt.

Not just by chance, institutions occupying the most strategic points in the Chilean public administration, such as the State Bank, the Central Bank, and the ministry of Finance, sat on the Economic Committee. Most incompatibilities between the agencies' demands and the Annual Operating Plan reduced to conflicts between the agency and one of the institutions on the Committee (e.g., CORA versus the ministry of Economy, the national airlines LAN-Chile versus the Central Bank, or the ministry of Public Works versus Finance). Under these circumstances, the hearings of the Committee might be construed as a Kafkaesque administrative court where the defendants sat before a tribunal of judges made up of the prosecutors, leading to quite predictable verdicts in favor of the prosecutors. The Committee's efforts at control were not always so successful, however, because of weighty extenuating circumstances that impinged on its recommendations.

For example, in 1969 the minister of Public Works visited the minister of Finance and asserted that he needed a budgetary supplement to raise the salaries of his engineers. He cited the deficit of engineers in the ministry and the impossibility of attracting younger professionals to crack the crust of ancient, tradition-oriented personnel in his departments. The minister of Finance felt that financing the request would have detrimental effects on other goals of government. If generous allowances were extended to the engineers in Public Works, a chain reaction would surely result. The engineers in the National Railways and Housing would demand an increase, encouraging even the Agricultural engineers to jump on the bandwagon. The total amount would be an astronomical sum which could not be absorbed by the system without completely destroying the short-term plan.

Encountering a stalemate, the two parties sent the problem upward. The minister of Public Works went directly to President Frei for a satisfactory hearing of his problem, but the chief of state always delayed making a decision until the Economic Committee had discussed the matter. The meeting of the Economic Committee was attended by the permanent members, the affected minister, and other officials closely linked to the problem, such as the Budget chiefs at the ministerial and national levels.

In this case, the Economic Committee found it difficult to rule automatically in favor of the Finance minister. The overriding extenuating factor was the real threat of a strike among the engineers in Public Works, which would paralyze construction in the country. The civil servants would not leave their jobs but simply decline to initial papers that approved each step of Public Works projects. Their refusal to stamp and sign would halt all construction in the country, all payments to contractors, all wages to workers, and engender social discontent possibly more serious than fiscal distortions emanating from across-the-board salary increases in the first place. Choices like these were the rule rather than the exception, and will be discussed in greater detail in the next chapter.

COALITION FORMATION IN THE ECONOMIC COMMITTEE

The best way to understand the Economic Committee's problem-solving approach is through the norms of the institutions represented, and the influence of these institutions within the Committee as a whole. The operational procedures and technical biases of the various organizations helped define the membership of two informal coalitions. One group was primarily concerned with monetary stability over the short term; it could be called the Restrictive Coalition. The other group was not unconcerned about inflation, but leaned preferentially toward the achievement of social and economic goals over the medium term; it could be labeled the Developmentalist Coalition. The relative power of the different institutions seemed to be based on their organizational resources, their technical criteria in defining short-term goals, and the personal compatibility between their representatives and the president of the country. The combined influence of the coalition members was almost always determinant in figuring which coalition emerged victorious, in the sense that the president adopted its point of view.[9]

Though there were some slight variations in emphases—depending on the institutional representatives, who changed occasionally over the six-year period—the organizations making up the Economic Committee can be scaled, as in Figure 11, from the most restrictive to the most

[9] Peter M. Blau observes that organizations "sometimes form coalitions committing them to joint decisions and actions. . . . Coalitions among organizations may become mergers that destroy the former boundaries between them." Blau, *Exchange and Power in Social Life*, p. 333. Guy Benveniste points out that no government, no matter how centralized, is of one mind on all issues; planners, like politicians and ideologues, must form coalitions within bureaucracy to implement their preferences. Benveniste, *Bureaucracy and National Planning: A Sociological Case Study of Mexico*. An ex-member of the Economic Committee, after reviewing this chapter prior to publication, commented that although two general orientations were indeed in evidence, and each was continuously defended by spokesmen from the same organizations, calling them "coalitions" may exaggerate the real situation. Other informed participants pointed out that the Restrictive group reflected more formal coalition-like behavior than did the Developmentalists.

developmentalist: the Central Bank, the State Bank, the ministry of Finance, the ministry of Economy, the Development Corporation (CORFO), the Planning Office (ODEPLAN), and the ministry of Agriculture. The two coalitions were fairly stable during the period; only the ministry of Economy was occasionally ambiguous in its attachment to the Developmentalist Coalition (because of its responsibilities for price control), and therefore marks the breaking point between the two groups.[10]

The coalitions that developed in the Committee were divided on the basis of a distinct conception of short-term planning. For the Restrictive Coalition, short-term planning meant the manipulation of gross economic variables, such as money supply, credit levels, fiscal expenditures in the current and capital account, the price of the dollar, and the foreign debt. Its theoretical economic model, using these independent variables as inputs, was highly accurate in predicting a series of the outcomes such as the rates of inflation, economic growth, and unemployment.[11] The Restrictive Coalition felt that the most important consideration was the rate of inflation and, appropriately, suggested credit and fiscal policies reducing the amount of money in circulation, dampening demand, and slowing the spiraling increases in the cost of living.[12] For the Developmentalist Coalition, the underlying conception of short-term planning appeared to be integral programming for the achievement of specific social and economic goals over the medium term. It tried to identify the components of programs which would best intermesh with other programs to lead rationally to the fulfillment of the plan. When referring to the economic model used by the Restrictive Coalition, the Developmentalists placed emphasis on economic growth rather than containing inflation.

[10] The apparent disinterest of the members of the Restrictive Coalition in sectoral programming may be attributable to their non-executing nature. The Developmentalist Coalition contained three executive organs (Economy, CORFO, and Agriculture), but its most technically qualified member, ODEPLAN, was only advisory and lacked responsibilities in implementing programs.

[11] See Jorge Cauas, "Stabilization Policy: The Chilean Case." This post-Keynesian model was designed to provide the president with at least six months of lead time to manage the economy.

[12] The model viewed structural forces as the basic causes of Chilean inflation. But it emphasized monetary policies over the short term as palliatives for inflation, while the government attacked the structural problems. Cauas states that the "approach adopted does not assume that a single theory of inflation—'structural' versus 'monetary,' or 'cost-push' versus 'demand-pull'—is valid as a basis for the stabilization policy, but rather that both kinds of approach should be considered. Structural problems are considered to be at the root of inflation, but demand and cost problems are closely related to the propagation and persistence of the phenomenon." See also Molina, *El Proceso de Cambio,* p. 69.

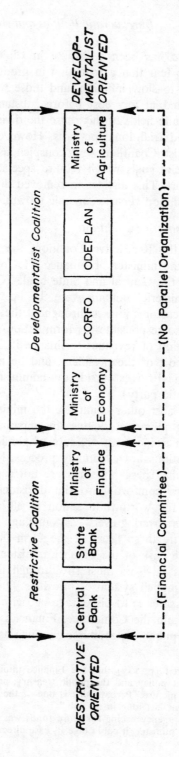

FIGURE 11.   COALITIONS IN THE ECONOMIC COMMITTEE

Historically there has been a dispute in Chilean economic circles between those who fear that a reduction in productivity is inherent in measures designed to slow inflation, and those who feel that inflation has to be eradicated at any cost before substantial progress can be made in the economic field. In this sense the division in the Economic Committee followed traditional patterns. However, some members of the Developmentalist Coalition were conspicuously committed to the achievement of social goals which require special types of investment and political support. This distinction removed the discussion from the standard one of inflation versus economic growth.

The Restrictive Coalition

Within the Restrictive Coalition, the top of the hierarchy was occupied by the minister of Finance. He formally outranked the presidents of both the Central and State banks. Other institutions falling within his ministerial domain were the tax bureau, the National Treasury, and the customs houses throughout the country. The minister of Finance was also responsible for formulation of the annual budget, and for the collection of revenues to finance it. The minister received the continual support of the president, and he maintained permanent contacts with political forces outside the administration (especially the Christian Democratic party).

In Chile, as in most other countries, the ministry of Finance has a reputation of being quite conservative, unsympathetic, and strong-armed in fiscal matters. The incessant pressure of public organizations to increase their allocations are eventually processed through decisions of the minister himself. These pressures are not easy to relieve, nor are the choices always comforting to the decision-maker.[13] The public sector's potential for worthwhile action is all-inclusive, and can be placed on long lists covering every economic and social need in society. Indeed, it is exactly these lists (in the form of budgetary requests) which arrive at the desk of the Finance minister and cause him headaches. He and his advisors must sift through them and allocate resources by some implicit system of priorities. One of the best ways to mitigate these pressures is to discourage agencies from even asking for supplements.[14] Within the Committee, Finance's position was oriented toward restricting public expenditures as much as possible.

[13] Molina complained (p. 135) that the Finance minister is "the last bulwark defending government policy and the public treasury, and usually ends up being the 'bad man in the picture.' Perhaps this is one of the reasons why Chilean Finance ministers do not last long in the job."

[14] Of course, if the agency asking for more funds was not satisfied with the decision of the Finance minister, it could take its case directly to the president. From

More so than even the Finance ministry, the Central and State banks continually presented the case for a restrictive monetary and credit policy. Economists who later became the highest officials in the Central Bank were the authors of the basic economic model designed to help reduce inflation over the six-year mandate of the Christian Democratic government. These men were firmly backed by President Frei, especially while the policies they put forth succeeded in lowering the rate of inflation without noticeably affecting the real growth of the gross national product.[15] The Central Bank was able to maintain an independent stance in the Economic Committee also because of its regulation over the exchange of foreign currency and its authority over the emission of newly printed money.

The State Bank tended to support the Central Bank in its unyielding line, although occasionally there were discussions as to the degree of restriction necessary. As the depository for all the current accounts of state agencies with their own bank accounts (decentralized agencies, autonomous corporations, and state industries), the State Bank consolidated this working capital into a single account (*Cuenta Unica*) for credit purposes. During this period it opened branches throughout the country as part of an energetic savings campaign to reduce consumer spending and encourage the creation of new investment funds. In the meetings of the Economic Committee, the State Bank reported on the margin of credit for making timely loans to the National Treasury or to public agencies. Its individual influence in the Committee was not great, but it teamed up with other members of the Restrictive Coalition in pushing the stabilization program.

Despite the consensus on generalities, some differences of opinion did exist in the Restrictive Coalition. These disagreements were usually between the Finance ministry and the Central Bank over unprogrammed emissions from the national mint, or between the Central Bank and the State Bank over the inflexibility of the credit policy. For example, during formation of the budget the Finance minister usually succeeded in resisting the onslaught of aggressive agencies pleading for more funds by being extremely adamant in his refusals. Occasionally, however, he was tempted to quell the demand somewhat with new emissions. For its part, the Central Bank was unsympathetic to Finance's allusions to pressures on the fiscal budget. Because it regulated the amount of

---

1964 to 1970, when the Finance minister was overruled by the president, he attempted to preserve a staunch image by sending a memorandum to the chief of state announcing his willingness to comply with the executive order, but only with his strongest misgivings about the wisdom of the decision.

[15] For an evaluation of the success of their model after the full period of government, see Jorge Cauas, "Política Económica a Corto Plazo."

money issued through the private banking system, the Central Bank was subject to the arguments of investors interested in cheap credit. If the monetary policy were going to be relaxed, it preferred to feed this money to its clients in the private sector, not to public agencies as did the ministry of Finance.[16]

An important reason for the eventual success of the Restrictive Coalition was that it met independent of the full Economic Committee to work out its differences. This caucus-like body, made up of the Central and State banks, the Finance ministry, the National Treasury, and the Budget Bureau, was called the Financial Committee (*Comité Financiero*), and met once a week on Thursdays to study two questions: the fiscal balance sheet and the credit situation. Within this subgroup the orientation of the Central Bank was distinctly rigid, while the positions of the State Bank and the Finance ministry tended to be more flexible.

The three major institutions used the preliminary sessions of the Financial Committee to agree on one general approach, so as not to arrive at meetings of the Economic Committee holding different viewpoints which, over the long term, would be to their joint disadvantage. Their compromises stressed control over inflation as the primary goal of the government's short-term program, and remuneration, monetary, and fiscal policies consistent with the stabilization drive. They were also anxious to use the power and prestige of the Economic Committee to enforce these principles. The high degree of interaction among the members of the Restrictive Coalition, along with its advantage in political resources, were instrumental in guaranteeing that the final resolutions of the Economic Committee invariably reflected the accords reached previously in the Financial Committee.

The Developmentalist Coalition

ODEPLAN, CORFO, and the ministries of Agriculture and Economy each placed emphasis on increased national growth, social development, and productivity, but did not meet separately to work out a single viewpoint defended by all of them in the Economic Committee. This lack of a unified front meant that they entered extraneous details and fragmented opinions into the discussion. The Developmen-

---

[16] In approaching short-term economic problems, the Central Bank tended to focus on three factors: foreign trade, the public sector, and the private sector. Information on each came from the balance of payments situation, pending budgetary deficits, and current employment figures. Other participants tended to concentrate discussion on the first two factors. The Central Bank did not want the third question to be ignored, because it felt that restricting credit to the private sector would lower employment figures.

talist Coalition was additionally handicapped because institutional rivalries weakened group bonds more seriously than in the Restrictive Coalition. These conflicts most frequently occurred between CORFO and ODEPLAN, and between the ministries of Economy and Agriculture. Partly for these reasons, the developmentalist approach to problems was considerably less articulate, forceful, and persuasive than that of their counterparts.

ODEPLAN was charged with designing a national economic plan over the medium and long term. It compiled information from sectoral and regional offices on current fiscal activities and tried to coordinate public projects with the targets of the plan and the necessities of the region. ODEPLAN could best test its methodology ofter observing the results of extensive investment in a whole range of sectors. Concern with expanding government activity, especially in social areas, lay at the base of ODEPLAN's developmentalist approach.

The fact that ODEPLAN acted as the technical secretariat for the Committee, and organized much of the statistical data on which decisions were based, did not guarantee it prominence in the Economic Committee. A new organization without political experience in the bureaucracy, it lacked the prestige of the president's support and did not interact with significant clients in the political community which depended on its activities. ODEPLAN did not have any control over financial resources, which put it at a distinct disadvantage in its relations with Finance, the State Bank, and the Central Bank.[17] Finally, it was deprived of its potentially most dynamic and effective spokesman with the untimely death of Jorge Ahumada in 1966. ODEPLAN often intervened in the meetings of the Economic Committee as a little boy might pull on the coatsleeves of his elder brother, struggling to be heard—a circumstance quite inconsistent with the technical capabilities of ODEPLAN's energetic and highly trained staff.

The ministry of Economy, with its three departments, two decentralized agencies, and thirty-nine state enterprises, is the superministry of the Chilean public sector. The ministry and its subsidiaries alone account for a significant percentage of the gross national product, which well justifies its importance in the elaboration of economic policy. However, under the Christian Democrats, other factors contributed to its profile in the Economic Committee. The centralized organs of the ministry, including the Industrial and Commercial Agency (DIRINCO), were only a small part of the sprawling organization. The most specific task of the centralized portion of the ministry, aside from attempting

---

[17] See Osvaldo Sunkel's comments on ODEPLAN in "Cambios Estructurales, Estrategias de Desarrollo y Planificación en Chile, 1938–1969."

to keep track of the other forty-three major appendages, was to regulate price control of consumer products. From 1964 to 1970 the position of the minister of Economy changed hands on four occasions. This turnover tended to blunt the ministry's ability to defend a consistent orientation toward economic development. During this period the ministry of Economy vacillated between its traditional job of spurring economic development and its immediate responsibility of controlling the price index.[18]

The formal subordinate to the minister of Economy, the vice-president of CORFO, actually had a larger staff, access to more information, and dependency relations with significantly more clients than the minister himself. The great majority of "mixed" industries, owned by both private and state capital, are under the auspices of CORFO. Because of its autonomy and its consistently dynamic leadership, CORFO has usually considered itself effectively outside of the orbit of the minister of Economy. To insure that its dependencies had sufficient working and investment capital, more liberal credit policies were the order of the day, and it was in CORFO's interest to argue for such policies in the Economic Committee.

The most fervent sponsor of an expansionary fiscal and monetary policy was the ministry of Agriculture. During much of this period agrarian reform was one of the top priorities of government. The expenditures of the ministry of Agriculture grew rapidly, as CORA absorbed a fair percentage of the cultivable lands in Chile and the Agricultural Development Institute (INDAP) organized a large number of campesino cooperatives and syndicates throughout the country. Although the budgetary allocations and public credits to the agricultural sector were quite generous, CORA and INDAP were voracious in their desire for more money. The executives of these two decentralized agencies used extensive political backing to apply unrelenting pressure on the minister of Agriculture. The minister was committed to the agricultural plan, and promoted the interests of CORA and INDAP in the meetings of the Economic Committee.[19]

[18] Under the Allende regime, this situation changed rather dramatically. Research by Lois Athey demonstrates that, because of legal dispensations stretching back to the 1930's which facilitated government "intervention" in and requisition of private industries, the ministry of Economy became one of the primary arenas for political action in the Unidad Popular government. From 1970 to 1972, the ministry of Economy subsumed its responsibilities in the realm of price control to using CORFO as an instrument to loosen private ownership over some 200 industries with sales accounting for 22 percent of the gross national product. See a complete description of this strategy in Instituto de Economía y Planificación, *La Economía Chilena en 1972*, p. 133, *passim*.

[19] See Molina, p. 93.

Specific issues sometimes weakened the informal bonds of the Developmentalist Coalition. The absence of regularly scheduled gatherings to iron out these differences meant that they were brought out into the open in the Economic Committee. Economy and Agriculture consistently disagreed over the question of agricultural prices in relation to inflation. DIRINCO prevailed upon its minister to insist on the stabilization of food costs to the consumer. Delaying price increases until the very last minute, however, placed a financial squeeze on the agricultural sector and meant that the cooperatives under the supervision of the ministry of Agriculture operated at a loss. When the costs of production on asentamientos were superior to revenues, CORA had to restrict new investment and appeal for deficit financing. The minister of Agriculture argued that the lack of economic incentives for the campesinos detracted from the social goals of the program.

Early in the period several jurisdictional problems caused tensions between CORFO and ODEPLAN, and their relationship did not begin on a good footing. Because the Development Corporation had been planning for the public sector since 1939, it naturally felt that ODEPLAN was usurping its functions. In a professional challenge to CORFO, and as a way to distinguish its modern outlook, ODEPLAN suggested a new, more socially oriented conception of planning. ODEPLAN felt that the credo of Chilean development planning in the past had been "industrialization," meaning the creation of any number or type of industries, just so they were industries. ODEPLAN questioned whether this bias was conducive to the long-term interests of the nation, or simply to the long-term interests of CORFO.

When ODEPLAN promoted social investment, however, it had to struggle with measurements of economic growth which favored the industrial orientation of CORFO. It was difficult for ODEPLAN to show how expenditures in education and medical services made an impact on the gross national product. Members of the Restrictive Coalition recognized that housing endeavors increased the satisfaction of their new occupants. But they believed that housing represented little in terms of national development, especially when compared with the output of CORFO and the ministry of Public Works.

The problem was compounded in the evaluation of programs such as Operation Sitio, which provided families of modest means with a plot of land on which they could build their own homes. When money was not used for construction, but to buy land parcels to be distributed to low-income families, the amount did not appear as capital increase, but as transfers. As such, Operation Sitio compared unfavorably with other projects, such as expanding a petrochemical plant of one of

CORFO's subsidiaries which appeared in the National Accounts as net capital increase. ODEPLAN helped fortify its arguments for social investment by manipulating the figures. In Operation Sitio, for example, when the family finished constructing the house, the original expenditures were classified as real investment, not transfers. This innovation helped ODEPLAN justify its predilection for social programs.

More serious than these semantic difficulties were conflicts stemming from proposals of ODEPLAN for organizational reform directly countering the interests of CORFO. In the 1940's, while CORFO was rapidly expanding, the central state ministries were quite lethargic and weak. Filling the vacuum, CORFO became a multisectoral institution. For a period of twenty-five years the organism thrived on effectuating positive action in building the country's economic infrastructure—in electricity, steel, fuels, communications, forestry products, transportation, agriculture, and mining—with little competition from the sectoral ministries. Eventually the various ministries became more organized and ambitious, and felt perfectly capable of directing all the activities related to their sectors. Consequently the overlapping responsibilities began to cause "territorial" disputes. In Agriculture, CORFO had eight subsidiaries involved in research, seeds, fertilizers, machinery, and distribution. Two major institutions, CORFO and the ministry of Agriculture, were responsible for agricultural development, and they were perpetually fighting over their respective domains. The same duplication also existed in the mining sector. When agencies of the ministry of Mining found themselves in conflict with one of CORFO's subsidiaries, they also found the full weight of CORFO behind the subsidiary.

Since this competition was counterproductive to coherent programming, ODEPLAN decided that the most logical arrangement was for CORFO to restrict itself to the development of manufacturing industries and hand over the other enterprises to the sectoral ministries. This proposal hardly met enthusiastic reception among the officials of CORFO, who felt that their patrimony over these industries and institutes was most desirable and had been legitimized over time.

These problems between ODEPLAN and CORFO, due to overlapping functions, incompatibilities in vocabulary, and interference in organizational prerogatives, resulted in an institutional rivalry during the early history of the Economic Committee. It was mitigated over time as some of the proposals became accepted as the new reality, and key personnel changes resulted in better working relations. More important, in 1968 the government's anti-inflationary drive took a dramatic turn. After three years of reduced inflation without a slowdown in real economic growth, the country began to suffer a complete reversal: rapid inflation coexistent with economic stagnation.

The Restrictive Coalition's proposals for fiscal restraint and a tight credit policy to fight the new surge of inflation jeopardized the interests of both ODEPLAN and CORFO. Their social and economic goals required continued expansion of fiscal expenditures and a more liberal monetary policy. Confronted with the conservative nature of the Restrictive Coalition, ODEPLAN and CORFO found that their mutual interests were more binding than the grievances that had separated them in the earlier period.

INSTITUTIONAL POWER AND DECISION-MAKING STYLE

The casual observer would probably not have recognized a situation of power differentiation in the meetings of the Economic Committee, which were quite informal, fairly unstructured, and often broken by humorous interludes. Recommendations emerged not after dramatic votes but from extensive dialogue, to which participants contributed supporting data pertinent to their sphere of knowledge. When the question under consideration was within the expertise of only a few Committee members, the others manifested confidence in their judgment by withdrawing from the mainstream of the conversation. While preparing for meetings with the president, discussion sometimes continued over several days until the final report was acceptable to all of the participants. When confronted by the selfish goals of public institutions undermining the short-term plan, the Committee members teamed together to give these agencies a pedantic lesson on the global aims of the government. Together they pointed out how certain behavior distorted those aims, and why these agencies had to mend their ways.

Power equality, however, was hardly characteristic of the two coalitions in the Economic Committee. In my reference to the influence of one coalition, conclusions are not based on an objective tally of recorded events but on the declarations of the participants. The president of the country, ultimately responsible for the government's short-term policies, was the kingmaker. And the fact is that *the Restrictive Coalition's orientation toward short-term planning always predominated.* The president always supported the ministry of Finance in discussions between it and ODEPLAN. When the Central Bank opposed new investment for CORFO and Agriculture in order to maintain its monetary policy, it was always upheld. If a meeting began by considering the fiscal or credit needs of a social program, the question was always decided on the basis of the program's effect on the rate of inflation.

It is easier to learn that the Restrictive Coalition was consistently the victor in the Economic Committee than to describe the reasons for Frei's preference. It appears that he aligned himself with the Restrictive Coalition because of the personal influence of its members, the organizational resources it commanded, and its technical orientation in the definition of problems.

Personalities and Institutional Resources

Personality seemed to play a major role in the sessions of the Economic Committee. Personality as an independent variable, however, poses difficult problems for the study of organizational power. The question is moot when there is a correspondence between important institutions and outstanding leadership. The economic resources and technical expertise of the organization are put at the disposal of a man who is in the post because of his outstanding personal traits. The appointee has the ability to influence the president both because he leads an organization with an ample array of resources not equaled by many of his colleagues and because it is through the president's confidence in him that he has been appointed in the first place. During these years, the men leading the ministry of Finance combined these two elements. On the other hand, it is possible that a man lacking in many of the more objective sources of institutional power could compensate by being endowed with quick intelligence, impressive forensic ability, human warmth, and other agreeable character traits. In all likelihood, such would have been the case had Jorge Ahumada lived to be the informal leader of the Developmentalist Coalition.

The importance of personal dynamism in gauging an organization's influence is borne out by many examples of weak individuals leading strong institutions, and vice versa. Often a political leader, insecure in his own position, will appoint lackluster executives to mitigate the real power of their organizations. Similarly, an aggressive personality can sometimes exploit insignificant organizational resources to give his point of view considerably more influence than it might warrant on a more objective scale.[20]

A review of this period, however, reveals that President Frei consistently appointed loyal, capable persons to powerful institutions and paid less attention to those individuals who represented lesser organizations. ODEPLAN was disadvantaged by being newly created, and the

[20] Despite their frequent occurrence, both situations have internal dangers. When a power vacuum develops at the head of an important agency, middle-level per-

potential influence of the ministry of Economy did not necessarily equal the sum total of all the agencies on its organizational chart. The economic power of both the Central Bank and the Finance ministry were more extensive than those of ODEPLAN, CORFO, and Agriculture, or even all of them together. While the Finance ministry maintained a strong hold over fiscal allocations, ODEPLAN had no formal authority to intervene in the distribution of funds.[21] The State Bank, with its subsidiaries in practically every town across the country, provided reports to the president on the real demand for farm credits, to counterbalance the prejudiced requests from the ministry of Agriculture. Although CORFO enjoyed considerable status in the society-at-large, and the activities of ODEPLAN were respected in academic and international circles, the prestige that counted in the meetings of the Economic Committee was that of the president of the republic. Frei backed those he liked, an important factor that should not be underemphasized. The fact that those whom he trusted most were leaders of the most powerful organizations in the Economic Committee is partial testimony to his personal political style.

Orientations of the Two Coalitions

In addition to nebulous factors of human compatibility, the organizational norms of the Restrictive Coalition helped it gain the president's support in the Economic Committee. Full delegation of financial authority in budgetary matters to the minister of Finance had the tangible benefit of reducing pressure on Frei from agencies forever requesting more. It became common knowledge within the administration that the Finance minister's opinion in the Committee was basically the last word. This relieved the president of having to say "no" again and again, which would have reduced his personal influence with those who were denied and turned away. Frei's apparent support of the Finance minister allowed him to lower the frequency of negative responses, but it did not prevent him from saying "yes" when he felt conditions warranted it. He could give extra satisfaction to the sectors that he preferred, such as Education and Public Works, while leaving

---

sonnel often formulate and carry out policies of their own choosing with little interference from a voice at the top. If repeated in many organizations, this behavior can seriously lessen the president's knowledge of, or control over, the activities of his bureaucracy. Likewise, the appointment of a strong personality sometimes lifts the influence of a weak organization beyond its ability to support the president in times of crisis.

[21] As part of its enabling legislation, Congress passed an amendment forbidding it from disrupting the normal administrative operations in the public sector, which reduced its influence even further. See Sunkel, "Cambios Estructurales," p. 46.

the fate of others for which he held no special sympathy, such as Lands and Colonization, in the cold hands of Finance. The word "apparent" is used above, since the appearance of delegating complete authority to Finance had to be preserved to give him the freedom needed to build compromises in private.

Could this strategy have been extended to the Developmentalist Coalition with the same results? If all requests for additional operating capital had had to be cleared through ODEPLAN, Frei could have avoided the ordeal of receiving delegations of top-level administrators with their urgent appeals. ODEPLAN could simply issue its recommendation, and he would give the appearance of automatically acting on it.

The fundamental difference between the two coalitions in this regard, however, is that the planning approach of the Developmentalist Coalition might have reduced the president's political options. Finance and the Central Bank made their decisions from a base of *global* figures— so much total expenditure, so much credit, so much total money in circulation, and so much inflation. ODEPLAN was concerned not only with the changes in overall economic variables, but also with the feasibility and advisability of the enterprises. The orientation of the Developmentalist Coalition included consideration of the *content* and *functional interrelation* of the programs suggested.

For example, the Central Bank and ODEPLAN began from different perspectives in considering the proposal to begin the Santiago metropolitan subway. The Central Bank advised the president that the metro would increase inflation by several percentage points each year for the duration of its construction. Because of his personal attraction to the subway idea, its alleged utility, and his political interdependency with those who stood to gain from its completion, Frei apparently did not find it overly agonizing to dismiss these arguments and order construction to begin.

On the other hand, ODEPLAN's argument considered opportunity costs and the subway's lack of integration with other programs under consideration. The underground would adversely commit the transportation policy for decades to come and seemed economically unjustified in terms of potential savings to future users, despite the extensive governmental subsidy for its operation. If the president were not worried about the inflation increase, a multitude of different programs could be implemented with considerably more advantageous long-term effects than the one he preferred.

In meetings of the Economic Committee, contrary opinions on suggested projects were voiced quite frankly and explicitly. Yet the fact that Frei continually supported the members of the Restrictive Coalition meant that the Developmentalist Coalition never mustered the strength to argue on equal terms. It also hinted that the president was not lending his prestige to institutions that, because of their technical orientation, complicated his decision-making tasks. From this perspective, the global figures of the Restrictive Coalition were much easier to accommodate.[22]

Decision-Making Norms of the Economic Committee

Whatever the precise reasons behind the fact, this power discrepancy between the two informal coalitions had very real implications for the decision-making style of the Committee as a whole. The hegemony of the Restrictive Coalition meant that the short-term policy-making activities of the Economic Committee were predefined in at least three ways: continuous obsession with the question of inflation, which overwhelmed many other considerations; a tendency to formulate the budget prior to setting down planning goals for the year; and a pattern of decisions made on a global basis, with little concern for detail. Had the Developmentalist Coalition maintained the upper hand in the Committee, it is probable that the preoccupation with inflation would have been tempered by letting the rate slide, in deliberate maneuvers to benefit certain economic or social goals; that planning targets would have been delineated prior to, and in association with, the formation of the budget; and that greater attention would have been paid to the detailed content of proposed public activities, to evaluate their functional integration with broader economic and social needs rather than just their effect on the rate of inflation.

The overriding concern of the Economic Committee was control over inflation. Though the Restrictive Coalition believed that marketing and income decisions in the private sector related more to the rate of inflation than government policies, it wanted to reduce the state's role as one of the causes.[23] The Central and State banks were not consciously against development per se, but they wanted to make the consequences of current financial decisions clear to the other committee members. They did not permit suggested changes in the monetary and fiscal poli-

[22] This is not to suggest that the variables put forth were too complex for Frei to grasp. It might even be said that on some matters, such as administrative decentralization, his political intuition responded to the ideas of the Developmentalists.

[23] José R. Ramos, in his study of the effectiveness of income policies from 1940 to 1969, concluded that the working population's expectations concerning the rate of inflation over the short term were more important than government wage policies in determining the actual increases in remunerations. Ramos, *Política de Remuneraciones en Inflaciones Persistentes: El Caso de Chile.*

cies until full analysis had shown their inflationary effect. They were adamant in assigning responsibility for the future state of affairs to the individual committee members who advocated a softer stance. The Central Bank usually went one step further by arguing quite insistently that policy not be altered, and that the Committee recommend that the original lines of the Annual Operating Plan be maintained. The president, who often stated that economic development could never take place in Chile without the systematic reduction of inflation, supported the hard line of the Restrictive Coalition.

The second implication of power differentiation in the Committee concerned the use of the budget to implement economic policy. In the protocol of the Chilean executive branch of government, the ministry of Economy was on a higher rung in the hierarchy than Finance. But Finance's dominance in the Committee placed the ministry of Economy and ODEPLAN at a relative disadvantage. Instead of the budget's being a tool of government for short-term policy goals, planning goals had to conform to the dictates of the budget. The principal question relating to the budget was *not* "What configuration of resources will move the country toward the social and economic goals of the regime?" but rather "How can economic maneuvers be employed to finance the budget?"

Finance decided the budgetary ceilings for each sector before the Economic Committee had the opportunity to discuss the goals of the next year's Annual Operating Plan. Although cursory discussion of the size of sectoral allocations occasionally took place, Finance and the Budget Bureau jealously guarded their authority to set the level of expenditures. The Committee's budgetary activities entailed little more than approving the size of the deficit and figuring out ways to finance it with the fewest repercussions on the stabilization drive. The Central Bank might inquire into the possibility of renegotiating loan payments of 100 million dollars to the Inter-American Development Bank over a period of three years, reducing the amount due for the first year to 33.3 million dollars. The minister of Economy might study the feasibility of readjusting salaries in the public sector by only 28 percent, against a 30 percent inflation figure, while increasing subsidies for family allowance by 35 percent. The State Bank might check its resources for a large loan to the National Treasury, and CORFO might suggest that the national railroads and other state industries float their outstanding debts to the private sector until the middle of the following year.

These helter-skelter activities, along with the emission of newly printed money from the national mint, served to scale down the size of the deficit to manageable proportions. The point remains, however, that the minister of Finance defined the budget in a way that left the other members of the Committee with the job of devising elegant tricks to legitimize his decisions. ODEPLAN and the ministry of Economy were not given the opportunity to evaluate the meaning of the budget for the social and economic goals of the middle-range plan.[24]

Third, the tendencies of Finance, the Central Bank, and the State Bank to view the economic situation in global terms carried over into the meetings of the Economic Committee. The relative efficacy of expenditures in education did not enter into the minutes of the meetings. Nor was the Committee as a whole seemingly interested in housing policy, urban works programs, the impact of Public Works investment on long-term transportation plans, agrarian reform as a social goal, the ambition to nationalize the large mining companies, the purposes of foreign aid, the orientation of community development projects, or the content of health policy for national development. The global position of the Committee almost obliged it to ignore these details of short-term policy in favor of the total level of investment, demand for credit, deficits in the state industries, the balance of payments, general remuneration policy, the size of the foreign debt, and the rate of inflation.

Again, there was latent disagreement over the meaning of short-term planning, and the Restrictive Coalition was able to make the whole Committee accept its approach toward problems. The Developmentalist Coalition did not claim that the rate of inflation and the level of unemployment were not matters of the gravest importance. Yet the probability remains that had the Developmentalists comprised the balance of power in the Committee, short-term policy-making would have conformed more to a programmed approach to planning. The Committee would still have dealt with global figures, but would also have made more effort to coordinate the activities of the different public agencies within the middle-term goals.[25]

---

[24] The preeminence of the ministry of Economy in the Allende regime helped account for a reversal of the situation: the Budget Bureau and the Central Bank faithfully served the regime's short-term political goals, such as nationalization of the large industries, radicalization of agrarian reform, and large wage hikes for the working class. Restricting the money supply was not an important consideration for the Economic Committee at that time.

[25] Such speculation may be beside the point, since the essential problem of ODEPLAN and the ministry of Economy was that they did not hold the balance of power under Frei. Accordingly, the operating procedures and the internal decision-making style of the Committee were more nearly as the Restrictive Coalition demanded, and not as the Developmentalist Coalition would have preferred. Given the technico-rational orientation of the Christian Democratic regime, ODEPLAN's position could not compare with that of the Central Bank, which

An Artificial Atmosphere of Equality

In this situation of extensive power imbalance, manifest hostility was minimal and the discussion was carried on in a spirit of apparent agreement, harmony, and shared value premises. However, the members of the Developmentalist Coalition were sensitive to the advantage of the more powerful organizations in the Committee and did not feel competent to fight for a general orientation countering that of their colleagues. First, the president's support reinforced the confidence of the Central Bank to amplify its cries for more stringent policies.[26] Second, the reality of the president's preference smothered the initiative of other members of the Committee to propose alternative formulae. Their restraint was not an offshoot of their agreement with the global position of the Central Bank. It stemmed from their inferior power base and their inability to construct a coherent model to counter the anti-inflation approach of the Restrictive Coalition. The members of the Developmentalist Coalition felt that they had nothing to gain by letting this conflict come forcefully to the surface.

The incompatibility of the core positions of the two groups also remained beneath the surface because of Frei's desire to maintain unity in the executive branch of government. In situations confronting two points of view, Frei was very cautious in judging the winners. He did not like to resolve differences between his advisors on a face-to-face basis, and often delayed several days before making a decision at all if it clearly favored one party. That is, he did not remark censoriously: "On this matter, A is correct and B is wrong." Frei had two general methods of making decisions in conflict situations which tended to dispel any feeling that he was overtly taking sides. In more minor disagreements, he listened to both points of view and then reworded the preferred argument in his own style, giving the impression that he had come to the opinion independently. Though it did not appear that he was supporting one individual over another, he invariably rewarded the position of the Restrictive Coalition. The second technique, more prev-

---

had an economic model predicting the inflationary effects of credit and fiscal policies in the future with remarkable accuracy, and the pertinent data to fit into that model. Internal decisions always tended to revolve around the variables that this coalition put forth.

[26] It appears that this resource discrepancy was so one-sided that some members of the Restrictive group failed even to realize that others on the Committee were not quite so dedicated to their interpretation of the national interest. Indeed, the backing of the president made the Restrictive position appear so impregnable that they were convinced that everyone listed priorities in the same way, with control over inflation a concern that admitted no exception.

alent in serious impasses, was to stop the discussion and ask the Committee to move on to another subject. Later, when he was alone, he made up his mind, and then telephoned the winner to say that his proposal would be accepted. Then he called up the loser and consoled him with the assurance that his ideas had considerable merit, but that it might be wise to wait a while before trying them out. This style preserved face for all parties and avoided feelings of persecution on the part of the perennial losers. Frei, through skillful management of human sentiments, tried to engender an atmosphere that artificially removed some of the barriers to free discussion among persons who were highly differentiated in organizational resources and in their capacity to convince.

DEVELOPMENT AND PLANNING

Why did ODEPLAN not lead the Developmentalist Coalition more successfully in the Economic Committee? At the beginning of the Christian Democratic regime, three propositions were put forth concerning the planning office's structure and location in the administrative hierarchy. The first presented the case for a small team of highly qualified advisors acting as watchdogs over the public sector. With offices in the presidential palace, these men would profit from continual access to the chief of state and be able to use his authority to orient the activities of the public sector toward identifiable developmental ends. A second alternative was to attach a middle-sized planning unit to the ministry of Finance and give it a predominant role in budgetary formation and execution—again with the aim of mobilizing the public sector toward the goals of the plan. There ODEPLAN would have a voice in managing over 30 percent of the gross national product and 70 percent of the country's investment. The first suggestion conceived of a planning elite at the top of the executive hierarchy, working with the president's authority; the second, a hard-working agency at the middle levels controlling extensive economic resources. Either of these arrangements would probably have given ODEPLAN more influence than it eventually had.[27]

Instead of patterning itself after either of these suggestions ODEPLAN evolved as a large bureaucracy under the presidency with sectoral and regional offices, but with no control over funds and very little access to the president. Following the trend inspired by international agencies, it became involved in global cybernetic planning, with

[27] Interview material. Also see Molina, pp. 163–165.

its national and sectoral targets, but was remote from daily decisions in the public sector. ODEPLAN's poor resource base placed it at a disadvantage in the bureaucracy, especially in its relations with Public Works and the decentralized agencies in Housing and Agriculture. ODEPLAN was not interested in the affairs of the weaker ministries, and was almost helpless to influence the stronger ones.[28]

When Frei asked ODEPLAN, in the Economic Committee, for an opinion on the level of salary adjustments for the coming year, he needed an immediate answer. When ODEPLAN said that it was planning for the coming years, Frei listened politely but then turned to the Central Bank and the ministry of Finance for the answer he needed. The Restrictive Coalition was willing to spell out those groups which would be advantaged and those which would not, and it defended its recommendations fervently. ODEPLAN was not ready to do this, and the possible value of its developmentalist approach was not reflected in most of the decisions of the Economic Committee.

ODEPLAN might have forfeited some economic decisions to the Central Bank and still used the Economic Committee to enforce its style of short-term planning. Since influence based on technical expertise is not an abstract commodity, ODEPLAN might have had more success if it had had full information on the affairs of the various ministries and state enterprises and had evaluated the effects of their programs on fulfillment of the medium-term plan. The subjects for analysis could have been rooted in the information it provided. Independent variables would have been: levels of sectoral investment, the types of programs being implemented, the interrelation of these programs among the sectors, and their comprehensive impact on society. Dependent variables would have been the relative progression toward the social, economic, and political goals of government. This is a defensible conception of short-term planning; and the Economic Committee, with the aid of the president, could have worked to implement it.

ODEPLAN's projections were relatively worthless as guidelines for action, if it had no idea what important agencies had done, were doing, or intended to do in the future. To operationalize its variables, ODEPLAN needed information from every corner of the public administration. It did not have this information because the high-investment agencies, relatively uninterested in the concept of overall plan-

---

[28] Sunkel, p. 47, attributes ODEPLAN's lack of influence to the fact that most of the regime's goals were made the responsibility of specialized agencies and commissions: CORA (agrarian reform), CORVI (housing), CODELCO (copper nationalization), CORFO (industrialization), and the Economic Committee (inflation).

ning and motivated to protect their organizational prerogatives, did not cooperate. ODEPLAN did not have the president's authority to force compliance, because it could offer him little in return. Nor could it trade financial resources for information as could the Budget Bureau, because it had no access to funds. ODEPLAN's incapacity to hold its own in the bureaucracy carried over into the sessions of the Economic Committee.[29] Compared to the Finance ministry, with its wide control over money, and the Central Bank, with its economic model and the information to complete it, ODEPLAN alone did not have a chance in determining the decision-making style of the Committee.[30] Its inability to operationalize overlapping goals with other Committee members into a winning coalition was significant for defining the types of economic and social policies that ultimately characterized the Frei regime.

[29] Why did not the less-favored participants in the Committee completely lose spirit and resign? Frei's careful efforts to give each party his say probably contributed to a phenomenon that Albert O. Hirschman has labeled the "member-of-the-team trap." Building on an observation of James C. Thompson, Jr., who saw "domestication of dissenters" in United States President Lyndon Johnson's National Security Council, Hirschman points out that policy dissenters overestimate their influence in mollifying extreme decisions, as well as their eventual ability to alter the course of events. These rationalizations, combined with loyalty to the president, induce them to remain "on the team" when resignation or threats of resignation are their most powerful weapons. Hirschman, *Exit, Voice, and Loyalty*, pp. 113–119. See also Guillermo O'Donnell, *Modernization and Bureaucratic-Authoritarianism*, pp. 106–109.

[30] These difficulties also characterized the Allende regime.

4

INCREMENTALISM
AND THE POLITICAL RESOURCES
OF THE ECONOMIC COMMITTEE

Recent Chilean presidential regimes, as Chapter 1 pointed out, have passed through discernible governing cycles. Soon after election the president's ideological precepts and campaign promises accurately reflect his party's or coalition's overall preferences. But when he passes directives downward to the bureaucracy, a lag in creating necessary expertise prevents immediate action on many of the fundamental changes promised. The inherent disadvantage of this gap between will and ability is that the time taken to fill it coincides with declining support for the regime. At the beginning the government has the greatest opportunity to make extensive headway on far-reaching programs; yet the incapacity to combine "high information" with "high legitimacy" attenuates reforms, development programs, and "revolutionary" initiatives before they can be carried to completion.

Exacerbating this tendency is the fact that sometime after its programs are deployed the government must contend with violent challenges to its authority, events almost unimaginable in the few months of euphoria immediately after taking office. Typically, in the latter half of the period, the regime's profile is considerably lower as it participates in a slower-paced, more deliberate style of consolidation and "nudged" changes in rather innocuous directions. The reduced efficacy of positional authority affects not only the president and his closest political partisans, but also important sections of public administration, especially those charged with implementing programs countering vested interests. The repercussions on bureaucracy can be illustrated through descriptive variables that alter from one period to the next.[1]

THE ECONOMIC COMMITTEE'S
DECISION-MAKING STYLE

The Economic Committee, for example, had the possibility of moving along three dimensions embodying its decision-making style: rational to political; restrictive to expansionary; and comprehensive to incrementalist. Its preferred decision-making style was rational, restrictive, and comprehensive.

What were the results when the Committee tried to make policies which reflected these criteria prevail in the real world? Here, as in the last chapter, we will treat the Committee's decision-making style as a dependent variable. Rather than focus on internal dynamics, however, we will evaluate the Committee when it confronted constraints in its task environment. The basic argument is that the Economic Committee was able to implement preferred decisions so long as it maintained access to a full range of political resources to back them up.

From 1964 to 1970, the Committee attempted to profit from its ties with outside groups, especially the Christian Democratic party, in order to bolster its influence vis-a-vis the bureaucracy and the private sector. Meanwhile, ambitious public agencies with extensive political support worked to disrupt the Committee's restrictive fiscal position, and organized labor challenged its stringent remunerations policies. During the first half of the period, the Committee's accumulated stock of resources was sufficient for decisions to be rational, restrictive, and comprehensive.

In 1967, however, the Committee overplayed its hand at a very important juncture. A frontal attack on inflation by means of a forced-savings plan aroused such resistance that the Committee exhausted all of its political capital. The consequences of this proposal were traumatic: mass rioting and the resignation of the Finance minister. The Committee abandoned its comprehensive and rationalistic decision-making style in favor of an incremental and political approach. Incrementalism, however, was not linked to the Committee's inability to gather and use information. It resulted from a lack of more important resources, such as money, prestige, and authority.

---

[1] A similar method will be employed in Chapter 8 to study the effects of urban violence on bureaucratic behavior.

Rational versus Political

One of the Economic Committee's characteristics was a rationalistic approach to problems. Committee members, upon arriving in power, purposefully abstracted themselves from day-to-day political realities. They designed a development strategy appropriate for a country with a five-hundred-dollar per-capita income, a relatively weak industrial infrastructure, uneven but not dichotomous income distribution (similar to pre-war Italy), advanced socialization of the economy, endemic inflation, and a very poor foreign trade picture.[2] They recognized Chile's long and active political history, but felt the moment opportune for a series of rational solutions to Chile's major problems. If interested parties would put aside their grievances over the middle term, the Economic Committee could prove the correctness of its measures. Within a rational framework and with the sympathetic understanding of the political community, it wanted to use the power of the state to advance on several fronts: a turnabout in foreign trade, increased industrial and social development, agrarian reform without bloodshed, and reduced inflation.

The members of the Committee understood their role to be that of technicians designing short-term policies in the public interest. Their bias toward formal rationality was consistent with the "sterilized" anti-inflation model of the Restrictive Coalition. Naturally it countered the substantive rationality of "unscrupulous" organizations in the public sector, and complicating human expectations and political drives in the society-at-large. These realities were deliberately ignored in favor of devising the optimal solutions to Chile's economic problems. The political leaders of the regime reinforced this orientation by telling the Economic Committee: You figure out the most rational economic course to take, and we will prepare the way to implement it.[3]

As long as the prestige of the president and the resiliency of the political party buffered the Committee from the political community, it could exercise a technical approach toward economic issues, despite the political ramifications. Eventually, however, this protective shield eroded and the Committee had to consider the political practicability of its suggestions. It no longer could hand over optimal decisions to a willing president and a cooperative party for implementation, nor ignore the fact that everyone outside of the conference room was screaming about the proposals that it was promoting. Subsequently, Commit-

---

[2] See Sergio Molina's description of the Christian Democrats' *"diagnóstico"* of the economic situation in 1964, in *El Proceso de Cambio en Chile*, pp. 40–64.

[3] Interview material. See also Molina, pp. 66 ff.

tee members had to study the political implications of their suggestions even while they were being formulated, and adopt the roles of political activists to have them implemented.

Restrictive versus Expansionary

A second characteristic of the Economic Committee was its restrictive position on issues. Frei's electoral platform was noteworthy for its wide scope and its lack of a dominating list of priorities. Education, housing, agriculture, industry, copper, and inflation all shared the limelight as part of his overall platform, but none was emphasized as the most important goal of the regime. The result was inevitable: different units of government and their clients adopted the goal that best suited their interests and tried to push it ahead of the others. Within the Economic Committee, the Developmentalist Coalition felt that social and economic development were the most important issues and that all others, inflation included, should be balanced off against programmed advances in housing, education, agriculture, and industrial growth. The Restrictive Coalition determined that control over inflation should be the top priority of government, and proposed that all other regime goals should be judged in terms of their effect on inflation. The previous chapter discussed several reasons why the Restrictive Coalition emerged victorious in Committee sessions and enjoyed the backing of the president.

Even those units at a disadvantage in the Economic Committee, however, had a vested interest in trying to implement its resolutions. Over the medium term a weaker institution such as ODEPLAN did not have much opportunity to impose its orientation on the Committee. But it could at least participate in the formation of Committee decisions, giving it some measure of influence at a very high level of government. It could also hope that, over the longer term, the political philosophy of government would change and its own resource base would improve, so that its possible predominance in some future Economic Committee would have real impact on the behavior of public and private sectors of the economy. Latent dissension on the internal workings of the Committee tended to dissolve when the Committee faced those individuals, groups, and organizations charged with complying with its decisions.

When political realities changed in the latter half of the Frei regime, the Committee's restrictive position became less valid. It had to compromise the goals of the short-term plan in order to relieve pressures from important institutions in the public sector. Printing up new money and imprudently releasing credits went against its own best advice and were measures of last resort through which the Committee could purchase breathing space. But as its resource base dropped toward zero, such means became the rule rather than the exception.

It is important to note that successful inroads against the Economic Committee's restrictiveness did not enhance the position of the Developmentalists. ODEPLAN was not programming public investment for key sections of the economy, but public agencies and private parties were gaining satisfaction for their credit and budgetary demands from a very reluctant Central Bank, State Bank, and ministry of Finance. The Committee's internal style was restrictive because of the influence of these latter economic agencies with the president.[4] When forces outside of the Committee challenged that style, relatively unregulated expansionary policies resulted. Neither the Restrictive Coalition nor the Developmentalist Coalition determined the direction of this expansion; the whole Committee was on the defensive.

Comprehensive versus Incrementalist

The Annual Operating Plan sponsored by the Committee purported to be comprehensive in three ways: through the large number of actors it affected; by the high degree of integration of the variables in the Central Bank's economic model; and in its goal of reducing inflation permanently in Chile. The committee members made decision-rules for all public agencies, despite the nature of their services; for the economy of the private sector, especially that part which was labor-intensive or dealt in credits and foreign trade; and for numerous organizations in the society with special economic interests to further, of which the most important were the labor unions. Although the quantity of variables in the theoretical model was insignificant compared to the infinite number of economic decisions that could be made in the society, the scope of these variables meant that they impinged significantly on a great proportion of these decisions.[5] In addition, these variables were highly interrelated within the economic model developed by the Restrictive Coalition. Movement in one had predictable effects on

[4] Molina, pp. 81, 98, hints quite strongly that the Committee, when faced with a choice between "development" and monetary stability, always elected the former. My interviews led me to just the opposite conclusion. This point represents the major discrepancy between this book and Molina's otherwise useful and entertaining first-person account of economic planning under the Frei regime.

[5] Martin Meyerson and Edward C. Banfield consider planning decisions more comprehensive if they indicate the principal acts by which all of the most important ends are to be attained, and more partial if they show how some but not all of the important ends are to be attained, or how subordinate ends are to be attained. Meyerson and Banfield, *Politics, Planning and the Public Interest,* p. 313. Amitai Etzioni suggests that working "toward the greatest combined service to a set of goals is an attempt to evolve comprehensive rationality." *The Active Society,* p. 261.

the others, and the Committee accepted the responsibility of controlling all of them simultaneously in order to reduce inflation.

Given the ninety-year history of inflation in Chile, and the numerous failures to put a stop to it, the Committee's commitment to succeed where others had failed represented another ambitious aspect of its orientation.[6] To definitively remove inflation, the Committee had to enforce rigid rules indicating precise behavior for the whole society. The 1967 forced savings program was such an effort.[7]

The Committee's comprehensive decision-making style was negated when the number of private and public actors abiding by its decisions lowered considerably, when pressures on every one of the variables so twisted its economic model that an image of the whole was lost, and when it gave up its attempt to eliminate inflation. Public and private clients continually attempted to induce the Committee to view their particular needs in isolated fashion. When the Economic Committee was pushed in one direction and then another, its Annual Operating Plan was reduced to a patchwork quilt, and the overall path of government was difficult to discern. The interrelationship of the variables in the economic model persevered, but with very little guidance from the Committee. Under such conditions, the Committee was forced to adopt an incrementalist approach—marginal, reactive, piecemeal changes, with low risk and low payoff, based on a recognition that it could only adjust to inflation, not reduce it systematically.

THE COMMITTEE IN THE FIRST HALF
OF THE FREI REGIME

In the years between 1964 and 1967, government revenue in Chile increased dramatically, giving the regime a wide array of financial resources to begin its programs for fundamental change. By 1966, because of a favorable price for copper exports, foreign aid, new and higher taxes, and an expansion of the economy after a period of stagnation, the Economic Committee had almost double the 1964 global

[6] Albert Hirschman provides a history of Chilean inflation in *Journeys Toward Progress*, pp. 129–223. For some measures to contain inflation, see Enrique Sierra, Sergio Benavente C., and Juan Osorio B., *Tres Ensayos de Estabilización en Chile: Las Políticas Aplicadas en el Decenio, 1956–1966*.

[7] Molina, p. 99, writes that the political dynamics of inflation in Chile remind him of the card game "Old Maid," whereby each player attempts to pass on the effects of wage and price rises to the others. The only difference is that the players who continually end up holding the Black Queen are the poorest and most defenseless, which eventually convinces them that the cards are marked and the rules systematically weighted against them.

amount of real governmental revenues.[8] During the first two years of the Frei government, the Economic Committee depended on the political party to insulate its rationalistic approach from disrupting influences in the political community. The Committee felt that the party had the right to provide the principal orientation for the government and call attention when the government seemed to be departing from its goals. In return, the party offered its structure as a depository for many sources of influence which the Committee could not hope to hold in perpetual reserve. The party's functional links with political actors from rural communes to the national capital were helpful to win compliance for the Committee's wage policies. The party votes in Congress, which constituted a majority in the Chamber of Deputies and about a third in the Senate, could be used to support the government's budgetary and legislative proposals. Its legitimacy as the standard-bearer for broadly based ideological principles helped bolster the Committee's moral authority, and its access to the mass media provided convenient means of reaching the population of the country to explain the more controversial aspects of the government's economic program.

The regime attempted to profit from its party backing in two ways. First, representatives from each sector of the executive branch participated in commissions with the party's congressmen to formulate laws, to follow their day-to-day progress through the legislature, and to discuss government programs that were of interest to the congressman in his home district.[9] On a second front, the minister of Finance was responsible for maintaining close ties between the party and the Committee. He attended meetings of the National Council of the party to explain the Committee's more significant decisions, such as the goals of the Annual Operating Plan. Broad policy lines were first approved by the party and then carried out by the Committee. For example, the foreign trade policy called for periodic devaluation. The Committee did not have to consult the party every time that small adjustments were contemplated in the exchange rate for the dollar.

The tremendous margin of financial liquidity, the favorable image of the president as the chief of state, and the firm support of the party meant two things for the Economic Committee: it could design strict anti-inflationary measures and have them enforced by a strong government and unified political party; and it could pump money in large quantities to sectors responsible for carrying out other aspects of the

[8] See the various *Exposiciones sobre el Estado de la Hacienda Pública*, 1966-1970. Also Tables 5 and 6.

[9] The 1965 activities of the Tripartite Commission (party, executive, Congress) for Public Works are discussed in the next chapter.

government's program, without having to abide by a fixed set of priorities. In addition, it could allow important public agencies pressuring
for budgetary supplements some measure of satisfaction, without upsetting the basic tenets of the stabilization program.

Throughout the six-year period, the Economic Committee had four alternative ways to subsidize agency deficits. In a few cases it was conceivable to ask the ministry to solve the problem by transferring surplus
monies from secondary priorities to the deficit account. Such self-
financing was the preferred way to maintain the short-term plan. The
second method was to lower the budgets of other ministries in order to
provide enough margin for the agency that was overspending. The sectors rarely cut were those with a very high proportion of expenditures
in the current account, such as Education and Health.[10] Third, the
Committee could cut those ministries that were somewhat behind in
their level of expenditures. The ministry's tardiness in spending its
monthly allocations provided a convenient margin to deduct and redistribute to agencies running deficits.[11]

During the first half of the period, however, a common solution
was to subsidize the agency's deficit with new government revenues, increases in the price of copper, or easy credit policies. Because of the
expansion of the economy at the time, these measures had virtually no
effect on the stabilization program (see Figure 4 and Table 5). At the
beginning of the regime, the economic model used by the Committee
proved to be

highly useful in designing a policy and explaining the results. . . . The main
discrepancies, from the point of view of short-term policy, were the wages
and salaries' behavior and government expenditure pressures. Both have deep
political implications and should be analyzed in that context, but the situation
was balanced by the favorable aspects discussed above. The results were
good in that a considerable reduction of the rate of inflation was obtained
simultaneously with an increase in production and no effect on employment.
Nevertheless, it became clear at the beginning of 1966 that in order to obtain
further improvements, measures should be taken to correct the elements gen-

[10] A second criterion employed: Cuts were not administered when the level of
employment in the private sector would suffer. It was not in the interest of the
Economic Committee to maintain a high level of employment in Public Works by
reducing it in Housing.

[11] This solution was fervently resisted by the ministries, and often provoked attacks on Finance for having changed the budgetary figures promised at the beginning of the year. The affected agencies claimed that they had made sincere efforts
to program their expenditures in line with the agency's goals, and that naturally
these expenditures would not be uniform, but seasonal. To punish them for not
keeping to the artificial schedule of the National Treasury was lunacy and undermined the whole programming effort.

erating pressures, inasmuch as the favorable aspects were assumed to be transitory by definition.[12]

After experimenting for two years, the Economic Committee was very confident that its model included all of the variables affecting Chilean inflation over the short term, and indicated their interrelationship accurately enough to predict price pressures with a high degree of accuracy. The next step was to implement a comprehensive program to systematically eradicate inflation from the economy. Within its model, the Committee assigned a preponderant role to the savings rate, which had to improve if demand were to lower and price pressures to reduce. The Committee worked during the better part of 1967 filling out the details of the forced savings program and linking it to other goals consistent with Christian Democratic ideology, such as increased participation for the workers and income redistribution through noncapitalistic means.

After 1967, the economy entered a recession which led to lowered government revenue.[13] The president's prestige and effective authority declined by natural atrophy, and the Committee could not count on such dependable flows of these resources to support its decisions. Already cracks were showing in the unity of the Christian Democratic party, which no longer was willing to insulate the Committee's "optimal" solutions from dissatisfied elements in political society. This last factor was especially important for the Committee's decision-making style, because its members had to learn the skills of political activists, lobby for its programs in Congress, and carry the issues to the people, whereas previously it had left these duties to the party.

The party was susceptible to political influences often incompatible with the technical orientation of governmental authorities in bureaucratic roles. Some party members, continually dismayed by the ideological image of their government, wanted to know whether it was heading further Right or Left every time it made a decision. For its part the Economic Committee was trying to devise workable instruments to cut inflation, and had difficulty empathizing with the ideological fervor around it. The Committee attempted to point out to rebels in the party that speed and revolutionary adjustment were not congruent with the multiple constraints on government, especially the need for monetary stability.[14] Individual members of the Committee concluded that the misunderstandings arose from the difficulty for any progressive

[12] Jorge Cauas, "Stabilization Policy: The Chilean Case," p. 825.

[13] See Osvaldo Sunkel, "Cambios Estructurales, Estrategias de Desarrollo y Planificación en Chile, 1938–1969," p. 47; Jorge Cauas, "Política Económica a Corto Plazo."

[14] Interview material. Also Molina, p. 142.

party, in the opposition for many years, to enter the executive mansion and learn quickly that the governing process implies inherent restrictions and responsibilities. Several of the more froward members of the party who were dissatisfied with the government, however, were not convinced that this cleavage derived exclusively from their own political immaturity. Their eventual divorce from the Christian Democratic movement substantiated the depth of their convictions.[15]

THE ECONOMIC COMMITTEE, THE PRIVATE SECTOR, AND THE FORCED SAVINGS PROGRAM

The Economic Committee's most comprehensive effort to eliminate inflation began in late 1967, and ended in complete defeat in the early months of 1968. The principal parts of the program involved an obligatory contribution by all salaried and wage-earning citizens to a Capitalization Fund for investment purposes. The justification of the program was that real income gains over the previous three years (11.3 percent in 1966 alone) would dissipate unless continuing advances were made to contain inflation. Cost-of-living increases had dropped from 45 percent in 1963 to 17 percent in 1966, but had jumped up to 22 percent in 1967 (see Table 6). The proposal, included in the Annual Operating Plan, was to dampen consumer demand by withdrawing money from circulation through the obligatory purchase of savings bonds. This money would be used to invest in capital projects with high productive or employment potentialities. Generally it might be said that those who opposed the Capitalization Fund attacked it principally on ideological grounds or for short-term political advantage, not on a technical basis. A description of the full events surrounding the capitalization program can help illuminate the Economic Committee's political weakness, and the reasons why it later adopted an incrementalist decision-making style.

On November 7, 1967, Sergio Molina, the minister of Finance, explained the reasons for the savings program in his yearly report to Congress on the state of the economy.[16] He noted that voluntary savings were not adequate and that increased taxes on the high income

[15] Among these were Jacques Chonchol (vice-president of INDAP), Rafael Gumucio (senator, and one of the founders of the Christian Democratic party), and Alberto Jerez (senator), who split off in January 1970 to support the presidential candidacy of Salvador Allende.

[16] Ministerio de Hacienda, *Exposición,* 1967. This plan actually had been discussed sometime earlier with members of the Christian Democratic party, who were reluctant to back it when it might have affected the results of the 1965 and 1967 elections. Interview material; also Molina, p. 144.

groups would not succeed in reducing inflation. At the same time, he was "convinced that all Chileans are willing to sacrifice a current, transitory advantage if through this sacrifice they could assure the future progress of the country." [17] The Capitalization Fund promoted by the Economic Committee was to have the following characteristics:

1. All workers would receive a salary increase in 1968 equivalent to the increase in the cost of living.
2. One-quarter of this increase would be deposited in the Capitalization Fund.
3. All employers would contribute to the Fund in amounts equal to that of their employees.
4. The workers would receive shares in the Fund representing both their forced savings and that deposited by the employers.
5. The Fund would be administered by a 50-man board, with 43 representatives from among the workers and 7 from the state.
6. The investment capital would be used for industrial development in housing, wood, petrochemicals, copper, and automobiles.

Molina argued that the Capitalization Fund was the best way to avoid cyclical inflationary trends: lower inflation in one period simply bringing it forth with new vigor in the next. The program would also have an income-redistribution effect, and would broaden worker participation in economic development. The Finance minister noted that if workers always spent 100 percent of their incomes on consumable products, there was no possibility of increasing their share in ownership of the national economy. Moreover, if they were frequently out on strike, the productive capacity of the country was seriously impaired. Molina's speech hinted strongly that the project would also place a prohibition on the right to strike.

The Reaction of the Opposition

The Communist party reacted most fervently against the proposal. Its newspaper, *El Siglo,* in referring to the Fund, continually used a derogatory name, *"chiribonos,"* which implied that they were practically worthless.[18] The party attacked the Finance minister's preoccupation with reducing national consumption, as if the poorest work-

---

[17] *Exposición,* 1967, p. 13.

[18] *Bonos* mean "bonds" in Spanish; *chirimoya* (cherimoya) is a popular fruit, and also Chilean slang for a bad check. *Chiribonos* conjured up the image of unredeemable pieces of paper. The Socialist tabloid, *La Ultima Hora,* can be credited with inventing this ingeniously ridiculous term.

ers in the country were buying televisions, refrigerators, washing machines, and imported food products by the truckload. *El Siglo* was the first opposition newspaper to suggest that the program had been foisted on the government by the International Monetary Fund, the World Bank, and the Alliance for Progress.[19]

In essential disagreement with the Economic Committee's whole interpretation on inflation, the Communists saw it caused by a monopolistic productive structure, by price hikes of middlemen in the wholesale market, and by the periodic revaluations of the dollar which continually increased the cost of imported products on which the country was very dependent. The Communists pointed out that foreign companies had taken 370 million dollars from Chile in 1966, more than twice the potential revenue of the Capitalization Fund. Instead of "chiribonos," they called for a 100 percent wage readjustment, measures against price speculation, no more dollar revaluations, no more profits for the foreign copper companies, a moratorium on tax breaks to large industries, and a suspension of the foreign debt.[20]

The Socialist party followed the lead of the Communists, stating that they were against any program which was inspired by international functionaires located in Washington, and which made the poorest pay most. The party expressed surprise that Sergio Molina should suddenly adopt the thesis that the high consumption power of the worker was the cause of inflation in Chile. The Socialists cited Molina's own book, *La Economía Chilena en el Período 1950–1953,* which showed that wage adjustments of 25 percent against a 1949 inflation of 20 percent preceded a 1950 inflation of 16.76 percent; and wage adjustments of 58.6 percent against a 1954 inflation of 71.1 percent led to a 1955 inflation of 83.8 percent.[21] The Socialist party concluded that the program was little more than a fraud to deceive the workers, when those who should pay were the rich and the Yankees.

The middle-class Radical party opposed the Capitalization Fund because it was regressive, coercive, and totalitarian. The measure took from the poorest, ignored foreign capital, and did not affect the high consumption of the rich. The Capitalization Fund would not lower

[19] *El Siglo,* Oct. 25, 1967, p. 6. Norman H. Keehn, in *The Politics of Fiscal and Monetary Stabilization,* discusses inherent conflicts of power and orientation between the International Monetary Fund and Chilean statesmen, although he does not describe the IMF's precise role in the forced-savings controversy (pp. 2–30, 77–119, 248–292).
[20] *El Siglo,* Oct. 28, 1967, p. 3.
[21] *El Siglo,* Jan. 15, 1968, p. 7.

interest rates, halt the flight of capital, end speculation, improve the management of state industries, contribute to development, or increase private investment. Besides, the economy could not afford to lower consumption further, which would hurt the small businessman.[22]

The rightest National party opposed the measure because it was simply a new tax in disguise, which would be used to finance the budget and lead to new bureaucratization. The Nationals said that they opposed all taxes because they had no confidence in the economic knowhow of the regime, and because money already in the central Treasury could be withdrawn from circulation to reduce the money supply. It was difficult for the National party to trust a government that would impose a tax just when the economy was going through a difficult period. The Nationals pointed out that the Christian Democrats had promised that only the first three years of their regime would necessitate sacrifices; this had turned out to be a lie. The accomplishments claimed by the Christian Democrats

exist only in the tropical imagination of our current leaders, with the simple object of justifying the economic aberration of having doubled the national budget in record time, with economic measures that no sensible country should have permitted. If some of what the minister of Finance said were true, the unemployment would not be so fearful, the drop in our mining and industrial production so drastic, the agricultural and commercial situation so lamentable, and the clamor and anxiety of the entire country so generalized.[23]

The labor unions, led by the Communist-controlled CUT (*Central Unica de Trabajadores*) adamantly opposed the Capitalization Fund. Beginning their political struggle as soon as they caught wind of what the Economic Committee had in mind, they even appealed to the International Labor Office of the United Nations to protest the measure. CUT was able to convince a broad spectrum of the working population to take part in a work stoppage on November 23, 1967.[24] These

[22] *El Siglo,* Nov. 17, 1967, p. 3.
[23] *Diario Ilustrado,* Feb. 3, 1968, p. 2.
[24] Participating unions were the Asociación Nacional de Empleados Municipales, Asociación Nacional de Empleados Semi-Fiscales (ANES), Asociación de Empleados y Profesionales de la Universidad de Chile (APEUCH), Federación de los Trabajadores de la Empresa de Transporte Colectivo (ETCE), Federación de Ferias Libres, Federación de Empleados Eléctricos, Federación de Obreros Panificadores, Federación Vitivinícola, Federación de Cuero y Calzado, Federación de Trabajadores de la Salud (FENATS), Federación Industrial Ferroviaria, Federación Nacional Textil, Federación Nacional del Metal, Federación de la Construcción, Federación Campesina e Indígena, Federación Minera, Unión de Obreros Municipales, Federación Bancaria, Federación de Empleados de Comercio, Confederación de Empleados Particulares (CEPCH), Federación de Técnicos y Profesionales del Servicio Nacional de Salud, Federación Lechera, Asociación de

violent street demonstrations against the "chiribonos," in which the armed forces had to back up the Carabineros, left at least five dead.

The Reaction of the Christian Democratic Party

Meanwhile, the Christian Democratic party was deeply divided over the issue. The president of the party, Rafael Gumucio, felt that the project was ideologically unpalatable, and the leader of the party's youth group denounced it as against the workers' interests. As early as October, and again in November, the National Council of the party voted unanimously against the project.[25] The Finance minister was continually lobbying in his own party to arouse some backing for the measure. Though he received support from most of the Christian Democratic senators, the deputies proved to be more resistant. The minister of Interior, recognizing the inconsistencies between the party and the government, indicated that the Capitalization Fund needed a vote of confidence from the party in order for the cabinet members to stay in their posts.[26] Many party members were waiting for the president of the country to commit himself before they decided their position. The Economic Committee had already softened its stance on specific aspects of the program, in order to remove some objections. The right to strike was still open for debate, and a scale was devised so that the poorest 15 percent of the workers would pay nothing, while the rest would pay between 3.7 and 7 percent of their total incomes.[27]

In the month of January, at the town of Peñaflor outside of Santiago, the Christian Democratic party held a plenary meeting of its highest officials and congressional representatives. In an impassioned speech, Eduardo Frei let it be known that he supported the Economic Committee and the Capitalization Fund.[28] He asked the party members to decide definitively whether they were with the government or secretly in the opposition. He said that he had never tried to dominate the party

Correos y Telégrafos, Federación Nacional del Dulce, Confederación de Hierro, Federación Electro-Metalúrgica (FETELMET), Federación Cervecera, Federación Nacional del Gas, Confederación Nacional de Obreros Molineros y Fideeros, Federación Nacional de Comercio, Federación Nacional de Suplementeros, Confederación de Trabajadores del Cobre, Unión de Estucadores en Resistencia, Federación Nacional de Construcción.
The only groups to approve the program publicly were the Asociación de Profesionales Universitarios del Servicio Nacional de Salud and the Frente Ferroviario Demócrata Christiano. For complementary analysis, see Alan Angell, *Politics and the Labour Movement in Chile.*
[25] *El Mercurio,* Oct. 24, 1967, p. 3; Nov. 14, 1967, p. 18.
[26] *El Mercurio,* Nov. 15, 1967, p. 1. Bernardo Leighton was minister at the time.
[27] *El Mercurio,* Nov. 17, 1967, p. 1.
[28] *El Mercurio,* Jan. 7, 1968, p. 1.

or force it to take an unswerving line. But a disorganized party heading in several directions at once was practically useless to the government. As president of the country, he had never had problems with his declared enemies, but when the attacks came from his own party they disconcerted and discouraged him. He warned that the leftist press was trying to split the party and was attacking him personally for that reason. This was to be expected, but when journals financed by loyal Christian Democrats joined in the parade of abuse, it was difficult to accept. The job of president was obviously a difficult one, but he had to carry it out as best he could, despite the fact that some people were bound to be hurt. The fact that the party was split, however, diminished the authority of the government.

If we don't have the backing of the party, you weaken the government. We have to eliminate the discrepancies at all costs. . . . I know that we have committed errors. But the party never in the history of Chile has had more power or more participation. [For five months we have been] looking for harmony in the plans that I have the obligation to propose and bring to the country, as is my duty as governor. But don't forget, *compañeros,* that we have constitutional deadlines for our economic projects. And I could not wait longer; I had to decide. . . . If the measure is unpopular, let me accept responsibility for it.[29]

At the Peñaflor meeting, Frei received a somewhat reluctant vote of confidence for the Capitalization Fund. The president of the party, Rafael Gumucio, resigned his post because of the government's refusal to delete the strike prohibition from the bill. Nonetheless, when the project finally arrived on the Senate floor, its prospects for success were dim. When none of the opposition parties could be convinced to support it, the president advised that the forced-savings program be withdrawn. CUT celebrated the event as a victory for the working population, and a vindication for the martyrs who fell on November 23. In mid-February, Sergio Molina handed in his resignation as minister of Finance.[30]

THE COMMITTEE AFTER THE FORCED
SAVINGS PROGRAM

Looking back, the members of the Economic Committee unanimously agreed that the defeat of the savings program was the major setback for the group during the six-year mandate of the Christian Democratic party. Some of them observed that the increasing rate

[29] *El Mercurio,* Jan. 7, 1968, p. 33.
[30] The ex-minister gives his interpretation of the events in *El Proceso de Cambio,* pp. 143–147.

of inflation—which by 1970 reached 35 percent—and the lower rate of economic growth after 1967 could be attributed in great part to the rejection of the Capitalization Fund. Others speculated that the defeat of the Christian Democratic candidate in the 1970 presidential elections was a partial consequence of this same lower productivity and higher cost of living.

As for their interpretations of the experience, the Committee members did not consider that the attitude of the newspapers was the deciding factor in the defeat of the project. Some expressed a certain disdain for the motives of the Chilean press, which at the time of the savings program was divided into at least six major orientations, all affiliated with political party lines. Likewise, the Committee was not entirely impressed by the declarations of union leaders in their opposition to the program, since it questioned the degree to which these leaders represented the labor sector as a whole.

During the national debate, each of the Committee members, as well as other cabinet officials, were assigned different areas of the country to tour and explain the significance of the savings proposal. Visiting cooperatives, unions, women's groups, schools, offices of the central government, municipalities, businesses, and factories, they came away encouraged by the fact that pro-Christian Democratic workers could often convince the Communist workers of the advisability of the program. After these tours the Committee members felt certain that they had received an overwhelmingly favorable response from the grass roots of the population. The general impression was that, had they started sooner in their attempt to mobilize support, the idea would have carried.

The street violence, resulting in the deaths of at least five persons, although universally lamented, apparently was not a factor to induce the Committee to withdraw its sponsorship of the savings program. The opinion was that outbursts of this type, resulting in personal injury at the midpoint of a presidential term, were not unique in Chilean history, nor even outside of the rules of the political game. In this case, the pressure exerted was unable to detract from the almost universal support the Committee felt it received for the proposal when it had a chance to talk with individual citizens on a face-to-face basis, rather than separated by a wall of armed police and agitated rioters. Violence did not seem to have much effect on the attitude of the Committee, though it may have helped solidify the intransigence of the opposition parties and the dissatisfied elements in the Christian Democratic party.

The principal reason cited for the failure of the project was the universal hostility of the opposition, from the far Left to the far Right, and the inability of the Economic Committee to garner support from its own Christian Democratic members. The seriousness of the situation was aggravated by public displays of no-confidence in the Committee. For example, while in the Chamber of Deputies collecting votes for the project, the subsecretary of Finance was confronted by a group of eighteen deputies of his party who had decided to reject the measure out-of-hand. A reporter from the opposition press was conveniently on hand to record the details of the subsequent verbal exchange.[31]

After the president of the country decided to forego the savings proposal, the Economic Committee was still supportive. In a special meeting, the Committee decided to send a letter to the president, delineating the precise effects that abandoning the program would have on the cost of living. The letter also pointed out that the underlying assumptions of the proposal were fundamentally sound, and that the Committee still believed the overall suggestion valid. At this point, early in the month of February 1968, the Economic Committee was virtually alone in its position. Lined up against it were the press, the labor unions, the opposition parties, its own political party, and even the president. Its leader was about to fall; it had lost the battle; its resources were exhausted.[32] Its further cry of alarm to the president was anticlimactic, at a point when the Committee's status was not much above that of a gathering of the local Odd Fellow's club. Despite the relative economic merits of the savings program and the Capitalization Fund, which may have been considerable, the Economic Committee had initiated an issue that eventually reached unmanageable proportions. From that point on, the inconsistent political support of the party, due in part to its problematic unity, became one of the constraints on the Economic Committee. It had to face a hostile environment with uncertain resources.

The savings program of 1967 was the Committee's comprehensive answer to the inflation problem, which had plagued the Chilean economy for almost a century. After three years of preparation and experimentation, the Finance minister was convinced of the economic merits of the forced savings program, regardless of its transcendental implications. He was willing to compromise on the formula by which the program would be implemented, but not on the concept itself, which

---

[31] *Diario Ilustrado,* Jan. 20, 1968, p. 2.

[32] "An actor has a limited stock of power which he gives up piecemeal or 'spends.' His power is like capital: he can either 'consume' it or 'invest' it." He seldom uses it all up on one issue. Edward C. Banfield, *Political Influence,* p. 312. In this case, the Economic Committee was an apparent exception to the last statement.

he never abandoned. Frei, while he still had hope that the program would be adopted, proclaimed to the nation,

I said once that I'd prefer a clear defeat to a compromised triumph, and that I would maintain the program even if I lost a million votes. I am not sorry for having said that. I say the same thing today.[33]

The position of the two men, and the Economic Committee as a whole, reflected neither haughty intransigence nor extreme ingenuousness, but simply their sincere belief that economically the moment was opportune for a definitive solution to inflation. Previously the Committee had made a series of important economic decisions without knowing the exact form that resistance would take. It was conscious that the political environment in which it worked was extremely uncertain in terms of the manner in which its decisions would be challenged. However, the committee members were confident that they could manage any situation simply with their institutional backing and the support of the Christian Democratic party. The environment continued to be uncertain; only when their own resource base also became uncertain did they give up their rational, restrictive, and comprehensive decision-making style in favor of a more incremental approach.

THE ECONOMIC COMMITTEE, SOCIAL ISSUES, AND THE PUBLIC SECTOR

After 1967 the problems of the Economic Committee were twofold: it was incapable of severely sanctioning public agencies that deviated from the norms of the short-term plan; and to relieve fiscal and monetary pressures, it had to use methods that deeply violated its own principles. The Committee looked to the president to provide the authority to conform the activities of public agencies to its precepts and to act as the intermediary between it and the society in explaining its policies. The president gave his unconditional support to the *internal* activities of the Economic Committee. In the latter period, however, he compromised when it came time to apply those internal decisions to an *external* reference group, whether in the public or private sector.

Chapter 2, on the budgetary process, described the tendency of agencies in Public Works, Housing, Agriculture, and others, to exploit their control over information to arrange budgetary *faits accomplis*. These tactics included the extension of roads past their budgeted destination (resulting in a floating debt to private contractors), overesti-

---

[33] *El Mercurio,* Nov. 29, 1967, p. 1.

mating independent income, creating imbalances in agency activity which acted like built-in deficits, and transferring money from account to account to require more capital if the investment were not to be wasted. When these agencies clamored for more money, the Finance minister brought the matter to the attention of the Economic Committee and the president as a means of incorporating other perspectives and broadening his base of support.

The first difficulty in applying sanctions to an agency upsetting the short-term fiscal program was to assign responsibility. The Economic Committee could rarely point the finger at an identifiable target, since those responsible were either hidden in the bowels of the ministry, obscured from view, or located at such high levels of confidence that an outcry would be self-deprecatory. In Public Works, for example, the minister often had little idea of what was going on in his ministry, since middle-level career functionaries struck bargains with obliging contractors to expand the public works program.[34] In Housing, the weight of the minister often did not equal that of the vice-president of the decentralized agency, who could easily conceal potential budgetary problems until it was too late to avoid a deficit. Quite often, the Economic Committee, the Finance minister and other cabinet-level officials were caught in a situation in which they could not admit that what was happening—widespread lack of control—was really happening, for fear of public ridicule.[35]

When responsibility for the overexpenditure was discovered, the Economic Committee expected that the president, at very least, would chastise the offending minister at the earliest opportunity. However, the president preferred not to criticize his appointees for several reasons, one of which was his desire to maintain some unity in the ranks. In addition, by finding a private solution he could be selective in the manner in which he handled the situation. On occasions he could use the complaints of the Economic Committee as an excuse to restrict funds to certain public investments. On others he could pardon the administrator in order to wield the maximum leverage when he wanted rapid completion of a project important for his personal image. One point more or less in the rate of inflation was unimportant compared to an additional public works project, consistent progress in agrarian re-

---

[34] See Chapter 7.
[35] The Committee's desire was to develop some system to control fiscal expenditures more fully. The minister of Finance wanted authority over all of the Budget offices in the public sector, and not to rely just on his cabinet-level contacts with the ministers to manage budgetary execution. In that way he could hold each Budget office responsible for guaranteeing that the ministry did not overspend.

form, disaster relief aid to a certain region, or enhanced possibilities for electoral success.

A more sobering factor was that the results of the sanction would have more serious effects than the problem the sanction was supposed to correct. By overspending, who was going to lose? And if the overspending was frozen, who was going to suffer? These questions gave the Economic Committee persistent headaches. It recognized that refusing funds to Agriculture, Housing, or Public Works would often have more detrimental consequences than even the unorthodox emission of new money and its impact on inflation. The penalty available to the president was available to both the Economic Committee and the Finance minister. But the risks were such anathema that the Finance minister sent the problem to the Economic Committee, the Economic Committee sent it to the president, and the president declined to accept responsibility for it.[36]

If the Committee cut off funds to Public Works, unpaid contractors would slow the pace of their projects and lay off workers until their activity ground to a halt. The pattern was well-known, and only the simple-minded would initiate the cycle out of spite against the ministry, just to call upon the ministry later to bail the government out of the unemployment crisis by speeding up its programs. As for Housing, the fulfillment of the housing plan had been a principal goal of the government's overall program. For the time being, marginal and dispossessed citizens were patiently waiting their turn for new housing units. The most seriously affected could not be convinced that slowing the housing program was necessary because of poor programming and budgetary vagaries.[37]

Agrarian reform, the government's pet program, which gave it a revolutionary facade, was widely supported by the leftist parties in the opposition, the campesinos, and international lending agencies. In presenting their case, representatives of CORA always reminded the Committee of the political significance of carrying the agrarian reform past the point of no return.[38] They proclaimed that it would be a catastrophe if the agrarian reform failed because of mere financial limitations.[39]

Of all agencies characterized by the latent tendency to break away, only certain ones could achieve that independence with any degree of

---

[36] In the end, instead of standing firmly by the Economic Committee, Frei acted like a referee between the Committee and individual agencies.

[37] Chapter 8 discusses the results when these pobladors lost their patience.

[38] Molina shows that he was swayed by these arguments in *El Proceso de Cambio*, p. 12.

[39] In the first year of the Allende regime this particular rationale, carried to an extreme, helped justify massive financing for many Unidad Popular programs.

impunity.[40] In the ministry of Public Works, those charged with the construction of irrigation projects, public buildings, and shipping and airport facilities were "controlled," and performed in exemplary fashion. The divisions of Roads and Sanitary Works, however, were "free-dealing," and continually caused difficulties. In the agricultural sector, the Cattle and Agricultural Service (SAG) was a model of restraint, while CORA's expenses perpetually outstripped its financing. In housing, the Corporation of Urban Works (COU) did not exceed normal administrative controls, but the Housing Corporation (CORVI) exerted tremendous pressures on the short-term plan.

The greater the importance of the social issue and the identification of the agency's activities with that issue, the easier it was for the agency to go its own way despite the Economic Committee's policy guidelines and the wishes of the president. In Agriculture, CORA (a decentralized agency) was manifestly responsible for increasing the agricultural production of the country, and latently for social and political revolution in rural areas; in Housing, CORVI (an autonomous corporation) was the most important institution for alleviating the shortage of dwelling units; in Public Works, the Roads division was latently linked to the issue of unemployment, and manifestly to the building of larger transportation networks.[41]

There was little that the Committee could do to neutralize these political realities. The variables in play were not included in its economic model, and it did not have the party and the president to back it up. Many agencies could not lose by overspending; indeed, they would always win. Organizations that programmed poorly, obfuscated information, and ran up deficits, knowing that their clients would support them, were going to do much better than those agencies abiding by the formal rules of the administrative process. Essentially, a shift in the balance of power took place between the members of the Committee, acting in concert, and the pertinent public agencies carrying out activities closely identified with national problems of the highest urgency.[42]

[40] These can be first scaled roughly from the weakest to the strongest, according to the sector in which they are located in Figure 1. Second, within each sector, some agencies had access to more resources than others.

[41] Besides these compelling reasons, ex-members of the Committee mentioned other pressures to approve supplements: the chief-of-state's own predilection for various social programs, such as education; the necessity to maintain the credibility of party electees who had committed themselves to special projects for regional benefit; and intermittent wage strikes by public employees, halting important government services.

[42] To illustrate, in March 1968 the Economic Committee attempted to economize by reducing the budgetary allocation of the Agrarian Reform Corporation. As is routine, the Finance minister invited the head of CORA to a private gathering to discuss the cuts he had in mind. Usually meetings of this type were conducted in relative secrecy, and the various allocation figures passed back and forth remained

Instead of coldly cutting payments, refusing credits, or berating the administrators involved, the Committee was forced to dig deep and locate the funds to allow the agency to continue its operations with the least slack. Because of the power differential, the Committee's new standards had little to do with stabilization per se. It acquiesced to meeting the demands of public agencies committed to resolving social issues, tried to maintain an image of unity within the ranks of government, and helped accumulate a record of visible public achievement, especially in capital works projects.

RESOURCE UNCERTAINTY AND AN INCREMENTAL
DECISION-MAKING STYLE

The Economic Committee's conception of short-term planning was comprehensive in the sense that it prescribed rules of behavior for virtually every unit of government, and dictated parameters for a great many economic decisions in the private sector. The Committee's short-term plan embodied its restrictive approach, and the economic

---

in the form of scribbled notes known only to the direct participants. In this case the head of CORA ignored this precedent and immediately called a press conference to announce that his budget faced a slashing which he claimed would sabotage the whole agrarian reform effort. The president had tacitly approved the cut; but the head of CORA, though one of the president's most loyal followers, was highly committed to the agrarian reform movement and was more willing to risk presidential censure than to let his agency be weakened.

After the news conference, the largest rural labor syndicate lodged vehement protests against the Economic Committee's decision, and the National Student Federation organized a mass demonstration of workers, campesinos, and students in defense of the agrarian reform. The leftist parties took the floor in Congress to express the opinion that the Finance minister had obviously been corrupted by rightist elements, which at the time were arguing quite persistently that the only way to balance the budget was through a reduction of CORA. Those groups in the Christian Democratic party who supported the agrarian reform began questioning both the wisdom of the proposal and the integrity of the Finance minister. In the turmoil over the question, it was the minister of Finance, not the head of CORA, who handed in his resignation. The opposition to Finance's intention was not orchestrated by the head of CORA. He did not have to do much more to protect his institution than to call the press conference.

For the major actors, see *El Siglo*, March 13, 1968, p. 5; March 15, 1968, p. 8; and March 22, 1968, p. 2. The conservative newspapers *El Diario Ilustrado*, May 10, 1967, p. 4, and *El Mercurio*, May 12, 1967, p. 3, contain interesting comments on CORA's assertion that it was *the* top-priority government agency. The editorial in the latter complained that the vice president of CORA was not really the appropriate person to announce this fact and that anyway, all knowledgeable persons knew that other problems, such as employment, stable production, and Latin American economic integration, were much more serious. Moreover, CORA's claim for more money to increase the number of its asentamientos from 96 to 400 was not reassuring to Chileans interested in stability in the countryside. See also Robert R. Kaufman, *The Politics of Land Reform in Chile, 1950–1970.*

model indicated exactly the degree to which projections were being achieved or subverted. But when the Committee conflicted openly with the private sector over the savings-bond issue, it lost not only the battle but also the war. The tremendous psychological pressures of the events of 1967 convinced the Committee to reduce the margin of its risk and seek certain boundaries in its decisions.[43]

As a consequence of this defeat, the decision-making posture of the Committee changed significantly. It became characterized by solutions that were partial rather than integral, flexible rather than firm, and subdued rather than dramatic. Assumptions for action evolved into "If the threat of political problems increases, lower your sights"; also "Keep things on an even keel," "The best decisions are small decisions," and "Recognize that nothing can be done according to one's wishes." [44] More than by the agrarian reform, the copper program, or the neighborhood political cadres law (*Juntas de Vecinos*), all of which eventually met some sort of success in Congress, the Committee learned to respect the constraints that the legislators posed for decisions affecting the private sector. Whereas previously it felt it could disregard the ideological bickering within the Christian Democratic party, the Committee was forcefully impressed with the necessity of party backing for its initiatives. More than its monetary, credit, or foreign exchange policies, the Committee discovered that some financial measures, because of whom they touched, could arouse a collective ire that was difficult to contain. In response, they concluded that "You cannot pressure the deputies too much, their parties' or ours" and "The workers never like the government, and in our case it was no different"; finally, "Do not start something you cannot finish." [45]

The Committee was not alone in feeling helpless when faced with the pressures of organized political groups. The president himself became more conscious than ever of the basic weakness of his government, especially when confronted with the wage demands of the unions. When labor disputes arrived at the level of the Economic Committee, the president invariably took a hard stand at first, declaring that he would tolerate no hikes that went above the real increase in the cost of living and were not matched by new productivity. But this first reaction never held. After a couple of days his position softened and he began giving in to the other side.

[43] Hints of the anguish and fatigue felt by the Economic Committee after 1967 are reflected in Molina's book, *El Proceso de Cambio en Chile*. For example, see p. 101.

[44] Interview material.

[45] Interview material.

The orientation of the Economic Committee in these last years of government was summed up in "The optimum may not have been reached, but the optimized possible was." [46] Read one way, this meant that the Committee thrived in an atmosphere of partisan-mutual adjustment, and put forth resolutions that represented mature and thoughtful compromise.[47] Read another way, the events of 1967 had infused the Committee with a cautious approach toward tackling either new or recurrent problems. In many instances in which the Committee had the legal authority to initiate an issue, it was convinced beforehand that it did not have the weapons to make the decision stick. Such a standard of sub-optimization tended to cancel consideration of problems susceptible to solutions with general benefits. The weakness of government faced with the strength of the unions was exemplified by the fact that it never made an all-out attempt to eliminate the underlying inequalities and inefficiencies in the workers' Social Security Funds.[48] Although the Committee was convinced that considerable financial resources could be located in the system and rerouted to more equitable and productive ends, the Committee did not feel that it had the power to change the situation. Its attitude toward questions such as this became basically very restrained. It had learned not to rush.

The above description is reminiscent of good old-fashioned incremental decision-making. Accordingly, the concept of incrementalism can usefully serve to summarize this section. The typical manner of defending incrementalism is through the impossibility of gathering all of the information required for making a *comprehensive* decision in a *rational* manner. The more comprehensive the decision, the more variables are entered, the more alternative paths are opened, the more direct consequences of each alternative are allowed, the more unanticipated results are engendered, and so on, until the uncertainty of outcome reaches gargantuan proportions.[49] The incremental decision, instead of being all-inclusive, minimizes the dangers of uncertainty and concen-

[46] Interview material.

[47] Charles Lindblom contrasts "successive limited comparisons (incrementalism)" to "rational-comprehensive method," in "The Science of Muddling Through." He examines the values of "partisan-mutual adjustment" in *The Intelligence of Democracy: Decision-Making through Mutual Adjustment,* pp. 207–225.

[48] See Jorge Tapia-Videla and Charles J. Parrish, *Clases Sociales y la Política de Seguridad Social en Chile,* pp. 15–16. These authors point out that although the system needs a complete reform, worker opposition is an obstacle, even though the workers who protest most would be the ultimate beneficiaries.

[49] "Rational" decision-making is discussed by James G. March and Herbert A. Simon in *Organizations.* Its requisites are examined critically in David Braybrooke and Charles E. Lindblom, *A Strategy of Decision: Policy Evaluation as a Social Process,* pp. 37–57.

trates on alternatives representing very little difference from the status quo, since the stable status quo is the most certain of all situations. Incremental decision-making is characterized by marginal changes over the short term, to maximize the decision-maker's ability to control the new situation he will create.

The rigor with which the argument is put forth is intellectually attractive when it is assumed that widespread information and accuracy of prediction are fundamental to "rational" decisions. At least two exceptions undermine this conception of rationality, whether for hypothesizing on political behavior or for suggesting policy-making norms. First, the values and ideology of leadership, especially in the way they represent social purposes and guides for action, indicate the scope of change sought (incremental-comprehensive) more faithfully than do constraints on information. Second, when information is perfectly *adequate,* incrementalism is better understood as resulting from a lack of other resources which precludes brusque changes.[50]

It is useful to remember that a lack of information per se was not the difficulty of the Economic Committee. The Committee members did not attribute their incremental decision-making style to a persistent uncertainty of the future state of affairs that they wished to create. They believed that their model predicting the beneficial economic effects of the savings program was highly accurate. Had the Capitalization Fund been implemented, it would have reduced inflation by the assigned amount as part of an integral solution to the problem. Likewise, had new economic resources been generated after 1967, the Committee could have continued satisfying the demands of important agencies without countering the stabilization program. Under these circumstances, it was not poor information that led the Committee to slip into a more incrementalist groove, but a deficiency of other resources which were even more important, such as legitimacy and finances.

It is worthwhile to continue in this line, since it is often intimated

---

[50] Amitai Etzioni, in *The Active Society,* notes that Lindblom's "incrementalism tends to ignore not only the underprivileged and politically-weak collectivities but also overdue societal innovations" (p. 273). Etzioni's model of "mixed scanning" encourages the decision-maker to look beyond incremental responses to problems in a way that does not overload his capacity to sort out data pertinent to the issue at hand. More significantly, Etzioni does not shy away from considering ideology and power as integral components of important decisions. "While knowledge, even when it is accurate, can be ignored, power cannot. A decision-maker may choose— because of normative commitments, psychological rigidity, or intra-unit politics— to ignore facts, but—by definition—he cannot ignore power" (p. 303). Conversely, when his power is sufficient to prevail over the opposition, one could expect him to be more willing to take a leap in the dark if he felt the direction of the jump was toward the fulfillment of an important ideological commitment or political goal.

that an incremental decision-making style results in the "best" decisions. The values of efficiency and stability underlying this contention can be substituted by other standards, such as social justice or even anarchy, especially if left to the political actor rather than the social scientist. In the case of the 1967 savings program, the Economic Committee was prepared to make a comprehensive decision on the basis of its relative certainty on the benefits of the proposal, combined with the authority of its institutional position, the legitimacy of the Christian Democratic party members, the prestige of the president, and, as things turned out, the temporary use of coercion by the carabineros and armed forces reacting to citizen protest. Events proved that the Committee did not prepare its strategies sufficiently for the contest, and it suffered the consequences. The Committee might have prevented many difficulties if it had either assured itself of more stable resources before revealing the proposal to the opposition; accurately evaluated the impossibility of its position at an early date, and skipped the issue; or sought an incremental rather than a comprehensive solution. Despite its failure, the attempt of the Economic Committee was comparable to other efforts at significant change that succeeded, because the decision-makers compensated for a deficiency in information with adequate amounts of other resources.[51]

The Economic Committee did not completely fail in its experiment to bring coherence to short-term economic policy in Chile. Rather, the strategies of public organizations and the combined resources of political elements in the society were such that a more total success was nearly impossible. The Economic Committee represented a notable improvement over a previous situation in which dominant political forces regularly overwhelmed and distorted short-term goals, even in the first part of the presidential period. The Committee nicely built up the foreign trade balance, which had been one of the traditional bottlenecks in the Chilean economy. Inflation was not handled so well.

Was there any way that the Economic Committee could have succeeded in implementing the forced-savings program? If the Christian Democratic government made extensive progress in agrarian reform, copper nationalization, industrial development, educational expansion, and administrative reorganization in the housing sector, a good part of

---

[51] Examples might be Gandhi (prestige), Castro (legitimacy), and Stalin (coercion). To what degree can lack of information be combined with conspicuous access to other resources for a decision-maker to proceed as if he were acting in a certain environment? Politicians use their intuition to deal with the problem. The question is at the core of the new political economy, and the means for answering it are still at a quite rudimentary level of refinement.

the reason can be attributed to the fact that these measures were de-creed or legislated early in the administration. As it turned out, during the latter half of the period the regime did not have the power to carry out new ventures implying far-reaching social change, and did not try. Attempts to focus public attention on the accomplishments of the regime were contained in low-risk projects of high visibility, such as a tunnel (Lo Prado) between Santiago and Valparaiso, and the breaking of ground for the Santiago metropolitan subway.

The fact that inflation has been the escape valve for virtually every Chilean government in the modern era did not help the Committee's task. Nor was it assisted by the prudence of some leaders of the Chris-tian Democratic party who, fearing repudiation at the ballot box, saw little reason for such a program while the rate of inflation was declin-ing, seemingly, of its own accord. Unfortunately for its ultimate in-tentions, however, the Economic Committee allowed itself to be stymied by these arguments until regime resources were insufficient to imple-ment any type of Capitalization Fund at all. Each semester that the president and his main economic advisors delayed in actively pursuing the plan—as they eventually did in 1967—the unity of the party weak-ened, the power of the opposition increased, and the chances for na-tional acceptance diminished.

5

BUREAUCRATIC POLITICS
AND ADMINISTRATIVE REFORM
IN THE HOUSING SECTOR

To this point, this research has dealt with general administrative processes penetrating Chilean bureaucracy as a whole: budgeting and short-term planning. No bureaucratic unit can escape interaction with the Finance ministry when it makes up its yearly budget. Those agencies powerful enough to take their case beyond Finance must contend with the Economic Committee members' insistence on maintaining the policy guidelines of the short-term plan. Now it is appropriate to examine public administration in Chile at a more detailed empirical level. The next four chapters will investigate the political connotations of administrative reform, coordination, and client relations in the high-investment ministries of Housing and Public Works.

This chapter begins from the premise that structural reform in the Chilean housing sector was desirable and necessary; an underlying theme in the next chapter is that coordination among bureaucratic units can lead to greater productivity. Within bureaucracy, however, judgments of this type are so difficult to substantiate that they are almost prejudices. They depend very much on the location of the observer and his particular interests in the affair. For example, the objective need for administrative reform is often not reflected in the behavior of public officials who are asked to cooperate.[1]

---

[1] This analysis will not emphasize cultural values particular to Chilean or Latin American bureaucrats, which elude measurement and are often indistinguishable from those held by bureaucrats in other settings. Lawrence Graham, for example, employs a Riggsian conceptual framework in his *Civil Service Reform in Brazil: Principles versus Practice* to try to link values with administrative behavior. He is

Given the poor record of most regimes in carrying out administrative reform, the experience of the Chilean Housing ministry offers clues to why some efforts succeed and others fail.[2] Administrative reform is not born in a political vacuum. Significant interests are always tied to the status quo.[3] The motives of the various adversaries may be self-serving or honest. But barring a dictatorial approach, opposition to reform represents a political reality that cannot be ignored if the desired change is to mature. It is incumbent on the "reformer" to map out strategies in advance to deal with both predictable and unanticipated nests of resistance.

From 1965 to 1968, urban planners and housing experts in the Christian Democratic party attempted to reorganize a multitude of public institutions and transfer them to a newly created Ministry of Housing and Urbanism (MINVU). This chapter begins by describing the motivations of the reformers in promoting this reshuffling. It then moves to general propositions concerning administrative reform which are based wholly on this experience. These generalizations may have comparative applicability, and their verification constitutes the basic objective of the chapter. The discussion then treats the two-part reform strategy employed by the founders of the Housing ministry and the various obstacles they faced, once their intentions were known. A major section of the chapter analyzes the tactics used by both proponents and opponents of the reorganization of the Sanitary Works agency; one theme will be that the reformers were unprepared for the tremendous resistance that developed, and managed their case poorly. The final observations may alert students and practitioners alike to some of the inherent difficulties in effectuating administrative reform, and how these problems might be anticipated.

CREATION OF THE MINISTRY OF HOUSING
AND URBANISM

Eduardo Frei first introduced the idea for a new Housing ministry during his unsuccessful bid for the presidency in 1958. Frei felt

---

forced to conclude, however, that "nothing in this material can be used to prove" that the modern "values of economy, efficiency, and rationality . . . conflicted with traditional values stressing personal and kinship" ties (p. 190). Kleber Nascimento uses a more structural approach in his article, "Reflections on Strategy of Administrative Reform: The Federal Experience of Brazil."

[2] Roderick T. Groves, in "Administrative Reform and the Politics of Reform: The Case of Venezuela," finds that in Venezuela failure was due to the reformers' shortcomings in timing, political skill, and preparation of general strategies.

[3] Indeed, Gerald Caiden, in *Administrative Reform*, goes so far as to define administrative reform as the "artificial inducement of administrative transformation against resistance" (p. 8).

that the government could not make headway against a housing shortage of some 280 thousand living units without an important structural reform.[4] Six years later, after the deficit had increased considerably, Frei promised 360 thousand houses if he won the September 1964 presidential election.[5] After his victory, lawyers and housing experts in the Christian Democratic party improved the 1958 proposal and submitted it to Congress in 1965.

The suggestion for a new ministry grew out of several administrative problems plaguing public housing at the time.[6] The ministry's founders concluded that the sector was afflicted with simultaneous crises of anarchical deconcentration, combined with stifling overcentralization, and scarcity of financial resources in the midst of plenty. They confronted each of these problems separately, with the intention of eliminating it permanently. At least on paper, the overall formula they devised was quite ingenious.

First, as for the problem of deconcentration, twenty-three public institutions under eight ministries dealt in housing and urban affairs.[7] This organizational scattergram resulted in extensive delays, because all project plans had to be approved in different jurisdictions and it was uncommon for officials to integrate their activities for the service of individual neighborhoods. Residents occupying new housing units often found no water, sewer lines, schools, medical clinics or lead-in roads. Simultaneously, these facilities were built on a grand scale in other urban areas where the small population did not justify them.

Second, a crisis of overcentralization affected the Housing Corporation (CORVI). From its offices in Santiago, CORVI handled every phase of housing construction for low- and middle-income families: land purchase, house construction, urban services, loans to families, assignment of the houses, and collection on the loans. In 1961 it had contracted a record number of housing units (22,504). By 1964, however, its executives believed that diversity of functions overwhelmed its responsive capacity, made it almost uncontrollable, and rendered it inadequate for the production challenges that lay ahead.

[4] See Raúl Sáez S., *Casas para Chile: Plan Frei.*
[5] See Frei's speech to the *técnicos* in the Sala Caupolicán, reprinted in *El Mercurio,* June 19, 1964, p. 25.
[6] Many of these problems were outlined by Modesto Collados, minister of Public Works, in his speech in Concepcion, "Exposición de Política Habitacional," on Dec. 4, 1964. He pointed out that there were serious peaks and troughs in housing construction, that money was not being freed opportunely, and that CORVI was overloaded with functions.
[7] These organizations are enumerated in Senado, *Boletín No. 21,776,* p. 24. For additional introduction to the housing agencies, see T. Robert Burke, "Law and Development: The Chilean Housing Program, Part 1."

Third, the apparent contradiction of scarce economic resources in the face a relative abundance stemmed from the fact that a large percentage of state investment was directed each year toward the housing sector. Yet once these resources were divided up among competing agencies, the part with which each worked was usually insufficient to execute its functions.[8] The amount received depended on the agency's competitive position inside its own ministry or its skillfulness in negotiating with the Budget Bureau. As described in Chapter 2, the ultimate size of these allocations was more a function of bureaucratic politics than of a cost-benefit analysis of investment. Economists in the Central Bank had created a concept of "housing sector" by aggregating financial data from the various institutions participating in the field, but the concept had absolutely no validity in terms of the administrative processes of planning, programming, and budgeting.

If the Frei government were going to succeed in building 360 thousand living units in six years, these shortcomings in the housing bureaucracy had to be eliminated. Given the political import of the campaign promise, special precautions had to be taken to insure that the institutional components of the new housing sector were given every advantage in dispatching housing services with a minimum of red tape. The challenges posed by the inadequacies of the existing framework led the founders of the ministry to include several administrative breakthroughs for improved output in the design of the new ministry of Housing and Urbanism. Among these were: a comprehensive definition of the housing sector; functional specificity among the various components of the ministry; autonomous status for the agencies; and a strong sectoral planning unit. These last three innovations will be discussed in the next chapter.

Traditionally, the housing problem in Latin America has been defined simply in terms of the lack of a house for family shelter. The Chilean housing advisors rejected this archaic physical interpretation and, in line with current developments in the discipline of urban planning, vastly broadened the concept. "Housing" meant not only houses, but also the social infrastructure making up the total community. The services of health, education, recreation, and personal security were necessary for the creation of an integral residential community.[9]

---

[8] Collados, in his speech celebrating the "Inauguración de la Comisión Coordinador Plan Popular de Viviendas," Santiago, March 25, 1965, noted that the total investment of the public and private sectors in housing was 800 million escudos, with no organization controlling or coordinating this investment. The official exchange rate in 1965 was 3.2 escudos to 1 U.S. dollar.

[9] See the comments of Federico Lorca in *AUCA*, 1:1 (December 1965), pp. 49 ff.

This definition was somewhat unwieldy in terms of administrative reform, however, because almost every unit of government impinged on family development and the residential setting in some way. Practicality forced the housing advisors to limit the scope of their concept. They identified eleven institutions in the Chilean public sector which carried out functions most important for the new ministry of Housing and Urbanism. These agencies were under the jurisdiction of five ministries.

1. Ministry of Public Works:

   a. CORVI (*Corporación de la Vivienda*) was the housing agency *par excellence,* charged with every aspect of housing construction from buying land to the collection of home loans. It was financed by transfers from the Social Security Funds, central subsidies, special taxes, and its collection of loans. CORVI's clients were solvent, low-income urban residents who signed up for houses and paid installments both before and after they were assigned a home.

   b. The Housing and Social Assistance Foundation (*Fundación de Vivienda y Asistencia Social*) was also known as the Foundation for Emergency Housing. The F.V.A.S. was founded by the wife of President Gonzáles Videla in August 1949 to supply housing and social assistance to persons too poor to be considered by CORVI, such as the aged, handicapped, or indigent. A somewhat paternalistic organization, it rented a small number of living units to these groups and "taught" them how to live in them, in the expectation that they would move out once their financial horizons brightened.

   The F.V.A.S. did not have a central office and the general quality of its administration was poor. Successive presidents filled the lower echelons of the agency with their own men to repay campaign debts. As a result, each level in the organization's hierarchy tended to have a different political orientation. The F.V.A.S.'s small volume of activity was financed by charitable contributions and a special tax on sweets and confections.

   c. The Urban Pavement agency maintained and improved the streets in the great majority of smaller municipalities in the country. The agency was subsidized from central government funds.

   d. The Sanitary Works agency distributed drinking water and built sewage facilities for practically the whole country. In water the agency's three branches were: heavy engineering, which captured the water at its source, treated it, and brought it to tanks on the outskirts of the cities; light engineering, which built pipelines under city streets and connected them to the homes; and operations, which managed the administration of water to the consumer.

e. The Santiago Water Company (*Empresa de Agua Potable de Santiago*) supplied water to several communities in the greater Santiago area in which the Sanitary Works agency did not have jurisdiction. El Canelo Water Company, a contracted subsidiary of the Santiago Water Company until at least 1994, made the home connections in these same communities.[10]

f. A very small number of individual water companies served single cities, groups of towns, or mining areas around the country, and were regulated by the government through the ministry of Public Works.[11]

g. The Architecture agency built public buildings in urban areas: schools, administration complexes, police outposts, courthouses, prisons, post offices, community centers, stadiums, firehouses, and recreation areas. This type of infrastructure is often referred to as "community development facilities" (*equipamiento comunitario*).

2. Ministry of Education: The Education Construction Society (*Sociedad Constructora de Establecimientos Educacionales*) planned and constructed schools in urban areas.

3. Ministry of Public Health: The Hospital Construction Society (*Sociedad Constructora de Establecimientos Hospitalarios*) constructed hospitals and medical posts in urban areas.

4. Ministry of Interior: The Electric and Gas Service agency regulated the provision of electricity and gas to urban areas.

5. Ministry of Finance: The Central Savings and Loan Fund (*Caja Central de Ahorros y Préstamos,* or CCAP) audited, regulated, and promoted the private system of savings and loan associations oriented exclusively toward the construction of houses.

CARDINAL ASSUMPTIONS OF ADMINISTRATIVE REFORM

Administrative reform is an extremely complicated business.[12] The type of agency reformed, the political conditions surrounding the

---

[10] These are Santiago, La Granja, Cisterna, Puente Alto, San Bernardo, Talagante, and Buín. Silvia Rodríguez G., *Análisis del Financiamiento del MINVU,* pp. 33–34.

[11] Approximately twenty-five of these private and semi-governmental companies in the country serve relatively small communities such as Chuquicamata and El Teniente. In Santiago, the Maipú, Colón, Lo Castillo, and Las Condes companies are examples. The government sets the rates and audits their books. In sewage, Maipú, the copper communities, Valparaiso, and Viña del Mar manage their own lines.

[12] See John D. Montgomery, "Source of Bureaucratic Reform: A Typology of Purposes and Politics," in Ralph Braibanti (ed.), *Political and Administrative Development,* pp. 427–471.

reform, the inherent logic of the reform, and the different attitudes taken by specific actors tend to make each effort unique. For these reasons it is often unwise to derive generalities from one experience to apply broadly to other cases. Nonetheless, the reform of the Chilean housing sector can be summarized in ten assumptions that appear to have comparative validity. The basic arguments of this chapter are outlined in these statements.

1. The relative success of an attempt at administrative reform has little to do with the technical or logical justifications of the suggested reform.
2. Rather, it is better to begin with the assumption that organizations are made up of people with different interests.
3. Actors at different levels of the organization (e.g., executives, professionals, workers) tend to have different categories of interests.
4. Groups outside the organization may have goals that reinforce the interests of actors inside the organization.
5. All of these groups have access to political resources that can be used to further and protect their interests.
6. The organizational reformer is confronted with the necessity of gaining compliance for his reform.
7. The more the reform is perceived to be favorable for, or neutral to, the interests of relevant actors, the less resistance the reformer is likely to meet.
8. Conversely, the more the reform is perceived to be contrary to the interests of relevant actors, the greater the resistance the reformer is likely to meet.
9. Depending on his skill in gaining access to and managing resources, the reformer can meet this resistance through a number of tactics.
10. The reform eventually implemented is a function of the desires of the reformer, his ability to persuade and coerce, the interests of the relevant actors, and their capacity to further and protect those interests.

The premise behind these statements is that organizational reform is a political, rather than technical, phenomenon. To many, this must seem extraordinarily obvious. Experience shows, however, that most efforts at administrative reorganization do not depart from assumptions similar to those above. Initiatives are undertaken with no preparation for the reactions bound to follow. The usual case is that the reformer is so ill-equipped to manage the resistance that his opponents emerge completely victorious, and the status quo is maintained. In other situations, possible benefits of the reform are distorted by debilitating compromise. Faced with entrenched opposition, the obstinate reformer may lose sight of his original intentions and become motivated simply to protect his prestige. His insistence on bringing his opponents to their knees may engender consequences far more damaging than the conditions he was originally trying to ameliorate.

The founders of MINVU conceived of the housing sector in terms of the construction of houses and community infrastructure, and the provision of urban services. They wanted eleven agencies in the new organization. Yet they succeeded in the case of only six. There was little in the intrinsic logic of the administrative reform which explains why some agencies submitted, and others did not (*assumption one*). In providing urban services, the Electric and Gas Service agency was in the same category as Urban Pavement. There were few differences between the Santiago Water Company and the Sanitary Works agency. Nonetheless, the response of the Sanitary Works and Electric and Gas Service agencies to the proposed reform was very different from that of the Santiago Water Company and Urban Pavement.

The objective functions of an organization, or the services it provides, sometimes describe very little about the organization itself. Especially in studies of the internal operations of bureaucratic units, it is useful to identify an organization's overall goals through the goals of the persons who make it up, weighted differently for the amount of power they have within the organization (*assumption two*).[31] The simple fact that the new ministry of Housing and Urbanism was going to give special attention to water and sewers in urban areas did not mean that the interests of everyone in Sanitary Works coincided perfectly with the interests of MINVU's founders. Similarly, personnel in the Architecture agency may have been conscious of the need for an organization such as MINVU in the Chilean public sector. They might even have accepted that the technically correct arrangement would be to locate planning and construction of community development facilities in MINVU. Those intellectual concessions, however, were not sufficient to guarantee smooth integration of the Architecture agency into the MINVU organizational chart.

Different outlooks distinguish persons at various levels of organizations (*assumption three*). These distinctions characterize the dynamics

[31] See Herbert A. Simon, "On the Concept of Organizational Goal"; Charles Perrow, "The Analysis of Goals in Complex Organizations"; Charles K. Warriner, "The Problem of Organizational Purpose"; and Lawrence B. Mohr, "The Concept of Organizational Goal."

of administrative reform and provide clues to the sources of probable resistance to change. They help predict the type of inducements that are most effective to carry out such reform. In the case of the Chilean housing sector, the most relevant actors were at three levels: the executive, made up of the different ministers of state and appointed heads of large agencies; the professional, comprised of those technicians, mainly architects and engineers, whose skills helped define the nature of the organizations' output; and the laborers and lower-level white-collar workers, whose services were instrumental for operation of the agencies.

The workers and lower-level administrators responded to organizational reform in terms of *job security* and *economic benefit*. Since they were mainly low-skilled personnel, the tremendous advantage of government employment was that they worked under the Administrative Statute, which protected them from the uncertainties of the general labor market.[14] The concomitant disadvantage was that salary and wage levels were inferior to those in the private sector. The interests of these lower-level governmental employees were in guaranteed job security and progressive headway on the wage and salary front.

Those at the professional level in these institutions were less concerned about job security, since their talents were scarce in the country at large. Even without the protection of the Administrative Statute, most engineers and architects had little reason to fear for their employment.[15] In fact, the agencies were desperately in need of their services, since the lower remuneration in the public sector meant that the agencies had a significant number of vacancies in key technical posts. The professionals tended to respond to *economic* and *prestige* inducements in defining their attitude toward suggested administrative reform. Technicians in the centralized sector of government were very sensitive to the fact that their pay was not commensurate with that of other professionals working in decentralized agencies or in the private sector. Inferior remuneration for equal work was a source of continual irritation. It served as a permanent point of contention with the upper levels of the agencies.

As professionals they also had certain ambitions intimately linked with the exercise of their labors. They were sensitive to the relative prestige of their specialty in comparison with other vocations. Within their own domain they preferred to work at the vanguard of the profession, using all

[14] *Estatuto Administrativo,* D.F.L. No. 338 (1960) (Santiago: Gutenberg, 1971), Title II, Paragraph 1, Article 37, p. 13.
[15] Of course, there were some exceptions to this rule. But generally job security appeared to be less important to these groups than salary and professional considerations. This view parallels that of Archie Kleingartner, in "Collective Bargaining between Salaried Professionals and Public Sector Management."

the skills they possessed, and not be relegated to projects of secondary physical or professional import.

The executives seemed to be motivated by considerations of *authority* and *prestige*. Unlike the workers, their principal concern was not job security or the level of their remuneration.[16] The ministers and agency chiefs wanted to know how the structural reform would alter their status and operating influence in government and among private clients. Reducing functions or prerogatives was a subtle censure of their abilities. Likewise, the stripping away of important components of the organization meant that their authority was reduced in value. There were fewer people to carry out orders and less money allocated according to their priorities. Fewer clients were able and willing to negotiate for access to their decisions and support their organizations in bureaucratic politics.

The preceding ideas are summed up in Figure 12, showing principal concerns of the housing administrators when they examined the relative merits of the proposed reform. The executives were preoccupied with their future authority and prestige; the professionals with prestige and remuneration; and the workers with remuneration and job security. Advantages for the upper two levels were often contrary to the interests of the workers, and important stimuli for the lower level were sometimes immaterial for the middle professional level. The workers acted to protect their Statute; the chiefs, their status. Despite some overlap in their motivations, the significant differences in orientation tend to belie the existence of a simplified "organizational" response to administrative reform. Even if all three levels fight for the status quo, it would seem that they do so for different reasons.[17]

It is worthwhile to note that job security, adequate economic compensation, and increased prestige and authority are conditions that ameliorate private situations. This is the sense in which they are employed in the figure. Each insecurity encompasses various issues, some of which apply

[16] These top administrative appointees, some of them from the private sector, had already reached a fairly high level of economic solvency; if still not satisfied, they would have sought well-paying positions through their personal contacts, or not accepted their government appointments. See the quote by Chester I. Barnard on p. 140.

[17] Although he did not trace out the political connotations of his observations, Martin H. Greenberg noted that workers and low-ranking personnel had drives centering on "security and convenience. . . . These workers . . . are greatly concerned with their day-to-day working conditions and the protection and retention of their jobs." Middle-level technicians "appear to be highly professional and (take) much pride in their work. . . . Although professional engineers can and do evince a desire for money income, many of them are prestige-conscious." As for the bureaucratic elite, Greenberg finds them "difficult to categorize, since they appear to be motivated by several seemingly contradictory desires." Greenberg, *Bureaucracy and Development: A Mexican Case Study*, pp. 104–105.

FIGURE 12.   CONCERNS OF DIFFERENT HIERARCHICAL LEVELS FACED
WITH ADMINISTRATIVE REFORM

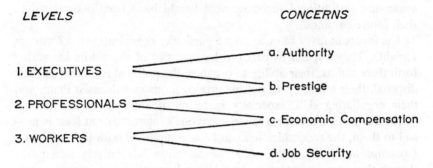

more to one set of actors than to another. For example, it will be seen
later that issues relating to prestige were not the same for the executives
as for the professionals. It is also useful to make the distinction between
motivating concerns and political resources. When they react to structural
reform, executives seem to be motivated to maintain a capital stock of
authority and prestige for indeterminate but generalized future use. Executives can use any combination of political resources to protect these
stocks, just as workers and professionals can use their power base to further their interests (*assumption five*).[18]

In other situations or other countries, outside interest groups might be
powerful enough to prevent or impose structural changes unilaterally,
against the wishes of all the actors inside the bureaucracy. Here, this was
not true. The pattern was as follows: as soon as political leadership
pushed for reform, bureaucratic actors forged alliances with outside supporting groups, and the weight of the outside group often tipped the balance of power in favor of those who were resisting (*assumption four*).

When such coalitions develop, one would expect the partners to be motivated by the same category of concern. Indeed, when the lower-level
personnel in Sanitary Works asked the unions to help protect their job
security and increase their incomes, the unions coming to their aid were
investing in the possibility that their members' economic interests might
be furthered by solidarity in some future confrontation. It is equally possible for a relevant group outside the organization to act in concert with
one level of the hierarchy, seemingly supporting the same aims but really
motivated by other interests. For example, the public works contractors
assisted certain executives in resisting organizational reform, on the pre-

---

[18] Executives can use prestige and authority to protect authority and prestige, but
it would be nonsensical to say that workers use job security and economic compensation to protect economic compensation and job security.

text that the latters' prestige and authority would be impaired. However, the motivating interest of the contractors was purely economic, in the sense that institutional rearrangement would have been detrimental to their future earnings.

The forces in favor of or against a particular organizational reform are variable. They depend in part on the intensity of the actors in putting forth their claims, their ability to organize the political resources at their disposal, their affinity with outside groups motivated to assist them, and their negotiating skill, especially in terms of anticipation and timing. When the particular reform favors everyone's interests, or at least is neutral to them, the reorganization can be accomplished with little difficulty (*assumption seven*). This particular situation is relatively infrequent, though there are examples in the Chilean housing sector. A more common occurrence is that the suggested reform serves the interests of almost nobody except the aspiring reformer. In this case the resources and strategies of the reformer must be of high concentration and quality for the change to be effected (*assumption eight*). The most unpredictable case is when pertinent aspects of the reform tend to favor some groups inside and outside the organization, yet are detrimental to others, and all the relevant actors square off for battle.

In such cases, the reformer has a certain amount of power at his disposal and is faced with a relative amount of opposition. He makes his job considerably easier if he takes the precaution of programming the probable reactions of different bureaucratic and nonbureaucratic elements into his reform strategy. In this way he can inform himself of their propensities for action, and avert stiff resistance which may suddenly appear. Naturally, if the reformer previously diagnoses the objections to his administrative reform and then alters it to neutralize the objections, or replace them with inducements, he is going to have much more success with his proposal than if he neglected to research the situation in advance.

In any case, a multitude of strategies and tactics are likely to result as the affected groups define and act on their positions. The critical variable is the manner in which the reformer manipulates his resources to counter opposition (*assumption nine*).[19] If he is skillful in predetermining the specific tactics of his adversaries, and outmaneuvering them in the subse-

---

[19] Perhaps the most detailed list of tactics for administrative reform (some thirty in all) has been compiled by G. N. Jones, "Strategies and Tactics of Planned Organizational Change." Strategies are either coercive (e.g., hierarchical pressure, stress inducement), normative (participation, value displacement, education and training), utilitarian (rewards, high placement), or neutral-like (charisma, catharsis, timing).

quent bargaining sessions, he can achieve his goals relatively cheaply.[20] If he enters the melee ill-prepared or with more good intentions than political skill, the attempt may prove to be a disaster. The suggested reform can be rejected or dangerously distorted, and the possibilities for future attempts greatly impaired.

INITIAL STRATEGIES FOR ORGANIZATIONAL REFORM

The housing advisors attached to the Christian Democratic movement in 1964 did not proceed from a preprogrammed battle plan for restructuring the housing sector. They began with the assumption that once their party entered government, everything on this front would fall neatly into place. There was little or no effort to determine where bureaucratic opposition might lie. This neglect is understandable, given the scope of their duties in planning housing policy and designing the formal structure of MINVU. But this same neglect contributed in great part to the difficulties they encountered later, when they tried to operationalize their formalized ideals. There is little doubt that different tactics would have been used had the whole episode been repeated.

The founders did base their hopes on two implicit strategies that, had everything gone smoothly, might well have led to the complete success of the reform. The first attempted to take advantage of the extraordinary amount of legitimacy that a new president has when he first comes to office. The founders expected that his authority, combined with comprehensive action right at the beginning of the presidential term, would create such momentum that any bureaucratic opposition would be cowed into compliance. The second strategy was to reduce prestige considerations to the minimum by insuring that the minister of Public Works, the sector that was to undergo the most severe alteration, would not be personally maligned by the loss of his prerogatives. The problem was not that these strategies were naive as far as they went. Rather, the founders of MINVU did not have back-up plans which could orient their tactics in

[20] Gerald Caiden, in *Administrative Reform*, states that the "reformers' overall strategy is to win over vested interests, opponents and neutrals if possible while strengthening support. . . . Reformers may deceive opponents and supporters alike by backing unsympathetic persons in power in order to influence, guide, or control the course of events. In so doing they may have to compromise over objectives to win greater support. In any event, they have to divert resources from direct advocacy to splitting the opposition. Should those tactics fail or appear unlikely to succeed at the outset, there remains the bludgeon—a direct frontal assault with the opposition struggling to the bitter end—and the rapier—a back-door entry when the opposition is off-guard" (p. 144).

the second go-around, once changing conditions undermined the relevance of the original thrust.

Approximately one month after taking office, Frei followed a precedent set by several of his predecessors and requested legislation from Congress which would facilitate the swift implementation of his campaign programs. First he asked for extraordinary powers (*facultades extraordinarias*) allowing him to proceed quickly with agrarian reform, Chileanization of the foreign copper holdings, and the assessment of new taxes on large enterprises. He also asked for the passage of certain normative laws (*leyes normativas*) giving him the right to implement far-reaching administrative reorganization with the least delay. Besides MINVU, he had in mind two other ministries: Transport, and Industry and Foreign Commerce. He also wanted to reorganize the Central Bank, to create ODE-PLAN (the national planning office), and to set up an advisory board to give the benefit of legality to cooperatives and neighborhood action groups in urban areas (*Consejería de la Promoción Popular*).

The ministry of Transport would have complemented the founding of MINVU, and the creation of both would have signalled the extinction of the Public Works ministry, one of the oldest in the Chilean public sector. In 1964 the subsecretariat of Transport was in the ministry of Economy, and the most important construction agencies dealing in transport facilities were located in Public Works. The idea was to correct this mislocation by elevating the subsecretary of Transport to the ministerial level, and moving the roads, ports, and airports divisions from Public Works to Transport. Simultaneously, those agencies dealing in urban or housing affairs would be transferred to the new MINVU. The ramifications of these changes are illustrated in Figure 13. Once Public Works lost roads, ports, architecture, urban pavement, CORVI, irrigation, sanitary works, and the various water companies, it would have ceased to exist. Its planning agency would have been split between Transport and MINVU.

If the normative laws had been passed very early in the new administration, the president and his housing advisors could have implemented their planned administrative reorganization almost immediately. The agency heads and ministers who were affected would not have had the opportunity to establish themselves in their new roles and to come to value the status quo as much as they did after several months on the job. Quick action would have kept the president one step ahead of his own appointees, since his relationships with his highest-ranking officials changed as the latter became key operating personnel. At the beginning they were dependent on the president for their appointments. As time passed, the president became more obligated to them as supporters and executors of his political program.

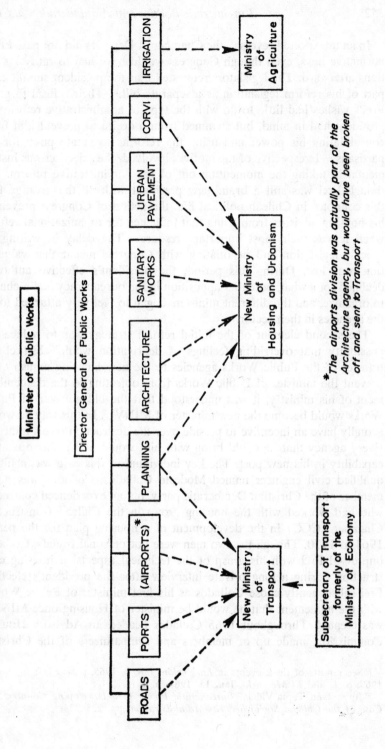

FIGURE 13. CONTEMPLATED REORGANIZATION OF THE MINISTRY OF PUBLIC WORKS IN 1964

*The airports division was actually part of the Architecture agency, but would have been broken off and sent to Transport

In an unexpected reversal, the Chamber of Deputies did not pass Frei's normative laws, even though Congress would have had to ratify his actions afterward. The legislators requested that the president submit each part of his reform legislation as a separate bill.[21] Their refusal to grant Frei's wishes had little to do with the type of administrative reform the president had in mind, but stemmed from a desire to prevent him from consolidating his power and using the reforms to create posts for his partisans.[22] Irrespective of the motives involved, the rejection was instrumental in taking the momentum out of the administrative reform. Although Frei was still a brand-new president with all the prestige that this connotes in Chilean political life, the action of Congress prevented his housing advisors from using that influence for organizational reform when it was their most important resource. The delay in writing up specific legislation and negotiating with Congress meant that valuable time was lost. During this period, the president's effective authority declined somewhat, potential opposition in the bureaucracy had a chance to organize, and the different ministers began to feel very attached to *all* the agencies in their sector.

The second element of the initial reform strategy was to reduce the possibility that overriding feelings of deprivation would obstruct the transfer of the Public Works agencies to the new Housing ministry. To prevent the minister of Public Works from objecting to the dismemberment of his ministry, it was understood that the old minister of Public Works would become the new minister of MINVU. In this way he would actually have an incentive to preside over the destruction of his ministry. Every agency that he could bring with him would add to his operating capability in his new post. The key individual in this case was a highly qualified civil engineer named Modesto Collados. Collados was not a member of the Christian Democratic party, but an experienced contractor who had worked with the housing group in the Chilean Construction Chamber (CCC) in the development of a housing plan for the period 1964 to 1970. Though the two men were not personal friends, Collados impressed Frei with his grasp of the technical aspects of housing construction during a long private interview after the president's election. Frei subsequently chose Collados as his first minister of Public Works, with the agreement that he would be minister of Housing once MINVU was created. Throughout 1965 Collados headed an Advisory Housing Commission, made up of members and sympathizers of the Christian

[21] See reports of these events in *La Nación,* Jan. 8, 1965, p. 4; *El Siglo,* Jan. 9, 1965, p. 1; and *El Mercurio,* Jan. 15, 1965, p. 1.
[22] Jorge Iván Tapia-Videla, *Bureaucratic Power in a Developing Country: The Case of the Chilean Social Security Administration,* pp. 223–224.

Democratic party who worked steadily on the projected law creating MINVU and the administrative reform filling out its organizational chart.

Ministerial Resistance

The eleven agencies that were to be transferred to MINVU can be divided into three groups according to their fate: those that remained firmly where they were, those that were relocated *in toto,* and those that became transaction or compromise agencies (see Figure 14).

By the time the law creating MINVU was passed by Congress in mid-December of 1965, each of Frei's ministers had had a full year to grow accustomed to all the agencies in his sectoral "family." The three agencies in Section A of Figure 14 remained where they were as concessions to the respective ministers: the Educational Construction Society (under the minister of Education), the Hospital Construction Society (Public Health), and the Electric and Gas Service agency (Interior). The executives of the first two, both long-time friends of the president, contended in front of the National Technical department of the Christian Democratic party that there were no compelling reasons for the agencies to move. If more coordination were needed, special new mechanisms between MINVU and their ministries would serve the purpose. They emphasized that health and education were as important as housing to the party's program. Taking the side of the ministers in its resolution of September 22, 1965, the party's Executive Council proposed that the Hospital and Education construction societies not be turned over to MINVU. The current structure facilitated maximum information flow between the planners, programmers, and project chiefs within each ministry; the status

FIGURE 14.   THE OUTCOME OF ADMINISTRATIVE RE-
FORM IN THE HOUSING SECTOR

A. Remained completely outside of MINVU:
  1. Education Construction Society
  2. Hospital Construction Society
  3. Electric and Gas Service agency
B. Integrated into MINVU:
  4. CORVI
  5. Housing and Social Assistance Foundation (F.V.A.S.)
  6. Central Savings and Loan Fund (CCAP)
  7. Urban Pavement agency
  8. Santiago and El Canelo water companies
  9. Other water companies throughout the country
C. Compromise or Transaction Agencies:
  10. Sanitary Works agency
  11. Architecture agency

---

quo meant faster administrative decisions and reduced costs; the change would disrupt the pace of construction; and it would be inadvisable to burden MINVU with affairs that were outside of its most urgent and fundamental responsibilities.[23]

The case of the Electric and Gas Service agency involved different reasoning, although the results were the same. The minister of Interior, responsible for the internal security of the nation, argued that electricity and gas ranked with communications as vital to the national defense. Transferring the agency to MINVU would lessen the minister's effectiveness in the case of natural catastrophe, threats to internal security, or foreign attack.

The personnel in the Advisory Housing Commission did not consider the arguments of Education or Health convincing. To them, the claims of Interior were not even plausible. The Commission's difficulties arose from the fact that it did not have sufficient power to bring all the relevant institutions into the fold. The minister of Public Works was not a Christian Democrat and had little political weight in the government. Frei had not just one but thirteen ministers to keep happy.[24] Asked to arbitrate, he settled on a compromise that legitimized the status quo. He decided that these agencies could remain where they were for the time being, but eventually they would have to transfer to MINVU. They never did.

Minimizing Resistance

Two easy ways to forestall resistance to change are to design a reform that is in the interests of all the affected parties, or is not a reform at all. These conditions were partially simulated in the cases of CORVI, the Central Savings and Loan Fund (CCAP), and the Housing and Social Assistance Foundation (F.V.A.S.). Opposition was nonexistent in CORVI and the F.V.A.S., and minimal in CCAP.

CORVI's architects felt uncomfortably disadvantaged in Public Works, an eighty-year-old institution dominated by engineers, where housing investment was inferior to the total capital budget of the other divisions. Since CORVI was to be the key component of the new housing sector, the reform would enhance their status in the country. CORVI's professional personnel in planning, programming, land acquisition, costs, and construction also saw that the reorganization provided fine opportunities for promotion to the upper levels of MINVU. For their part, the lower-level

[23] Partido Demócrata Cristiano, "Memorandum sobre el Artículo 5 del Proyecto de Ley sobre el Ministerio de la Vivienda y Urbanismo," Sept. 22, 1965.
[24] Richard F. Fenno, Jr., speaking of the United States bureaucracy, observes: "It is not realistic to expect the President to give strong support to those pet projects of a Cabinet member which affect so many of his fellows." Fenno, *The President's Cabinet*, p. 233.

workers would suffer no adverse change by moving to the Housing ministry. In Public Works, CORVI workers were governed by the dictates of the private Labor Code, which would also prevail in MINVU.[25] Their job security would neither improve nor suffer because of the reform.

Personnel in the F.V.A.S. had little reason to fear a drop in the organization's prestige, since it had very little to begin with. Its charitable status, commendable for a previous era, was incongruent with the image of social reform that the new government was propagating. In MINVU, the members of the technical staff of the F.V.A.S. would no longer be almoners associated with an organization based on paternalistic legal precepts, but social workers engaging in more modern expressions of their profession.

Arguing that CCAP was a financial, not a constructing concern, its executives were somewhat dismayed at the prospect of moving to MINVU. In order to preserve their excellent working relations with the major source of economic power, they preferred to remain in Finance, where the Fund's budget was firmed up over the intercom. They also predicted difficulties in inducing the Finance minister to approve special transactions, such as increasing CCAP's floating debt or letting its reserves slip a bit below the legal minimum. The transfer was finally effected by guaranteeing that CCAP would remain completely intact with no changes whatsoever in its structure or its personnel. Its executives especially insisted on a continuance of its decentralized status, which helped it qualify for grants and loans from international agencies.

The prospective transfer of these three organizations either had beneficial results for all their personnel or made little difference. Moreover, there were no outside clients whose interests would be impaired by the change. The dismemberment of the old CORVI would actually improve the housing contractors' relationships with the corporation. The overburdened CORVI had become so mired in the multiplicity of its functions that budgeted funds often lay dormant for many months until administrators untangled the mess and solicited bids. If CORVI could be the center of a new ministry, the contractors felt that they would be able to get their hands on CORVI money much more quickly. They were thus favorably disposed toward the reorganization and subsequently helped carry it out.[26]

[25] The Labor Code (*Código de Trabajo*) governs the private sector and most decentralized agencies, and is less stringent on the question of termination than the Administrative Statute.

[26] The contractors' design for the formation of MINVU, published in the CCC's journal, *La Revista de la Construcción*, No. 30 (November 1964), pp. 61–69, was nearly the same one that eventually emerged. As a former CORVI contractor, Collados had contemplated the detrimental effects of an overclogged administrative unit from the outside.

Another set of institutions eventually passed over to MINVU, but not as smoothly as CORVI, the F.V.A.S., and CCAP. In the Urban Pavement agency, and the Santiago, El Canelo, and other water companies throughout the country, resistance to the proposal did not go beyond mutterings of discontent among the personnel or relevant interest groups outside of the bureaucracy. In Urban Pavement, for example, each specific pavement contract was relatively small, involving a patch here and there or asphalting only a few streets in widely scattered cities. This meant that there was a great dispersal of power among the contractors who might have supported those engineers who felt they were dealing in "public works, not housing." [27]

The main difference between the two groups of agencies in Section B of Figure 14 was that the bottom three (Urban Pavement and the water companies) were used as negotiating pawns in the chess match between the MINVU founders and Public Works over the fate of the Sanitary Works and Architecture agencies. MINVU wanted them all transferred; significant forces inside and outside of Public Works wanted them all to stay. The compromise eventually reached was that Urban Pavement and the water companies would go, but on the condition that the bulk of Architecture and Sanitary Works would be allowed to remain in Public Works. The agreement also included provisos permitting MINVU to set up parallel organizations for sanitary works and community infrastructure if it felt that they were badly needed. But under no circumstances would Public Works be stripped of two of its most important components—Sanitary Works and Architecture.

This case merits further examination.

THE SANITARY WORKS ISSUE

The period from November 1964 to December 1965 was somewhat painful for many executives and professionals in the Sanitary Works agency. In late 1964 the agency lost quite a bit of its autonomy because of Law 15,840, which established the General Public Works agency and placed a general director of Public Works between the agency chief and the minister. In late 1965, despite a fervent effort to preserve the integrity of the agency, Sanitary Works was split in two, and part of it sent to the General Urban Works agency in MINVU. Many engineers who were knowledgeable on the earlier history of water and sewers in Chile complained that the agency was beginning to head backward.

[27] Interview material.

In 1906 all sanitary works facilities in the country were managed and owned by the municipalities. The most important were in Santiago, Valparaiso, Concepcion, Talca, and Punta Arenas. Water tariffs were controlled by the central state, and were pegged more for electoral purposes than to keep the companies solvent. Around the turn of the century, most of these municipal companies were suffering financial crises because of their incapacity to keep up with the pace of increased industrial and consumer demand. From 1906 to 1915 most of these companies were "intervened" by the central government.[28]

From 1915 to 1953 the functions of construction of sanitary works and management of services to the consumer were handled by separate entities under two ministries. The Hydraulic department in the ministry of Public Works built all sanitary works projects. The General Water and Sewage agency in the ministry of Interior managed the water and sewer operations. These two offices operated relatively successfully side by side for several decades. Gradually, however, it was necessary for the officials of each organization to sustain more permanent dialogue with their colleagues in the other ministry. Interior had to inform Public Works of the type of water services solicited by their clients. The engineers in Public Works had to explain more modern sanitary techniques to the managers in Interior. The ever-increasing population led to amplifications of existing networks and more projects with special requirements.

In August 1953, sanitary engineering in Chile took a significant step forward with the integration of the Hydraulic Department and the General Water and Sewage agency. Baptized the Sanitary Works agency and located in the ministry of Public Works, its formation led to more efficient coordination for construction and consumer service.[29] The agency also set up an elaborate decentralized system to bring the organization closer to the local consumers.

During the last two years of the Alessandri regime, Congress discussed a law altering the structure and statutes of Public Works. The original intention was to make a large autonomous agency out of all the agencies of the ministry to allow faster financial transactions, fewer preaudits, and payment of bills from a special bank account separate from the National Treasury. The new agency would also move toward greater decentralization by setting up zonal delegations, and its personnel would

[28] Raúl Montesinos G., "Organizaciones que hasta la fecha han tenido a su cargo en el país las obras de agua potable y alcantarillado," in Obras Civiles, Sección Sanitaria, *La Ingeniería Sanitaria en el País y su Enseñanza.*

[29] Horacio Lira D., "Características que debería reunir una organización a cargo de las obras de agua potable y alcantarillado del país," in *La Ingeniería Sanitaria.*

work under the Labor Code. Because of the opposition of the lower levels of the ministry to the Labor Code, the original bill was watered down and the autonomous status was eliminated. When Law 15,840 was finally passed in 1964, it retained some aspects of the suggested reform, including the General Public Works agency with zonal delegations and headed by a director general positioned between all the agency heads and the minister (see Figure 13).

The engineers in Sanitary Works were very unhappy with the final version of Law No. 15,840. For many years they had wanted a state enterprise for Sanitary Works (ENOS), with the right to fix tariffs and set salaries at a scale commensurate with those of engineers in private employment. An autonomous agency for Public Works would have been a step in that direction. But the prostitution of the original bill left the situation worse than before. An intervening authority between the head of Sanitary Works and the minister meant that the local offices had to submit to the whims of the representatives of the zonal delegations who worked under the director general.

A thorough probe into the events of 1965 identifies at least ten actors and eight major issues linked to the Sanitary Works affair. The immediate question at hand pertained to the future location of Sanitary Works, but for different actors this question aroused other tangential issues. Each of these issues helped spur coalitions among the ten actors, and the different tactics were related to the coalitions' political resources.

The executives of the ministry of Public Works, supported by large construction firms and influential members of the Christian Democratic party, judged the reform by its effect on the level of total investment centered in Public Works, and the organizational integrity of the ministry. The Sanitary Works engineers' attitude toward the reform was related to a long-standing rivalry between architects and engineers; their possibilities for professional expression in projects of significant scale and technical challenge; general working conditions necessary for their personal dignity; and their relatively low level of remuneration. They were supported by the Association of Engineers inside of Public Works, the College of Engineers, and the Institute of Engineers—the latter two groups operating on behalf of engineering in general. The workers in the agency responded to changes in their family allowances that raised their real incomes, and the general legal regulations affecting their work status (the Administrative Statute versus the Labor Code).

Actors and Coalitions at the Executive Level

The first issue of major import was the future status of the ministry of Public Works and its control over the distribution of public investment in Chile. Earlier it was pointed out that the creation of the ministries of Transport, and of Housing and Urbanism, would have signified the virtual extinction of the ministry of Public Works (Figure 13).[30] Those who were attached to Public Works for sentimental and economic reasons naturally felt threatened by an administrative reform that would be the death knell for Public Works and the fine tradition it represented. When the reformers had the impertinence to reply "So what?" the infighting began in earnest.

The attitude of the general director of Public Works, one of the actors most committed to the preservation of the ministry in its existing form, can be understood against the background of his career. A confessing Catholic, he had been a functionary of Public Works since very soon after receiving his engineering degree. He entered the ministry on the heels of the 1925 Constitution, which definitively separated Church and State in Chilean public institutions. During most of this period, the Radical party controlled the government. Aggressively laic and anti-clerical Radicals opposed the future general director at practically every turn. His high technical qualifications tended to be ignored, promotions were continually delayed, and he had to struggle for every advancement he achieved.

While in Public Works, he became a personal friend of Eduardo Frei, who was first elected to Congress in 1949 as a senator from the northern mining provinces of Atacama and Coquimbo. The general director worked on many public works projects benefiting the area and sponsored by the Christian Democrats' rising political star. When the party entered government in 1964 he was with them, and had accrued sufficient political capital to qualify for an upper-level position. It was widely believed that he would end up as minister of Public Works, but Frei passed him over. If he had had ministerial rank from the beginning, he could have moved easily to another important post once Public Works was disbanded. However, it would have been nearly impossible for him to fill another second-level post with equal authority and prestige. As head of the General Public Works division, he had executive authority over six major agencies which in 1965 invested approximately 36 percent of the central government's total budget.[31]

Given his long trek to reach this apogee of prominence, and the emotional bonds he felt with "his" ministry, it was only natural that he responded negatively toward the prospect of effacing his administrative slot, despite the fact that he is credited as the originator of the idea to

[30] In advocating the reform, Frei was not preparing a vendetta against Public Works. Indeed, he had been its minister in the late 1940's.
[31] Ministerio de Hacienda, *Ley de Presupuesto de la Nación.*

create Transport along with MINVU.[32] Accordingly, he and his allies fought to preserve the whole, presumably on the assumption that by waging an all-out campaign they would remain with more at the end than if they negotiated each agency separately. They erected a solid front to defend all the agencies that were going to be stripped away, including Urban Pavement, Sanitary Works, Architecture, and Irrigation. It was partially for this reason that the Agricultural Planning Office (ODEPA) could not induce the ministry to relinquish jurisdiction over Irrigation, and was finally forced to settle for just some seats on the agency's future directorate.[33]

The general director of Public Works, a mild-mannered and gentle man, could hardly have carried out this herculean resistance without some help. Support was forthcoming from a variety of sources, including the groups inside Irrigation, Sanitary Works, and Architecture who felt insecure about their futures; in turn, their interests were reinforced by the general director's persistent efforts to preserve the overall status quo. He profited from more specific support from the National Technical department of the Christian Democratic party and the public works contractors in the Chilean Construction Chamber (CCC).

After the Christian Democrats came into power, they formed tripartite commissions to orient the government's activity in each sector. The Tripartite Commission for Public Works consisted of the minister and his advisors, the highest-ranking party congressmen sitting on the public works committees in parliament, and representatives from the National Technical department of the Christian Democratic party (see Figure 15). Since there was no MINVU at the beginning of the regime, the *party's* housing policy was hammered out in the public works subdepartment of the National Technical department, headed by a major contractor for Sanitary Works who was an influential member of the party and would later become minister of Public Works. This arrangement put the reformers at a distinct disadvantage, because the Advisory Housing Commission could count on almost no support from the party in the meetings of the Tripartite Commission. Their opponents were very partial to Public Works and later prevailed upon the Executive Council of

[32] This was in the pre-electoral period, before it was known that he would be critically affected by the change.

[33] The 1967 Agrarian Reform law called for creation of the National Irrigation Enterprise (ENR), a state industry that presumably would be linked to the ministry of Agriculture. But during the full period of the Christian Democratic government, the status of Irrigation did not change. Public Works would not even discuss the possibility of Irrigation's becoming a state industry unless it would remain under Public Works, with at least four members of the directorate appointed under the minister of Public Works, no more than four named by Agriculture, and one by the president.

the National Technical department to accept the general director's views as the party's position.

Approximately one month before the government sent the formal version of the MINVU law to Congress, the Executive Council listed the reasons why the ministry of Public Works should remain in its existing form, except for minor alterations.

1. If other ministries such as MINVU needed community facilities, the agencies inside Public Works were perfectly capable of projecting, constructing, and maintaining any projects that were assigned. Accordingly, there was no need for a massive reorganization.

2. If the government wished to act rapidly, it was necessary to take full advantage of the efficiency and potency of Public Works. Any tampering with its structure would destroy that capacity.

3. There was a grave shortage of professionals, architects, and engineers within the current Public Works organization. If the ministry were split up, that deficit would simply be more serious.

4. It was technically, materially, legally, and administratively inconvenient to pass Public Works through another restructuring while it was still recovering from the throes of Law 15,840.[34]

The National Technical department did offer some concessions, such as the possible transfer of several city planning units and Urban Pavement to MINVU. Also, it did not deny MINVU's right to design its own agencies for water, sewers, and community development facilities if need be. But it was adamant in preserving the major part of Public Works as it was. This accord of July 28, 1965, was contrary to Frei's stated intentions on administrative reform and had to be retracted and redrafted for public consumption.[35] Meanwhile the party engineers on

[34] Partido Demócrata Cristiano, "Acuerdo del Departamento Técnico Nacional del Partido Demócrata Cristiano en relación con la creación del MINVU," July 29, 1965.

[35] Frei's position was published in *La Revista de la Construcción,* No. 27 (August 1964), p. 51. "We have decided that it is necessary to study a structural change of this ministry. . . . We see no reason to leave in the same organization an Architecture agency, which is constructing public buildings, schools, and carabinero outposts, and a Roads division, which must resolve the problems of the country's road network. Similar considerations can be made with respect to the Urban Pavement agency and the Irrigation agency. Moreover, today there is no effective coordination between Roads and Railroads, and air transport and coastal trade. . . . Therefore, I will redistribute the current agencies of the ministry of Public Works, creating the ministry of Transport (roads, railroads, ports, airports) and the ministry of Housing and Urbanism (CORVI, Sanitary Works, Architecture, Urban Pavement, etc.). The Irrigation agency, most probably, will be subsumed under the ministry of Agriculture."

FIGURE 15.   THE TRIPARTITE COMMISSION FOR PUBLIC WORKS, 1965

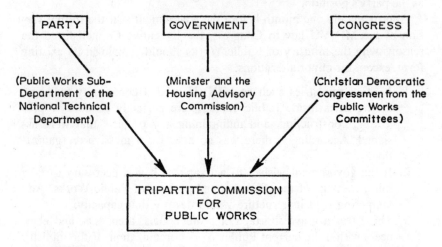

the Tripartite Commission were maneuvering behind the scenes in support of the director's position.

The major contractors joined the movement against dismemberment of the Public Works ministry, motivated in part to preserve one of the main byproducts of Law 15,840, the general directorship. Through this key nexus of authority they could exercise additional influence over decisions made in the various agencies of the ministry. When their problems were not solved satisfactorily by the respective agency head, the contractors could try to convince the general director to bend a bit on contract regulations and the amplification of capital projects.

The public works contractors apparently came to an agreement with the housing contractors in the CCC on the best way to proceed. The housing contractors were most concerned about restructuring CORVI, less concerned about transferring the Architecture agency, and minimally preoccupied about the fate of Sanitary Works. As long as CORVI's future was secure, the housing contractors let their public works colleagues use the weight of the guild organization to protect the rest of the ministry, with the understanding that Architecture would probably pass over later. The CCC prepared reports against a comprehensive administrative reform, emphasizing future budgetary difficulties for Public Works, deterioration in the cash-flow position of the agencies, and the inconvenience of upsetting the progress of initiated works.[36] The CCC pre-

[36] See their editorial in the May 1965 issue of *Construcción*, No. 36, p. 17.

sented its arguments to the minister of Public Works and had a private interview with President Frei.

The interests and orientations of the general director of Public Works, the National Technical department of the Christian Democratic party, and the CCC led to a coalition which consistently argued that the organizational integrity of the ministry of Public Works should not be violated. Obviously the general director was aware that the CCC always watched out, first and foremost, for the overall economic interests of its members. Part of his job was to keep vigil over the propriety of the relations between his ministry and the contractors. On some occasions, however, such as during this challenge to the existence of Public Works, their concerns were mutually reinforcing.[37] The Technical department of the party wanted Public Works to remain as principal constructor of the country's infrastructure, and supported the general director in his attempt to preserve the ministry intact. The civil engineers in the party felt that it was necessary to maintain the heritage of a large and powerful Public Works ministry, which had traditionally brought together the nation's best engineering skills to collaborate on large capital projects that had placed Chile near the forefront of Latin America in roads, bridges, sanitary works, and irrigation.

This coalition was rather successful in its resistance. Throughout the years 1965 and 1966 the Frei government gradually became preoccupied with more important matters, and possible creation of a Transport ministry became more and more remote. The idea was virtually abandoned when the subsecretary of Transport was transferred to the ministry of Public Works on December 13, 1967. The continued existence of Public Works was no longer in doubt, which had a remarkable effect on the campaign to preserve the totality of the ministry's organizational chart. In 1968, the Public Works agency had a change of heart and was suddenly willing to throw the Architecture agency into a package deal involving a slight reshuffling of functions between MINVU and Public Works.[38] This more benign attitude of the executives in Public Works

[37] Many of these transactions were of the positive exchange variety. For example, in late 1965 the CCC gave the new general director favorable publicity in an interview written up in its prestigious journal, *Construcción*, No. 41 (October 1965), p. 14. Other transactions resemble joint payoff, to be discussed in Chapter 7.

[38] This was Decree Law No. 323 (*Diario Oficial* of Aug. 24, 1968) which established the Urban Works Corporation (COU), the successor to the General Urban Works agency, of which Architecture was to have been a part. By this date MINVU was moving along at a fast clip, and Collados' replacement, Juan Hamilton, did not want to slow the pace to ease Architecture into the organization, especially since the agency's deficits would place heavy strains on MINVU's budget. Meanwhile, MINVU had turned over the function of constructing community develop-

contrasted sharply with their intransigence three years earlier, when the disappearance of the ministry was a real possibility.

Actors and Coalitions at the Professional Level

The engineers in Sanitary Works were the most intimately affected by the proposal to transfer the agency to MINVU. Most of them were strongly opposed to the suggested change, and solicited support from the Engineers Association in Public Works, the Institute of Engineers, and the College of Engineers in an attempt to remain where they were. The resistance was hardly a reflection of infatuation with their current situation. Indeed, they were very dissatisfied with the way sanitary engineering was being abused inside the Public Works agency. First, their salaries were very low: their engineering colleagues in state enterprises and the private sector earned from one and a half to two times as much money. Second, the profession of sanitary engineering had not been given sufficient stature in the hierarchy of engineering in general. They felt that the agency should be transformed into ENOS, the *Empresa Nacional de Obras Sanitarias,* a state corporation operating with a minimum of government interference. ENOS would consult with Public Works for purposes of overall planning, not be dependent on it administratively, and would have the power to set tariffs for its services.[39]

How could ENOS benefit the sanitary engineers? It would have provided them with an organization of their own to deal with all the sanitary problems of the country in an integral fashion. Its autonomous status would have helped enhance the prestige of sanitary engineering, probably attracting a greater number of prospective engineering students to that specialty. By using its power to set rates for water services and sewage disposal, it could have increased capital investment independent of political pressures and competition from other sectors. This added capacity would enable it to engage in second-generation sanitary projects in Chile, especially the tapping of underground water sources and the construction of sewage treatment plants, almost completely absent in Chile at the time.[40] Most of all, the change would have meant a pay increase.

---

ment facilities to one of its own planning units, the *Dirección de Planificación de Equipamiento Comunitario,* whose activities will be discussed in the next chapter.

[39] "Proyecto de la Empresa de Obras Sanitarias," in *La Ingeniería Sanitaria.* It is interesting to note that the forum from which this document emerged purported to bring high officials together to discuss the *teaching* of sanitary engineering. The engineers took advantage of the occasion mostly to voice their complaints and extol the virtues of ENOS.

[40] Almost all sewage is dumped into rivers or the ocean, including the systems of Santiago, Valparaiso, and Concepcion. Sanitary Works manages a pilot treatment plant in Melipilla serving 40,000 people, one of eight plants in the country. Another installation in Cartagena is overloaded to the point of becoming a cesspool.

By being an autonomous agency, ENOS could set its salary scales above those of the centralized ministries.

It was not difficult to see that the suggested transfer of the agency to MINVU would not result in any of the advantages that the engineers sought in ENOS. There would be no change in salary. The engineers in MINVU would earn exactly the same as in Public Works. There would be no progress toward autonomous status. In MINVU the agency would be subsumed under the General Urban Works agency, even more centralized than the General Public Works division. There would be no improvement in highlighting the special characteristics of sanitary engineering. In MINVU the agency would be thrown together with Urban Pavement, a significant comedown from its usual contacts with the Irrigation agency, the River Defense department, and the General Regulator of Waters, all in Public Works.

The proposed reorganization aroused a series of other worries among the engineers. The first related to a longstanding mutual lack of confidence and professional jealousy in Chile between the engineers and the architects.[41] Engineers considered architects fanciful dreamers with little respect for reality; architects maligned engineers as obsessed with numbers and petty detail. This tension between the two professions was so prominent that it even raised its head in international conferences. Chilean architects were known to have denounced the engineers publicly, to the amazement of their colleagues from other countries who did not share such animosities.

The origin of the overt dispute is difficult to ascertain. Because of the seven-year length of study, engineering is generally considered, with the medical profession, one of the more exclusive occupations in Chile. Despite the greater number of years required to become an engineer, the College of Architects predated the College of Engineers, and for a long while engineers had to be members of the College of Architects to practice their profession. The College of Architects was so protective of its prerogatives that it did not recognize a separate College of Engineers for two decades. Some engineers were fearful that the architects were going to use MINVU to aggrandize their power. Not content just to build, they were going to insist on administering the post offices, clinics, and schools as well. Some engineers sensed in the tone of the architects'

[41] The founders of MINVU were not architects in the traditional sense, but urban and community planners with advanced training. The split between architects and planners is treated in Enrique Browne, "A propósito de un Dilema: Arquitectos y Planificadores." However, here we are dealing with subjective prejudices. The engineers looked upon all professionals with degrees in architecture as "architects," despite more recent advances in the field stressing the social, economic, and administrative connotations of physical construction.

language that they wanted to transfer the total activity of government to their jurisdiction.[42] Others, not quite so obsessed by the power factor, were still convinced that it was important to maintain an institutional division between engineers and architects, just so long as it did not impair the profession of sanitary engineering in general.

Second, the reform had implications for the personal expression of their trade and the size of the projects they would undertake. In Sanitary Works, they received special satisfaction from working with powerful firms and a host of qualified engineers on large capital projects that were technically challenging. If they were relegated completely to the city, they would be dealing in programs of relatively small size calling for little professional excellence. The contact would be with less well-established contractors; the tasks would be easier and considerably less demanding intellectually. Collaborating with highly skilled colleagues on stimulating investments was much more interesting than checking up on the daily output of a journeyman.

A related problem was the engineering focus of Sanitary Works projects. The founders of MINVU continually proclaimed that the Sanitary Works agency would complement CORVI in the construction of new housing. The engineers, on the other hand, emphasized Sanitary Works as a technical unity, including the location and exploitation of new water sources, purifying plants, and feedlines to populated areas. They felt that service to existing neighborhoods was more important than that to the new dwelling, and wondered whether being at the beck and call of the architects would work to the detriment of their traditional activities.

When the division of Sanitary Works was imminent, additional factors relating to the engineers' working conditions became points of contention. Some realized that in MINVU they would have fewer telephones and vehicles, less office space and furniture. In Public Works there were always good chances of pursuing postgraduate studies abroad for the advanced technical training needed for complex engineering problems. In MINVU, these opportunities would be gone. Many engineers could not understand why anyone would want to go to MINVU to provide miniscule rations of water to new shantytowns when he could remain in Public Works and help plan reservoirs for the future of all Chile.

In sum, the majority of engineers in Sanitary Works saw significant

---

[42] For some engineers, this distrust of the motives of competing professionals extends to economists and medical doctors, who they believe want to control the country. Engineers have accused doctors of trying to monopolize social assistance programs so they can manipulate the community through their penetration of individual family units.

disadvantages in moving to MINVU. They would have to subordinate themselves to the authority of the architects. The content of their work would be reoriented toward smaller projects. They would not share in the benefits of working together with teams of engineers from prestigious firms. Their undertakings would not substantiate the excellence of their profession. All these eventualities had negative connotations for their personal self-esteem, along with the continuance of a dismal pay scale which was an insult to their abilities.

The engineers worked through several established channels to put forth their opposition. Within the ministry of Public Works, the labor union with the most members is the Federation of Workers. It joins several more specialized syndicates, such as the Administrative Employees Union (workers and lower-level personnel), the Association of Professionals (lawyers, engineers, civil constructors, architects, accountants, social assistants), and the Association of Engineers. The sanitary engineers worked mainly through the Association of Engineers, a tightly organized union sometimes referred to as the *Cosa Nostra* of Public Works, with the reputation of waging frontal battles when ministerial or governmental authorities ignore the engineers' wishes.

The College of Engineers was created in 1958 as legal overseer of the profession in Chile.[43] It attends to maintenance of the high standards of the university titles awarded in engineering; the salaries of engineers in the public sector; and fees to the engineers working in the private sector, to assure that they are commensurate with those of other professions, such as medicine.[44] Though the Association of Engineers is not officially affiliated with the College, the engineers in Sanitary Works solicited its assistance to prevent transfer of the agency. In presenting its case to the minister of Public Works, it was hoped that the College would be considered more disinterested than the parties directly involved. The College argued that the intentions of MINVU's founders would irrevocably weaken the profession of engineering.

The Institute of Engineers is not considered as impartial as the College, but traditionally has exerted more political clout. The Institute was

[43] Law No. 12,851 (*Diario Oficial* of Feb. 6, 1958). The engineers are divided into several specialties. In 1965, there were 4645 members of the College in the following categories: Civil (2075), Commercial (472), National Defense (318), Electric (367), Mechanical (582), Mines (324) and Chemical (507), with approximately 75 percent of the members residing in Santiago. *El Mercurio*, Dec. 5, 1965, p. 51.
[44] "When professions seek governmental help, they do so . . . (1) to control preparation, entry, and practice; (2) to maximize favorable public opinion and so obtain guarantees of freedom on the job; (3) to rationalize work; (4) to maximize economic terms; and (5) to facilitate their work." Corrine Lathrop Gilb, *Hidden Hierarchies: The Professions and Government*, p. 135.

founded in 1882, with the intention of furthering the profession in Chile.[45] Its active membership draws together the engineers from the large contracting firms, who consider the Institute more of an interest association than the College. Its usual tactic is to prepare a study of the issue and present the report to the government as an official petition for action, backed by the full weight of its membership. In the case of Sanitary Works, the Institute took a firm stand against any reform implying a breakup of Public Works or a division of the principal agency dealing in sanitary engineering.

The basic tactic of the Association, College, and Institute of Engineers was to confront the minister of Public Works with their intense displeasure over the proposed transfer. In the first half of 1965, the engineers told the minister as often as once a week that they were opposing the changes he was promoting. Later they asked him to defend his position in front of a plenary meeting of the Institute of Engineers. This concerted agitation succeeded in impressing Collados with the tremendous undercurrent of discontent over his ideas. Eventually he decided that the resistance was too great. The compromise solution would be to establish a separate office in MINVU to install water networks and manage distribution, from half of the old Sanitary Works agency. He would allow the large investment projects to remain in the ministry of Public Works.

The engineers obligated the minister to alter his position without going to extremes. But it is important to point out that the methods used by the various engineering groups were remarkable for their timidity. The Association on other occasions had called a strike to protect its members. This time the word "strike" was barely mentioned by the rank and file, much less by the union leaders. On another issue relating to a dispute over fees paid to private engineers, the executives of the College were so intransigent that the government began proceedings against them for violations of the Law for the Internal Security of the State.[46] The Institute waged an all-out campaign, including use of the mass media, to prohibit giving the status of their profession to commercial engineers. On the reorganization of Public Works, although the ramifications would have been more damaging to their interests, the campaign was much more low-keyed.

The restrained attitude of the interest groups had much to do with the timing of the reorganization. These events were unraveling immediately after Frei's election. At the start of presidential terms there is

---

[45] Instituto de Ingenieros de Chile, *Estatutos*, Decree 2926, July 13, 1961.
[46] See *El Mercurio*, Aug. 11, 1967, p. 24; Aug. 13, 1967, p. 47; Aug. 14, 1967, p. 34; Aug. 21, 1967, p. 25; and Aug. 27, 1967, p. 47; and *La Nación*, Aug. 21, 1967, p. 17.

always a political breathing spell during which the president is backed simply because he is president. The reorganization of the housing sector was at the heart of one of Frei's most specific campaign promises. Under these circumstances, it was inappropriate for the guild associations to protect the parochial interests of the engineers in too forceful a manner.

Actors and Tactics in the Reform Coalition

If the authority of the Christian Democratic government was so strong in its first year, why did the minister of Public Works feel he had to compromise at all? The answer relates to his inability to claim a portion of that authority for the execution of the housing reform. His two potential bases of support were the Christian Democratic party and the Advisory Housing Commission affiliated with the party. The National Technical department of the party sided with the general director and the engineers in Public Works against reorganization. Since he was not a party member, it was difficult for the minister to appeal to other Christian Democrats, nor did he have the full support of the Advisory Housing Commission.

In the interim between the September election and the November inauguration, the ultimate designation of the minister of Public Works remained a question mark long after other positions were filled. The eventual appointment of a contractor to become minister of Public Works caused extensive consternation among the housing advisors. The architects on the Commission were displeased that Frei had chosen a "big-money man" who had been on the directorate of the CCC, and was neither a party member nor a professional architect. They were upset that an engineer with strong capitalistic interests in CORVI contracts was to be their future boss and the personification of the ministry they were creating. Several of the housing advisors drafted a letter to Frei asking him to reconsider a choice not representing their aspirations.[47] The action of the housing advisors was probably shortsighted for their own ultimate aims. Their wavering support prevented the minister from claiming a unified front before the opposition, and reduced his chances of carrying out the very reorganization that they earnestly desired.

In response to the situation, the minister followed a policy of appeasement and abandoned the idea of transferring *all* of Sanitary Works to MINVU. The persistent opposition of the general director, the National Technical department of the party, the professional personnel in Sanitary Works, the CCC, the Association, the Institute, and the College of Engineers convinced him that there were just too many interests aligned

[47] This letter was never sent, but the agitation over the affair was well-known in the grapevine of the party and the upper levels of the public administration.

against that particular outcome. The counterproposal would be to transfer just *parts* of Sanitary Works to MINVU. The resulting organization would be called the Sanitary Services agency. It would only install networks in the cities, and manage the administration of water to the consumer. Projects of capital infrastructure would remain in Sanitary Works. Thus the engineers who dealt in the "heavy" aspects of their profession would be happy, and CORVI would have an agency to urbanize its new neighborhoods.

This compromise solution was not banged out as a common accord between the two opposing points of view. It was a resolution that the minister and his advisors came to on their own, unilaterally, after weighing the different options open to them. The minister then dedicated his efforts to imposing the "compromise" on those same groups who had opposed him earlier on the original idea of transferring all of Sanitary Works to MINVU.

It would be erroneous to assume that this compromise was welcomed as an improvement over the previous suggestion. There was a strong outcry against the administrative and technical problems inherent in the division of Sanitary Works. The engineers emphasized that this change would turn back the clock on the history of sanitary engineering in Chile to the pre-1953 era, when the different functions were split between the ministries of Public Works and Interior. The engineering groups felt that it was highly irrational to divide an organic body that was operating normally. Most sanitary engineers felt that even the *complete transfer* of Sanitary Works to MINVU was *preferable* to the unnatural division of the agency.

Technical difficulties on how to divide the existing agency into two units, Sanitary Works and Sanitary Services, soon presented themselves. The first suggestion was for Works to handle everything between the Andes Mountains and the storage tanks outside of cities; and Services, everything between the tanks and the consumer. Because of an inconsistent definition of "storage tanks," this idea was discarded. The next suggestion was to give all installations connected by pipes of less than ten centimenters to Services, and all connected by larger pipes to Works. This solution was called the "Faucet Theory," on the presumption that faucets would be installed where larger pipes split into smaller pipes in order to place boundary markers on the domain of each agency. Eventually it became obvious that any precise technical distinction would be artificial. The heads of both agencies would have to get together to work out where the jurisdiction of one stopped and the other started.

Once the idea of a separate Sanitary Services agency was fixed in the minds of MINVU's founders, they devised two strategies for its acceptance. Because they felt they were operating from a deteriorating power base, their efforts to defuse the opposition and win their point engendered rather blunt tactics. One strategy was to restrict information flow on their intentions; the other was to "borrow" authority for their move.

While the legislation for MINVU was being drafted, the articles pertaining to sanitary works were clothed in relative secrecy. The minister either did not provide any information at all, or leaked out information that would bolster his position. The professional level was informed that MINVU had advantageous regulations for speeding administrative processes, although it would have been difficult for them to be more favorable than those accorded Public Works by Law 15,840. There was also an effort to have people commit themselves to the law by suggesting additions and modifications. However, the net worth of this type of participation was reduced when each successive modification nullified the one that came before. Finally, some behind-the-scenes negotiations filled the top positions in the Sanitary Services agency in exchange for support for the division of Sanitary Works. This tactic fomented a good deal of distrust and recrimination inside the agency, which later proved to be difficult to smother.

The final decision on whether to divide Sanitary Works took place in the Tripartite Commission of Public Works. The Commission had its first meeting on July 19, 1965, some four months before the MINVU law was passed by Congress. It held meetings periodically thereafter to follow the progress of the law in Congress and to determine the government's "final indications" or definitive desires in regard to the new housing ministry. At the meeting of September 28, 1965, the Commission still had not decided which institutions would be included in the law. At that point the pending agreement was that the Electric and Gas Service, National Hotels, National Monuments, Atmospheric Health, Railroad Construction, and National Parks were "in"; while the Health and Education Construction Societies, and the Valparaiso and Viña del Mar, Santiago, El Canelo, and other water companies were "out." [48] For the final indications, after all negotiations and transactions were completed, the situation was very much reversed. All of these "ins" were out, and all of the water companies were "in." As of September 28, no decision had yet been made on the Sanitary Works question.

The final meeting of the Tripartite Commission to resolve the fate of the agency took place in October 1965. Officials from the General Pub-

---

[48] The party's treatment of the question is summarized in Partido Demócrata Cristiano, "Antecedentes sobre la Creación del MINVU," which discusses the proceedings at the September 28 meeting.

lic Works agency, Sanitary Works, and the Santiago Water Company, and the minister of Public Works and his advisors attended from the government side. Members of the National Technical department represented the party's position, and ranking Christian Democrats from the Public Works committees in both houses came from Congress. This added up to approximately twenty-five regular Commission members. The representatives from the National Technical department and the General Public Works agency were already committed to opposing the division. The head of Sanitary Works had persuaded the congressmen and all the government representatives, except for the minister and his advisors, of the inadvisability of the proposal. As things stood at the beginning of the meeting, those against splitting Sanitary Works made up the majority, and the minister of Public Works would have lost in the final vote.

Notwithstanding, the minister pulled a surprise move that caught his adversaries completely off-balance. He executed a coup that covered up for his deteriorating position in the Commission. Prior to the meeting he had visited the presidents of the Senate and the Chamber of Deputies, as well as the president of the country, to convince them of the need for a separate sanitary agency in MINVU. The presidents of both houses of Congress attended the meeting and gave their personal support to the minister's position, claiming it was a good way out of an impasse. The minister of Public Works then announced to those present that he also had the personal backing of the president of Chile, Eduardo Frei, who felt that MINVU should have its own agency to urbanize lands for CORVI. After these declarations there was little that opponents to the division could do. Although they were certain that the national leaders had poor information, their continued resistance would have brought into question both their party loyalty and their patriotism. By entering the meeting with three new cards in his hand, the minister proved to be skillful in mobilizing support when he needed it most. The artifice enabled him to "borrow" authority to achieve his aims. He timed this perfectly to overcome entrenched opposition.

The Costs of Poor Resource Management

Although the founders of the ministry were able to impose their compromise solution on a hesitant Tripartite Commission, they still had failed in their initial ambition to transfer all of Sanitary Works to MINVU. One reason for the failure was that they did not prepare their strategies with sufficient attention before the encounter. They did not anticipate resistance within the bureaucracy and had no comprehensive backup strategies devised, in case they did not win in the first go-around. The standard "assumptions" of administrative reform outlined at the beginning of this chapter were badly ignored. The reformers had no idea of the propensities and aspirations of the different levels of Sanitary Works until those immediately affected laid them out on the table. The reformers forfeited leadership roles to the opposition and had to rely on relatively makeshift techniques to gain acceptance for even their diluted proposal.

In this case the costs of poor resource management were rather high. The bungling of the reform effort marked a sad chapter in the history of sanitary engineering in Chile. The morale and effectiveness of the personnel responsible for sanitary works were much lower after the imposition of the "compromise" solution than when both activities were joined in Sanitary Works. The founders first justified the division on the pretext that the rivalry between the two institutions would lead to greater levels of productivity. The resultant experience showed, however, that it led only to unfortunate feelings of resentment among engineers who previously had worked together in close harmony. The law establishing Sanitary Services transferred certain functions, buildings, furniture, and personnel from the ministry of Public Works to MINVU. Sanitary Works, however, refused to vacate their buildings, forcing Sanitary Services to operate in painfully cramped quarters. The meetings between the directors of both agencies to resolve jurisdictional ambiguities soon broke down. Though this personal interaction was supposed to take place at least biweekly, at one point several years passed before communication went beyond a cold memorandum.

Consequently, a very poor working relationship developed between the two agencies and they began to duplicate each other's work. Cases occurred in which both Sanitary Works and Services installed water and sewers on different sides of the same street. Sanitary Works had a much larger budget and more personnel than Services. By default, it had to carry out many projects that should have belonged to the MINVU agency. In 1966 the government issued Decree Law No. 492, in an attempt to clarify the division of functions. But the confusion of the situation was perfectly reflected in the wording of the law. The two main articles were pristine examples of "double-talk": the activities of the agencies were described in exactly identical terms.[49] Though the decree called for the joint signature of the ministers of MINVU and Public Works to settle who built what and where, no such procedure was ever followed. From 1965 to 1970, whichever agency happened to be working in the locale at the time installed sanitary facilities.

[49] *Diario Oficial* of Sept. 23, 1966. This particular decree must be one of the most extraordinary in the annals of Chilean jurisprudence.

The most distressing aspect of this redundancy was that the principal objectives of the compromise solution were not realized. One of the intentions of the reform was to divide exclusive duties between the two agencies. The reformers argued that the distribution of water to satisfied clients entailed a whole series of different problems from capturing water at the source and leading it to the city. After the reform, the ministry of Public Works was supposed to concentrate on the heavy engineering aspect, and Sanitary Services in MINVU was to handle the light engineering and administration of the system. Nonetheless, the transfer of administration never took place, and it remained in Sanitary Works. The failure to apply this aspect of the compromise meant that the overlapping of functions was complete. Sanitary Works built in the Andes Mountains and dealt with the consumer. Sanitary Services operated in between, placing networks under city streets.[50]

The second intention of the reform was to use the Sanitary Services agency to provide CORVI neighborhoods with water and sewers. But the Housing Corporation continued to issue contracts for these installations through its own Costs department. In the end the splitting of Sanitary Works was wholly purposeless. The waste, unhappiness, and sacrifice were for naught.

Several years later, objective analysis would conclude that the division had been irrational and ridiculous, and that it was imperative to bring the two agencies together again. Personnel in both Sanitary Works and Services agreed in theory that a recoupling would be an intelligent move. Yet when talk circulated that someone upstairs was going to try to rationalize the situation, personnel in each agency became quite nervous, believing they would be worse off under any other arrangement. Rather than risk submitting themselves to the authority of persons they disliked, many administrators concluded that the status quo was both the worst and the best situation.

Other Possibilities[51]

Were there any other exits to the perplexities posed by the reform of the Sanitary Works agency? The priorities of the Advisory Housing Commission were ordered as follows:

[50] Another anomalous characteristic of Decree Law No. 492 (1966) was that it ordered the immediate transfer of operations (*explotación*) to Sanitary Services, in Article 1 of its *Disposiciones Generales*. Sanitary Works chose to ignore this provision, with the backing of its minister. At the same time, Sanitary Services could not obtain the support of the Housing minister to defend its legitimate right to this activity.

[51] Albert O. Hirschman, in *Journeys Toward Progress,* pp. 251–275, employs an approach similar to that of the next four paragraphs.

1. Transfer all of Sanitary Works to MINVU.
2. Divide Sanitary Works and bring Sanitary Services to MINVU.
3. Leave all of Sanitary Works in the ministry of Public Works.

As described earlier, the minister of Public Works determined on his own that the second alternative represented the compromise solution. On his scale of preferences it fell into the middle range.

The priorities of the engineers in Sanitary Works were different:

1. Leave all of Sanitary Works in the ministry of Public Works.
2. Transfer all of Sanitary Works to MINVU.
3. Divide Sanitary Works and bring Sanitary Services to MINVU.

The desire of practically all the sanitary engineers in 1965, and the interest groups that supported them, was to preserve the unity of the agency dealing in sanitary engineering. The transfer of Sanitary Works to MINVU would have been highly distasteful. The consensus nevertheless was that it would have represented a better solution than the establishment of parallel organizations.

If the minister had reviewed the situation in either of two ways, and planned his action accordingly, he might have increased his chances of coming to an agreement more favorable to his own interests. First, he might have mapped a strategy playing only with the priority list of the sanitary engineers. If he had pushed the division of Sanitary Works while the engineers were attempting to protect a whole organization, it is conceivable that the engineers would have compromised for the complete transfer of Sanitary Works to MINVU, the second choice on their list. Naturally, this outcome was the top preference of the founders of MINVU.

Second, if the minister had assigned interval values to the two sets of preferences, the combined total value for each alternative could have been considered an indicator of the *optimal solution possible,* given the interests of both parties. The first priority for each party would receive a value of 3; the second priority, a value of 2; and the third, a value of 1. Table 11 reveals the subtleties of this mathematical gymnastics. If the minister could have operationalized the assumptions of this construct—namely, power equity between the two parties and a similarity of intensity for each level of priority—he again would have come out on top. The most "popular" solution was the transfer of all of Sanitary Works to MINVU, with a total of five points. In second place was the status quo, or leaving the whole agency in Public Works, with four points. Interestingly enough, the solution ultimately imposed would have emerged worst, with a total of only three points.

TABLE 11. CALCULATING THE OPTIMAL SOLUTION IN THE SANITARY WORKS QUESTION

Preference	Priority for MINVU	Point Value	Priority for Engineers	Point Value	Total
Transfer all	1	3	2	2	5
Leave all	3	1	1	3	4
Divide	2	2	3	1	3

It is not presumed that the minister and his advisors needed only to draw a chart such as this and all would have been rosy for their ultimate aims. The previous discussion has shown that the dynamics of the situation were considerably more complicated. However, it could safely be stated that the overlap in the positions of MINVU and the engineers left room for maneuvering, which MINVU could have exploited better by managing its resources and strategies more skillfully.

By their own admission, the engineers found it difficult to resist wholeheartedly a reform that had been an important part of the president's electoral platform. With the benefit of hindsight, they conceded that after the initial defense of the status quo their potential influence was significantly spent. Relative weakness in later negotiations prevented them from avoiding the division of Sanitary Works, imposed by MINVU but anathema to them. The minister and his advisors committed their first tactical blunder when they abandoned, early in the game, the goal of transferring all of Sanitary Works. It removed from negotiation the solution most advantageous to MINVU. And it eliminated the possibility of implementing the one outcome that had real possibilities for becoming the "true" compromise between the two parties. The minister's second mistake was to underestimate his access to authority. He later proved that he could borrow authority at a crucial moment to force the division of Sanitary Works. He might have used that technique equally well for the last-minute transfer of all of Sanitary Works to MINVU.

Why could not the founders of MINVU offer the Sanitary Works engineers what they really wanted—namely, ENOS? This alternative had previously been eliminated by the one level in the hierarchy whose interests have not yet been examined—the workers. Discussion of their position will round out this study of the Sanitary Works agency and lead to the conclusions drawn from it. The main obstacle to providing the General Public Works agency with autonomous status in Law No. 15,840 was the opposition of the workers. The decentralization of Public Works (or of Sanitary Works into ENOS) would have meant that its personnel chart (*planta*) could have been modified every year and that its workers would have been under the dictates of the Labor Code, not the Administrative Statute. This provision was in the interests of the executives, since they could hire and fire their employees like a private company. It was neutral to the interests of the professionals, since in general their skills were scarce. However, the provision was very much *against* the interests of the workers. They would lose the overriding advantage of their employment in government, their job security.

Ironically enough, by pursuing their interests, the workers represented a permanent nemesis for the sanitary engineers.[52] First, they were a barrier to what the engineers wanted most, the creation of ENOS. Second, they almost accomplished what the founders of MINVU wanted most, the complete transfer of Sanitary Works to MINVU. In 1968 the executives of the General Urban Works agency changed their organization from a centralized agency to a state corporation, the *Corporación de Obras Urbanas* (COU), which had some, but not all, of the characteristics of a decentralized agency. On the one hand, the personnel in COU qualified for increases in their family assistance allowances. COU's lower-level employees earning 650 escudos as a base salary could increase it by 200 via a favorable family subsidy, meaning a gross pay raise of 30 percent. This significant income differential applied only to the lower levels; for a professional earning 6,500 escudos, the increase was only 3 percent. On the other hand, COU did not change over to the Labor Code. Its employees were still protected by the Administrative Statute.

Word of this development caused an uproar in the Sanitary Works agency. Suddenly the workers, through the Administrative Employees Union, saw significant advantages in being attached to COU rather than Sanitary Works. In COU they would have higher remuneration with no loss in job security. Serious talk of a strike to pressure for the move caused near panic among the engineers in Sanitary Works. The loss of this large group of underlings would deprive them of much of their line support, without which they could not operate. Much against their will, they would have been forced to follow their subordinates into Sanitary Services.

In response, representatives of the sanitary engineers immediately tried to convince the Administrative Employees Union to withdraw its demand. They pointed out that the workers wanted this change for their own personal convenience, despite its detrimental effects on the rest of the organization. They also argued that MINVU did not have the funds to pay this higher family allowance to such a large group and had given no guaran-

[52] David Mechanic emphasizes the role of the workers in "The Power to Resist Change among Low-Ranking Personnel."

tees that it would. Finally, to seal off the main sources of dissidence, the Christian Democratic engineers resorted to demands for party obedience to bring the leaders of the union into line.

THE COMPLEXITIES OF ADMINISTRATIVE REFORM

This final turn of events was not deliberately planned by those who wished all of Sanitary Works in MINVU. But its near success emphasized that the founders of MINVU had mismanaged the implementation of their reform. There was probably little they could have done to placate the general director of Public Works and the CCC, who were bound to lose prestige and authority through the move. However, they might have mapped obstacles and inducements more adeptly in negotiating with the engineers and the workers.

If a multi-faceted reform program, such as that initiated by the Christian Democrats in 1964, must be carried out through political bargaining in an atmosphere of relative power equality, the change agents are faced with a difficult task. For resistance to be reduced to zero, the suggested modifications must be neutral or provide concrete advantages to every party involved. Since this is improbable, the simpler procedure is to conduct an extensive preliminary study of the ills of the current situation, order the reforms by priority, and then execute them quickly and decisively to outflank the opposition.

In discussing this question, Samuel P. Huntington suggests that in theory two broad strategies are available to the reform leader. One is "to make known all of his goals at an early time and to press for as many of them as he [can] in the hope of obtaining as much as possible"—the blitzkrieg. The alternative is the "foot-in-the-door approach of concealing his aims, separating the reforms from each other, and pushing for only one change at a time"—the Fabian technique. Huntington goes on to say that the most effective reform method is

the combination of a Fabian strategy with blitzkrieg tactics. To achieve his goals the reformer should separate and isolate one issue from another, but, having done this, he should, when the time is ripe, dispose of each issue as rapidly as possible, removing it from the political agenda before his opponents are able to mobilize their forces. The ability to achieve this proper mix of Fabianism and blitzkrieg is a good test of the political skill of the reformer.[53]

The failure of the Christian Democratic regime to transfer more than six of eleven agencies to MINVU resulted from the error of combining

[53] Samuel P. Huntington, *Political Order in Changing Societies,* p. 346.

an overall blitzkrieg strategy with Fabian tactics within the housing sector. Frei did not assign relative priority and order the implementation of his programs by sequence. Rather, he presented them simultaneously, became somewhat disoriented when resistance appeared, and concentrated too much attention on various battles in Congress, while almost totally ignoring such items as the structural reform in the housing sector.

The Christian Democratic maxim of appointing *técnicos* and giving them a free hand to carry out their administrative responsibilities was probably inadvisable in the case of the minister of Public Works, charged with implementing one of the regime's fundamental objectives. The president did not offer sage counsel and consistent backing to compensate for the minister's political naiveté, and did not foresee the mismatch when the minister was opposed by several of the most powerful interest groups in the country. Lacking a certain measure of political skill, the Advisory Housing Commission used Fabian tactics (e.g., wavering on the inclusion of certain agencies in MINVU, compromising on Sanitary Works) when it should have used the blitzkrieg. There is good reason to believe that the outcome would have been considerably different had the general director of Public Works been appointed minister, and had the president monitored the emergent situation in the Tripartite Commission more sedulously.

Huntington does not offer a label for the third stage in a reform process, relating to appropriate political behavior if the first and second thrusts fall short. If the reformers are serious about their intentions, they must have backup strategies prepared in case initial momentum is lost. In administrative reform, these should reflect the basic concerns of the hierarchical levels of the organization and include preprogrammed tactics to overcome or lessen resistance. Figure 16 presents a summary matrix of actors, supporting groups, and interests in the Sanitary Works affair.

The scheme illustrates quite vividly the parallel relationship between hierarchy and types of political motivation. The differences are probably sharpest at the two extremes. The executives seem relatively unperturbed by job security, and the workers are uninterested in the prestige of the organization. The middle-level professionals share preoccupations with both the executives and the workers and, when battle lines are drawn, often determine the fate of the reform effort. The coalitions that the professionals set up can represent an irresistible force in favor of the status quo; conversely, if provided with sufficient inducements, they can lead the way to the new system.

The founders of MINVU did not construct such a scheme before undertaking the reorganization. If they had, their chances for success, even as late as early 1966, would have increased considerably. In this critical

FIGURE 16. ACTORS, SUPPORTING GROUPS, AND ISSUES IN THE SANITARY WORKS QUESTION

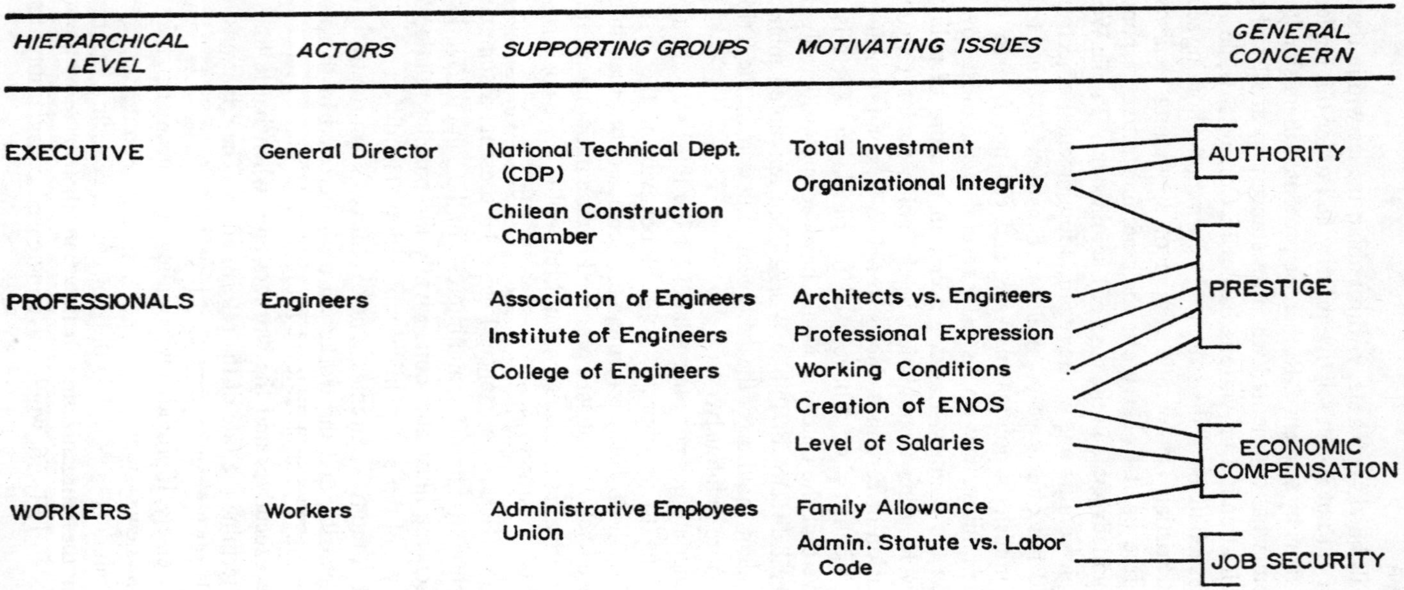

HIERARCHICAL LEVEL	ACTORS	SUPPORTING GROUPS	MOTIVATING ISSUES	GENERAL CONCERN
EXECUTIVE	General Director	National Technical Dept. (CDP) Chilean Construction Chamber	Total Investment Organizational Integrity	AUTHORITY
PROFESSIONALS	Engineers	Association of Engineers Institute of Engineers College of Engineers	Architects vs. Engineers Professional Expression Working Conditions Creation of ENOS Level of Salaries	PRESTIGE ECONOMIC COMPENSATION
WORKERS	Workers	Administrative Employees Union	Family Allowance Admin. Statute vs. Labor Code	JOB SECURITY

third stage, they did not attempt systematically to forge coalitions to make the change prevail. They did not recognize that if the executives' desire for prestige and authority was not neutralized, the costs of compensating the workers probably had to be borne by the state. Failing that, special concessions, such as the formation of ENOS, had to be granted to the professionals.

   This discussion of administrative reform reaffirms that organizational prerogatives and goals are not abstract concepts separate from the interests of the human beings who are members of the relevant organization. They are a result of the interaction of executives, professionals, and workers who, when faced with administrative challenges, tend to respond dissimilarly and with different resources. The next two chapters will revert to studying organizations as integrated units. Chapter 6 will discuss the way that decentralized corporations, by augmenting their control over authority, prestige, information, and finances, have been able to aggrandize their power base inside the new ministry of Housing and Urbanism.

6

POWER, AUTONOMY,
AND COORDINATION IN THE MINISTRY
OF HOUSING AND URBANISM

Most complex organizations are confronted by the challenging problems of coordination and control, and the Chilean Housing ministry from 1965 to 1970 was no exception. The specificity of functions included in the original scheme meant that there were a number of key points at which coordination was crucial. The various units charged with implementing housing policy (CORVI, CORMU, CORHABIT, CCAP) profited from legal dispositions and financial resources enabling them to act with extreme independence if they so desired. As it turned out, these corporations *did* tend to go their own way, subjecting the whole ministry to serious centrifugal forces.[1] These events brought about a crisis in coordination for the central ministerial authorities (MINVU), which responded to the situation in two ways. The main control unit, the General Planning and Budgeting agency, responsible for monitoring and guiding the programs of the corporations, tended to withdraw from the conflict and pursue narrow but technically interesting minor programs. Later a a surrogate control unit, the Subsecretariat, counterattacked the independence of the corporations politically, using a decentralization program to try to bring them under better supervision.

The main proposition examined in this chapter is: The more powerful the organization, the more autonomy it can achieve, and the more difficulty other units will encounter in coordinating its activities.[2] *Power is*

---

[1] John Friedmann, in "Urban-Regional Policies for National Development in Chile," takes a somewhat less critical view of MINVU's early history. Also see T. Robert Burke, "Law and Development: The Chilean Housing Program."
[2] Edward C. Banfield, in *Political Influence*, pp. 318–323, fills out this proposition

represented by the types and combinations of political resources at the organization's disposal, especially in relation to those of other entities and actors in its environment. *Autonomy* describes degrees of freedom in the orientation of the executive organization compared with the policies, directives, and orders of the controlling or monitoring unit.[3] It also refers to the organization's ability to operate relatively independently when faced with contingencies in the task environment. *Coordination* suggests a situation in which complementary functions of distinct organizational units merge at the appropriate time and location to achieve recognized goals with the least operating uncertainty.[4]

In the case of the Chilean ministry of Housing and Urbanism, these variables cannot be treated empirically without going into extensive detail.[5] The underlying assumptions of MINVU's organizational design related both to autonomy and coordination, but not to factors of variable bureaucratic power. It soon became obvious that MINVU, the monitoring unit, was operating without one single resource advantage over the corporations it was supposed to be controlling. From the beginning, the corporations maintained near monopolies over authority and finances, and had tremendous leeway in defining who would control information and status accrual within the organization. Because of uncertainties in their task environments, and their general antipathy toward unsolicited interference from MINVU, the corporations attempted to increase their autonomy as much as possible. Not all employed the same tactics, but their general strategy was similar: Increase control over scarce organizational resources, both to increase their performance before relevant publics and to reduce even more MINVU's precarious influence.[6]

CORMU led the campaign against MINVU's claim of authority over the corporations decisions; CORVI, CORHABIT, and CORMU all

---

with a series of hypotheses such as: (1) the wider the distribution of authority, the larger the stock of power required if proposals are to be adopted; (2) as the number of autonomous actors increases, the probability of adoption decreases; and (3) as the number of autonomous actors increases, control mechanisms tend to be less structured.

[3] For an instructive brief on coordination, see Paul Hammond's "Foreword" to Basil J. F. Mott, *Anatomy of a Coordinating Council: Implications for Planning.*

[4] See Wilbert E. Moore, *Man, Time and Society.*

[5] Some of the complexities in the study of housing policy and institutions can be appreciated in Gabriel Pumarino, "La Política de Vivienda como Instrumento de Desarrollo Urbano."

[6] This analysis will skirt a borderline between "intention" and "response." No doubt some of the events and tendencies stemmed from the explicit desires of principal personages in the ministry. But much resulted from the fact that, given the conditions, the officials felt they had no other choice. The study focuses on bureaucratic entities containing human actors with policy goals, and not on men consciously manipulating institutions for capricious personal reasons.

moved quickly to create an informational capacity superior to MINVU's; CORMU and CORHABIT strove to embellish their reputations in the community-at-large; and CORVI and CORMU used political means to consolidate their finances. These strategies reveal different facets of the tendency of organizations to aggrandize their power base. Their effect on MINVU was nearly devastating, and led to a wide confusion of roles within the monitoring agency. As a result, three of its four main divisions headed down paths of least resistance in defining their activities, paying informal homage to the hegemony of the corporations, to the detriment of sectoral coordination.

This chapter presents this wealth of material in a way that stresses the relationships between organizational power and coordination. First, some of the working assumptions of the ministry's founders were at the heart of weaknesses in the organizational design. Second, conventional wisdom suggests three theories for the breakdown of the original system—the most satisfactory one being that overwhelming resource advantages allowed the corporations to increase their autonomy in the ministry and the sector. Finally, MINVU responded to the power imbalance in several ways, including avoidance, withdrawal, goal displacement, and counter-attack. The concluding discussion on organizational rationality and coordination links the Chilean data with current administrative theory.

FUNCTIONAL SPECIFICITY

The ministry's founders, while still engaged in the institutional reform described in the previous chapter, were also designing an organization to centralize government activity in the housing sector. They wanted to reduce demand overload on the old Housing Corporation and eliminate all confusion over priorities within each administrative unit. Their answer was functional specificity, whereby each agency concentrated on just one type of output in a linear housing process.

By this working concept, they divided the functions of the old CORVI among a number of agencies and corporations inside the new ministry. Before these changes, CORVI had separate departments for acquisition of land sites; sewer and water works; project development; housing construction; assignment of completed houses; collection of home-owners' loans; and planning, programming, and budgeting. These tasks were distributed among the Urban Renewal Corporation (CORMU); the General Urban Works agency (later called COU); CORVI, a new rendition of the old Housing Corporation; the Corporation for Housing Services (CORHABIT); and the General Planning and Budgeting agency.

CORMU assumed the function of acquisition, and was given special powers for the expropriation of private property.[7] Its immediate job was to purchase or expropriate lands for CORVI housing developments on the periphery of urban areas. As its full name implies, CORMU was also given the task of urban renewal, through contracts with municipalities, private consortiums, and regional development committees. Though this was a new undertaking not previously handled by CORVI, the original concept of functional specificity was not broken, since CORMU would *not* deal in contracting. After it had taken possession of the land and outlined the renewal project, other public and private institutions would be responsible for excavation and reconstruction.

The General Urban Works agency was originally intended to install sewers and water lines, before CORVI began to construct the houses. Previously CORVI had contracted pavement, water, and sewage facilities through its Costs department. The founders hoped that Urban Works would also contain Sanitary Works and the Architecture agency from the ministry of Public Works, as well as the Electric and Gas Service agency from the ministry of Interior. The previous chapter discussed in some detail why this ambition was not realized, and sewer and water works remained inside CORVI.

After the land had been urbanized, CORVI would build the houses. CORVI—stripped of most of its previous functions—would project basic housing design and accept bids for their construction.[8] Subsequently, CORHABIT would carry out the old CORVI tasks of housing assignment and loan collection, as well as finance home construction for neighborhood cooperatives.[9] By combining the old F.V.A.S. (Housing and Social Assistance Foundation) with CORHABIT, the enlarged unit was also given a responsibility not emphasized by CORVI—that of social assistance to poorer families. Finally, the Planning and Budgeting agency would coordinate the different activities of the ministry.

AUTONOMOUS STATUS

Once the ministry's founders had decided on the functions of the various institutions, they were concerned about making the system operative. They wanted the organization to be characterized by "administrative agility" and not bog down in debilitating bureaucratic detail. The solution was to liberate many of its divisions from the central administra-

---

[7] The original law creating MINVU, No. 16,391 (1965), gave powers to the president to establish each of the corporations within certain guidelines. CORMU was created by Decree No. 483 (Aug. 25, 1966).

[8] Decree No. 508 (Sept. 26, 1966).

[9] Decree No. 485 (Sept. 15, 1966).

tive structure by making them autonomous agencies or state enterprises. The founders' prejudices against the centralized structure were based on several considerations. First, the central budget had to be approved by Congress, which had the right to determine how many houses of what quality would be built in each area of the country, and the ministry's founders feared that the legislators would use the housing budget to serve their own clienteles. Second, the General Comptroller's office required the centralized agencies to submit to pre-audits for all payments, in both current and capital accounts, which slowed the pace of work and prevented rapid execution of decisions.[10] Third, personnel policy was highly circumscribed in the centralized agencies where public employees were governed by the extremely protective Administrative Statute (*Estatuto Administrativo*), with its tendencies to limit upward mobility for qualified persons, to lower initiative by requiring similar salary scales for equal grades, and to prevent firing. For an agency to increase or decrease its number of personnel entailed a long-drawn-out process, since the staff organization (*planta*) could be changed only by law.

The founders chose autonomous status for the executing agencies because they believed that the housing sector needed institutions that could respond very quickly to changes in their task environments. Congress reviewed only the global amounts of central subsidy allocated to the agencies. The president, or the minister in the sector, approved the allocations to the different programs. The General Comptroller's office performed only a post-audit on the expenditures of the agency, which freed it from several days' delay each time it made a financial transaction.[11] Finally, the workers in the decentralized agencies were usually regulated by the Labor Code (*Código de Trabajo*) which also applied to the private sector. The decentralized agency could change the number of persons in its *planta* each year, with only the approval of the minister of Finance. This proviso greatly aided the agencies in reconciling their human resources with changing institutional requirements.

[10] The general rule was that *all* decrees, vouchers, and resolutions of *centralized* agencies must be sent to the General Comptroller, but only the *most important* of these from decentralized agencies. The General Comptroller's office could take up to thirty days to pass on these decisions.

[11] Nonetheless, many financial transactions had to be approved by the General Comptroller's office, because contract bids and modifications were not exempt. The Comptroller's office passed on some 9,000 decrees and resolutions from the housing sector each year. The founders of MINVU were so concerned about this procedure that they convinced the Comptroller's office to include the housing agencies in a special section with Public Works for more individualized attention, and reduce the maximum period from thirty to fifteen days, and five days on special request. Also, in cases of extreme urgency (e.g., signing a large materials contract for disaster victims), MINVU could proceed without consulting beforehand. "Extreme urgency" was defined in the ministry, not the Comptroller's office.

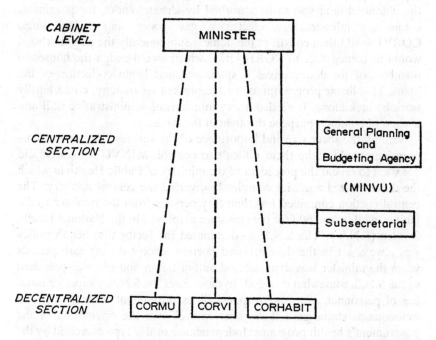

FIGURE 17. AN EARLY CONCEPTION OF MINVU'S ORGANIZATIONAL CHART, 1964–1965

A partial organizational chart of the ministry is presented in Figure 17. CORMU, CORVI, and CORHABIT were made decentralized state enterprises, associated with the government through the minister of Housing and Urbanism. The vice-presidents (chiefs of *decentralized* agencies are called *vice-presidents* in Chile; heads of *centralized* agencies are *general directors*) were appointed by the president of the country. The Planning and Budgeting agency and the Subsecretariat, which dealt in legal and administrative matters, were located in the centralized portion directly under the authority of the minister. This centralized section of the ministry came to be known as MINVU, an acronym for the *Ministerio de Vivienda y Urbanismo*. The Technical Secretariat for Coordination (later eliminated) and the General Urban Works agency (later made into a state corporation, COU) were also located in MINVU. In addition, the decentralized sector included the Central Savings and Loan Fund (CCAP) and the various water companies mentioned in the previous chapter. The discussion here will be restricted to MINVU, CORMU, CORVI, and CORHABIT.

The founders were conscious of two potential difficulties in their conception of the ministry. First, the sector's productivity was handled sequentially—the outputs of one unit were the basic inputs of the next. To begin the process, CORMU bought or expropriated the land. Originally the untreated land was to be absorbed by Urban Works, for pavement, community infrastructure, electricity, gas, water, and sewage lines. CORVI would then construct the homes. Subsequently the neighborhood would be turned over to CORHABIT, which would assign the houses to members of the cooperatives it sponsored and begin collection of the loans. This linear programming, or long-linked technology, could hardly work by luck alone. It needed heavy infusions of administrative skill and a sense of common purpose throughout the ministry.

Second, the sheer size and importance of the various autonomous corporations could make them difficult to control. MINVU's founders did not want to repeat the precedent of the ministry of Public Health in which the decentralized agencies completely dwarfed the central ministry. The central portion contained less than fifty persons from the minister to the janitor, while some 60,000 persons were employed in the National Health Service (S.N.S.). The S.N.S. so dominated the sector that health policy was always set in the decentralized portion, except during rare periods when the minister was dynamic and authoritarian and the vice-president of the S.N.S. somewhat of a dud. In most cases the S.N.S.'s superior number of personnel, extensive responsibilities throughout the country, and autonomous status gave it *de facto* control over the orientation of the government's health programs. Independence of this type exercised by the different corporations in the future MINVU would have had disastrous results, since each organization was so highly dependent on the others to carry out its functions.[12]

To prevent this, MINVU's founders placed a tremendous amout of responsibility in the offices of the Planning and Budgeting agency. Its central functions were to advise on policy, formulate the annual program, and coordinate the output of each corporation during execution. This arrangement can be visualized in Figure 18, which describes the functions of the planning units.[13] Housing planning would integrate the activities of CORMU and CORVI, principally to assure that CORMU supplied CORVI with sufficient land several months before CORVI was ready to begin construction. Urban Development's principal responsibilities were to establish urban policy and raise the general viability of the Chilean municipalities. It would also assess the impact of CORMU,

[12] Richard Fenno might have called the ministry of Public Health and MINVU, as it ultimately emerged, "holding company" types of departments, and predicted their difficulties. See Fenno, *The President's Cabinet.*

[13] In Spanish, these are the Direcciones del Desarrollo Urbano, de Planificación Habitacional, de Planificación de Equipamiento Comunitario, and de Finanzas.

CORVI, and Urban Works' organizational output on urban settlement patterns, and coordinate the annual housing plan with general urban policy. Community Development Facilities would inform Urban Works of each neighborhood's needs in public buildings and urban services, based on the size and location of the CORVI project and CORHABIT's assessment of the social development of the community. Finally, Finances would supervise the income and expenditure schedules of all the agencies, to keep them in line with the respective emphases in housing policy and the dictates of the Annual Operating Plan.

In this manner MINVU's founders hoped to cure every ill in the past experience of CORVI, add new activities such as urban renewal and social assistance, and indicate precise roles for the different agencies in the ministry. They founded the organization on a series of modern assumptions: a comprehensive definition of housing, functional specificity, autonomous administrative status, and integral sectoral planning. Any inherent inconsistencies in the organizational design would be corrected by the prestige of the minister and the technical qualifications of the planning body which would enforce the exclusive functions of the corporations and their sequential programming.[14]

THE BREAKDOWN OF THE ORIGINAL SYSTEM

The system devised by MINVU's founders was extremely innovative. The immediate question is: Did it work? The answer is: No, the overall arrangement did not operate as intended for more than a few months after it was set up. The officials who took over the various executive positions were unable to uphold the ideals implicit in its creation, principally because of certain structural weaknesses that may already be obvious to the reader. There were many more inducements and pressures to abandon the original scheme than to stick to it. With the specificity of functions, a strong control over the actions of the corporations was mandatory. The efforts of the Planning and Budgeting agency to coordinate were largely ineffectual, which led to reduced integration of tasks at the boundaries of the organizations. Increased contingencies for the corporations encouraged an expansion of functions, of which the most dramatic was a ubiquitous mania for construction. CORMU began to build its own living units. CORHABIT started to assemble homes

[14] Some of these functions are outlined in MINVU, *El Ministerio de la Vivienda y Urbanismo: Instrumento de la Política Habitacional* and, Gustavo Reyes y Adriana Kohán F., *Política Habitacional y el Ministerio de la Vivienda y Urbanismo.* For earlier housing practices, see Luís Bravo H., *Chile: El Problema de la Vivienda a través de su Legislación, 1906–1959*, summarized in Burke, "Law and Development."

FIGURE 18. ORGANIZATION AND MONITORING FUNCTIONS OF THE
GENERAL PLANNING AND BUDGETING AGENCY, MINVU

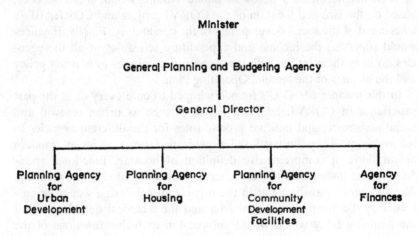

A. ORGANIZATION

Minister

General Planning and Budgeting Agency

General Director

Planning Agency for Urban Development   Planning Agency for Housing   Planning Agency for Community Development Facilities   Agency for Finances

B. MONITORING FUNCTIONS

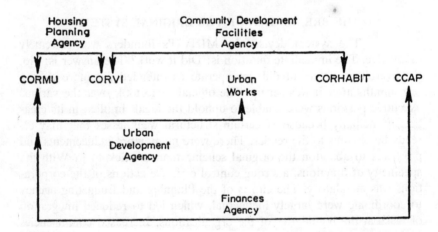

Housing Planning Agency   Community Development Facilities Agency

CORMU   CORVI   Urban Works   CORHABIT   CCAP

Urban Development Agency

Finances Agency

at a rapid rate. Even within MINVU, one of the planning agencies, Community Development Facilities, began constructing schools, medical facilities, and recreation areas by direct bid.[15] It seemed that the only

[15] Here the comment in footnote 6 bears repeating. Community Development Facilities officially protested against having to exceed its functions before actually undertaking construction activities.

group not engaged in construction tasks were the lawyers in the Subsecretariat.

CORMU displaced its interest from land purchases to grandiose urban renewal projects. The most important of these were the San Borja complex and the Santa Lucía underpass. San Borja is a series of tall apartment houses practically in the center of Santiago, soaring above older buildings in its midst.[16] The Santa Lucía project is a major underpass for the city's main boulevard, the Alameda Bernardo O'Higgins, which was needed in order to ease traffic congestion in the immediate vicinity of San Borja. Not satisfied merely with designing these undertakings, CORMU called for bids and began constructing them. It financed the San Borja towers in part with down payments from their future occupants. In the end, CORMU was involved in projecting urban renewal, constructing living units, and apartment sales. According to the intentions of the ministry's founders, the first part of this process definitely belonged to CORMU—but the second part belonged to CORVI, and the third to CORHABIT.

Of all the agencies, the Housing Corporation, CORVI, stayed most within the bounds of its original functions, designing and constructing houses and apartments. But because CORMU became engrossed in San Borja, CORVI could no longer count on it to provide sufficient stocks of land for its new neighborhoods. As a result, CORVI had to assume the task of buying land for itself.

The Corporation for Housing Services, CORHABIT, did not concentrate exclusively on financial and social services. Instead, it entered a whole range of activities including construction, land purchase, and the sponsorship of local factories producing housing materials. It claimed that CORVI was ineffective and could not provide houses quickly enough for CORHABIT's poorer clients. Consequently, it gave major emphasis to a widespread program whereby *pobladors* (urban residents with modest incomes) would build their own homes under CORHABIT supervision. When this program also proceeded at too slow a pace for CORHABIT's liking, it began to ask for bids for prefabricated housing materials. From there it was a small step to setting up factories in the poorer urban areas of the country, in part to avoid paying retail prices for the prefabs.[17] CORHABIT also began buying land for its projects, since neither CORMU nor CORVI gave its needs sufficient priority. Eventually, CORHABIT was participating in all the housing services,

[16] For pictures and layout, see "Remodelación San Borja," *AUCA*, N. 16.
[17] See *CORHABIT, Operación 20,000/70.*

with very little reliance on its partners nor regard for the original spirit of the housing laws.

Since all three institutions were building, the sequence of the original scheme was broken and internal competition tended to disrupt administrative coordination. The difficulty in purchasing land was one outcome. There were also deficiencies in effective integration of housing supply and demand; the timely provision of materials and services; even distribution of tasks among ministry personnel; and rational allocation of financial resources among institutions with similar functions.

In a number of cases, CORVI built large houses while CORHABIT was collecting payments for much smaller units. The families who signed up and deposited money with CORHABIT had no homes when CORVI finished construction, since the amount they had paid was insufficient to qualify for the larger houses. CORHABIT often ended up with a surplus of materials, such as windows, from one of its projects. CORVI might have a housing complex in the same region which was completed except for windows. With no communication between the two corporations, the CORHABIT windows rotted in the open while CORVI waited several months for new windows to be ordered from Santiago. Each corporation inspected its own construction. Yet teams from both CORVI and CORHABIT would pass in and out of the same locale, when one team could have completed the whole job in each province. It cost CORMU much time and money to train the technical crews needed to supervise construction of the San Borja and Santa Lucía projects. CORMU created these teams from scratch, despite qualified underutilized personnel in CORVI.

At budget-making time, each corporation attempted to obtain as much money as possible by emphasizing the cost advantages of its approach compared to the others. CORHABIT pointed out that its budget should increase because it could build houses much more cheaply than either CORMU or CORVI. If CORVI's least expensive house started at about 56 thousand escudos, CORHABIT could produce them for 20 thousand escudos. Using prefabricated products from its own shops, the cost could be reduced even more, to about 10 thousand escudos. CORVI, as defender of the more orthodox approach, felt that its vast experience in the sector justified giving added impetus to its programs. Its homes were solidly built and completely urbanized, and formed part of well-integrated communities.

CORMU insisted that CORVI and CORHABIT were obsessed with a *"viviendista"* orientation toward living units—building houses side by side until they covered the whole national territory. It claimed that the housing patterns in greater Santiago had been too extensive, resulting in a city with an area larger than Paris but only about half the population.[18] As an alternative, CORMU suggested an *"urbanista"* approach, with emphasis on high urban density through more vertical expansion.[19] CORMU felt that the "viviendistas," in pushing for a house that cost 10 thousand escudos, ignored that sooner or later another 20 thousand escudos would have to be spent on maintenance and urban services. With 30 thousand escudos, CORMU promised a highrise unit that would last twenty-five years.

It was not the responsibility of the corporations to integrate their own activities, but of MINVU to enforce that coordination. Officially, CORVI did not depend directly on CORMU for land; it was MINVU's job to take that land from CORMU and turn it over to CORVI for its projects. Likewise, it was not necessarily incumbent on CORHABIT to accept a conservative and limited definition of its functions; MINVU had to tell it what it could and could not do. As a supervisory body, MINVU was charged with estimating housing demand and determining levels of public housing, scheduling the utilization of materials and the provision of services by the corporations, dividing tasks evenly among ministry personnel, and indicating the most efficient allocation of financial resources among the corporations. Any disappointments in these facets can be attributed to the failure of MINVU to do its job properly.

REASONS FOR FAILURE IN COORDINATION

The problems faced by MINVU in coordination are not uniquely Chilean nor restricted to social services in general. Bureaucratic forces impeding coordination and structures designed to mitigate them exist in practically all complex organizations. Despite their frequency, surprisingly little academic attention has been dedicated to their analysis. Aaron Wildavsky believes that the concept of coordination has developed almost whimsical connotations.

Coordinate! Coordination is one of the golden words of our time. I cannot offhand think of any way in which the word is used that implies disapproval. Policies should be coordinated; they should not run every whichway. People are supposed to be coordinated; no one wishes his children to be described as uncoordinated. Many of the world's ills are attributed to a lack of coordination in government. Yet . . . there has never been a serious effort to analyze the term. It requires and deserves full attention.[20]

---

[18] Francis Violich provides excellent background material on the Santiago metropolitan area in *Urban Planning in Latin America.*

[19] Speech by Gastón Saint-Jean to the Chamber of Deputies on June 25, 1969.

[20] Naomi Caiden and Aaron Wildavsky, *Planning and Budgeting in Poor Coun-*

Sideline observers and participants in Chilean public bureaucracy have not developed a foolproof theory of coordination. But three generalizations commonly emerge to explain varying degrees of functional integration among organizations. The first observation is that the *personality characteristics* of the different actors in key positions determine whether coordination can be achieved. When energetic personalities with high need-achievement have to cooperate with other agencies, coordination is bound to decline. The second observation suggests that when a planning unit has the job of integrating bureaucratic activities, the level of coordination depends on the quality of the *planning methodology* employed. Many times these methodologies fail to link theory and practice, which leads to artificial norms for action. The third hypothesis is that *political factors* within bureaucracy tend to govern the level of coordination. If the array of political resources available to the coordinators is superior to that of the institutions with complementary output, functional integration is more likely.[21] Though none of these three propositions can stand alone in explaining all the problems of coordination in MINVU, it would appear that the last contains more elements of fact and explains more variance than do the first two.

Personality and Coordination

The personality argument maintains that "good" individuals can work wonders with "bad" structures, while poor administrators will ruin even the best institutional arrangement. Whether the structure is good or bad, coordination is maximized when meek, cautious, and self-

---

tries. Harold Seidman is of similar persuasion: "The quest for coordination is in many respects the twentieth-century equivalent of the medieval search for the philosopher's stone. If only we can find the right formula for coordination, we can reconcile the irreconcilable, harmonize competing and wholly divergent interests, overcome irrationalities in our government structures, and make hard policy choices to which no one will dissent." Seidman, *Politics, Position, and Power: The Dynamics of Federal Organization,* p. 164.

[21] A variation of this theme applies to coalition governments in Chile. When appointees from different political parties are distributed vertically within the public bureaucracy, coordination is more difficult to achieve. To prevent agencies from becoming political party enclaves, posts must be assigned on a horizontal basis, creating a set of cross-cutting cleavages between party and institution. In this way, the degree of coordination among agencies theoretically reverts to a function of variable bureaucratic power. The Allende regime demonstrated, however, that arrangements in which no individual is directly above or below a member of his own party can institutionalize skipped relays and skew "normal" communication pathways between hierarchical levels. Though results were mixed, the Unidad Popular apparently devised an innovative administrative principle to take advantage of this tendency: Assign one party a predominant number of similar functional posts (e.g., appoint Communists as budgeters throughout the bureaucracy) with the aim of increasing data flow and a more global outlook.

deprecating persons are located in key exchange points, and dynamic, strong-willed individuals occupy supervisory posts. The latter can lord over their colleagues and insure that coordination prevails. Here the control mechanism is said to stem from the zeal of the watchdog rather than the objective power he commands. Many of the officials in MINVU felt that personal factors were of overriding importance in explaining the independence of the corporations.

My opinion is that CORHABIT was given a big push to start constructing prefabricated units when the first vice-president was a civil constructor, and the second an architect. Naturally, they were more interested in building housing units than in social or accounting problems.

Most of the reasons for the lack of coordination can be traced to one source: the personality of the vice-president of CORMU. He was an architect, extremely imaginative, creative, and highly qualified professionally. He was a person blessed with a great capacity for achievement and a man who could overcome obstacles. He just went off by himself.

In great measure, the weakness of coordination depended on the personal behavior and the administrative style of the heads of the different organizations. The highest authorities in the ministry, instead of demanding that they stay within their limits, accepted certain initiatives in the corporations' activities which destroyed coordination.

The lack of coordination in MINVU was based on a number of factors, many of them human. If the people in the Planning and Budgeting agency had had a clearer vision of things, the result might have been different. Generally they were young, idealistic, and had little political experience. They were too good-natured. There wasn't a cunning instinct among them.

You have to work with the people you have. If the personnel in the Subsecretariat are strong and dynamic, and get things done, you are going to give them the role of coordination. If those in the Planning and Budgeting agency are technicians without the right personality, they are not going to be as valuable.

Once MINVU succeeded in changing three of the four vice-presidents, coordination improved considerably.[22]

The personality characteristics of the main actors did seem to be related in some way to the level of functional integration within the sector, yet it is open to question whether this factor played as large a role as indicated by these comments. The lack of coordination within the sector did not reach its apex with the appointment of the vice-presidents of the corporations and the general director of the Planning and Budgeting agency. It developed gradually over a period of time and was accom-

[22] Interview material.

panied by almost imperceptible moves by the corporations to protect their borders and increase their operating capacity. As they became more autonomous, MINVU was less able to monitor their activities, and the level of coordination declined. It may be true that coordination improved with the change of the heads of CORMU, CORHABIT, and CORVI in 1969. But these turnovers were the outcome of bureaucratic maneuvering by MINVU with the precise intention of better regulating the sector's output. If MINVU had not attempted to change the balance of power, the vice-presidents would not have resigned and no new personalities would have appeared on the scene.

The personality argument is given some substance by the fact that MINVU's counterattack was spearheaded by energetic and daring individuals. These persons, located in the Subsecretariat, tended to replace the officials in the Planning and Budgeting agency as the ministry's main coordinators. It is doubtful, however, whether the relative success of the subsecretary, contrasted with the relative failure of the personnel in the Planning and Budgeting agency, can be attributed solely to the personalities of the men involved. The period from 1966 to 1969, which saw Planning and Budgeting lose hold of the organization, also marked the incumbency of Juan Hamilton, an up-and-coming young politician with senatorial aspirations. Hamilton gave very little overt support to the Planning agency in its attempts to coordinate. He apparently found it politically advantageous to strike individual agreements with the vice-presidents of the corporations, allowing them to function more or less at will within a self-defined sphere of action. These informal coalitions between the minister and the corporations were much too powerful for the planners to combat. Perhaps not unexpectedly, they became a bit disheartened and looked to other, noncoordinating activities to keep themselves occupied. Later, when the subsecretary took the initiative, he had the full support of Hamilton's successor and the indirect backing of the president of the country. This time the alignment of forces was too much for the vice-presidents, three of whom resigned. The tipping of the balance in MINVU's favor tended to change the outlook of all parties involved, and the corporations felt more obliged to conform their activities to MINVU's policy directives.

Planning and Coordination

The question of political backing was also closely related to the second piece of conventional wisdom: In institutions divided between *planning* units and *action* units, the twain will rarely meet. The unstable nature of the latters' task environment often places a premium on expediency, reducing the role of the former and necessarily upsetting coordination. While the housing corporations felt that they were politically responsible for carrying out policy, the Planning and Budgeting agency worked at a higher level, away from the public eye. The corporations argued that the irrelevance of planning concepts to real problems forced them to proceed according to their own criteria. Some officials in the ministry felt that this division between planning and execution provided basic reasons for the lack of coordination.

The situation was that you had a theoretical planning process on one hand, and the responsibility to perform on the other.

The novel concept of central planning and programming, and corporation execution, was not absorbed by the corporations until the very end.

For the minister and vice-presidents, urban development theory and integral national planning were very vague and abstract. Now housing *construction, that* was something they could understand.

The urgency of certain problems, such as the land invasions, the demonstrations of pobladors without homes, floods, earthquakes, and droughts, did not leave time for the functioning of an elaborate planning system. Even if the corporations had wanted to wait and consult with MINVU, they couldn't do it. They had to work as best they could.

A major difficulty in coordination stemmed from the fact that there just was not enough time for reception of the information, formulation of a policy response, and projection of construction—and the long route that this process entailed from the corporation up to MINVU and back again to the corporation. It was a case of a doctor treating a cold, when suddenly there is a serious attack to the liver. Naturally the cold is forgotten in favor of immediate attention to the liver.

This incapacity of MINVU was a failure in the concept of planning they used. They were too rigid, and didn't provide sufficient flexibility to mold the plans and programs to new situations. Planning must be a dynamic process.[23]

The methodology of the Planning and Budgeting agency began with indicators from the National Planning Office (ODEPLAN). After reviewing the national accounts over the previous decade, ODEPLAN predicted the probable gross national product for the coming year by multiple regression analysis. To improve this figure, it assigned a tentative investment goal for each sector of the economy in twelve zones of the country. Those figures were sent to the different ministries and state industries for review. The ministerial planning offices calculated the level of production that they believed the sector could achieve, given probable

[23] Interview material.

fiscal subsidy and the known levels of independent income. They also determined what changes would have to occur to reach the levels of production indicated by ODEPLAN. These estimates were then sent back to the central planning office, where specialists estimated whether it was possible to achieve the desired levels of national growth without creating distortions in the economy.

MINVU worked with ODEPLAN through the sectoral housing office at the central level. Eventually this office informed the Planning and Budgeting agency of its definitive investment goal for the year. The last step in the process was to formulate the annual plan. Given the works already in progress and those committed the previous year, the Planning and Budgeting agency assigned a certain number of new works to each zone. Committees from the local areas put together a list of projects by priority. The top priorities in each region were included in the plan until their cost reached the zonal investment ceiling. The local areas were informed which projects they could count on for the year, and the programs were then sent to the corporations for implementation.

Though the corporations may have found this routine technically interesting, quaint, or even admirable, they did *not* feel that it had much relevance for their specific purposes. Their emphasis was on actual performance and production, not the execution of a preliminary list of projects that had some abstract link with the gross national product. For them, national interest was defined in terms of providing massive housing solutions at a rapid pace. While others may have been planning, their job was to execute.

Coordination might have improved if MINVU had changed its methodology to correspond more to the wishes of the corporations. But most evidence points to the fact that it was not the methodology that bothered the corporations, but the very existence of MINVU itself. When the corporations asked for more flexibility in the plan, they were in essence requesting that MINVU give them a completely free hand to do as they deemed necessary. When they complained that the urgency of problems left no time to consult with the planning unit, they felt that MINVU could only complicate their jobs. By claiming full responsibility for the actions of their organizations, they suggested that the less contact with MINVU, the better. The corporations resented any obstacles to their independence, and MINVU was one of the most troublesome.

Politics and Coordination

MINVU officials admitted they had not learned everything about producing an annual plan that was technically perfect and realistically in line with the corporations' executing abilities. But they were also confident that their approach was superior to other programming efforts in the Chilean public sector, and to the *ad hoc* methods commonly used in the corporations. Though the annual plan may have contained some flaws, MINVU did not consider that the results of its labors deserved such summary treatment at the hands of the corporations, whose officials often belittled it as a bad joke. If the plan was impractical in some respects, it was because MINVU had faulty or insufficient information from the corporations, poor financial control, little knowledge of local land and drainage conditions, no way to oblige the corporations to fulfill preconditions of the plan (e.g., buy land), and restricted ability to keep a step ahead of program revision. These problems stemmed *less* from the methodology they used, and *more* from the power wielded by the corporations.

MINVU's founders cannot be completely exonerated from responsibility for this predicament. They apparently neglected to distribute resources within MINVU in any purposeful fashion. They felt that freeing each corporation from the hindrances of the central bureaucracy would give it a certain performance capability in its task environment. But in their organizational design they never contemplated the balance of power within the sector itself. They failed to deal with the question of who was going to control finances. They did not meditate long on the matter of information flow or the consequences of bureaucratic prestige for administrative processes. The system of authority they perpetuated was hardly consistent with their ideal of sequential interdependence among the housing corporations. All of these factors eventually led to disruptions in MINVU's operations, and to greater autonomy for the corporations.

The autonomy exercised by the corporations had to have a political base. The corporations, to perform effectively in their task environment, were given access or potential access to authority, finances, information, and prestige. To improve this performance, they needed to manipulate an even greater array of economic and political resources; i.e., they needed to become more powerful. During much of this period, they pursued goals that consolidated their position by increasing their resource stocks. The less the corporations' influence was counterbalanced by commensurate strengthening of MINVU, the more they were able to ignore the planners with impunity.

THE CORPORATIONS' INITIAL ADVANTAGE

The first and foremost advantage of the corporations was clearly their legal structure, which allowed them to expand their functions within the ministry. The spirit of the original legislation was that each corporation's range of activity would be kept distinct. Unfortunately, the founders did not dedicate enough effort to translating the spirit of the law meticulously into the articles of the actual legislation. Because of the requirements of Chilean public law (or an unfortunate oversight), the corporations' enabling legislation gave each the right to partake in all activities within the ministry. In Chilean private law, the individual or organization can do anything not specifically prohibited by the law. In public law, the situation is reversed. The public official or organization can do only what the law explicitly allows. The founders felt that the regulations for each corporation would have to be written with wide latitude so as not to limit their performance artificially.

CORHABIT needed the power to buy and expropriate land in order to establish commercial centers in poorer neighborhoods. It needed the right to construct, so it could deal in emergency housing after earthquakes or floods. CORVI had to be able to buy, or else it could not renovate, equip, and redesign neighborhoods, which were among its secondary functions. CORMU was given the power to construct and sell, to facilitate its assistance programs with municipalities. All three corporations, CORMU, CORVI, and CORHABIT, were empowered to buy, expropriate, renovate, construct, and sell property. They actually had the law on their side when they wished to expand their prerogatives.

The authority available to MINVU to counter the independence of the corporations was extremely vague. The specific functions of the units in the Planning and Budgeting agency were never delineated.[24] No article in the original laws indicated the precise powers of the general director of that agency. As a matter of fact, the legislation gave the vice-presidents practically the same responsibilities as the general director for integrating the activities of the ministry. The corporations were placed directly under the authority of the minister, which put MINVU in a most untenable position to enforce its directives. It could not legally enjoin the corporations to comply without receiving the formal backing of the minister. But MINVU did not have exclusive access to the minister's attention. The vice-presidents had a good chance of holding sway politically over the technical criteria of the Planning and Budgeting agency, especially since they were appointed directly by the president.

Another decisive advantage of the corporations was their access to independent funds. This income bypassed MINVU and went directly into their bank accounts. In 1967, for example, only 31 percent of the

[24] The enabling legislation setting up the Planning offices did mention their general functions, but these were not elaborated to any degree. See Decree No. 632 (Nov. 25, 1966) and Decree No. 670 (Jan. 13, 1967).

TABLE 12.   SOURCES OF CORPORATION INVESTMENT INCOME IN 1967
(*In percent*)

Source of Income	Institution CORVI	CORHABIT	CORMU	CCAP
1. Central Government	22.9	31.6	56.9	42.8
2. External Credits	—	15.1	—	7.5
3. Transfers from Other Public Institutions	59.7	—	—	—
4. Special Taxes	15.1	—	—	—
5. Savings Quotas	—	10.2	—	—
6. Loan Recuperation	.2	20.1	16.2	11.1
7. Bonds	.5	1.0	—	28.9
8. Excess from the Current Account	(−3.8)	(−10.5)	25.7	9.0
9. Other Income	1.6	22.0	1.2	.7
Total in Millions of Escudos, 1967	*495.5*	*230.9*	*43.7*	*123.9*

SOURCE: Derived from Silvia Rodríguez G., *Análisis del Financiamiento del MINVU*, p. 39.

corporations' financing in the capital account originated from fiscal subsidy. The rest came from transfers from other public institutions (36 percent), recovery of loans (8.2 percent), special taxes (7.9 percent), external credits (4.9 percent), sale of bonds (4.3 percent), and savings quotas and miscellaneous (7.7 percent), all of which was channeled directly to the corporations. Table 12 breaks down the sources of this revenue for the major corporations.[25] CORVI received approximately 60 percent of its capital subsidy, and 50 percent of its total budget, from the excess collections of the Social Security Funds. CORHABIT depended on MINVU officials for only about 30 percent of its investment. Over 40 percent of CORMU's building funds came from outside sources.

MINVU's founders disregarded the fact that without complete control over the release of funds, the Planning and Budgeting agency lacked an important element of influence. Though the correlation is not perfect, the more these funds went directly to the corporations, the less the planning officials could influence how the money would be used. The officials who tried to manage from above, without continual access to

[25] Silvia Rodríguez G., *Análisis del Financiamiento del MINVU*, p. 77. In 1969 these figures changed somewhat. CORVI (28.3 percent) and CORMU (44.7 percent) maintained similar percentages of their income from MINVU. Because of an emphasis on Operation Sitio, CORHABIT's central subsidy rose to 61.3 percent of its total budget. See Octavio Cabello, *Informe sobre Misión de Asistencia Técnica al Ministerio de la Vivienda y Urbanismo de Chile,* p. 8.

the pursestrings, had considerably less say in how the money was spent than those who actually had the checkbook in hand. In addition, an organization such as CORVI might feel more loyalty to the Social Security Funds, which provided almost 60 percent of its investment, than to MINVU, which gave only 23 percent.

The decentralized system designed by MINVU's founders meant that the Planning and Budgeting agency had the right to approve the corporations' total budget once a year. But afterward the corporations could spend the money as they saw fit. Since the ministry's output was determined by the spending patterns at the lower levels of the corporations, it was difficult for MINVU to administer programs through execution of the budget. The corporations could manipulate the pace of work, their payment schedules, and their projects in order to receive maximum utility from their budgets. It mattered little that the corporations' criterion of utility might not coincide with MINVU's. They felt no need to consult with MINVU, because the founders did not make MINVU's authorization necessary to spend the money.

The corporations began with advantages over MINVU in two other areas: information and prestige. The fact that the corporations were implementing policy meant that they were in direct contact with the ministry's task environment. The work site was the most fertile and volatile source of new information. MINVU had to have access to this information in order to judge the nature and level of output and to enforce standard interaction between the corporations. The less these data left the corporations' domain, the more independently they could act.

Similarly, the corporations were engaged in productive activities leading to quite concrete results. Their assigned functions had much more prestige value than the administrative routine of MINVU. CORVI was given the task of building thousands of houses and apartment units; CORMU of buying huge quantities of land and eradicating the blights of urban decay; and CORHABIT of spawning community organizations throughout poorer neighborhoods. The Planning and Budgeting agency was oriented toward nothing more than the creation of a plan. If the various organizations in the sector had operated as originally envisioned, no doubt the Planning unit would have been the system's cerebellum. Nonetheless, the corporations would still have received the accolades and paeans from the community: their productivity was more visible, spectacular, and identifiable than that of MINVU.

MINVU often responded to the corporations' initiatives by accusing them of stepping out of bounds and creating deficits for the sector. The corporations maintained a generally negative attitude toward this kind of commentary. In handling their daily affairs and when coping with emergencies, they preferred to act with complete independence, regardless of the planners' opinion on the subject. To broaden their resource base and increase their autonomy, the corporations did not sit idly by and let their initial power advantage slip away.

CORPORATION ATTEMPTS TO CONSOLIDATE
AUTHORITY

MINVU's principal control mechanism during this period was the weekly staff meeting, held every Wednesday over lunch on the sixth floor of the ministry. These meetings were specifically intended to inform the corporations of current policy guidelines and increase the flow of communication between MINVU and the executing agencies. They brought together the general director, the subsecretary, the heads of the planning units, the minister, and the vice-presidents of all the corporations.

These lunches never served the function of high-level council meetings, nor did they lead to firm decisions on policy-making. Attendance was theoretically obligatory, but MINVU always had difficulty bringing all the major personages together at once. At least one of them was always absent because of travel, illness, or simply because he felt that he had more significant items on his agenda.

Apart from the weekly meetings, MINVU often sent directives to the vice-presidents, or to a middle-level official in the corporation, concerning the implementation of policy; but the corporations were conversant with tactics undermining the efficacy of this procedure. When a vice-president received messages from MINVU which were not consistent with his views, he either disregarded them or passed them downward until they lost their force. When no notable response occurred at the middle levels of the corporation, the general director would call up the relevant official to learn the reasons for the delay. The official could claim quite legitimately that the vice-president had not liked the directive and had told him to postpone its implementation indefinitely. Since MINVU had no authority over the corporations, it had no direct way to redress such lack of cooperation.

When serious discrepancies occurred between what was ordered and what was done, MINVU would complain to the minister. The minister sometimes placated the Planning and Budgeting agency by requesting an explanation from the vice-president. A short report justifying the actions of the corporation generally ended the matter. The minister was seldom in a mood to rebuke the vice-president's behavior.

The precarious authority position of the general director was con-

tinually exploited by the corporations. He might determine that Policy
A was most advisable for the ministry as a whole. After gaining the
minister's acceptance for the measure, he then promulgated it as government policy for the sector. However, a corporation vice-president, without consulting the general director, might announce that Policy A was
unacceptable, and that his organization was going to work with Policy
B. Unless the minister was willing to engage the vice-president in a
head-on battle, which he rarely was, the declaration of the vice-president
prevailed and the general director was tacitly overruled.[26] It was little
wonder that Planning and Budgeting's enthusiasm for issuing authoritative orders to the corporations declined over time.

The vice-presidents increasingly considered themselves the supreme
authority over their own affairs. The minister himself was not immune
to frustration when he tried to gain their attention. Sometimes he would
fully support a MINVU decision, only to wait a year before anything
was done by the corporations. One cabinet official claimed, in an interview, that nearly all his time was spent on the telephone, trying to get
people in the corporations to heed his instructions. Eventually new decrees and laws placed more encumbrances on the corporations' independence and reduced the scope of their authority. To maintain their
autonomy, however, the vice-presidents simply bypassed new, super-
imposed authority links and talked directly with the middle-level officials
in MINVU who had to approve certain of their procedures.

On the whole, the corporations' legal status provided them with convenient mechanisms to escape untoward interference from the control
agency. They used well-known tactics, such as agreeing but not implementing, and disregarding legitimate communication channels. In such
an atmosphere, coordination within the sector did not result from the
weekly meetings over lunch, the stream of memoranda from MINVU, or
even the authoritative word of the minister himself. It depended on the
possible conformity of all the vice-presidents with MINVU and their
voluntary restraints on their corporations' behavior. To the extent that
everyone agreed, coordination occurred. To the extent that some did not,
autonomy predominated and functional integration declined.

Control over Information

Another strategy used by the corporations to achieve greater
autonomy was to improve their access to and control over valuable
information. An important tactic in this strategy was the creation of
their own programming offices. This move reduced their dependency on

---

[26] Interview material.

the Planning and Budgeting agency for designing their yearly programs. It also gave them an informational depository near the base of their operations. This new capacity improved their position in the task environment, but it also facilitated the perpetuation of *faits accomplis* in the execution of the program. These offices transformed the corporations' *potential* advantage in information-gathering to an *operational* reality.

One of the original ideas of the ministry was that the Planning and Budgeting agency would plan the corporations' activities down to the minutest detail. The original law did not include any special mention of programming offices in the corporations, because the founders did not consider them necessary. MINVU would handle all the thinking; the corporations would limit themselves to executing MINVU's program. The corporations soon claimed, however, that MINVU had neither the personnel nor the time to carry out comprehensive cost studies, PERT (Program Education Review Technique) designs, soil assays, drainage measurements, weather conditioning checks, and other shop details. The corporations felt that they needed their own units to imbue MINVU's program with the expertise necessary to make them workable. MINVU officials actually encouraged the idea in the belief that they would have counterparts in the corporations with whom they could use the same technical language.[27]

Over time, however, these offices tended to expand their staffs and areas of concern. Their improved technical skills won respect inside of the corporations, and the vice-presidents insisted on filtering all MINVU projects through their own programming offices before accepting them. The more confidence the sectoral planners gained, the less they wished to exist in the shadow of the Planning and Budgeting agency, and they progressively asked for less guidance from the parent institution.

With the aid of their own programmers, the corporations began to intervene much higher in the planning process. Though MINVU's list of projects was as specific as before, its annual program came to be considered "indicative planning." The programming offices simply picked out those "indicators" most consistent with their own models and neglected the rest. Not unexpectedly, the projects ultimately executed by the corporations were quite different from the annual programs developed in MINVU. If MINVU complained, the corporations could always say that their list was "more feasible." In the end, the programming offices had more influence in setting policy than did MINVU itself.

The importance of these offices in the evolving relations between

---

[27] Only to discover later that, in the words of one participant, they had helped create "Frankenstein monsters."

MINVU and the corporations should not be underestimated. Given its ambiguous authority and deficient financial control, information management was MINVU's most effective weapon to wield influence over the executing organizations. Initially it was almost obligatory for the corporations to carry out MINVU's program, for they had no substitute. When they created their own information-gathering arm, however, the intervention of the Planning and Budgeting agency was no longer necessary. The programming offices could provide an alternative to MINVU's plan, and as this program corresponded much more to the interests of the corporation in reacting to its task environment, it had a much greater chance of being implemented.

The creation of these programming offices meant that the direction of communication between MINVU and the corporations was turned about almost completely. Instead of the corporations' soliciting its advice and orientation, MINVU became involved in a running battle to find out what was going on inside the corporations. MINVU's planners were continually analyzing what the corporations had *already* done, rather than what they were *about* to do. The corporations consulted with their own programming offices before acting, but found a thousand excuses not to keep MINVU abreast.[28] They claimed that six years was a very short time in which to accomplish all their goals. If MINVU were informed of every change in corporation policy, the presidential term would be reduced to two months of effective action. The time-consuming "memorandum routine" resulted in lost reports at critical moments. The useless "meeting routine" meant elliptical discussions on whether projects should be painted black, red, or striped. If the corporations did not act quickly, money would lie dormant, practiced construction crews in the private sector would be disbanded, catastrophe victims would go unsheltered, pobladors would invade land, and houses just would not be built. The corporations preferred to make a hundred mistakes in terms of sectoral coordination rather than be tied up in purposeless entanglements with MINVU.

The concentration of information in the corporations, and their unwillingness to share decision-making with MINVU, meant that *faits accomplis* became quite frequent. The corporations completed early

---

[28] In the case of CORHABIT, many officials did not even consult the programming office before acting. The CORVI programming office, in the second year of the Allende regime, further loosened its ties with MINVU by establishing a time-sharing arrangement with COMECON, the government's central computer facility. CORVI officials advised the Housing Planning office that MINVU's computer was too small to handle the complicated programs it needed to implement the annual operating plan.

stages of a project in relative obscurity, not to reveal the full implications until a point after which it could not very well be stopped. The losses incurred by eliminating it would be greater than the net benefits gained from substituting some other project more consistent with the sector's policies. Such was true of San Borja.

During the year, CORMU, CORHABIT, and CORVI frequently asked MINVU to provide funding for items they had failed to include in the original programs. CORMU would sign a contract to purchase a tract of land, would take possession of it, begin excavating it, and then ask MINVU for the money to pay for it. CORHABIT would under-estimate housing demand in certain locales, but not close family enroll-ments until they several times surpassed the allocated funds. CORVI would incur extensive cost overruns in leveling land, digging foundations, or providing urban services, but not inform MINVU until its budget was totally assigned. In all these cases, the "forgotten" commitments of the corporations opened up Pandora's box for MINVU. The corporations always apologized for the oversight, but the seriousness of the situation usually meant that MINVU had no alternative but to play along, put aside the original program, and attempt to subsidize the corporations' deficit as best it could.

Glorification Moves

The corporations also attempted to improve their power posi-tions by raising their prestige, i.e., associating their names with major accomplishments widely heralded in the community-at-large. It was partially for prestige reasons that CORHABIT and CORMU deempha-sized their original functions and moved into construction. These more visible endeavors tended to be highly satisfying to their self-esteem. They also contributed to the sector's output in a way that added to the good reputation of the Housing minister and to the luster of the government party. The minister, the party, and the president were not blind to the fact that their political future depended in great part on the image of their regime in the eyes of the voters. Accordingly, they upheld those corporations whose operations were most supportive of this image. In turn, the backing of these political actors was quite helpful to the corporations in bureaucratic politicking. For one thing, it enabled them to resist unwanted interference from MINVU.

The corporations felt that it was much more impressive to boast "We constructed these buildings" than to say "We bought land for these buildings" or "We gave loans for them." Construction was considered a real accomplishment; the latter, merely necessary steps. CORMU should

not have built San Borja; it should have expropriated the land and designed the buildings and turned the project over to CORVI. In principle,
CORHABIT should not have been building prefabs, but providing
services and credit. However, to justify their existence both neglected
their initial functions and became involved in more noteworthy undertakings. The two losers were CORVI and MINVU. CORVI lost its
monopoly over construction and had trouble getting land from CORMU;
MINVU had to contend with two brand-new corporations that soon had
considerable status in the political community.

With the San Borja project, CORMU was motivated to gain a name
for itself and give rise to a favorable culture for urban renewal in Chile.
It felt that it could not achieve these goals without leaving an indelible
trademark on the Santiago skyline. By means of the project, CORMU
wanted to dethrone the reigning conception that urban renewal consisted
of nothing more than tearing down a decrepit apartment house and
erecting a seven-story office building in its place. It did recognize that
there were serious arguments against placing San Borja next to the
Catholic University on the Alameda. Apartment costs would be high,
a hospital would have to be moved, and in reality no buildings in the
vicinity warranted condemnation. Population shifts and very poor residential conditions in much older areas of Santiago should have suggested any one of a number of alternative locations for the project. But
CORMU refused to tuck San Borja away in a forgotten marginal section
of the city where it would not have earned a second glance. For urban
renewal to make headway, CORMU felt it was imperative to design an
outstanding project for the middle of town. On the Alameda, twenty
times more vehicles would pass San Borja than in any other section of the
city. The public would not have to imagine what urban renewal was
like; they would be able to see it in front of their eyes. The sheer size of
the project would guarantee a permanent association in people's minds
between CORMU and comprehensive urban planning.

Once CORMU finished the designs for the twenty-four towers and expropriated the lots, it suddenly became very reluctant to turn San Borja
over to CORVI for execution. It wondered whether San Borja would
receive any priority over CORVI's single-family dwellings. It pointed out
that San Borja entailed construction problems never before confronted
by a Chilean housing organization; CORVI, comparing these difficulties
with its antiquated techniques, would find innumerable reasons not to
proceed. In addition, Urban Renewal officials expressed misgivings about
CORVI's administrative capacity. CORMU, with a staff only a fraction
the size of CORVI's, felt that CORVI was "ossified," or heavily encrusted with bureaucratic lethargy and inefficiency. CORMU feared that

San Borja would die before inception, a victim of CORVI red tape and incompetence.[29]

Part of CORMU's insistence on constructing San Borja was based on its jealousy of CORVI's receiving any credit for the accomplishment. The San Borja affair began a rivalry between CORMU and CORVI for status in the housing sector.[30] The Housing Corporation was upset that CORMU had begun to build, ignoring its rightful role in the process, and sent a letter to the minister of Housing complaining that the intention of MINVU's founders was being vitiated. The architects in CORVI felt that CORMU was trying to corner all the projects of major technical challenge and leave them the duty of meeting the bulk of the housing demand with ticky-tacky houses in monotonous rows. In private, some CORVI officials stated that the enthusiasm of CORMU's vice-president had gone too far; it was pretentious of him to exaggerate the importance of San Borja. By the end of this period, CORVI expressed pride that it had built towers similar to those of San Borja in the project Los Militares, but more quickly and less expensively. In turn, CORMU tried to develop a reputation of outperforming the older institution in several areas: apartments at a lower price, shorter time for construction, and releasing units to owners more quickly. As for Los Militares, CORMU retorted that if CORVI put the buildings up more quickly, it was only because CORVI did not have to design the original blueprints; if more cheaply, it was because CORVI left out air conditioning and a central hot water system! [31]

The prestige value of San Borja proved to be a political boon for CORMU. The head of CORMU introduced the project to President Frei by saying he could offer the country a masterpiece that interested CORMU from the urbanist point of view, and would surely interest the president and his party from the political point of view. Frei apparently recognized San Borja's potential political impact, and his intuition

[29] The decision on who was going to build San Borja went to the highest levels of government. CORMU's vice-president, Gastón Saint-Jean, eventually succeeded in convincing both the minister of Housing and the president that San Borja would never be completed if given to CORVI.

[30] "This very looseness around the joints . . . made public service attractive to men of a certain boldness and imagination. It also spurred them on to better achievement. How to tell which man, which approach was better? One answer was to let them fight it out. This solution might cause waste but would guarantee against stagnation." Arthur M. Schlesinger, Jr., *The Coming of the New Deal*, p. 535.

[31] However, the CORVI units were occupied much more rapidly than San Borja. Because of technical difficulties with the electrical system and elevators, and political indecision after the Allende regime took office, the San Borja towers still sat empty three years after their construction.

proved correct when the Communist and Socialist parties later complained that the Christian Democrats had initiated urban renewal on the fringe of the northern part of the city, where national economic and political power was most concentrated. Frei gave CORMU his verbal backing on San Borja, as well as on the Santa Lucía underpass.

This support naturally altered the relations between MINVU and CORMU. Officials in the Planning and Budgeting agency felt that urban renewal should have started in another part of Santiago where the need was more urgent. They were also distressed that CORMU was creating a new high-rent district on the Alameda, which would be considerably beyond the economic means of those families with the most desperate need for new houses. MINVU wanted CORMU to renew properties that would serve primarily lower-middle-income groups, and concentrate on areas such as Plaza Chacabuco, Barrio Cívico, Mapocho, and Santiago Poniente.

Practically every Wednesday at lunch, personnel from MINVU asked CORMU's representative when it was going to get started on the other projects. CORMU continually requested a postponement, at least until it could put San Borja behind it. Because of the political prestige of San Borja, the minister tended to go along with CORMU just so long as it promised that the other projects would not be completely forgotten. But they *were* forgotten, as were most of MINVU's directives sent to the organization. It was no secret that the opinion of the Planning and Budgeting agency meant very little compared to the support given CORMU by the president and many other elements of the Christian Democratic party.

CORPORATION ATTEMPTS TO RESIST FUND TRANSFER

MINVU's founders wanted each corporation to have a certain percentage of guaranteed income so that it could face its difficult task environment with a relatively secure economic base. Because of legal restraints and organizational pride, the corporations' independent funding could not easily be shifted to other entities or even other program areas. It was MINVU's unenviable task to try to transfer the corporations' finances to bring them in line with housing policy.

Operation Sitio and the Social Security Funds

By the second year of government, when the officials in MINVU realized that they would never be able to keep Frei's campaign promise of building 360 thousand houses in six years, they reviewed the corporations' budgets to determine whether a more productive allocation could be devised to meet the changing conditions. They were attracted to a program called *Operación Sitio* (Operation Homesite) as a partial answer to the ministry's resource scarcity and the growing insistence of popular elements on government action in urban areas.[32] The basic unit of supply in Operation Sitio was not a completed house, but simply an urbanized plot of land. The government surveyed the land, lay down boundaries, marked off dirt roads, and installed minimal electrical, sewage, and water facilities. The family occupied the plot and built its own home, either through a CORHABIT cooperative or self-construction program. Shelter and urban services were then improved, as the government and the family, through its own savings, could afford them.

Though buying land and urbanizing it was much cheaper than putting together comprehensive housing projects, there was not sufficient margin in the budgets of either CORMU or CORHABIT to underwrite the program. CORVI had the largest budget in the ministry, but the structure of its income made it difficult to free money from special accounts, as 50 percent of CORVI's income came from surpluses in the operations of the eight largest Social Security Funds in Chile.[33] In theory, CORVI was supposed to return housing units to the Funds in exchange for this subsidy. MINVU, however, was convinced that this money was badly invested in terms of general housing policy. While the Funds generally wanted houses of middle- and upper-middle-class quality, the Planning and Budgeting agency felt that the country's housing deficit was greatest among families with more modest incomes.

The planners were very interested in using some of these Social Security Fund surpluses for Operation Sitio. Since all CORVI expenses came basically out of the same account, MINVU claimed that no one would ever be able to prove that the money coming from the Funds was being used indirectly in the homesite program. The Funds, however, immediately protested that CORVI had never built all the houses it owed them and insisted that it repay these debts before em-

[32] See Antonio Labadía C., "*Operación Sitio:* A Housing Solution for Progressive Growth." The end of this article contains passing reference to the "viviendista–urbanista" dispute inside of MINVU.

[33] The pertinent Social Security Funds were the Cajas de Previsión de Empleados Particulares (EMPART), Nacional de Empleados Públicos y Periodistas (CANAEMPU), de Retiro y Previsión Social de los Ferrocarriles del Estado (CAPREFERRO), de Retiros y Previsión Social de los Empleados y Obreros Municipales de la República (CAPREMU and CAPRESOMU), de Previsión de Carabineros de Chile (CAPRECA), de Previsión de la Defensa Nacional (CAPREDENA), and de Previsión de la Marina Mercante (CAPREMER), and the Servicio de Seguro Social (S.S.S.). After deducting their operating costs and pension payments, excesses were sent to CORVI. See Jorge Iván Tapia-Videla, *Bureaucratic Power in a Developing Country: The Case of the Chilean Social Security Administration*.

barking on any new adventures. Initially, CORVI expressed interest in the goals of Operation Sitio but asserted that it did not want to do anything obviously illegal.

To counter these legal restrictions, officials in MINVU developed a special interpretation of CORVI's obligation to the Funds which they hoped would free some of this money for Operation Sitio. MINVU argued that the crucial question was whether CORVI owed houses to the Funds, or whether the Funds owed money to CORVI. If all of CORVI's subsidies were compared to the houses they returned directly to the Funds, CORVI most certainly was in debt. But if all of CORVI's subsidies were balanced against the houses they turned over to the Funds, and the Fund *members,* CORVI was the creditor by a large amount. MINVU noted that approximately 85 percent of the working population in Chile belonged to one of the Funds. Practically all of CORVI's houses went to working families, and almost all of these were members of one Fund or another. This meant that CORVI's debt to the Funds was being repaid, but through indirect means. In fact, the final balance sheet revealed that CORVI had paid back too much and that this credit could be used for Operation Sitio.

Once this interpretation was sanctioned by decree, the great *surprise* for MINVU was that CORVI was *not* in a mood to cooperate. CORVI was not overly attracted to the idea of urbanizing plots of land that would be turned over to CORHABIT for housing construction. Operation Sitio would represent an indirect transfer of its funds to CORHABIT, which would receive the major credit for the program. Instead of forming a coalition with MINVU to confront the objections of the Social Security Funds, CORVI joined the side of the Funds, and both of them teamed up against MINVU. This alliance helped CORVI protect its budget and preserve its freedom of action on how to spend it. Eventually it did transfer some Fund subsidies to Operation Sitio, but not nearly as much as MINVU would have liked.

MINVU always had the alternative of forcing a showdown with the Funds. But without CORVI support it felt that it could not run the risk of a public demonstration in which Fund members could very well carry signs saying, "MINVU's housing policy is a fiasco." These practical considerations induced it to follow a zigzag course of compromise and accommodation with both CORVI and the Funds, to the detriment of its main policy line.

CORMU's "Landlocked" Budget

A second example of a corporation's resisting MINVU pertained to the transfer of money from CORMU to CORVI for the purchase of land. Over time CORMU increasingly emphasized urban renewal as its principal activity, especially in the San Borja area. A series of problems accelerating this trend eventually worked to the detriment of CORVI, which was quite dependent on CORMU land to operate. First, to build San Borja, it was necessary to tear down and relocate a complete hospital. Feeling that such a major disruption of medical services was ill-advised, the ministry of Public Health and medical interest groups lodged strenuous protests. The vice-president of CORMU found himself engaged in continual meetings with these groups and others to convince them of the need for the San Borja renewal.

Second, even though CORMU should have been working to provide both CORVI and CORHABIT with a suitable stock of land, it could not cover all of its responsibilities with its small staff. In order to take over tracts of land, CORMU had to perform a topographical survey of the site and have its lawyers begin legal proceedings. But the vice-president chose to hire technicians to study projects in metropolitan areas, not to test the soil composition in smaller provincial centers; and, he preferred to use the services of his few lawyers for CORMU's expropriations, not CORVI's. Third, since the central government did not have sufficient resources to build all of San Borja's twenty-four towers, CORMU was obliged to enter into complicated financial and credit arrangements to underwrite construction. It struck agreements with the future apartment owners, who paid 20 percent down on the project design and the remainder in monthly installments over the next five years; with the building contractors, who financed 30 percent of the construction with loans from the private banking system; and with the ministry of Finance, which seeded the project with a loan of one hundred million escudos, to be repaid in two years. Finally, many parts of CORMU's regular budget, such as that allocated for CORVI land purchases, were being used indirectly to support the San Borja project.

When CORVI faced its land crisis, it asked for the right to buy its own plots. MINVU, impatient with CORMU's self-styled housing program, granted this faculty and ordered CORMU to relinquish all the lawyers, technical teams, and budgeted funds that theoretically were being used for land purchases. The vice-president of CORMU was highly displeased with MINVU's decision, since his organization was quite dependent on this money for progress at San Borja. He pointed out that CORVI's new land-purchasing office would not achieve full operating capacity for at least five months; in the interim, CORMU could continue to use the money to maintain the rhythm of construction on the project site. When CORVI proved that it was ready to spend the money, he would then be willing to transfer it.

On this basis the vice-president of CORMU refused MINVU's directive. When the Housing minister insisted, the vice-president tried to gain support from his friend, the Finance minister. Furious, the Housing minister felt that this disrespect of his authority was intolerable and went to the president for action. After a month or so of behind-the-scenes negotiations in the political party and the executive branch of government, the president felt obliged to ask for the vice-president's resignation. The president pointed out that, as the top administrator of the country, he had to keep the hierarchy of command intact. Nonetheless, he praised the tremendous achievements of CORMU during the vice-president's term of office.[34]

Subsequently, MINVU and the Housing minister prevailed upon CORMU to allow this money to be transferred, but the victory was almost pyrrhic. The sector lost one of its most dynamic executives as a result, and MINVU gained enemies in the party and in the housing sector who had supported the vice-president. The eventual resolution of the land-budget issue hardly changed the balance of power between CORMU and MINVU; MINVU could not very well ask that the vice-president be fired every time it wanted to use a corporation's budget to implement policy. The insubordination of CORMU was indicative of the forcefulness with which the corporations protected their financial prerogatives.

CORPORATION POWER AND AUTONOMY

The Corporation for Housing Services (CORHABIT) provides a typical example of many of these tendencies emerging together. At birth it was endowed by MINVU's founders with certain functions. However, to reduce its level of dependence on other bureaucratic units, it used its wide legal faculties to pursue a policy of rapid task expansion. Not wholly by accident, many of these activities received

---

[34] *Diario Ilustrado*, Sept. 16, 1969, p. 3; Oct. 12, 1969, p. 3. Note the parallels in Richard Neustadt's observations on bureaucratic–presidential relations in the United States. "Honorable and able men inside departments fume in frustration at White House 'unwillingness' to be 'decisive,' while their White House counterparts fume in frustration at bureaucracy's 'unwillingness' to be 'responsive.' Why do these feelings persist (and grow)? For answer one must probe beneath the surface of 'machinery,' even beneath the surface of 'personality,' to the perspectives and compulsions generated by the combination of 'big government' and 'separated' powers. . . ." Neustadt, "Approaches to Staffing the Presidency: Notes on FDR and JFK," p. 863.

In the Chilean case, officials in CORMU felt the president had not been 'decisive' in his support of San Borja, while presidential spokesmen did not believe that CORMU's vice-president was being sufficiently 'responsive.'

considerable support in the political community. This political backing, and CORHABIT's administrative disorganization, removed it from MINVU's tutelage. The predictable result was its dedication to its own priorities rather than to the integration of its output with that of the other housing corporations.

CORHABIT's first function was to issue loans, collect them, and handle the financial aspects of CORVI housing construction. In principle, while CORVI constructed the houses, new home owners were depositing money with CORHABIT to pay for them. Eventually this money was to revert to CORVI to provide a continuing source of fresh capital for future housing starts. CORHABIT's second function was to organize the population to achieve greater participation in the society. In this area it counted on a special subagency, Popular Promotion, which administered the Juntas de Vecinos program. Its third task was to help lower-class families adjust to the responsibilities of home care and community living. As in the case of the old F.V.A.S., it introduced family groups to their home before handing them the keys.

Being the agency in most direct contact with the pobladors, COR-HABIT could not avoid being subject to urgent pressures stemming mostly from the critical housing conditions of a great number of urban families with modest incomes. The pressures were aggravated by the direct action of the pobladors, often led by political party organizers, to win immediate solution of their problems. The corporation was also responsible after landslides, torrential rainfalls, floods, volcanic eruptions, or earthquakes, for providing temporary shelters to the victims. In attending to emergencies, CORHABIT wanted the capacity to make its own decisions and not to wait for others to act, especially if this would entail delays and force it to make concessions to policies determined elsewhere. CORHABIT was always striving for an increased capacity in land purchase, rapid construction, prefabricated products, and trucks to deliver these products to the project site.

It did not take long for CORHABIT's activities to spread into new areas not contemplated by MINVU's organizers. One of the more effective programs inherited from the Alessandri regime was self-construction, through which families saved time and money by putting up their own homes. In line with the separation of functions, MINVU decided that self-construction should be divided between CORVI and CORHABIT. CORVI would supervise the work details at the site, while CORHABIT would organize the community and handle the financial aspects. CORHABIT claimed, however, that the two parts of the program could not be separated in practice, and prevailed upon MINVU to turn over the entire program to CORHABIT. The subdepartment of self-construction in CORVI duly passed to CORHABIT in 1965.

After the major earthquake in that same year, CORHABIT turned over 40,000 prefabricated houses to families left homeless. From the purchase of prefabricated products, it next began to manufacture these materials itself, by means of factories set up in poorer neighborhoods. The intention was to absorb local unemployment and spur economic development while facilitating less expensive home construction. COR-HABIT began as a social assistance agency and a bank for low-income social groups; it turned into a construction firm and a government enterprise. By the end of the period, most of CORHABIT's attention was focused on self-construction, with prefabricated material produced in CORHABIT's own factories.[35] These programs were outside the framework of MINVU's intentions for CORHABIT and represented a very loose definition of housing services. But given the organization's wide legislative dispositions, they were perfectly within the letter of the law.

While CORHABIT was engaging in these other activities, its political influence was rising. Its capacity to act quickly on a massive scale brought a good measure of prestige inside and outside of government. Its success in providing cheaper housing than CORVI qualified it for a larger portion of the budget than if it had restricted itself to its original jobs. CORHABIT officialdom could use its authority over funds for more purposes. Congressmen prevailed on CORHABIT to help them fulfill their commitments in certain regions of the country, in return for continuing support of the agency on other fronts. When the minister of Housing was a man with political ambitions, he could not avoid being impressed by the number of exchange relations COR-HABIT maintained with pobladors in key electoral districts. These contacts made it possible to dot the country with CORHABIT neighborhoods named after the minister, which would help his chances in future electoral campaigns. The innovation of workers' factories for prefabricated materials also attracted attention, even internationally. Housing officials from other Latin American countries toured the workshops to see if the concept was applicable to their own situations.

Despite the enthusiasm of CORHABIT personnel in attending to the urgent problems of the pobladors, the whole agency tended to be highly disorganized. First of all, the personnel coming originally from the F.V.A.S. were not accustomed to working within the legal requirements of a public organization. They had not had contacts with the General Comptroller's office and were not attuned to the necessity of

---

[35] CORHABIT, *Operación 20,000/70.*

integrating their policies within any set plan. Second, the officials of CORHABIT tended to be oriented more toward social problems than to administrative detail. They preferred talking with the pobladors in the shantytowns and at the construction sites to sitting behind a desk.

These activities were commendable from the point of view of serving the needs of the ministry's poorest clients. But they were detrimental for enforcement of a sectoral housing plan. During this whole period, the Planning and Budgeting agency had a very difficult time monitoring CORHABIT, which flew more and more out of MINVU's orbit. The most frustrating problem for the planners was their inability to obtain consistently accurate information on CORHABIT's activities. Without these data it was almost impossible to coordinate its actions within the housing plan. Telephone calls and memoranda went unanswered because people were away from their desks; money was spent without a precise idea of where it went; records were misplaced, and statistics were not kept. Organizational stability was impaired by high turnover in both the upper and lower levels of the agency. Not only did the organization as a whole go its own way, the individuals in CORHABIT were encouraged to develop their own job descriptions. Many of them considered CORHABIT a political action organization. Perhaps it was not unusual that MINVU's requests for information were ignored; no one person in CORHABIT could provide much more than a vague idea of what it was doing.

These problems also became very troublesome for other corporations that depended on CORHABIT's output to operate properly. As it expanded its functions, CORHABIT began to neglect its original duties. The assignment of CORVI houses became mired in confusion. Although CORHABIT should have been distributing the houses as they were being built, this long process would often not begin until the homes were finished and ready for occupancy. Houses often sat empty for a year or more while CORHABIT personnel rushed about trying to straighten out the situation: locate registration lists, calculate individual family payments, and assign the homes.[36] CORHABIT's role as a collector of savings suffered in quality. It had difficulties predicting housing demand (mainly through a system called the Popular Savings Plan, or PAP), and was incapable of providing CORVI with an accurate estimate of how many houses to build in specific areas.[37] Its level

---

[36] This delay, added to the normal amount of time needed by CORVI to construct the house, meant that the process from beginning to end could take two and a half years. The different steps are described in Cabello, *Informe*, pp. 39–41.

[37] PAP is described in Charles A. Frankenhoff, *Hacia una Política Habitacional Popular: El Caso de Chile.*

of collection fell off considerably, leading to a serious lack of self-generating capitalization in the sector. People received houses or land sites on the condition that they would pay an installment every quarter, but CORHABIT was not collecting.[38]

CORHABIT had more activities proceeding simultaneously than any other housing corporation. The dominant impression inside of MINVU was of an unfathomable organization doing a great many good things, but doing them badly. On the one hand, the Planning and Budgeting agency had difficulty controlling CORHABIT because its authority, finances, and access to prestige enabled it to act independently. On the other hand, its generally disorganized administration meant that it could not provide MINVU with details on exactly what it had done, was doing, or would be doing in the near future. This peculiar type of resource management helped it to both achieve its self-defined goals in the task environment and resist any unwanted interference from the central ministerial officials.

DIVIDED MINVU REACTIONS

Before continuing further, it would be useful to clarify the roles of the different planning units in their relations with the corporations. For the sake of simplicity the preceding discussion implied that all of them joined ranks on housing policy and were then united in their efforts to try to enforce policy on the corporations. This is a false impression. Of the four main units in the Planning and Budgeting agency, only one, Housing Planning, was methodically concerned about providing norms for the corporations' behavior. Of the rest, Community Development Facilities was building inexpensive schools, Urban Development was heavily committed to the municipalities, and Finances represented the corporations' interests before the ministry of Finance.

---

[38] In 1968, Frankenhoff estimated recoveries at 35 percent in his report to the Ford Foundation, "A Strategy of Decentralization and Housing Policy Decision-Making in Chile" (March 1968, mimeo), p. 5. Robert N. Merrill, *Towards a Structural Housing Policy: An Analysis of Chile's Low-Income Housing Program* concludes (p. 51) that one of the reasons for payment delinquency was that "not only are there often not enough [State Bank] branches at which to pay, but also that these branch offices are only open two to four hours a day. Consequently, it is often extremely difficult for working-class families located on the urban periphery to get to the offices during [banking] hours and wait in the inevitable line to pay." The reasons cited for poor payment by CORVI clients in three Santiago districts were as follows: don't have enough money each month (46 percent); no information on the amount owed, total cost of site, lack of monthly bills (13 percent); difficulties in paying, CORHABIT hours, location of offices (23 percent); isn't necessary to pay (2 percent); because almost no one pays (5 percent); don't like housing solution obtained (8 percent); other (3 percent). Merrill, p. 50.

For the full six years of this period, the precise functions of the different planning units were never specified. One planning executive even admitted that he did not have a clear conception, until the last months of the regime, of what his office was supposed to be doing.[39] Much of the confusion stemmed from the ambiguous position of the general director of Planning and Budgeting. He was theoretically charged with guiding output, through systematic coordination of the ministry's activities. However, he never gained any momentum in this job. On the one hand, he wanted to preserve a global perspective of the overall situation and not be distracted by the daily decisions made in the corporations. Yet he did not want to lose too much contact with the action, since he realized that problems ignored could return to haunt the ministry. He tried to travel a middle road by concentrating his attention on the special projects going on within MINVU. But it was not long before he became extremely bogged down in the immediate financial and technical details of the Planning and Budgeting agency. The mountains of paper crossing his desk did not allow him breathing space to contemplate the sector's global policy. His dedication to the agency left him no opportunity to observe and evaluate the actions of the corporations. In the end he occupied a no-man's-land between two planning styles.

MINVU's slow start, which forfeited policy formation to the corporations, was partially attributable to the government's decision not to adopt a basic plan for the six-year period. Many of MINVU's officials came from the department of Planning and Economic Studies in the old Housing Corporation. There they had put together the *Proposición del Plan Sexanal del Sector Vivienda* (Proposed Six-Year Housing Plan), which contained broad policy norms and specific guidelines for action. The personnel in MINVU expected that this white paper would serve as their working document during their full term of office. Though the plan was discussed quite extensively, it was never formally approved. The opposition of the minister himself to certain parts of the plan proved a hard blow to the spirit of the officials in the Planning and Budgeting agency. In a short while the commitments made by the corporations meant that a comprehensive plan was no longer feasible.

Subsequently, the planning units in MINVU started to define their activities in haphazard, piecemeal fashion. Each unit reached an independent agreement on what activities it would undertake, without considering the role of the other planning units or who was going to try to control the corporations. The administrators in MINVU did not

[39] Interview material.

form a team: they had little idea of what they wanted to accomplish together, and their actions were not mutually reinforcing. To the relative advantage of the corporations, but probably to the disadvantage of the housing sector as a whole, a policy vacuum developed in MINVU which was never successfully filled.

Community Development Facilities

The most unusual case of goal displacement was that of the agency for Community Development Facilities, which was originally designed to be the planning brain of the Architecture agency (see Figure 13). In Chapter 5 we learned the reasons why this agency never passed from the ministry of Public Works. Consequently, the Architecture agency was taken out of the organization chart of the Urban Works agency. Its elimination meant that CORVI had no separate agency to construct public buildings and recreational areas for its housing complexes. It also meant that Community Development Facilities would have very little to do, since it could not very well be the brain of an imaginary body. It first attempted to place construction directly in the hands of CORVI. But CORVI was completely engrossed in housing programs and did not wish to accept additional burdens. For lack of an alternative, the planning office took the job itself and began to build schools, clinics, sport fields, gardens, squares, and cultural centers in CORVI neighborhoods.

Before the Community Development agency started building, its officials had aspirations of forming a coordinating committee with representatives from the ministries of Education (for schools), Health (for medical posts), Interior (for police, civil registry, postal, and telegraph offices), and National Defense (for sports), and with the Catholic Church (for cultural and religious buildings). This committee would agree on certain formulae for how many of each facility were needed for each thousand homes, and Community Development would distribute them in old and new neighborhoods all around the country. However, the planning agency was soon disappointed by the realization that this idea was impractical. As a small office in the Housing ministry, it could not possibly wield authority over powerful ministries in other sectors. Even though its executives obtained a presidential decree for this regulatory control, their efforts at application met with little success.

Quite prudently, the unit lowered its sights and absorbed the functions of the Architecture agency within MINVU. In 1966 it began the job of supplying community buildings and facilities to the CORVI housing complexes. It also complemented the efforts of Urban Development at the municipal level by offering a series of loans to small communities to construct theaters, gymnasiums, and other buildings for public use, without having to wait for the Architecture agency to fit their specific needs into the national plan. Its staff developed the first standard methodology in Latin America for community infrastructure policy correlated with population density. Its daily routine in carrying out these tasks, however, effectively removed it from trying to coordinate the output of the different corporations in the sector.

Urban Development

Urban Development was another planning unit that blazed its own trail. It became deeply involved in two programs, both of which related only indirectly to the activity of the corporations. The first of these was technical assistance to the Chilean municipalities: Urban Development tried to encourage local initiative, raise the technical standards of municipal administration, and improve city plans in order to increase their operational capacity. The planning office wanted to help city governments to gain greater marginal utility from their meager budgets and to requisition funds from the central government in more sophisticated language. Second, Urban Development embarked on a series of "pre-investment studies" conducted by foreign and national consultants who were experts in urban and regional planning. These studies were designed to set priorities and standards for regional investment and urban land use over the long term.[40] They outlined preferable growth patterns in the regions and prescribed the best transportation, employment, industrial, and social policy over the coming years. Very soon after its formation, Urban Development was directing its attention away from Santiago and the corporations, toward the provinces and municipalities.

It was expected that Urban Development would establish general urban policy for Chile; subsequently, it would make sure that the actions of CORMU, CORVI, and CORHABIT were aligned with that policy. Urban Development did recognize that population density was too low in Chilean urban areas. To correct the situation, it could have insisted that in Year One, 20 percent of new public housing would have to be highrise; in Year Two, 30 percent; in Year Three, 40 percent, and so on. But Urban Development never elaborated or defended a firm urban policy that would have changed traditional housing expansion from a horizontal to a vertical basis. It justified the corporations' disparate policy lines by saying that urgent problems had to be solved

---

[40] Peter S. Cleaves, *Developmental Processes in Chilean Local Government*, pp. 54–57.

immediately; later, more time could be dedicated to a rational land-use policy.[41]

Within the ministry, the most important reference group for Urban Development should have been CORMU, which was responsible for the renovation of Chilean urban areas. But Urban Development never handed specific policy guidelines to CORMU to indicate how it believed urban renewal should proceed. For five years it worked in smaller cities, such as Osorno, Talca, and Puerto Montt, completing one pre-investment study after another. Some of these documents were extremely informative, but they had little relevance to the areas where CORMU had the greatest responsibility, such as the metropolitan regions of Santiago, Valparaiso, and Concepcion. Urban Development wanted to test the methodology in the smaller regions and then apply it to Santiago; but while it was doing this, CORMU was embarking on a controversial urban renewal scheme and CORVI and CORHABIT were proceeding full speed ahead with a "viviendista" approach.

The regional activities of this planning office took it almost completely outside the domain of MINVU. Its pre-investment studies, for example, were more characteristic of ODEPLAN, with its clearer regional responsibility, than of MINVU. Urban Development's sponsorship of this project seemed to dismiss the reality that regional investment in industry, transportation, power, and tourism were determined in the ministries of Economy, Public Works, Interior, and Finance, not in Housing. Despite their quality and the fact that they were sent to these ministries, the pre-investment studies alone could not assure that this investment would be rational. These decisions had to be enforced. ODEPLAN might have controlled this investment if it had been more influential.[42] But one person who certainly was *not* going to make

[41] Enrique Browne and Guillermo Geisse use the example of lower-class public housing on the outskirts of the Santiago metropolitan area to criticize an incremental approach toward planning. "These decisions are justified over the short term by the cost and availability of land, the popularity of single-family dwellings, and low population density, fewer direct construction costs, and other similar considerations. Nonetheless, over the longer term, the irrationality of the situation has been proved by the ecological segregation of the Santiago metropolitan area, the enormous indirect costs due to extended urban services and transportation lines, the elimination of fertile farm land used for supplying food products to the metropolis, and other negative effects." "¿Planificación para los Planificadores o para el Cambio Social?" p. 15. It is interesting to note that Urban Development *knew* the disadvantages of horizontal growth. If it followed incremental and accommodating policies, it was not lack of information, but of other resources, which prevented it from altering the trend. Its ability to enforce policy on the corporations and the pobladors was circumscribed by a severe power imbalance. Its incrementalism stemmed from the same factors inducing the Economic Committee to give up the battle against inflation (Chapter 4).

[42] Officials in Urban Development did hope eventually to move the bureau to ODEPLAN.

these decisions was the minister of Housing. His sway over the corporations in his own sector was irregular, and it was difficult to imagine his wielding extensive influence over public organizations in other jurisdictions. Revealingly, Urban Development did not even try to use the minister to influence the corporations: it apparently sensed their superior resource base and chose not to begin any battles it might not be able to finish.

Finances

The founders of MINVU assumed that the centralized section of the ministry would supervise execution of the corporations' budgets as one means of coordinating their activities. But the high percentage of income channeled directly to the corporations' bank accounts deprived the planning unit of any real possibilities of day-to-day control over their financial affairs. Consequently, budgetary supervision for planning purposes never progressed much further than scheduling monies provenant from the central government and representing the corporations' claims for higher allocations before the ministry of Finance.

The office of Finances was faced with quite perplexing cash-flow problems that dominated its attention. In 1967, for example, the central government provided a subsidy of 256 million escudos to the capital account of the ministry's four largest corporations. Of this amount, 104 million was for CORVI, 74 million for CORHABIT, 25 million for CORMU, and 53 million for CCAP. Ideally this total should have been divided evenly into twelve monthly parts and paid proportionally to each corporation. However, the Finance ministry's tax revenue was not consistent throughout the year. It might be able to provide MINVU only one million in January, two million in February, three million in March, and then 30 million in April, 50 million in May, and 50, 50, 20, 20, 10, 10, and 10 millions for the remaining months of the fiscal year. In the end, the total of 256 million would be the same, but the payment would have been very irregular.

During the period of budgetary execution, the corporations continually badgered for funds, and the planners had to justify why money duly budgeted was not available to cover expenditures. The office of Finances had to juggle accounts to try to cover each corporation's most pressing needs as opportunely as possible. Often it had to deprive one corporation of part of its monthly quota to help another cancel a debt. It had very little time to try to coordinate actual expenditures within MINVU's annual program.

The corporations had every reason to feel more confident about the arrival of their independent funds than those from MINVU. CORVI knew that the Social Security Funds would provide about 60 percent of its capital budget at an even 5 percent per month. MINVU might give 23 percent, but on a very inconsistent basis. The inability of MINVU to provide regular subsidies seemed to reduce any indebtedness the corporations may have felt toward it. Partially to augment their status with the corporations, officials in Finances expended much energy in trying to extract more money for them from the national Budget Bureau. The power imbalance between the corporations and MINVU seemed to convert the role of the sectoral budgeting office from that of a strict financial regulator into that of a junior accountant or a courier in the service of the corporations.

Housing Planning

Only one planning office regularly attempted to orient the corporations' activities along a series of consistent norms. The Housing Planning unit tried to measure the housing demand in localities throughout Chile, and then convince CORVI, CORHABIT, and CORMU to provide their services accordingly. Its approach was premised on a desire to increase participation of the community in decisions which affected its collective well-being, but which traditionally had taken place behind closed doors in the central bureaucracy. After MINVU received its indications from the Finance ministry on its probable subsidy for the year, and from ODEPLAN on regional investment goals (discussed above), the office for Housing Planning began the task of calculating the real housing needs in each area of the country. Its procedure began with questionnaires sent to special local committees made up of provincial officials, mayors, municipal councilmen, and pobladors. These committees formed a list of the most imperative housing requirements of their regions and fixed a priority for each. Housing personnel sometimes traveled to the different locales to meet directly with the committee representatives, in order to see that the forms were being completed properly and that all pertinent information was being passed upward.

When the forms came back to Santiago, officials from the corporations eliminated those grass-roots projects that seemed technically unfeasible. Housing Planning then evaluated the remaining pre-programs via computer to ascertain per-unit costs. Simultaneously, the corporations were asked to calculate the total cost of their works already in progress and the backlog of approved projects that had to be initiated in the coming year. Once these values were set, the whole package was turned over to Finances for the total cost of the *projected* housing plan for the year. Finances used these data to try to increase the ministry's allocation in the *oficio final* that the ministry of Finance sent to Congress in late December. Meanwhile, Housing Planning scratched projects from the local lists from the bottom upward, until their total cost equalled the probable income of the ministry. The remaining projects represented the annual housing plan, which was distributed to the corporations for execution.

At this point Housing Planning ran into real difficulties. Despite the enormous amount of work going into the housing plan, the corporations did not consider it a serious document. In the first place, they had done a sloppy job of figuring the total cost of their backlog. The underestimate of these obligations meant that much less money was available for new works than MINVU believed. Second, their general disrespect for the Planning and Budgeting agency meant that, although they had participated tangentially in the formation of the program, the corporations felt no commitment to it. The persons who handled the feasibility studies were not the most qualified in the corporations. Indeed, sometimes they were the ones who could be spared for this kind of "minor" task because they were the least needed at home. The result was that many approved projects should never have been included in the program.

Because of these financial and technical miscalculations, many of MINVU's projects were simply never executed by CORVI, COR-HABIT, or CORMU. Each corporation made up its own program and then modified it slightly according to what MINVU put forth. In each province there was at best an 80 percent overlap between the lists of the Planning and Budgeting agency and the corporations. It was questionable whether even this congruence was due to the corporations' attentiveness to MINVU's annual program, or simply because they arrived at similar conclusions through their own means. Each time a discrepancy existed, it lowered the validity of the type of institutionalized participation that MINVU was trying to generate. When MINVU said that something would happen that did not happen at all, it gave increased credence to those political actors who claimed that violence was a more effective means to achieve housing goals.[43]

Despite the problems with the corporations, the Housing Planning office followed the planning process through to its conclusion. It swallowed its pride, and turned its annual program into a loose-leaf notebook. It replaced many of its programs with those indicated *post facto* by the corporations. Though it did not have the authority to oblige the corporations to inform it of subsequent changes, it tried to

[43] See Chapter 8.

keep the program lists up-to-date and maintain some conception of the global housing picture. It tried to time CORMU's buying of land with the initiation of project design and CORVI's issuing of bids. It worked to integrate the termination of construction with CORHABIT's assignment of homes to their new occupants. It pleaded with and cajoled the corporation vice-presidents to sacrifice their parochial interests from time to time for the general benefit of the sector. Although everyone was aware that it lacked sanctions, Housing Planning censured them verbally when it felt that they were deviating from the ministry's basic norms.

It would be foolish to speculate if Housing Planning's attempt was either naive or courageous. On the one hand, the initial political advantages of the corporations were enormous. The tools given MINVU in the original legislation were completely inadequate to control them in any meaningful way. The other planning units apparently understood this fact quite early in the administration and displaced their goals toward endeavors in which they would have at least some influence. On the other hand, the relative failure of Housing Planning to enforce its politics and programs did not negate the validity of its earnest intentions. It felt that if no one in MINVU tried to coordinate the ministry's output, the result would be chaos.

MINVU COUNTERATTACK

Eventually the lack of coordination led to efforts by the Subsecretariat, the Housing Planning office, and the general director of Planning and Budgeting to bring the decentralized sector under better control and end their feelings of engaging in useless work.

Authority by Fiat

The Planning and Budgeting agency had discovered that whenever the corporations found its directives too meddlesome, they simply brandished the original legislation bestowing their autonomous status. Therefore, MINVU's first campaign measure strengthened its imprecise authority over the corporations. Early in 1968 Congress passed a law making any orders of the minister, subsecretary, or general director mandatory for the vice-presidents.

This law was submitted with considerable back-room fanfare and expectation; soon afterward, however, it was filed away and used only sparingly. If the intention was to slap the corporations with the hand of authority every time they deviated from MINVU's program lines, this proved more difficult in practice than at first imagined. The law did not give MINVU direct authority over all personnel in the corporations, but only over the vice-presidents. The only punishment implied for refusal to execute an order was dismissal of the vice-president. However, as evidenced by the CORMU affair, firing the head of the corporation was easier said than done, and it was not a procedure easily standardized in everyday routine. The upper-middle-level executives in MINVU had fewer personnel, office facilities, vehicles, responsibilities, and clients than the vice-presidents, yet suddenly they were supposed to have more authority. The obvious inconsistency was not lost on the participants, and the law's forcefulness declined considerably in face-to-face encounters between the major actors. The corporations were accustomed to acting independently, and they simply continued in the same vein. The planners in MINVU were accustomed to having little influence over the corporations, and their inferiority complex tended to persevere. Though MINVU found the law useful on some specific program points, such as having CORMU buy a certain tract of land, it was not sufficiently broad to tip the overall balance in MINVU's favor.

Decentralization

Because of the relative ineffectiveness of the 1968 authority law, MINVU launched a second counterattack to increase its influence in the housing sector. Officials in the Subsecretariat of MINVU felt that decentralization of the corporations' activities was the most suitable manner of deflating their autonomy. The new program entailed restructuring on two fronts. First, the corporations were asked to beef up their staffs at the regional level, and assign them functions such as land purchases, issuing bids, and evaluating works, previously centered almost exclusively in Santiago. Second, MINVU appointed an official from its home office to take up residence in the local area. He ascertained housing demand, supervised the corporations' productivity in the region, and maintained direct links with the central ministry. The decentralization program was designed to concentrate practically all the functions of the ministry in regional organizations which would be self-contained units with financial autonomy.

This power move was considerably more subtle than the authority law passed sometime earlier. Based on technical criteria, it was reminiscent of a liberal ideology in Chile that paid tribute to regional autonomy. In addition, the program received important support from the president of the country, who was interested in using the Housing ministry as a pilot program for decentralization in the whole public administration. The Subsecretariat of MINVU was most active in sponsoring the effort in the housing sector. In 1968 and 1969, a series of decrees were enforced which made the program a legal requirement for the corporations.[44] In describing the program, MINVU pointed out that it was a simple extension of measures already in force, such as the regional pre-investment studies and the local committees that helped Housing Planning formulate its annual plan. Through a transfer of just a few officials, the ministry could proceed beyond local planning and programming, to execution.

Decentralization did not originate wholly from MINVU's raw desire to impose its will. The program was also conceived as the best way to attend to regional needs. In practice, MINVU felt that these two goals were inseparable. Programs could not suit local needs if the land bought was inappropriate for the housing designs, if communication snags meant that people were not attracted to the type of house programmed for the area, if contractors brought their workers from Santiago rather than hiring locally, if construction was postponed because central officials suddenly transferred money to new priorities, or if houses sat empty for long periods until they were assigned. In the provinces, the local representative of the corporation had traditionally looked to his head office in Santiago for guidance and instructions, and no one was programming the interaction of the different entities on the construction site. MINVU expected that the decentralization program would correct these deficiencies and have other positive spin-off effects, such as more citizen participation, efficacy, and regional consciousness.

Obviously the full enactment of this system would also have a remarkable effect on the nationwide power relations between MINVU and the corporations. Once the yearly plan was established, the local MINVU delegates could exercise far-reaching financial control, and see to it that budgeted funds were actually being spent on the local projects indicated. Instead of harassing the corporations for information in Santiago, MINVU could depend on its local officials to provide all pertinent data on the corporations' past, current, and future activities in each zone. MINVU's wide information-gathering capacity would soon supersede that of the individual corporations, preventing the perpetuation of *faits accomplis*. MINVU could back up the local delegates by referring to the 1968 authority law on a whole range of items.

The local officials could use their on-the-spot location to have land purchased with ample anticipation, bids issued promptly, and houses

44 Decree No. 289 (April 2, 1969); Decree No. 678 (Sept. 26, 1968).

assigned with minimum delay. As pobladors and contractors realized that final decisions were being made by MINVU, not the corporations, the planners' prestige would increase significantly. The eventual improvements in coordination and efficiency would result in a greater number of housing solutions, enhancing the government's reputation and resulting in political backing for MINVU in any disagreements with the corporations. The central planners could insist on policy norms, and question the vice-presidents directly when these norms were being violated. Once the system was internalized, the planners would have an enormous capacity to monitor daily decisions and orient them to current and future sectoral needs.

The corporations, correctly assessing the power connotations of the decentralization program, were completely against the reform. CORVI and CORHABIT, which had the most to lose, thought it was a grave error that would reduce the prerogatives of their vice-presidents with absolutely no guarantee that the resultant housing projects would be any more suited to local conditions. They felt that the program was a disguised attempt by the planners to finally achieve their goal of managing the affairs of the corporations. They argued that their local representative would be confused by a double hierarchical structure, not knowing whether to follow the orders of the head office or those of the local MINVU delegate. With only eighteen months left in office, and an election on the horizon foreboding grave distortions in the sector's budget, they doubted that the program would ever get off the ground. The next government's appointees would pay it no heed, continuing to work through the corporations.

The vice-president of CORVI, Hector Valdés, indicated that he was not against decentralization as a concept. Indeed, he would abide by a system that delegated the functions, personnel, budget, and projects to regional organizations, along with *responsibility* to the local MINVU chief. But as the program was described, he felt that it placed grave legal burdens on the vice-president's office: The funds would be controlled and spent by the local MINVU officer but the vice-presidents would still have to account for them before the General Comptroller's office. Rather than submit to the program, the vice-presidents of both CORVI and CORHABIT resigned their posts.[45] The main advocates of the system in the central ministry saw these resignations as a first indication of the new power relations between MINVU and the corporations, and proceeded to implement the system as well as they could in the short time remaining before the change in government. Regional

[45] *El Mercurio,* July 25, 1969, p. 36; Dec. 6, 1969, p. 31.

offices were established in Arica, Antofagasta, Valparaiso, Concepcion, and Punta Arenas.

COORDINATION AND RATIONALITY

In an earlier quote, Aaron Wildavsky pointed out that little serious analysis has been dedicated to the concept of coordination. Parts of James Thompson's work help fill this void and can serve to conclude this discussion of coordination in MINVU. Thompson looks for coordination whenever interdependence exists between organizations, or branches within the same organization. Three typical kinds of interdependence are *pooled, sequential,* and *reciprocal.* Thompson assumes that an organization will move naturally toward that type of coordination which contributes most to its bounded rationality—to the reduction of uncertainty, or increased certainty, in its internal operations and relations with its task environment.[46]

The most diffuse type is *pooled* interdependence. Each organizational unit contributes to the welfare of the whole, but its activities are virtually self-contained. Like one store in a chain under common ownership, a branch need not interact with its counterparts; in fact, competition is often encouraged. In *sequential* interdependence, one branch produces parts or outputs that are the inputs for the next, as in an assembly-line factory. The first must act before the second; but unless the second acts, the first may have difficulty solving its output problem, and the third may be inoperative for lack of inputs. *Reciprocal* interdependence refers to a situation "in which the outputs of each become inputs for the others. . . . Under conditions of reciprocal interdependence, each unit involved is penetrated by the others," such as within an airline.

Thompson then observes that each type of interdependence implies an appropriate method of coordination. The *rational* organization facilitates coordination in the following combinations: *Pooled* interdependence evokes a need for standardization, or "the establishment of routines or rules which constrain action of each unit or position into the paths consistent with those taken by others in the interdependent relationship." *Sequential* interdependence needs coordination by planning, or "the establishment of schedules for the interdependent units by which their actions may be governed." And *reciprocal* interdependence

[46] James D. Thompson, *Organizations in Action: Social Science Bases of Administrative Theory,* pp. 54–56.

requires a system of mutual adjustment, which "involves the transmission of new information during the process of action." [47]

To place this study in the context of Thompson's nomenclature, it is useful to recall that MINVU's founders defended a classic conception of *sequential interdependence*. CORMU purchased the land; Urban Works was to urbanize it (install sewer and water lines and lay pavement); CORVI was to construct the houses on the urbanized plots; and CORHABIT was to maintain relations with the home-owners to finance, assign, and service the houses. Urban Works never fulfilled its original function, but the basic sequential nature of the process nevertheless remained intact. CORMU's output (land) became CORVI's input. CORVI's output (houses and urbanized sites) were the inputs for CORHABIT. Without land, CORVI could not function; and without houses, CORHABIT would be unable to carry out its tasks.

According to Thompson's criteria of appropriate coordinating structures, sequential interdependence requires an elaborate planning instrument. In 1965, MINVU's founders recognized that each corporation's specific dependence on its counterparts down the line meant that finely detailed schedules were necessary. They institutionalized planning in MINVU precisely for purposes of coordination, and thus adopted the means appearing most rational in terms of Thompson's propositions.

Lack of coordination in the Chilean housing sector stemmed from two sources. First, the corporations attempted to increase their autonomy to confront their task environments with maximum capabilities. In doing so, they expanded their functions, undermined coordination, and shattered the sequential assumptions on which the ministry was founded. Several of the control units in MINVU were interested in operationalizing Thompson's ideal coordinating mechanism, but a discriminatory locus of power in the sector left them in total disarray. This second source of functional disturbance within the ministry was not mitigated until MINVU disregarded the relative importance of planning skills and looked more to planning power to reach its goals.

One element is often underemphasized in treatments of planned coordination: the step between organizational rationality and bureaucratic power. What might be *certainty* for one part of the organization may well represent *uncertainty* for another—i.e., rationality for the corporations was not the same thing as rationality for MINVU. One unit's justifiable attempt to monopolize access to a series of operating

[47] Thompson, pp. 54–56.

resources can starve the organization as a whole. This phenomenon
was also quite evident in the earlier description of the Chilean budgetary process. The contradictory strategies of the Budget Bureau and
the agencies tended to increase their respective certainty, but led to a
generally irrational situation in which uncertainty was maximized for
the bureaucracy overall.

Like good or bad budgeting, coordination or the lack of it can be
judged on the basis of which unit's definition of rationality finally prevails. It may be in the rational interest of certain administrative units
to resist coordination with complementary structures, despite the objective nature of their interdependence. The resisting organization would
hardly call Thompson's coordinating mechanisms "rational." Standards
and rules can easily be considered "arbitrary," scheduling and control
"meddlesome," and mutual adjustment "unacceptably compromising."
Though an enthetic standard of organizational rationality is valuable
in offering clues to long-term tendencies, the realization of the standard
rarely comes about through passive evolution. Bounded rationality, the
reduction of uncertainty, and the enforcement of coordination cannot
be separated from the power moves of the actors involved. When one
unit succeeds in imposing its definition of rationality on another, a
political act has taken place.

Though a lack of coordination, serious problems of control, duplication of functions, and a certain policy vacuum were shortcomings of
MINVU during its infancy, these growing pains did not prevent it
from fulfilling a certain measure of promise. CORVI and CORHABIT
built 220 thousand living units and provided 280 thousand additional
housing solutions, meaning that they directly improved the habitational
environment of over 25 percent of the country's population. CORMU
made positive strides in the area of urban renewal, and Urban Development revitalized interest in the Chilean municipality, which for too long
had been stagnant and neglected by central authorities. In addition, with
no precise measurement for slippage, waste, or efficiency, it is difficult
to determine exactly how much productivity was lost as a result of lack
of coordination. Yet in the Chilean Housing ministry at the end of
the period, feelings of unease were pervasive and there was a general
consensus on the need for drastic structural and functional changes.[48]

[48] For example, in a personal letter to the author (July 8, 1971), César Díaz-
Muñoz, the former subsecretary of Housing, suggested that two of the corporations
that caused MINVU the greatest difficulty, CORMU and CORHABIT, as well as
COU, should be disbanded. He would have redistributed the ministry's functions as
such: (1) land expropriation exclusively to CORVI, (2) urban renewal to Urban
Development, (3) urban services to CORVI and the Sanitary Works agency in the
ministry of Public Works and Transport (thus rejoining the agencies split in the

Much more so than in 1965, these suggested modifications were based on assumptions of bureaucratic power, and deliberately strove to attain a delicate balance between the monitoring and executing units without destroying the latters' capacity to perform well in their task environment.[49]

---

circumstances described in Chapter 5), (4) savings deposits for CORVI houses to CCAP, and (5) social assistance to a new subsecretariat of the Family, an idea promoted during the presidential campaign of Salvador Allende.

[49] Amitai Etzioni, in conceptualizing a solution to this problem, finds it useful to consider monitoring units as the "controlling overlayer." "So far as the autonomy of the overlayer (its relative power versus that of the members) is concerned, a *medium amount*, we suggest, would make it more responsive than either a low or high degree. If the overlayer's power is low, the system will *drift*, reacting to changes in the environment and the members with little 'creative' or anticipatory capacity and, therefore, at the mercy of the more powerful members. If the overlayer's power is great (not only greater than that of any one collectivity or subset of collectivities, but greater than that of all of them together), it will *overmanage*, imposing policies that run counter to the members' needs." Etzioni, *The Active Society*, p. 519. If only a "medium amount" of autonomy were simple to operationalize!

7

THE CONTRACTORS
AS PUBLIC CLIENTS

       Whatever the club-like aspects of employer associations, or
their functions as internal regulators of the sector, no one doubts that
they are formed to foster a working environment clearly favorable to
their members. Because one of their primary purposes is to intervene
in the policy-making and executing phases of governmental activity,
interest groups provide fascinating opportunities for empirical research
and intellectual speculation.[1] Analyses of their activities invariably lead
to observations on political motivations and mores. They offer insights
into the nature of cooptation, its uses and abuses, and they can dis-
credit traditional conceptions of organizational boundaries. They also
provoke discussion on the relationship between back-room wheeling
and dealing and the public interest.

    The dependent variable in most client studies is the ability of the
outside actor to break away from being a simple "subject" of the whims
and rules of officialdom and become a real "participant" in bureaucratic
and legislative decisions. One popular notion is that when an individual
citizen meets success in this realm, the system is just and democratic; a
high incidence of interest-group intervention, however, hints that evil
is lurking somewhere in the background. A complementary claim is
that when the individual is using a privileged status to gain access to
public decision-making (e.g., he comes from the upper social groups,
or his brother is prime minister), an injustice is probably occurring.

---

[1] See, for example, Abraham Holtzman, *Interest Groups and Lobbying,* for a
summary of interest group literature. Also Joseph LaPalombara, *Interest Groups
in Italian Politics,* and Philippe C. Schmitter, *Interest Conflict and Political Change
in Brazil.*

Likewise, if the interest association is made up of the right kind of people (e.g., a consumers union or a collectivity of shantytown dwellers), the system is showing positive symptoms of responsiveness. What is often ignored is that the relative success of all of these actors tends to be determined by similar factors.

Bureaucratic or legislative relations with powerful clients and interest groups hardly exhaust the ways in which government authorities interact with the public. Even within a relatively closed political system, their contacts with individual citizens are always more frequent and affect a much broader spectrum of the population. Unfortunately, there is a dearth of serious material—perhaps reflecting a lack of academic sympathy—on bureaucracy's treatment of the individual as a claimant, plaintiff, or petitioner. For the layman who has infrequent but generally unpleasant encounters with public administration, this subject can represent a more agonizing problem (and a matter crying more for reform) than the ability of self-interested firms or tightly knit, mafiosa-type pressure groups to turn public decisions to their liking (often accepted as an inevitable fact of life).

This chapter on construction interests in Chile will suggest that an important variable affecting client relations is the *functional interdependence* between the pertinent outsider and the government unit. Functional interdependence can lead to coalitions of *joint payoff* between the public and private actors.[2] These particular concepts seem most appropriate for the case at hand. One observer has commented that the Chilean construction sector has

perceived with absolute clarity its links with the state. . . . The Chilean Construction Chamber [is] the only interest group that has succeeded in forging stable alliances with the public administration. . . . The Chamber has been able to design successful strategies emphasizing common objectives between itself and important sectors of bureaucracy. The former responds to the legitimate proposition of a larger volume of expenditure and, in consequence, more profit; and the latter to an interest in obtaining more administrative and institutional prestige and, in many cases, a political prestige for the minister, the vice-presidents, and their immediate collaborators.[3]

---

[2] William F. Whyte observes that success or failure in the parties' activities is determined by the rewards-penalties in which they share, and these rewards-penalties are provided by individuals, groups, or organizations outside of the immediate joint-payoff relationship. Whyte, *Organizational Behavior: Theory and Application*, p. 153.

[3] Genaro Arriagada, *La Oligarquía Patronal Chilena*, pp. 35–36. Disappointingly, the author does not describe these alliances nor offer such perceptive comments on the political style of other Chilean interest groups. His book pertains mainly to voting procedures inside these employer associations.

Functional interdependence, as it is used here, indicates a relatively frequent exchange of resources between at least two actors, each attempting to reach his individual goals. *Joint payoff* connotes that this exchange also advances a set of mutually reinforcing objectives. The preceding quote points out that the interaction of contractors and public officials leads to a distribution of profits and prestige consistent with the basic aims of each. This reciprocal relationship is characteristic of the way in which *construction, bureaucracy,* and *politics* are intermeshed in Chile (and probably elsewhere too), making for a relatively happy love triangle. While the music is playing, at least two of them are dancing. Individual firms do use some standard tactics to try to gain an upper hand over bureaucracy, but this facet of the story is not as revealing as the consistency of institutional goals common to private clients and public officials, and its effect on bureaucratic behavior.[4]

BUREAUCRACY VERSUS THE CLIENT
AND THE INTEREST GROUP

The plight of relatively powerless individuals who take their requests to bureaucracy leads to generalizations about the client and the interest group. For many persons bureaucracy is an appropriate synonym for exasperation. Bureaucracy's bad name comes from the fact that citizens, when they go to it for basic services, seldom leave without feeling severely mistreated. Public offices tend to be plagued

[4] Ricardo Lagos E., *La Concentración del Poder Económico*; Ben G. Burnett, *Political Groups in Chile,* pp. 146–151; and Rosemond Cheetham, "El Sector Privado de la Construcción: Patrón de la Dominación," ascribe to the theory of overlapping directorates to explain manipulation of power and political influence on government. Cheetham, for example, painstakingly quantifies the contractors' participation on the boards of private banks to sustain her conclusion that they are model members of the "dominating class" in Chile.

Approaching the problem from a different angle, Jeffrey Pfeffer explains the composition of directorships through the corporation's dependence on certain resources, one of the most important being finances. Pfeffer, "Size and Composition of Corporate Boards of Directors: The Organization and its Environment." As elsewhere, banks and construction firms in Chile have encouraged overlapping to further their operating goals in their respective task environments. Construction firms face a perpetual necessity for credit, because fiscal payments always run behind current expenditures. One of the principal functions of banks is to lend money. This interdependence was demonstrated after the Allende regime bought controlling shares in most Chilean banks. Although they were in the hands of the state, and contractors no longer sat on their boards of directors, the banks still issued loans to the construction firms in large amounts to cover the latters' short-term obligations. The earlier statement on the interrelationship between politics, construction, and bureaucracy includes banking as well. The congruence of interests generally has little to do with the class membership of the principal actors.

by long lines, delays, confusion, arbitrariness, and plain rudeness.[5] The acrimony of the occasional visitor, as he waits in line, is often heightened by his realization that some persons seem to have the magic ability or unrestrained gall to bypass the line, walk straight to the director's desk, finish their formalities in record time, and leave with happy smiles. It is not an accident that some stand in line and others do not. There is a fundamental difference in the relationship of the two actors with the bureaucracy: the first could be called a *petitioner,* and the second is probably an *administrative broker.*

Low frequency of interaction and a reduced power base pose continual quandaries for the petitioner. He may be an elderly person at the post office who wants to send a slightly oversized package by air; a foreign resident at the Central Bank who would like to liquidate his belongings for hard currency; the returning traveler at the port customs house who attempts to clear his personal effects in one afternoon; the parent at the health clinic who asks for a definite appointment for his child's examination, so as not to lose a day's wages; or the upper-middle-class housewife at the social security office, trying to pay her maid's allowance quickly before the butcher shop closes. In Chile, sympathy is extended to individuals in these circumstances. Their possibilities for success are very limited unless they can appeal to some outside source to break through bureaucratic obstinacy and delay. For the agency personnel administering these services, the satisfaction is hardly greater; the prevailing structure of supports and incentives leads to a frictional, stifled, and essentially inefficient performance of duties with the majority of their public.[6]

When the interaction is more predictable, regular, and permanent, these norms tend to change. Politicians who invent "duties" requiring a mandatory pilgrimage of citizens to public offices, and then use the resulting departments to distribute jobs to their partisans, are actually serving broader employment goals. Clogging the internal administrative machinery often increases the need for even more personnel to achieve some modicum of effectiveness.[7] An outward-directed multi-

[5] Differences within a country often depend on how well an agency can afford to staff the administration of these services, while differences between countries depend on the distribution of power in the society and the degree to which "citizen efficacy" is perceived by both the claimant and the bureaucrat. Germán Urzúa has compiled a source booklet, *Prensa y Administración Pública Chilena,* on the reactions of the Chilean press to *"burocratismo"* from 1925 to 1967.

[6] See Germán Urzúa V. and Ana María García Barzelarro, *Diagnóstico de la Burocracia Chilena, 1818–1969,* pp. 159–180.

[7] While the Chilean population has increased by about 35 percent since 1940, employment in public bureaucracy has grown by some 400 percent. Charles J. Parrish, "Bureaucracy, Democracy, and Development; Some Considerations Based on the Chilean Case," p. 18.

plier effect also creates job opportunities on the immediate borders of the organization, where the beleaguered petitioners stack up on top of one another waiting for attention. Parallel structures made up of specialized brokers tend to evolve at the very points where demand for improved service is greatest. Brokers (*tinterillos* or *corredores*) are experts in bureaucratic formalities in specific realms of government activity who tend to develop integrated links with lower- and middle-level bureaucrats. For a fee they aggregate a number of claims, requests, or tributes, saving individual petitioners from presenting them in person.

Permanence of contact is the clue to the broker's success and the element enabling him to obtain the permit, stamped form, or signature quickly for petitioners who can afford to hire his expertise. His customers are either ignorant of the intricacies of the bureaucratic maze or know all too well what awaits them when they enter a public office as individuals. The frequency of the broker's visits means that he becomes familiar with the internal folkways of the bureau. This knowledge allows him to compensate for weak links and to skip steps in ways not available to the individual client. By maintaining close contacts with agency personnel in the Central Bank, Internal Revenue, Customs House, Social Security agency, etc., this middleman can speed through the formalities at a pace impossible for a mere petitioner.

Another difference between the petitioner and the broker pertains to their power bases. All else being equal, the broker, by aggregating the claims of several petitioners, carries a heavier "weight" or influence than the individual petitioner. The broker's requests are magnified by some variable coefficient of the number of customers he represents on that particular occasion. Extra-salary incentives may oil the gears, but these are by no means necessary. More regular contacts can help build close social bonds. The broker's recognized utility for the smooth functioning of the office arouses positive attitudes toward his activities; when he performs efficiently, he offers valuable services that reinforce the relationship. He can assist the agency officials in performing routine tasks (e.g., typing up the forms, moving paper from desk to desk, pasting stamps) which lowers the office's total workload and liberates more time for the perpetual backlog. Because he responds to definite needs in the bureau, the broker is viewed not as a parasite but as a symbiotic agent whose contribution to the bureau is almost crucial. The evolution of this interdependency, based on aggregation of interests and frequency of functional exchanges, gives the broker considerable advantage over the lone petitioner.

These observations can be summarized in a series of propositions that help to explain bureaucracy's tendency to fragment the attention it offers its clients. The petitioner suffers from a low frequency of contacts with bureaucracy and offers little compensation in return. In such cases one might expect:

- lower psychic satisfaction on the part of both the petitioner and the bureaucrat;
- a more marked prevalence of official norms governing the relationship (bureaucratism, red tape, delay);
- a greater incidence of tangential inducement mechanisms to receive preferential treatment (family contacts, political pull or *cuña,* friendship, bribery, violence); and
- less likelihood of a mutually supportive relationship defined in terms of the agency's output.

The broker profits from frequent interaction and a routinized interdependence. In his case, one tends to find:

- greater psychic satisfaction on the part of both the broker and the bureaucrat;
- less rigorous application of official norms to govern the relationship, more improvisation, and looser interpretation of regulations;
- a lower incidence of tangential inducement mechanisms to gain special treatment; and
- more likelihood of a mutually supportive relationship defined in terms of the agency's output.

Discussion of the petitioner and the broker introduces the subject of broader client relations. Most people share a universal experience as petitioners, and have probably worked through brokers at one time or another to achieve limited goals within public administration. In a certain sense, the *petitioner* is to the *broker* as the *client* is to the *interest group.* Here clients are conceived to be private actors in the society (this includes not only business firms, but also scattered, isolated groupings such as neighborhood committees or local labor syndicates) who depend on government regulations and decisions in some fundamental way. The large manufacturer, the importer-exporter, the wealthy agriculturist, the pobladors living in a shantytown, and the shop union each make periodic, particularistic demands on government in regard to a wide range of economic and social measures. The main difference between the individual petitioner and the client is the latter's enlarged power capability. But this distinction is attenuated by the client's tendency to submit his request to the upper-middle levels of bureaucracy; while access is pre-restricted to the more influential, competition for valued preferences can be just as frantic as for the petitioner standing in line in front of a first-floor window. When the client interacts infrequently with the bureau and does not engage in activities which contribute to achievement of the agency's goals, the encounter is usually characterized by a strict application of official norms, low psychic satisfaction for both actors, little mutual servicing and support, and necessary recourse by the client to some tangential inducement mechanism (political pull, family contacts) to receive special treatment.

Clients are motivated to join interest groups for reasons similar to those that attract petitioners to brokers. Interest groups claim to be representative of the aggregate desires of the sector, and attempt to impress the upper-middle and upper levels of government with the combined political power of their membership. Clients appreciate the utility of their guild association for its frequent interaction with government and for any interdependence it can build with public authorities that has marginal utility for their interests. Brokers can usually boast of a higher "success quotient" in their limited aims than interest groups can in influencing government on matters of great importance. Yet the analogy is valid, to the extent that both brokers and interest groups function as aggregators, maintain frequent contacts with access points in the decision-making process, lay claim to a greater array of resources than the individual petitioner or client, and often identify mutually reinforcing goals with public agencies. In the end the relative efficacy of outside actors to influence bureaucratic and legislative decisions is contained in the power relationships between the petitioner, broker, client, and interest group, on the one hand, and the lower, middle, upper-middle, and highest levels of government, on the other.

ORGANIZATIONAL ACCESS TO AUTHORITY

Some 700 firms and independent professionals belong to the Chilean Construction Chamber (*Cámara Chilena de la Construcción,* formed in 1951, and referred to here as the CCC). Members of the CCC monopolize approximately 90 percent of the total volume of contracts and fixed capital in three branches of activity: the general contractors in housing and public works; the specialized subcontractors in heating, plumbing, gas, electricity, elevators, plastering, etc.; and the materials industry—producers of cement, bricks, wood, windows, and hardware products.[8]

Despite the CCC's leftist critics, power in the construction sector is rather deconcentrated.[9] The economically powerful, however, tend to

[8] Estimates of the CCC.
[9] The list of registered contractors for the ministry of Public Works contains approximately 500 firms in five size categories and nine specialties.

dominate the upper echelons of the CCC through a weighted voting system placing about half the electoral strength in the hands of 15 percent of the members. These votes elect a ninety-man General Council for a three-year term (one third renewed each year), which subsequently chooses a president and a seven-man directorate for a one-year period.[10] The Directorate selects two vice-presidents who, with the president, dedicate themselves full-time to the activities of the CCC. These three men constitute the Executive Board of Directors, the outward face of the Chamber before the public and the upper levels of government. The CCC also forms working committees for each of various types of construction activity (Public Works, Housing, Industrial Products, and Specialized Subcontractors). These committees meet weekly, settle disputes in the sector, and help lobby for construction interests.

The CCC is typical of a number of interest groups in Chile because it has made a wide range of demands on government; has developed a style to present them; has access points at several policy-making nexuses; and has had more veiled successes and failures than clear victories or smashing defeats. The CCC and other interest groups, such as the National Agricultural Society (SNA), the Industrial Development Society (SOFOFO), the National Mining Society (SNM), and the Central Chamber of Commerce (*Cámara Central de Comercio*) are all affected by the government's regulatory decisions over the economy (taxes, foreign currency, tariffs, credit, investment, income policy, price controls, and other measures to break inflation).[11] To the extent that the CCC has political capital to mold these decisions to its interests, it is in the same category as its sister organizations. Each lays claim to a certain amount of prestige, information, and economic strength that can be used for influencing public policy.

The distinguishing feature of the CCC's membership is its high frequency of contacts with government at all levels. The Chilean state originates some 80 percent of all construction investment in the country.[12] The construction firms, their suppliers, and their subcontractors down the line are almost completely dependent on government bids and contracts. The CCC is also unusual in that it represents a sector that is not only critically important for the economy, but also serves as a flexible instrument for implementation of the government's economic policy, especially with regard to employment. Unless the private construction firm is totally effaced from the scene, the interaction between the CCC and

[10] Arriagada, *La Oligarquía Patronal*, pp. 130–140.

[11] For an introduction to these other groups, see Constantine C. Menges, "Public Policy and Organized Business in Chile: A Preliminary Analysis," and also David F. Cusack, *The Politics of Chilean Private Enterprise under Christian Democracy.*

[12] Arriagada, p. 34.

government is a permanent fact of life; it is legitimized as a functional necessity for both the contractors and high public officials.

This frequency of contact is important for separating the CCC conceptually from the SNA, SOFOFO, and the other interest associations in Chile. Whereas the others have focused their lobbying efforts on Congress, the CCC and its members look first to the bureaucracy for influence; the halls of Congress are only secondary launching pads for their initiatives. The high frequency of contact intimates a broad functional interdependency between construction and government which is helpful for understanding coalitions based on joint payoff between public actors and private clients.[13]

The issues motivating the CCC to intervene in the policy-making process have grown out of the difficulties of its client members as they attempt to produce, earn profits, increase their capital base, and remain liquid in their task environment. A first category of major concern has been the general level of construction in the country, determined in great part by the size of the budgets for Public Works and Housing, and the structure of government incentives for private investment in construction (interest rates, taxes, rents). A second type of motivation has stemmed from dissatisfaction with administrative obstacles to carrying out major public works projects in Chile. Inefficiency in the public sector is manifest in extensive documentation, a complex set of norms, orders, and requirements, barriers against the importation of parts and machinery, delays in obtaining municipal permits for the installation of electricity, gas, and water mains—in sum, a surfeit of bureaucratic red tape at all levels. Third, a lack of adequate and timely credit, cyclic instability in the selling market, a low capital base in the society, irregularity of pay-

[13] This might be called a kind of *clientela* relationship in which an interest group succeeds "in becoming, in the eyes of a given administrative agency, the natural expression and representative of a given social sector, which in turn constitutes the natural target or reference point for the activity of the administrative agency" LaPalombara, *Interest Groups in Italian Politics*, p. 262. LaPalombara succeeds in exculpating client relations in a "rule-making" bureaucracy by indicating that transactions between the executive branch and interest groups can be mutually beneficial. His analysis places more emphasis on *quid pro quo* exchanges than on overlapping goals and joint payoff. Schmitter, in *Interest Conflict and Political Change in Brazil* (p. 303), backs up LaPalombara's assertion that when an interest group is too thoroughly dependent upon the public administration, there will be no client relationship because there is no bargaining between independent actors.

The CCC is not covered by this rule because it has a "distinctive base of influence (wealth, status, strategic location, legitimacy, numbers, etc.)," and hence is able to offer certain segments of bureaucracy with resources "they could not gain more easily elsewhere." However, the unique characteristic of joint payoff is that no bargaining needs to occur. The CCC and the Public Works ministry, by aggressively pursuing their organizational goals, naturally reinforce each other's position with no need for trade-offs.

ment from public offices, unpredictable return on investment, and long delays before the definitive acceptance of completed projects and settling the accounts have been traditional hindrances to production and profits.[14]

Because of the characteristics of their production and the fact that the majority of their activity is sponsored by the state, contractors have been obliged to build bridges from the heights of government down to quite subordinate levels of authority. The objectives of the CCC and its members have been: to increase the magnitude of construction investment in the country; to facilitate their working relations with public administration; and to improve their profit margins. These issues, which are interrelated and point toward furthering the ultimate welfare of the contractors, have been conveniently divided up within the contractors' formal and informal hierarchy. Functional specificity and division of labor for influence-seeking have facilitated the contractors' close and frequent contacts with decision-making centers in bureaucracy and Congress.

Important targets for the contractors have been: the president of the country; congressional leaders; the minister of Finance; the ministers of Housing and Public Works; the head of the Budget Bureau; the head of the Internal Revenue agency; the president of the Central Bank; the director general of Public Works; the vice-presidents of CORVI, CCAP, CORMU, and other decentralized agencies (ENDESA, ENAMI, ENAP, CAP, etc.); the heads of the public works agencies (Roads, Irrigation, Ports, Architecture, Sanitary Works, Airports); the chief construction engineers of all of these agencies; the regional engineers who supervise construction of a number of projects; and the inspecting engineers, who maintain constant vigil over the project at the work site.

Figure 19 indicates the manner in which this lobbying effort is distributed. At the top, the CCC president and board push for a high level of construction activity in the country. They make appointments with the president (to solicit his sponsorship for major savings, credit, or investment programs), the Congress (mainly for defensive actions, such as the maintenance of tax incentives), the ministry of Finance (on budgetary and payment questions), Internal Revenue (tax breaks) and the Central Bank (imports and credit). At the middle level, the Committees for Public Works and Housing from the CCC try to facilitate the contrac-

---

[14] All these issues have repeatedly been emphasized in editorials in the CCC's magazine, *La Revista de la Construcción,* and speeches of its top officials. Other matters mentioned less frequently are the competition of foreign engineers and contractors, a lack of skilled labor, burdensome but ineffective social laws, and inflation.

FIGURE 19. CONTRACTORS' MULTIPLE ACCESS TO DECISION-MAKING POINTS IN GOVERNMENT

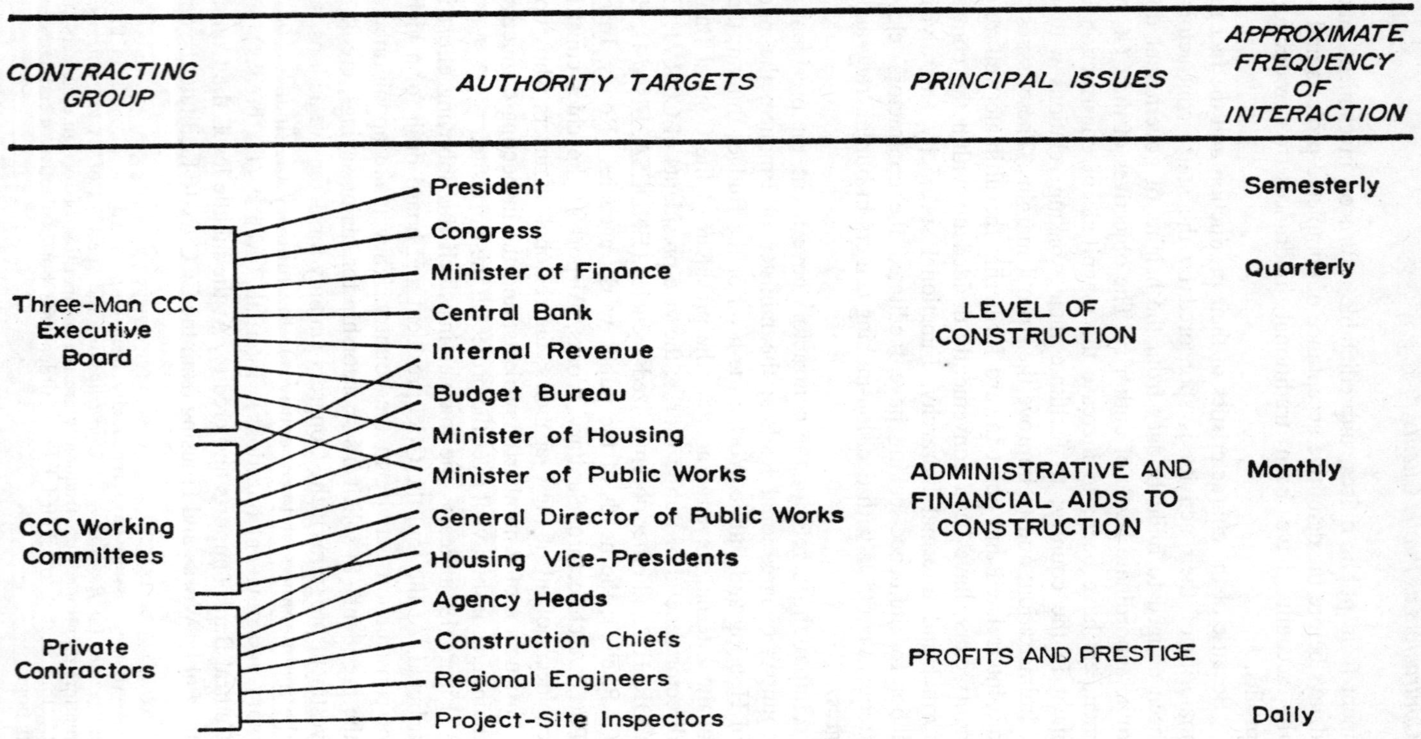

CONTRACTING GROUP | AUTHORITY TARGETS | PRINCIPAL ISSUES | APPROXIMATE FREQUENCY OF INTERACTION

Three-Man CCC Executive Board

President — Semesterly
Congress
Minister of Finance — Quarterly
Central Bank
Internal Revenue
Budget Bureau — LEVEL OF CONSTRUCTION
Minister of Housing

CCC Working Committees

Minister of Public Works
General Director of Public Works — ADMINISTRATIVE AND FINANCIAL AIDS TO CONSTRUCTION — Monthly
Housing Vice-Presidents
Agency Heads

Private Contractors

Construction Chiefs — PROFITS AND PRESTIGE
Regional Engineers
Project-Site Inspectors — Daily

tors' relations with bureaucracy so they can perform with a minimum of administrative and financial hangups. They visit the ministers (to encourage them to fight for budgetary supplements), the director general of Public Works and the vice-presidents of the MINVU corporations (for faster payment and more liberal contract regulations). The construction firms themselves act as individual clients, separate from the CCC, to protect and further their own economic interests and prestige. They talk frequently with the general director, the agency heads, the vice-presidents, and the construction chiefs (for faster payment and the expansion of works), the regional supervising engineers (for approval for unforeseen but "necessary" work), and the inspectors at the site (for support for costly additions, and manipulation of the vouchers to increase their working capital).

Though precise averages are difficult to compile, construction interests face a curve of increasing interaction from those officials at the very top to those at the bottom of the column "Authority Targets" in Figure 19. There appears to be relatively infrequent discussion over the level of construction in the country between the Executive Board and the president of the country (semesterly), the minister of Finance (quarterly), and the head of the Budget Bureau. Interaction over matters of more minor import tends to increase gradually further down the hierarchy, to the point at which the contractor and on-site inspector are in daily discussion over the progress of individual projects. The figure is perforce impressionistic, because some presidents of the CCC have had much more frequent access to the president of the country (when they were friends, or the country was shaken by grave construction crises).

CCC SUCCESSES

The CCC has met notable success increasing the level of construction by means of three programs which it counts among its major accomplishments. First, Decree Law No. 2 of 1959 provided special tax breaks for construction firms, economic incentives for home investment, and new capital for this sector of the economy. Second, the National Savings and Loan System (SINAP), begun in 1960, gave tremendous impetus to housing starts by stimulating regular savings that were channeled directly to middle- and upper-middle-class homes. Third, plans for building 360 thousand houses and creating the ministry of Housing and Urbanism, submitted by the CCC to Eduardo Frei in 1964, formed the bases of the programs that were ultimately adopted. All these measures represented advances for the construction industry.

Decree Law No. 2, drafted originally by President Alessandri and the

CCC to promote "low-cost" housing, is an excellent example of legislation favorable to construction interests. Defining "low-cost" housing in terms of units of less than 140 square meters of interior floor space (by no means a one-room shack), the law included a number of provisions to encourage their proliferation. It exempted the construction firms from some income taxes on their materials and reduced or eliminated several small, bothersome surcharges applied to their activities. To make the purchase of these homes more attractive, it relieved them of all inheritance taxes and rent controls. It also liberated them from property taxes for certain periods according to their dimensions: twenty years for those under 70 square meters, fifteen years for those from 70 to 100 square meters, and ten years for those between 100 and 140 square meters.

A series of provisions also facilitated the transfer of fresh capital to the construction sector. The owners of *plata negra,* or capital undeclared to Internal Revenue, were exonerated if they invested this money immediately in housing construction. This *"blanqueo"* accounted for an estimated 15 to 20 percent of the sudden surge in housing starts in the first year; more investment was forthcoming from small and large capitalists who saw that housing could bring a profitable return. Another important disposition required industrial, commercial, agricultural, and mining firms to "obligate" 5 percent of their profits. These companies could pay this amount to the state as a tax, return it to their own employees in a complicated home-loan arrangement, or invest it in SINAP or tax-exempt private enterprises dedicated exclusively to financing housing units (e.g., ENACO, Cervantes). Most firms chose this last alternative. The larger contractors invested heavily in these "five-percent" enterprises, which increased the volume of their work and gave them yet another source of nontaxable income. The main purpose of Decree Law No. 2 was to give quick impulse to the sector by offering both the firms and the public generous incentives to build and invest in housing. The law, succeeding in its original intention, also improved the profit statements of the great majority of CCC members.

The second breakthrough for the CCC, coming soon after the initiation of Decree Law No. 2, represented a further operationalization of some of its principles. The CCC was afraid that the five-percent enterprises, which sold their houses commercially, would not have enough customers from among the middle class. The private banking system in Chile at the time was dominated by large borrowers, consisting of well-established industries and commercial magnates (often members of the CCC itself), and ignored the small, individual borrowers despite their credit rating. Many financially solvent middle-class families naturally could not afford to pay the entire cost of their home in one lump sum.

After visiting several countries with savings and loan systems, CCC executives, with the encouragement of the A.I.D., devised a plan for creation of a nationwide savings and loan system (SINAP), linked to the government through the Central Savings and Loan Fund (CCAP).[15] Near the beginning of Jorge Alessandri's presidential regime, this plan was decreed virtually in the form presented by the CCC.[16] The loans provided by SINAP could be used only for houses, guaranteeing that the fruits of the CCC's labors would not be diverted to other sectors of the economy. The system was soon responsible for the construction of approximately fifteen thousand houses per year, about 30 percent of the total housing construction in the country.[17]

The CCC considered its Housing Plan of 1964 its third major success, although in this case the victory celebration did not last very long. The Chamber believed strongly that only it could transform Frei's ambitious goals for housing from a politician's dream to an attainable reality. The contractors' answer was a fairly sophisticated document containing four major sections.[18] The first part of the plan specified the distribution of housing units among social strata and regions of the country, and between the private and public sectors. The second analyzed the compatibility of the target of 360 thousand houses with managerial capacity, the work force available, current production levels of materials, and its effect on the balance of payments. Third, it outlined supply and demand curves for housing over the next six-year period, and suggested means of keeping the market flexible and consistent. Finally, the plan emphasized the norm of decentralized agencies for the new ministry of Housing and Urbanism. Though the plan was favorably received by the president, members of the CCC felt that they were later betrayed by economists in government who convinced the Economic Committee and the ministry of Finance that investment in housing was inflation-producing and counterproductive for overall economic growth. They were also disappointed by the distortions in the functioning of MINVU, discussed in the previous chapter, which they blamed on the use of political rather than technical criteria in decisions made at the highest level of the ministry.

[15] CCAP supervises SINAP, aids in the financing of the regional associations through short-term loans and purchase of bonds, insures the depositors' savings, and provides home-coverage insurance. CCAP, *Asociaciones de Ahorros y Préstamos: Disposiciones Legales que Rigen su Existencia y Funcionamiento*, p. 7.

[16] Decree Law No. 205 of 1960, creating SINAP, was almost an exact reproduction of the CCC's "Proyecto de Ley sobre Asociaciones de Ahorros y Préstamos" of Dec. 15, 1958.

[17] See Servicio de Cooperación Técnica, ODEPLAN, *El Mercado de la Vivienda en Chile*.

[18] "Plan Habitacional: Proyecto Entregado por La Cámara Chilena de la Construcción al Presidento Electo antes de su Asunción al Mando."

Almost as important to the contractors as these quite dramatic successes have been many small items of a practical nature, handled either by members of the Executive Board or the committees of the CCC, which keep the machinery running smoothly more or less in the contractors' favor. These matters pertain to regulations on bids, payment of vouchers, solicitation of budgetary supplements, reduction of red tape, small tax or credit breaks, and other measures to increase the volume of resources, speed of payment, or rapidity of decision-making. In these more routine affairs, officials of the CCC have estimated their historical record of success in the range of 60 to 70 percent.

Interdependence and Joint Payoff

Reasons for the extensive penetration of government by contracting interests lie in the degree of functional interdependence between the two parties. The fact that the contractors represent an important link between the government's economic policy and short-term employment trends represents the first element of this relationship. Second, construction activities respond to the interests of some of the poorest citizens in the country, wanting houses, and of most politicians, needing public works projects associated with their names, who make construction a continual preoccupation for government officials. Third, whenever political leadership has floundered in the face of serious depressions in the economy, or has extended itself in promises that went beyond its knowledge of what could be accomplished, the CCC has suggested timely proposals that filled the policy void and, not unexpectedly, corresponded to the interests of its members. These three conditions have helped foster mutually supportive roles between government and the CCC. They also tend to explain the high degree of CCC access to elected officials and to the middle levels of the ministry of Public Works, where reciprocity is the rule rather than the exception. The CCC has been skillful in maximizing its initial advantages by not soiling its reputation in its contacts with governmental authorities.

In relatively stagnant economies, construction and the tertiary sector are typical, albeit temporary, job havens for low-skilled and marginal workers. In Chile, the average level of unemployment in construction runs about 18 percent (versus a 5 percent average for the rest of the economy). Because the government is the main customer of construction services, unemployment figures tend to be sensitive to changes in fiscal policy, especially in the capital account of the ministries of Housing and Public Works.[19] Figure 20 indicates the high correlation between

[19] Jaime Cisternas Pinto, "Antecedentes sobre el Sector de la Construcción de Viviendas: Dinámica de Concentración," p. 5.

FIGURE 20. TRENDS IN THE GROWTH INDEX OF INVESTMENT AND
OCCUPATION IN THE CONSTRUCTION SECTOR (THREE-YEAR AVERAGES
FROM 1960 TO 1968)

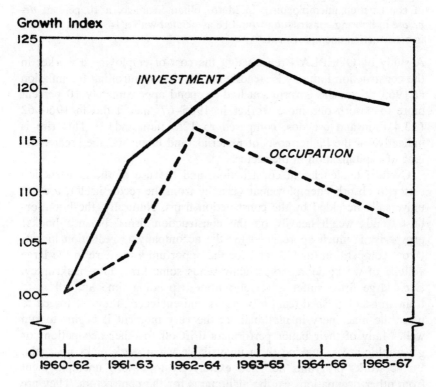

SOURCE: Fernando Tagle Yrarrázaval, "Modernización en la Construcción, Un estudio de Caso: Empresa Constructora de Vivienda."

NOTE: The indicators have been divided into three-year periods to compensate for the sensibility of both variables to annual changes in public expenditures and the lag between fund allocations and subsequent employment.

investment in construction and the construction unemployment index for the period between 1960 to 1967. The government uses massive public works to manipulate the employment figures, without committing itself to keeping those workers employed indefinitely. Once the level of unemployment reaches acceptable proportions and the drain on the national treasury becomes detrimental for other economic goals, the regime skims resources from construction and moves them into other priorities. When a new crisis occurs, the cycle is repeated.

Clearly, this game is fraught with dangers. Robert Merrill has pointed out that in Chile employment in construction increases at a less rapid rate with new investment than it falls when investment is cut back.

Larger percentage increases in housing activity coincide with smaller percentage increases in employment, while the pattern during declines in housing volume is mixed. . . . In other words, according to the limited evidence of construction unemployment in Metropolitan Santiago, a 10 percent *decrease* in housing construction would be associated with a 14 percent *increase* in construction unemployment.[20]

A study by ODEPLAN reveals that the cost of employing a worker in the construction industry is steadily on the rise. Controlling for inflation at 1965 prices, the government had to spend approximately 10 percent more to absorb one more worker in 1965–67 than it did in 1960–62 (13.4 thousand escudos, compared to 12.2 thousand).[21] This rise is indicative of the higher costs of materials and labor and the greater degree of capitalization in the sector.

Cyclical tendencies in construction, and the use of the construction sector to absorb unemployment (usually from the sector itself), are not universally heralded by the construction firms. Naturally, the boom-or-bust trends weigh heavily on the construction firms' balance books: prosperity is much appreciated for the accompanying reduction in cutthroat competition for bids and for the opportunity to share in the large volume of work; depression usually sends some firms into bankruptcy. Even large firms suffer adversely: after expending time and effort to train an accomplished team of workers and engineers, they are forced to place the machinery in mothballs at the very moment it begins to run well. Many of their better performers drift off to other occupations or geographic areas, making them unavailable when work picks up again. Public works programs designed exclusively to absorb unemployment from other occupations can be nightmares for the contractors. They are obliged to hire tailors, butchers, typists, waiters, and farmers to carry out functions that are completely foreign to these persons' skills, physical capacities, or ambitions. In some cases the use of motley groups of laborers for simple repair of a bridge has cost as much as completely replacing the bridge with the benefit of experienced crews.

Though the CCC may complain heatedly about the irrationality of middle-range investment trends in construction, its members do not deny that they hold a rather privileged position when employment crises confront the government. Marcos Mamalakis has stated that the industry, by the nature of its output, has the "clear ability to awaken public con-

[20] Robert N. Merrill, *Towards a Structural Housing Policy: An Analysis of Chile's Low-Income Housing Program*, pp. 132–135.

[21] Fernando Tagle Yrarrázaval, "Modernización en la Construcción, Un Estudio de Caso: Empresa Constructora de Vivienda," p. 2.

science with its power to bring the economy to the brink of collapse" whenever attempts to invest in more stable sources of production or to apply short-term anti-inflationary measures lead to reductions in construction activity.[22]

Though only about 5 percent of the working population is associated with construction firms, the CCC has always emphasized the forward and backward economic linkages of its trade.[23] When challenged by assertions that construction has almost a minus effect on increasing the gross national product, leaders of the CCC beg to differ, pointing to charts such as Figure 21, tending to prove that Chile's current state of development is highly interrelated with the country's capacity to build. They claim that Chile's industry consists of little more than middle-sized enterprises in iron, steel, cement, wood, transport, textiles, petroleum, and the "white-line products," such as refrigerators, televisions, stoves, washing machines, and other kitchen appliances. Public works projects and building construction require wood, cement, steel, and petroleum-burning trucks to deliver these materials to the site. The new house eventually requires furniture, curtains, and white-line products. If construction rises, consumption of all of the other products and services rises as well, leading to increased investment in these areas. Also, unless the worker is given an adequate house that endows him with personal dignity, he is not going to break out of the vicious circle of poor earnings, low purchasing power, fatalism, and laziness. Unambitious workers are not going to contribute to a high gross national product.

The construction sector also establishes interdependence with the government through its contribution to the supply curve in the housing market. For the past few presidential regimes, the housing issue has received an extraordinary amount of attention, for both humanitarian and political reasons. The governments of Alessandri, Frei, and Allende have committed themselves to build ever greater numbers of living units, eradicate the housing deficit, and provide each Chilean family with a wholesome residential environment. Though impressions of mass misery and imminent revolution in the *poblaciones callampa* (mushroom settlements) have been shown by sociological studies to be somewhat overdrawn, given the values of their inhabitants, the expectation of a large percentage of urban dwellers for improved housing conditions has been

---

[22] Marcos Mamalakis and Clark W. Reynolds, *Essays on the Chilean Economy*, pp. 83–85.

[23] From 1960 to 1968, the percentage of the working force in construction fluctuated from 4.08 to 5.30 percent. In 1968 it was 4.7 percent, representing about 140,000 workers. Cisternas, "Antecedentes," p. 6.

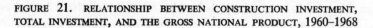

FIGURE 21. RELATIONSHIP BETWEEN CONSTRUCTION INVESTMENT, TOTAL INVESTMENT, AND THE GROSS NATIONAL PRODUCT, 1960–1968

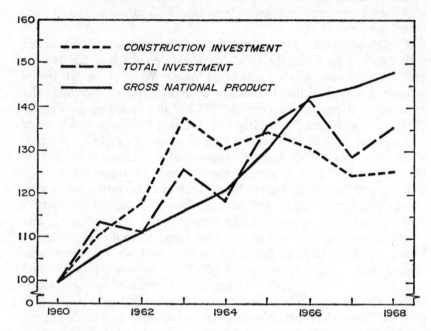

SOURCE: "La Construcción en Cifras," *Revista de la Construcción*, No. 100-1 (October–November, 1970), p. 28.

a Chilean political reality for some time.[24] The situation engenders an unusual meeting of the minds between pobladors and large construction firms. The pobladors can arouse a commitment from political leadership for positive action that eventually results in profits for the contractors.

Though this coalition is informal (more so than that joining construction interests with middle- and upper-level bureaucrats in the heavy-investment ministries), it again calls to mind the fortuitous meshing of the CCC members' financial welfare with the political solvency of the

[24] For the values of pobladors, see William P. Mangin, "Latin American Squatter Settlements: A Problem and a Solution," and his later "Poverty and Politics in Cities of Latin America," in Warner Bloomberg, Jr., and Henry J. Schmandt (eds.), *Power, Poverty and Urban Policy*. Also see Denis Lambert, "L'urbanisation accélérée de l'Amérique Latine et la Formation d'un Secteur Tertiaire Réfuge," and the more optimistic point of view of Milton Santos, "Le Rôle Moteur du Tertiaire Primitif dans les Villes du Tiers Monde." For Chile specifically, see Bruce H. Herrick, *Urban Migration and Economic Development in Chile*; Daniel Goldrich et al., "The Political Integration of Lower-Class Urban Settlements in Chile and Peru"; and Oscar Cuellar et al., "Experiencias de Justicia Popular en Poblaciones."

regime. The massive presence of pobladoṛs in inadequate housing throughout urban areas, their voting strength, and their occasional recourse to violence, speak more eloquently than all the charts and technical studies the CCC can present linking construction with development. The utility of public works for the electoral success of politicians in scattered districts also plays nicely into the hands of the builders. The prospects for individual firms may be buffeted by cyclical uncertainty, over the middle term. But public works and housing construction are advantageous occupations when the social stakes are high and political competition sharp.

The generally recognized import of physical infrastructure and housing for economic development and social progress have permitted the CCC to approach its lobbying tasks in the same way it might defend the national interest. When the CCC insists on the overriding importance of new roads, dams, water facilities, houses, airports, and irrigation works, it cannot be accused of looking after parochial interests whose benefits will accrue only to an entrenched clique of leeching capitalists. Physical infrastructure and housing are beneficial for the whole country, even though their marginal utility may decline as volume climbs.

The CCC has been quite careful not to engage in any dealings that would shatter its naturally favorable lobbying image. Its generally moderate pressure tactics, such as press campaigns, have earned it respect no matter what the political leanings of the party in power. The CCC has never used the weight of its organization to gain undue favors for individual firms. It never discusses the fate of one company unless the case can be generalized to the whole. If a firm has miscalculated a bid, lost its credit rating, suffered a reversal due to technical error or a reckless attempt to cut costs, the CCC does not intervene to have public officials grant it a special break. Responsibility for these setbacks must be assumed by the firm and worked out with government alone. On the other hand, if a contractor has been following the rules of the game and is surprised by an unjust governmental decision that sets an unhappy precedent, the CCC attempts to rectify the situation. Here it acts not for the exclusive benefit of the injured firm but for the membership as a whole.

All of these factors serve as partial explanations for the relative success of the CCC. The functional interdependence of its activities with the goals of the regime have made it an unavoidable partner in implementing national economic and social policy. It has preserved a high degree of access to government, at least for the purpose of explaining its point of view, even when the regime contained officials who were motivated to destroy the capitalistic base on which construction firms are founded. The prescience of keeping its hands clean has shielded it from scandals shaking public confidence in other Chilean interest groups.[25] These factors have served as necessary prerequisites for the CCC's three major accomplishments, but they do not tell the whole story. The CCC participated in the formation of Decree Law No. 2, SINAP, and the Housing Plan of 1964 at a time when the government was looking for technically crafted programs to solve specific problems. The Chamber's cause was furthered by a type of *pantouflage* (skipping from private to public employment) by which sympathizers to construction interests were conveniently located in top authority posts.[26]

Technical Expertise and Pantouflage

The proposals for Decree Law No. 2 and SINAP were developed when the government faced a serious economic crisis and measures had to be implemented to salvage the construction sector before it suffered a serious breakdown. In its 1956 report, the CCC complained of credit restrictions, delays in government payments, and unpaid debts of state organisms. In that year issuances of building permits had fallen 42 percent below the levels of 1955; unemployment was on the rise; orders for industrial iron were down 25 percent; building supplies sales had fallen by 32 percent; and the production of sanitary pipes and fixtures had dropped by 55 percent. The CCC warned that the country faced a "situation of extreme difficulties . . . as a consequence of the imminent paralysis of construction, given that this sector constitutes the nervous system of the national economy." [27] Some short-term palliatives were tried in 1957, but the uncertainties of the 1958 elections sent construction to new lows. Jorge Alessandri entered office with a generally depressed economy that needed fast attention. The executives of the CCC supported Decree Law No. 2 and the SINAP as their kind of comprehensive solutions.

Initially Alessandri was not favorably disposed toward either the final

---

[25] This is not to suggest that the CCC is immune to criticism. A June 1965 editorial in the *Revista* commented on a "violent campaign" against the CCC as an organized pressure group operating in the shadows to satiate its interminable desire for profits. The CCC has usually answered such attacks by pointing out its many achievements in the area of social welfare for construction workers, including accident insurance, medical services, generous family allowances, and the School for Foreman Training, which place it head and shoulders above the record of other employer associations.

[26] For the generic use of the term, see Henry W. Ehrmann, *Politics in France,* pp. 134–135.

[27] "Testigo de la Historia" is a valuable summary of the CCC's activities on the occasion of its twentieth anniversary. *Revista de la Construcción,* 9:108–109 (May–July 1971).

versions of Decree Law No. 2 or the SINAP proposal. He felt that the former gave far too generous tax breaks to the contractors, and the latter would never work because the country did not have sufficient savings potential.[28] Some officials of the CCC attributed their ability to overcome these objections to a standard rule: when the government has no priorities or programs, any idea pertinent to the situation which is not inherently bad will be accepted. Decree Law No. 2 and SINAP were coherent, intelligent, and extremely easy to execute, and they were handy. On that basis they were put into force.[29] Decree Law No. 2 might have been better balanced with the public interest, and SINAP might have been improved in certain technical respects. But they were drafted at a critical moment when action was at a premium; by solving one problem (even though they ignored or caused others), they won by default.

The CCC also profited from the location of some of its own members in key authority positions during the early years of both the Alessandri and Frei regimes. Ernesto Pinto was a vice-president of the CCC before Alessandri appointed him head of CORVI and later minister of Public Works. Modesto Collados was an electee to the General Council of the CCC before Frei made him minister of Public Works and then MINVU. To the extent that the CCC's proposals had merit for increasing the general level of construction in the country (a principal concern of *any* minister of Public Works or Housing), there was a friendly ear on the inside to listen to them. Pinto was able to convince Alessandri to promulgate Decree Law No. 2 in 1959 and form SINAP in 1960. Collados worked with the fundamental aspects of the CCC's plan for the new housing ministry. The idea of a series of autonomous agencies unencumbered by central bureaucracy was a long-standing desire of the housing

[28] Actually, the situation was a bit more complicated. When he directed the Chilean Paper and Carton Company, Alessandri had taken a personal interest in the loan and construction program providing all of the company's tenured workers with their own home. The success of this program was one of the reasons he was favorably disposed toward the housing sector during his administration. Once Alessandri was convinced that construction had to rise if the economy were to recover, the main question revolved around the means by which the housing plan would be managed. The first draft of Decree Law No. 2, written under the supervision of Alessandri himself, countered many of the contractors' interests and contained technical flaws. The CCC worked frenetically for a year to turn the situation around before the law was promulgated. In the end, Decree Law No. 2 aided the middle and upper-middle classes, not those groups most desperately in need of minimal living units.

[29] It was also helpful that Alessandri had been given special powers which precluded a congressional debate before the measure was implemented. Different kinds of presidential decrees are outlined in Cecilia Loma-Osorio Pérez and Benjamín Moreno Ojeda, *Los Decretos.*

contractors, promoted by Collados while the ministry was being designed.

It should be pointed out, however, that there were no "funny deals" based on this arrangement. Collados opposed the CCC on the question of transferring Sanitary Works to MINVU. Both Collados and Pinto were adamant in protecting the best interests of government during their tenures in office. Both tried to reduce the contractors' practice of increasing their profits unfairly at the expense of the public treasury. Since they had been on the other side of the fence, they were more qualified to recognize these tactics than the best-intentioned layman. The functional interdependence between the CCC and government, however, was clearly assisted by the favorable location of these men. They relied heavily on the advice of an organization that was technically sophisticated, though somewhat biased, when the government needed programs to solve important problems in the construction sector.

Working Committees of the CCC

The CCC fits into a natural situation of reciprocity with upper levels of government. Near the middle of the parallel hierarchies, this interdependency is operationalized by the CCC's working committees. On the surface, the routines of the committees are simple and undramatic. Approximately once a month, the Public Works and Housing committees visit the minister of the sector, the vice-presidents of the corporations, or the general director of Public Works, in order to review the current status of the agency's or ministry's projects. Discussion evolves around up-dating bids eroded by inflation, the level of official unit prices, changes in bidding procedures, payment delays, budgetary supplements, transferring funds to alternative projects, and other matters pertaining to scheduling, programming, and regulating. The possibility always exists that conflicts over these items can work their way up the hierarchy until they reach the president of the country—culminating in a critical, rather than an informational, press campaign on the part of the CCC. However, the working relations between the committees and the middle and upper-middle levels of bureaucracy tend to be so healthy that cooperation is much more prevalent than dissension.

The fact that agencies in Public Works and Housing are basically motivated to pursue their institutional interests is quite conducive to joint-payoff relationships, defined in terms of bureaucratic output, with the committees of the CCC. The contractors are interested in larger investment in public works and housing, rapid completion of work, and quick payment for work completed. Authorities in the ministries of Housing and Public Works are interested in larger budgets for their agencies, progress on a good number of works simultaneously, and financial liquidity and a maximum of flexibility in execution. Together they want budgetary supplements, rapid payment, legal facilities for increased construction, a minimum of red tape, projects of large importance and employment potential, and smooth professional interaction with their colleagues. Although all the agencies, ministries, and construction firms are competing with each other for valued resources, great possibilities for cooperation exist between the firms acting together and the individual agencies. Indeed, the aims of the ministry of Public Works and the contractors merge more consistently than the interests of Public Works and the ministry of Public Health, even though both of them form part of the state. The coalition between Public Works and the CCC is more stable than that between Public Works and the ministry of Finance, which ultimately is called upon to subsidize their extravagances.

Previous chapters described the manner in which many functionaries try to advance the prestige and financial capacity of their agencies. In budgetary matters, agencies generally subscribe to a Darwinian interpretation of administrative competition. It is a rare public official in Chile who voluntarily abnegates some of his organization's prerogatives for the general good. No official in Public Works, for example, would announce to the ministry of Finance that he believed that his agency was overfunded and that it might be more fruitful for the country to invest in education.

Once the public budget is duly divided among different agencies and ministries, bureau chiefs not receiving their desired allocations do not usually resign in protest or express extreme acrimony over the decisions of their superiors. The Sanitary Works agency, Architecture, and the Roads division readily admit that the government's priorities have been oriented toward other sectors over the past few years.[30] Irrigation may lament that Education and Agriculture have received more of a boost; but it is preparing for the day, not too far distant, when the agrarian reform will have generated a much greater demand for irrigated farmland, significantly raising that agency's importance. In the meantime, the

[30] A common tactic to remain on the offensive is to link the agency's output with whatever happens to be the priority at the moment. For example, a *Revista* article entitled "The Crisis in the Chilean Road System" made the following points. "The Roads division has been hindered by cost factors and by the necessity of the government to confront other tasks as important as the widely-discussed Educational Plan, Industrial Development Plan, agrarian reform, and increased mining production. At the same time that these plans apparently constitute a direct competition for resources with the Road Plan, they are direct or indirect consumers of roads, a type of infrastructure indispensable for any kind of development undertaken." *Revista de la Construcción*, 8:77 (October 1968), p. 27.

execution of the budget continually provides new opportunities for supplements.

Officials at the middle level of Public Works have taken advantage of the CCC's technical expertise and easy access to high governmental circles to press for goals internal to the bureaucracy.[31] The elaborate studies of the CCC, programming greater levels of physical infrastructure or housing units, are helpful in outlining the agencies' own plans for the future.[32] When CORVI needs a budgetary amplification it informs the CCC, which visits the Budget Bureau and its acquaintances in Congress to push the agency's request. If the Roads division learns of a movement to check construction-linked importations, reduce allowable expansion of works in progress, or eliminate some of its guaranteed income, the CCC begins to lobby in the Central Bank, Internal Revenue, or Congress. If Sanitary Works is threatened by a budgetary cut, the CCC may begin a protest that goes all the way to the president of the republic. The CCC has also tried to elevate the abysmally low salaries of the engineers in Public Works, for which attempts those professionals are quite grateful. In turn, these different agencies and ministries receive the working committees of the Chamber on a regular basis to iron out more routine matters in bidding and payment procedures. In essence, the mutual aid relationship is based on the fact that the interests of the contractors and the public agencies are more congruent than diverse.

Much of the effort of the CCC in recent years has been to consolidate and protect those favorable decrees already obtained. It has adopted a defensive attitude when initiatives in Congress, Internal Revenue, or the Central Bank intimate restrictions on the generosity of Decree Law No. 2 or the independence of the savings and loan system.[33] The legal department of the CCC maintains continual contact with informants in Congress who advise whenever a congressman begins agitating for stringent modification of the two programs. In such cases, the committees appoint member contractors sympathetic to the congressman's political party to try to convince him to change the more detrimental aspects of

[31] Holtzman, *Interest Groups and Lobbying*, pp. 114–121, indicates various ways that agencies exploit their interest-group contacts: pressure the political executive; consult for information and advice; build strength in the legislature; coopt to reduce the incidence of criticism.

[32] See, for example, CCC, *Análisis de la Infraestructura del País.* The first volume of this impressive document brings together valuable statistics, in-depth analyses, and future projections of roads, ports, irrigation, airports, public buildings, and sanitary works, correlated with the gross national product. The second volume is a twenty-year plan for port construction.

[33] By 1969, Decree Law No. 2 had suffered 105 modifications, many of them unfavorable to construction interests. See Luís Bulnes A. and Diego Barros A., *El D.F.L. No. 2 y sus 105 Modificaciones.*

his suggestion. When the Internal Revenue agency promotes a tax regulation with untoward effects on the construction industry, the executive board or a committee of the CCC tries to improve the dictum according to its own set of assumptions. The CCC generally does not ask that a tax be eliminated altogether, but reduced in certain respects, modified to make its payment more convenient, or freed from retroactive clauses. Since great new victories are not on the horizon for the CCC, its defensive posture is designed to prevent a total loss of the programs initiated in the early 1960's, all for the ideal of maintaining and increasing the level of construction in the country.

The committees of the CCC are more at ease inside the ministries of Public Works and Housing than in Internal Revenue or testifying before Congress. A 1964 forum sponsored by the CCC's monthly publication, *Revista de la Construcción,* came to the conclusion that the contractors and their representative committees were almost part and parcel of the high-investment agencies. One participant from government stated:

The contractors must be considered indispensable collaborators in the accomplishments of the ministry of Public Works. If we consider it right and just that most works are executed by contract, the contractors represent a crucial part within the ministry; they bring activity to our engineers and technicians, and provide private capital for the construction of projects.[34]

There are always some discrepancies of opinion. This gentleman complained of the contractors' lateness in beginning assigned work, the occasional slowness with which it was carried out, and the irrepressible desires of some construction firms to amplify their works, which led to disequilibria in the budget. This last allegation can be challenged by showing that distortions in the budget are often in the interests of the agencies themselves.

CONTRACTORS' EFFORTS TO INCREASE PROFITS

The previous chapters on the Chilean budgetary process indicated the manner in which agencies, especially in Public Works and Housing, employ tactics allowing them to apply pressures for supplements during the year, even though their original budgets were quite small. Now we offer more details on this phenomenon, in light of the fact that contractors are often willing partners in withholding information and perpetuating *faits accomplis* as a means of increasing agency funding. Individual contractors (acting independently of the CCC) employ a series of techniques which take advantage of internal bureaucratic

[34] D. Pedro Alvarez, in *Revista,* 4:22 (March 1964), p. 17.

politicking and contribute to their own profit aims. The most common of these are: submitting bids with deliberately unrealistic unit prices; transferring private capital to public projects and then agitating for cancelation of the floating debt; and inducing the on-site and regional inspectors to support complementary or extraordinary works. It will be shown below that these practices are much more prevalent in Public Works than in Housing. But collusion among contractors to divide up public bids, and corruption of public officials, are apparently *not* very widespread. These mechanisms are generally unnecessary because bureaucratic strategies and profit-oriented tactics combine naturally to achieve the goals of the agency (increase the magnitude and scope of projects undertaken) and of the contractors (more profit with less risk).

The problem of unrealistic bids begins with formation of the project plan. The publicly employed engineer who estimates costs for an important construction is encouraged to be very economical in his projections. The lower the total figure, the greater the chances the project will be included in the agency's budget and accepted by the ministry of Finance. He elaborates a project plan estimating a minimum amount of site preparation, dirt movement, cement used, pavement laid, foundations dug, and so on, for the project to be completed successfully, at current unit prices.

The Costs department of the agency combines the engineer's estimates of the total work volume with the unit prices for each item and arrives at an Official Bid. The different items in the Official Bid are considered fixed prices (*precio unitario*) or adjustable prices (*suma alzada*). In the former case, the estimates are fixed and the amount paid does not vary. In the case of adjustable prices, the regulations allow for an increase in the volume of work performed at that price according to the actual project requirements (to compensate for possible errors in the original plan). When they compete for the public contract, the construction firms can submit bids either above or below the Official Bid, always remembering that the lowest bid wins. A much simplified Official Bid, representing adjustable prices, might be:

Piece of Work	Volume	Current Unit Price	Official Bid
Moving Type A Soil	100,000 m³	10 escudos/m³	1,000,000 escudos
Moving Type B Rock	10,000 m³	60 escudos/m³	600,000 escudos
Total	110,000 m³		1,600,000 escudos

Upon inspecting the site, Construction Firm X may discover that the engineer had made a serious miscalculation in the type of earth to be moved; indeed a total of 110 thousand cubic meters had to be removed, but the proportion of Type B Rock, the more expensive of the two, was grossly underestimated. In such cases, Firm X applies a standard bidding rule that serves both to increase its chances of winning the bid and to open the way for extraordinary earnings once the project is executed: undercharge for that item whose volume has been overestimated, and overcharge for that which has been underestimated. Implementing this principle, Firm X submits a bid below even the Official Bid.

Piece of Work	Volume	Submitted Bid	Total Owed
Moving Type A Soil	100,000 m³	5 escudos/m³	500,000 escudos
Moving Type B Rock	10,000 m³	80 escudos/m³	800,000 escudos
Total	110,000 m³		1,300,000 escudos

This bid of 1.3 million escudos, almost 20 percent below the Official Bid, is extremely artificial and does not represent the real costs of this project. But it is nevertheless conducive to the aims of the agency, because it consumes even a smaller portion of its initial budget and allows it to give the go-ahead to Construction Firm X to begin work immediately. It is also quite consistent with the profit outlook of Firm X, since it opens a marvelous opportunity to make a considerable amount of money when the error is discovered. Not long after execution begins, the firm runs into rock where the government had predicted soft dirt and points out to the on-site inspector that Type B Rock constitutes a large portion of the total amount of earth to be moved. The agency is then responsible for paying Construction Firm X its unit price for each additional cubic meter of Type B Rock removed.[35] This could result in a balance sheet at liquidation resembling the following:

Piece of Work	Real Volume	Contracted Unit Price	Total Owed
Moving Type A Soil	60,000 m³	5 escudos/m³	300,000 escudos
Moving Type B Rock	50,000 m³	80 escudos/m³	4,000,000 escudos
Total	110,000 m³		4,300,000 escudos

Whereas it originally appeared that the project would cost 1.6 million, and that Construction Firm X would lose .3 million on its contract, the real cost of the project turned out to be 3.6 million (assuming

[35] In reality, the process is complicated by the use of the "compensated bid." The agency first calculates the percentage of the Official Bid represented by the winning bid; or 80 percent in the example. The agency then pays the firm 80 percent of each unit price as indicated in the Official Bid, or 8 escudos for Type A Soil and 48 escudos for Type B Rock. However, the agency can pay the firm at the compensated price for only 30 percent more volume than the original estimate for that piece of work. Thus the agency pays 48 escudos for only 13,000 m³ of Type B Rock. It must then negotiate with the firm for the price of the remaining 37,000 m³. In these negotiations, bargaining begins at the price initially included in the winning bid, or 80 escudos/m³, and the firm usually receives that price for the rest of the work.

that the unit prices of the Official Bid represented true costs). The distortion in X's "low" bid increased the project cost to 4.3 million, leaving the firm with a potential windfall of .7 million. Of course, the miscalculation in the original project plan is embarrassing to the engineer who made the first estimates. However, he cannot be criticized too severely, since he was given neither the time, equipment, or finances to do a more thorough job. The error actually plays into the hands of the agency, since an original estimate of 3.6 million might have encountered obstacles under the scrutiny of the Budget Bureau. For its part, Construction Firm X is not displeased with the outcome: the extra margin in the contract means not only more profits but an opportunity to spend a little more money on inspection, frills, and safety, and to leave the agency a truly superior product. This extra care is seldom manifest when there is no cushion in the bid, and it is satisfying to the agency, which is always concerned about the engineering quality of its projects.

Another area of potential cooperation between the contractor and the agency revolves around their common incentives to terminate capital projects as quickly as possible. It is economically damaging for the firm to underutilize its men and equipment on the project site when it has a backlog, has other contracts with rewards for fast completion, or is generally overextended. The expense of moving workers and machinery around the country encourages the firm to finish one project completely and move lock-stock-and-barrel to the next. For its part, the agency must contend with political groups also interested in the rapid completion of their pet projects. Especially in transit or central-city programs, constituents and parliamentarians expect to see steady progress until the job is finished, eliminating inconveniences and dangers as rapidly as possible.

The financial situation of the agency does not always permit a payment schedule that corresponds to the termination date of the construction. Indeed, the public works contracts signed by the Chilean government never obligate the state to pay more than one escudo per year on each project, no matter what the size of the total bid. Conceivably, the ministry could take several million years to pay off a dam costing that number of escudos. All works are eventually paid from the ministry's *"disposición de caja,"* or cash-flow margin in the capital account, on the basis of verbal assurances from the agencies to the private contractors on their probable payment schedule. For example, it might be feasible to complete a stretch of highway costing 10 million in one construction season, but Roads can extend only 5 million per year to the firm winning the bid. To induce the firm to sign the contract and to finish the project quickly, drawing on its checking account and sources of credit, Roads further promises that it will try to obtain financing to repay the debt before the next year's budget is issued.

If the firm goes on to another publicly sponsored project and runs into a severe economic squeeze, low working capital will threaten the continuance of the second job: the pace of work declines and workers are dismissed. Construction firms are forever calling up the agency to say, "We're afraid we're going to have to let a number of men go on Friday unless something is done about the money you owe us." The agency then asks the ministry of Finance to eliminate the floating debt. Finance reprimands Roads for getting into such a fix, but when several firms begin laying off workers in unison, the discussion is elevated from the administrative to the political sphere. Such deals arranged with enough firms induce the CCC to lobby in the ministry of Finance and Congress for an emergency supplement to cancel these obligations, and sometimes to launch a press campaign linking the plight of the contractors with the construction worker's vain search for employment. Though the firm's pace of work and the agency's cash liquidity are temporarily stymied while this process works itself out, the sagacity of the original agreement is usually confirmed when Finance comes up with the money.

A third tactic used by the firms is to come to favorable accords with the regional and on-site inspectors. This interaction can help gain approval for complementary or extraordinary works not contemplated in the Official Bid. Most complementary works stem from the inaccuracy of the Official Bid let by the public agency. Firms often find it necessary to detour a canal, widen a roadway, level a grade, insert deeper foundations, dynamite a hill, create a new access road, or perform any one of a number of jobs not included in the original plan. Another cause of these amplifications comes from the simple desire of the contractors to have more work, leading to such "extraordinary" undertakings as paving a road originally planned to be dirt, extending a road several kilometers to reach another town, or building a four-lane instead of a two-lane bridge. The responsibility of the on-site inspector, a paid employee of the agency that let the bid, is to approve or deny amplifications in the category of complementary works and advise on the question of extraordinary works. The tactic of the contractors is to convince the inspector that the modification is a *good* idea, and then convince him that it is *his* idea. In this way, the inspector presumably will approve complementary works more quickly and fight much harder for the authorization of extraordinary works.

The high degree of congruence in the interests of the officials of

Public Works and their client contractors tends to minimize conflict over these matters. Since the inspector is oriented more toward engineering feats than budgetary constraints, he usually has few objections to these additions even though they may entail a considerable new investment—from an engineering point of view they are all justifiable. Approval of extraordinary works must be made higher in the hierarchy, where the executives are preoccupied with the prestige of their agencies. They maintain a favorable attitude toward all visible expansions of works in progress, but generally look for outside support before giving their authorization. This outside support can come from the political party or coalition in power, influential members of Congress, or the president of the country. On occasion, when a contractor senses that a potential project expansion is not arousing enough interest on its own, he will make a point of meeting with opinion leaders in the local community and Congress to generate some pressure for continuation.

When projects of discernible public utility are inflicting deficits on the national treasury, it is difficult to ascertain who is watching out for the public interest.[36] The construction chief, the director of the agency, and the general director of the ministry cannot possibly keep abreast of all projects being carried out simultaneously in their jurisdictions.[37] Since even the regional inspector is not in daily contact with each project, the upper officials in the ministry are forced to delegate wide leeway to the on-site inspectors' judgment. From the vantage point of central control, the most vulnerable link in the chain of command appears to be at the local level, where the inspectors are persistently bombarded by requests from the contractors to approve complementary or extraordinary works.

Under the current rules of the game, the respective agencies simply rubber-stamp the opinion of the inspectors in decisions on complementary works, and the contractors carry them out without waiting for formal approval from Santiago. The inspectors compensate for being low man on the totem pole by having a near monopoly over information pertaining to what the contractors are really doing at the work site. Because of the technical complexity and unstable conditions of construction activity, this information can virtually negate the value of their superiors' authority on many matters with major financial implications.

[36] Compare with J. Stefan Dupré and W. Eric Gustafson, "Contracting for Defense: Private Firms and the Public Interest."
[37] In 1969, for example, Irrigation was involved in 9 major programs, Airports in 16, Ports in 35, Sanitary Works in 195, Roads in 213, and Architecture in 619. Ministerio de Obras Públicas y Transportes, *Memoria,* 1969, *passim.*

Far from their homes and their boss, the inspector's immediate reference group is made up of personnel from the firm. This isolation can make him susceptible to helping the contractor in ways that assist the project. A friendly inspector, partial toward the firm, can render a number of services stretching strict interpretation of regulations, but probably not constituting corruption or betrayal of the public trust. For example, if a firm has completed 90 percent of a given item in the contract and will obviously complete the rest in a couple of days, the inspector can report that the total job has been finished, advancing partial payment to the firm by as much as two weeks. Since the firms are usually pressed for working capital, small favors such as these can prove an enormous benefit in reducing administrative headaches. The inspectors often reflect as much dissatisfaction as the contractors with the high bureaucratism of the public sector. Slow payment and paperwork complicate their jobs and often impair the rate of progress on the project.

In general, construction firms attempt to facilitate this interaction with inspectors by means of special favors. The construction firms try to include the inspector in the "corporate family" by lending him vehicles on his day off, giving him access to the company canteen, sending him gifts on customary holidays, repairing his automobile in the machine shop, and perhaps even lending him money in moments of family emergency. It should be stressed that there is very little evidence that these services pass beyond the point of probity. There is no expectation that the inspector, because of them, will deliberately perpetrate a fraud in the company's behalf: e.g., reporting that the firm moved twice as much earth as it actually did. The construction firm, however, is well aware that a stubborn, picayune inspector can greatly hinder its job. These services are conceived as means of improving the firm's "public relations" with government. Though these practices are accepted as facts of life by most contractors, some do not believe that they are totally ethical and refuse to participate in them.

The looseness of the relationship between the inspectors and the contractors is recognized as a source of potential trouble by officials in the ministry of Finance, but they never broach its seamier connotations directly with the agencies or the contractors. The millions of escudos involved mean massive opportunities for corruption. Probably the outstanding phenomenon is the remarkably low degree of bribery, or requests for payoffs, despite the very poor remuneration of the engineers in Public Works. This "anomaly" is another credit both to the traditional honesty of career bureaucrats in Chile and to the desire of most large construction firms to protect their prestige, which act as deterrents against letting the situation get out of hand. The argument sustained here is that there is little reason for contractors and inspectors to resort to salary supplements to come to a meeting of the minds. Their professional and institutional goals lead to a perfect congruence on a wide range of substantive matters.

CORVI EFFORTS TO REDUCE DEPENDENCE

CORVI, facing somewhat different problems with the housing contractors, repeatedly tried from 1964 to 1970 to neutralize their influence in its internal operations. While Public Works seemed motivated to take advantage of its mutual interests with the firms, CORVI tried to reduce these links somewhat, in order to remain clearly on top of the game. CORVI was always appreciative of any help the CCC could provide in raising its budget, estimating housing demand, or providing data on the costs of materials and building supplies. But it was wary of becoming too dependent on a small group of contractors who could dominate its bidding process. Fortunately for CORVI, it was feasible to achieve this goal because the cost of its product was more predictable than the variable output of Public Works. This lessened interdependence resulted in strained working relations between CORVI and the construction firms, which contrasted with the camaraderie so prevalent between the two in the Public Works sector.

As in Public Works, Housing contractors are divided into several categories according to their capital base, their years of experience, and their performance in previous dealings with CORVI. The largest, most established firms are in Category 1; progressively smaller firms occupy Categories 2 through 4. Firms in each category are allowed to sustain contracts with CORVI up to a fixed maximum: e.g., 30 million escudos for Category 1, 20 million for Category 2, 15 million for Category 3, and 10 million for Category 4.[38] No single firm can have total contracts superior to the limit of its category ranking at any one time. Until 1966, this top figure was readjusted each year by the rate of inflation. If the rise in the consumer price index had been 30 percent, a firm in Category 1 with a maximum volume of contracts could immediately submit bids on 9 million escudos more work, since the limit would have increased from 30 to 39 million escudos.

During the nine years from 1960 to 1968, there was a gradual concentration of CORVI bids in a continually shrinking circle of housing contractors. Of 79 firms that won CORVI bids from 1960 to 1964, 41 had fallen by the wayside by 1964, going bankrupt, merging with one

---

[38] These are hypothetical figures.

of the larger firms, or simply dropping out of competition. The top 18 contractors, only 12.4 percent of the 145 firms who presented bids from 1960 to 1968, built 60.3 percent of the CORVI houses during the period.[39] Because of the financial solvency, diversification, and access to credit of the top contractors, it became increasingly difficult for the small firms to win bids. The more modest contractors could not afford to bid too close to the break-even point, for fear of miscalculating and going under. CORVI felt that the size and liquidity of the larger firms were allowing them to eliminate all competition and control the market. The practice of increasing the maximum volume of work for Category 1 firms each year contributed to this trend.

To forestall the eventuality that CORVI would be at the mercy of a small group of large producers with excellent possibilities for collusion and price fixing, in 1967 it froze the top figures in each category. This action effectively barred larger firms from bidding on an ever-increasing number of projects, since they could not sign new contracts until they finished projects already underway. This decision spread work among a wider group of contractors and gave CORVI more breathing space in handling its clients.

CORVI was also interested in reducing costs in order to better program its finances and lower the profit margin of firms who depended on the public wealth for their existence. Before 1965 each CORVI bid had represented a brand-new design that was the latest brainstorm of the architects drawing up the project. Once in execution, the programs always encountered innumerable cost overruns because design errors and supply needs were never completely worked out. Housing contractors took advantage of this situation in the same way as their colleagues in Public Works—exploiting weaknesses in the adjustable costs and piling a good many complementary works onto the original plans. To eliminate these practices, CORVI began working with standardized housing designs (*viviendas tipos racionalizadas*) in four basic units: a house and an apartment for workers, and a slightly larger house and apartment for white-collar employees. Large blocks of these standardized units were offered for bid on a repeated basis, which allowed past learning to contribute to improvements in their blueprints and layouts.[40]

The program was a tremendous success in predicting true costs and reducing the portion of the bid consisting of adjustable costs. This dis-

---

[39] Cisternas, "Antecedentes," p. 33.

[40] The smallest unit, Vivienda Tipo Racionalizada No. 132, reduced construction costs 30 to 45 percent. It used the cheapest materials available locally, eliminated all luxury items and accessories (interior doors, locks), and left termination to the owner. CORVI eventually knew exactly how many bricks, boards, beams, and nails were needed for each unit. *Revista de la Construcción*, 7:57 (January 1967), p. 35.

couraged contractors from carrying out amplifications at the site, since unanticipated expenses in the fixed costs could not be initiated through simple approval of the on-site inspector. They had to be passed all the way up to the General Comptroller's office for the requisite stamps and signatures. Unlike Public Works contracts, complementary works became rather bad business for the housing contractors. Because they entailed long delays and payment with depreciated money, many firms did their best to refuse accepting them. Often they had to be literally obliged to provide better insulation or rain protection when the standardized design did not account for local climatic conditions.

However, after issuing a massive number of bids for *viviendas tipos racionalizadas* from Arica to Punta Arenas, CORVI soon discovered that a reduced number of large firms were again dominating the competition. Knowing that each design was going to be a repeat of the previous one, some of the larger firms invested in vertical industries, reducing costs still further. They began to manufacture certain modular parts on a prefabricated basis, such as molding, tiles, and drains. They imported equipment ideally suited for the standardized designs, allowing them to increase the speed of construction and reduce labor overhead. The concurrence for bids started to drop off, because only the strongest firms could push their profit margin down to near the base price.

Table 13 points out the degree to which the four largest firms were able to outstrip their smaller competitors in reducing costs from 1960 to 1968. The total level of CORVI investment in 1968, distributed among all of the contractors in the sector, had risen by 315 percent compared to 1960 (controlling for inflation). At the same time, the total increase in square meters constructed was only 28 percent, and

TABLE 13. LARGE FIRMS CONSTRUCT HOUSES MORE CHEAPLY THAN THEIR SMALLER COMPETITORS
(*In percent*)

	All Firms That Won Bids	Four Largest That Won Bids
Increase in the Real Value of Bids Issued from 1960 to 1968	315	177
Increase in the Number of Square Meters Constructed, 1960–1968	28	51.8
Increase in the Number of Houses Constructed	5	26.4

SOURCE: Jaime Cisternas Pinto, "Antecedentes sobre el Sector de la Construcción de Viviendas: Dinámica de Concentración," p. 23.

only 5 percent more houses were built. The four largest firms taken alone showed a much better record. With an increased investment of 177 percent, they were able to augment the volume of floor space by 51.8 percent and the number of houses by 26.4 percent. The four largest firms were approximately three and a half times more effective in keeping prices down than the average for the whole construction sector. CORVI was pleased with the reduced costs, but was again worried that smaller firms would be put completely out of the running, leaving the agency in a one-sided wrestling match with the four or five "big daddies."

CORVI felt that smaller firms would bid on standardized units if they gained an idea of their production costs without risking huge losses in open competition with the largest contractors. CORVI located vacant plots of public land in urban areas which were adequate for the construction of one or two of these apartment buildings, or a small complex of the single-family dwellings. It then contacted several medium-sized firms and arranged for them to construct them on a cost-plus basis. The program was designed to give them practical experience with the designs and first-hand data on how much margin they needed to come out in the black.

The cat-and-mouse game between CORVI and the construction firms resulted in generally cooler working relations than in the Public Works sector. Housing inspectors tended to be more rigorous in applying strict norms to the conduct of the contractor at the work site, and the higher officials were less sympathetic to project amplifications. Individual contractors seemed to feel a little less certain of their standing inside of CORVI, and could not count on being defended by its authorities as trustworthy collaborators in carrying out housing plans. There was considerably more interest in CORVI than in Public Works in experimenting with a state construction company that would absorb all public housing construction, altogether eliminating the need for the private firm.

INTERDEPENDENCE AND ACCOMMODATION
IN CLIENT RELATIONS

At the beginning of this chapter I suggested that some of the same factors governing an individual citizen's treatment by bureaucracy help explain the nature of client relations. Several hypotheses generated from observation of the petitioner and the broker were applied to the client and the interest group. In his interaction with bureaucracy, the outside actor can improve his bargaining position in three ways: (1) high frequency interaction in function of the agency's output, leading to routinized contact, joint payoff, and a partial disappearance of the boundary separating organizational insiders and outsiders; (2) using his capital stock of resources to support the political actor, agency, or regime, and reduce contingencies for their operations in the political or economic community; and (3) intervening on the basis of tangential inducements having no direct relationship with the stated goals of the public organization (indeed, favors based on political pull, bribes, or family or social contact can easily subvert these goals).

The outside actor who is most successful in influencing bureaucratic decisions has to lean on one or more of these factors to support his claims. If not, he operates from a rather precarious position. The first two sources of influence are more orthodox than the third and insure a more stable participant status. They are based on obligatory interaction with the public organization and can be justified by legal, technical, or cost-reduction arguments. The efficacy of the third fluctuates with the turnover in administrative posts, the problematic chance of locating linkages to the key official, the social composition of the bureaucracy, the political style of the regime, and the bureaucrat's evaluation of the risks involved in forgetting ethical standards in favor of short-term personal gain. As examples of (1) and (2) above, both housing and public works contractors, through their representatives in the Chilean Construction Chamber, have developed mutually supportive roles with the upper- and upper-middle levels of government. At the work site, however, there is considerable evidence that a different situation prevails: the housing contractors have been "participants" in fewer and "subjects" to more bureaucratic decisions than their counterparts in public works.

During the period under examination, CORVI was ideologically displeased with the capitalistic bases of the private firms and viewed its interdependence with them more negatively than did Public Works. This skepticism of the good intentions of the large housing contractors prompted CORVI to freeze the category maximums, introduce the *viviendas tipos racionalizadas,* and attempt to spread the work among smaller firms. Ideological discrepancies with their private clients, however, was a necessary though not sufficient condition to change these relationships. First, the nature of CORVI's output made it relatively easy to upset the formation of coalitions between contractors and the on-site inspectors. CORVI produced basically the same product repeatedly, making it much simpler to standardize costs than in the case of Public Works. Even if the latter had wished to do so, it could not have achieved such a high degree of price sophistication. Dams in the Andes Mountains or bridges over riverbeds pose new technical challenges and cost contingencies every time they are constructed. A more elaborate control system to monitor the real costs of major public works would be expensive to set up and probably counterproductive to implement.

A second explanation for the different working relations is that possibilities for joint payoff were less pronounced in housing than in public works. The ministry of Public Works could gain prestige and financial flexibility by cooperating fully with the contractors, who had professional expertise and private capital to contribute to the relationship. The public works contractors, agencies, and inspectors were attracted to significant engineering projects of technical complexity and high public benefit. They were interested in rapid completion, turnover, and liquidation, at a time when they were not a high-priority sector for the regime. The agencies were somewhat restrained by a diminutive original budget, but they cooperated with the contractors to make the most of that base, which invariably increased during the year. The low project estimates, the high number of project starts in the annual operating plan, the financing of projects from private credit sources, the contractors' cash-flow crises threatening employment levels, the necessary and unnecessary project amplifications, *all* had positive connotations for both the agencies and the private firms.

In housing, CORVI could actually lose prestige and financial capability by cooperating too much with the organizational goals of individual contractors. *Reducing* interdependence with the contractors served to increase CORVI's possibilities for prestige and financial flexibility, since it meant more houses at a much lower price. Each escudo saved could be put into other projects with a fairly certain idea of the return on investment. The number of houses programmed for a neighborhood was fixed—there was no opportunity for CORVI to continue building houses beyond the boundaries of the plot of land. The ploys and tricks of the contractors were quite damaging to CORVI in internal bureaucratic politicking. The house represented a much smaller unit of production than an irrigation system, reservoir, or port. If CORVI overextended its budget, Finance could shut off money much more easily than in the case of large public works. For these reasons, CORVI's relations with individual construction firms, compared with those of the ministry of Public Works, were characterized by lower psychic satisfaction, a more marked predominance of official norms governing the interaction, and less likelihood of a set of reciprocal supports defined in terms of the agency's output.

For those committed to rapid social upheaval, the reality of functional interdependence facilitating joint-payoff coalitions is both reassuring and frustrating. The pervasiveness of overlapping organizational goals insures that the social system will not collapse if previously outcast elements suddenly occupy elite administrative posts. Yet standard patterns of exchange are so mutually self-serving that simply changing the faces will not alter the system's substantive operation.

In the three years of the Allende regime, many newly appointed bureaucrats in Public Works experienced role tension in their day-to-day work schedules. While they recognized the value of sustaining functional links with professional contracting firms for the purpose of carrying out projects of national significance, their Marxist interpretation of Chilean history militated against such collegial transactions with successful capitalists, many with last names of an oligarchic hue. The prevelent rationalization for such dealings was the necessity for temporary, though vigilant, collaboration with these elements to maintain uninterrupted economic activity in the sector and to continue building the country's infrastructure. Despite claims that cooperation at one point in time did not rule out the axe later on, this particular argument fell within the same paradigm of politics, construction, and bureaucracy described throughout this chapter, and most upheld by none other than the Chilean Construction Chamber.[41]

The definitive route for eliminating undesired coalitions based on joint payoff is to undermine the conditions of functional interdependence— i.e., induce or enforce a redefinition of the goals, and the exchanges based on them, orienting the public organization's output. In Public

---

[41] Under the Allende regime, relations between the contractors and officials in the ministry of Public Works continued to be much smoother than those between their colleagues in Housing. A CCC report on March 23, 1973, revealed that after October 1972, "The minister of Housing and the heads of all the housing corporations completely cut off conversations with representatives of the Executive Board of the CCC. . . . The interruption of dialogue has prevented the solution of fundamental problems affecting activity in this sector. Quite an opposite attitude has been adopted by the various ministers of Public Works and the other high officials in that ministry. Although we have not been able to establish standard criteria for how to handle recurring problems, we have been able to resolve technical difficulties as they come up." CCC, "Informe Final: Conclusiones y Acuerdos de la 56a. Reunión del Consejo Nacional de la Cámara Chilena de la Construcción." While this report accused MINVU of arbitrariness and chaotic substitution of political for technical production norms, it reflected the gratitude of the CCC that Public Works was sympathetic to cost pressures on the contractors due to runaway inflation. For projects not commissioned on a cost-plus basis, upper-level officials of that ministry typically allowed for complementary works under the category of adjustable costs to permit the contractors to break even in purchasing materials, the increasing cost of which in 1972 ran approximately 20 percent ahead of the official cost-of-living index.

Works, for example, the ministry would have to cease measuring its achievements through traditional standards such as engineering excellence, efficiency and effectiveness of construction, rapid completion of works, a large operating budget, and continual professionalization of its personnel. A substitute ethic might be high employment and social welfare, regardless of the utility of the fiscal expenditures in terms of projects completed. The ministry's acceptance of an amalgam of objectives almost totally inconsistent with the aims and capabilities of the CCC would not only break functional interdependence but also obviate the need for any contact at all with large contractors. From the bureaucratic point of view, the revolutionary challenge lies less in a rapid rotation of elites than in a drastic definitional shift in the basic functions of public organizations.

8

POBLADOR VIOLENCE
AND ADMINISTRATIVE RESPONSE

Besides the contractors, the other important client group for MINVU consists of the *pobladores* (generally defined as poor urban dwellers living in substandard housing). During the Frei regime, pobladors played roles of both petitioner (acting alone) and client (through their cooperatives or neighborhood organizations).[1] Though a study of the alliances between pobladors and public officials might serve as a replication of the observations in the previous chapter, it probably would not arrive at any new insights. CORHABIT was designed to be the ministry's open face to the marginal shantytowns, and as such was in continual contact with pobladors, whose organization, agitation, and demands were conducive to its short-term bureaucratic objectives. Within MINVU, CORHABIT could use the dramatic living conditions in urban settlements for strategic advantage to counter the technical and rationalistic orientation of CORVI.[2]

Poblador agitation at its extreme, however, offers an excellent opportunity to enter into another theme covered only intermittently in previous chapters—the relationship between *violence* and *administration*. This is not to suggest that pobladors commonly use physical force to achieve their aims; quite the contrary. However, an identifiable cycle

[1] The *Federación Nacional de Juntas de Vecinos* could not be called an interest group because it never effectively aggregated poblador demands and impinged on public policy-making.

[2] Chapter 6 also discusses interaction between the pobladors and CORHABIT. It should be noted, however, that the mutual assistance pact was quite primitive compared to the relationships between the contractors and officials in the Public Works ministry.

of authority and coercion in the housing sector is instructive for understanding outbreaks of poblador violence and the behavior of organizations in highly volatile environments. *Poblador violence* is manifested by the invasion or usurpation of private or public lands for the purposes of erecting a living unit. *Government authority* pertains to the ability of government officials to make decisions that are binding in areas in which public offices claim jurisdiction. *Coercion* is the use of physical force (police, military) to oblige the acceptance of official decisions. *Administration* refers to the utilization of standardized regulations to implement policy.

These definitions are not all-inclusive, but help orient a study of land invasions (or *tomas,* as they are known locally) in Chilean urban areas from 1964 to 1970.[3] Opposition groups sponsoring illegal tomas challenged the authority of the Christian Democratic government throughout this presidential period. In the years 1965 and 1966, there were very few invasions and the outcomes were detrimental to the perpetrators. The reaction of the government (ministry of Interior) was to proceed immediately with eviction and put any entrenched resisters under siege until they capitulated from lack of food and materials. In the early years there was very little relaxation of the regulations and requirements of the Housing ministry in response to the pressure. Gradually, an increasing incidence of tomas coincided with a deterioration of support for the government. The culminating blow to the regime's use of physical force occurred in 1969, when ten pobladors were killed by the police in the southern city of Puerto Montt. The public outcry discredited the regime's policy of forceful eviction and initiated a pre-electoral interim when not only authority, but also coercion, became problematic resources for the regime.

At the end of the six-year period, violence in the form of land invasions was tolerated and administrative processes within MINVU were subjected to grave distortions. Tomas became an everyday event and the government no longer dared use force to dislodge the occupants. The carabineros practically withdrew from the scene, leaving the situation completely in the hands of MINVU personnel. MINVU abandoned its traditional rules in the face of the onslaught and resorted to bizarre negotiating mechanisms to reduce conflict and reach accommodation. During this process, outside political agitators and organizations constituted a type of surrogate government in competition with

---

[3] The pervasiveness of housing as a social issue has added words to the Chilean vocabulary: *poblador, población callampa* (mushroom village), *loteo brujo* (land speculation), *toma* (usurpation), *campamento* (a settlement on usurped property).

the legal regime. Great masses of pobladors learned that they could receive their homesite more rapidly by adhering to these counter-elites than by passing through formal bureaucratic channels.

A POSSIBLE FORMULA FOR URBAN VIOLENCE

The subdiscipline of political sociology dealing with the consequences of rapid urbanization has passed through several stages of refinement. The first writers on the subject saw large shantytowns as potential hotbeds for violent revolution directed against the existing social order.[4] Analysts from both the far Right and the far Left concluded that the pobladors represent a lumpenproletariat ripe for revolt, unleashing a wave of violence that would be difficult to contain.[5] A more sophisticated body of literature rejects the simplistic generalizations of the "lumpen" school, explaining poblador passivity through their predominant values and the structural environment of typical shantytown settlements. According to this approach, the "available mass" conception is untenable in view of the fact that social disintegration in shantytowns is not as pronounced as first suspected.[6] Once pobladors succeed in obtaining a plot of ground and a house, no matter how

---

[4] William P. Mangin refers to these writings in "Latin American Squatter Settlements: A Problem and a Solution." See also Tad Szulc, *The Winds of Revolution*; Franz Fanon, *The Wretched of the Earth*, p. 103; César Pinto Quesada, "Le Phénomêne d'immigration dans l'agglomeration de Santiago du Chili." Also, footnote 24 of Chapter 7.

[5] After 1940, Chile would have been a typical country for such violence to occur. In that year, 54.7 percent of the national population lived in municipalities containing fewer than 25 thousand persons. By 1960, only 31.4 percent of the populace lived in these smaller towns, and 52.9 percent were in cities of 50 thousand or more. In the province of Santiago, where much of the urban growth took place, the percentage of the population consisting of potential lumpen elements (low-class, low-income) increased dramatically during this period. Whereas the lower and middle classes were somewhat balanced percentage-wise in 1940, in 1960 the lower class outnumbered the middle and upper strata by approximately three to one. See Table 2 in Peter S. Cleaves, *Developmental Processes in Chilean Local Government*, p. 23. The fact that widespread violence failed to materialize in Chilean urban areas confutes the causal model, Rapid Urbanization → Violence. Also see Lars Shoultz, "Urbanization and Political Change in Latin America."

[6] Shantytown dwellers rarely come directly from the countryside. They are not highland or rural villagers incongruously residing in the city, attracted, awed, and fascinated by automobiles and bright lights. Much of their motivation stems from economic factors, and they are susceptible to the same inducements that affect the behavior of more integrated members of the social community. They have moderate aspirations for themselves and higher ambitions for their children. Their nominal allegiance to radical movements seems to be more a means to consolidate, protect, and further their most immediate goals than a symptom of pent-up feelings of vengeance.

deficient, they begin to reflect conservative political attitudes.[7] Very rarely are they desperados with nothing to lose by taking up arms. The neighborhoods themselves can be subdivided into "slums of despair" and "slums of hope" (Charles J. Stokes); into "the squatter settlement," "the decaying housing project," and "the new resettlement area" (Alejandro Portes); or into as many as eight different types of shantytowns (Carlos Delgado), depending on structural factors.[8]

The remarkable implication of much of this later literature is that most pobladors are oriented toward the same values as middle-class urbanites, and represent an aspiring bourgeoisie camouflaged only by depressed living conditions. This tentative conclusion fits in well with Chilean social history. The "value leaders" in the society have consistently been the upper strata—the traditional aristocracy in the colonial period, the oligarchy in the nineteenth century, followed by the commercial, industrial, and mining plutocracy dominating economic, political, and social life in the twentieth century. A basic consensus on the parameters of social and political behavior has led to facile cooptation of troublesome power contenders and contributed to a remarkable stability in the system.[9] Those counter-elites who totally reject the status quo (from the Carrera brothers to the M.I.R.) generally have encountered difficulty winning broadly-based support, mainly because they oppose exactly what their potential followers earnestly desire.[10] In housing, this historical tendency has not yet been broken. The demands of pobladors connote final ends emulating the life-style of higher levels on the social hierarchy, though naturally on a more modest scale. Specifically, this means that pobladors demon-

[7] John Turner, "Uncontrolled Urban Settlement: Problems and Policies"; Wayne A. Cornelius, Jr., "Urbanization as an Agent in Latin American Political Instability: The Case of Mexico"; Daniel Goldrich et al., "The Political Integration of Lower-Class Urban Settlements in Chile and Peru"; Irving L. Horowitz, "Electoral Politics, Urbanization, and Social Development in Latin America"; John Friedmann, "The Role of Cities in National Development."

[8] Charles J. Stokes, "A Theory of Slums"; Alejandro Portes, "The Urban Slum in Chile: Types and Correlates"; Carlos Delgado, "Three Proposals regarding Accelerated Urbanization Problems in Metropolitan Areas: The Lima Case." See also Jorge Balán, "Migrant-Native Socioeconomic Differences in Latin American Cities: A Structural Analysis."

[9] This argument is developed by James Petras in *Politics and Social Forces in Chilean Development*.

[10] The Carrera brothers were Chilean independence fighters described by many as Jacobins. The *Movimiento de Izquierda Revolucionaria* (M.I.R.) is a paramilitary group founded at the University of Concepción and similar to the Uruguayan Tupamaros. It rejects a peaceful or electoral road to socialism, has participated actively in urban and rural tomas, and has financed many of its activities through "expropriation" of bank funds.

strate for a plot of ground, title to it, a fence around it, and a garden in it.[11]

If pobladors are middle-class suburbanites in disguise, we would not expect them to be attracted to violence as a means of achieving their ends. Many of the studies referred to above do predict that widespread violence will not be a characteristic of Latin American urban areas in the near future.[12] Three field surveys of political attitudes conducted in urban settlements in Santiago reinforce the impression that pobladors are not prone to use violence to solve their problems.[13] The first study was carried out by a team headed by Daniel Goldrich, from May through July 1965, the initial year of the Frei regime.[14] The second was conducted by Alejandro Portes in 1969, and the third in the same year by a research group from the Interdisciplinary Center for Urban and Regional Development (CIDU), led by Franz Vanderschueren.[15]

Daniel Goldrich noted that the "Chilean political system has a considerable cushion of legitimacy vis-a-vis the settlers." [16] In response to the statement "Violence should never be the way to resolve political problems" an average of 72 percent of his informants from four different shantytowns agreed strongly, and only 14 percent disagreed. Both

[11] It is interesting to note that some leftists in Chile used this type of carrot to mobilize pobladors to take part in tomas. Once in government with the Allende regime, this same ideal countered their goals for new housing developments: apartment buildings with collectivized services (nurseries, restaurants, entertainment) which would facilitate a *"concientización"* of working-class unity. See "La Firme," No. 13 (Santiago: Quimantú, 1970), a government comic book for mass distribution. An interview with Jorge Wong, vice-president of CORMU ("La CORMU Construye Ahora para el Pueblo," *El Mercurio*, Dec. 30, 1971, p. 11) revealed that "construcción en altura," although advantageous from both ideological and technical points of view, was still losing out to the "viviendista" approach because of short-term political necessities.

[12] Some studies have suggested that while upheaval is not an immediate prospect, it could occur in the next decade if the second generation of pobladors is suppressed in achieving broader middle-class goals in education and status. Other research argues that employment is the key: the traditional agricultural and tertiary sectors currently provide only a "sense of employment" to much of the laboring force; as these sectors modernize and become capital-intensive, massive unemployment will result; the economic system will be at the command of a diminishing number of capitalists; and the urban under-class will lead a violent upheaval. However, the scientific validity of these propositions cannot be tested until an indeterminable number of years have passed. See Goldrich et al., "Political Integration"; also W. P. Armstrong and T. G. McGee, "Revolutionary Change and the Third World City: A Theory of Urban Involution."

[13] Unfortunately, violence is not well defined in these questions. Is it land invasion, confrontations with police over specific issues, or guerilla warfare?

[14] Goldrich et al.

[15] Portes, "Urban Slum in Chile"; Franz Vanderschueren, "Significado Político de las Juntas de Vecinos en Poblaciones de Santiago."

[16] Goldrich et al., p. 18.

the Portes and the CIDU surveys indicated similar attitudes. To the question "What would be the best form in which to influence the government to change a decision?" only 22 percent of Portes' respondents and 16 percent of CIDU's felt that violence was the suitable method.[17]

The theoretical quandary associated with answers such as these is that land invasions have taken place in Chile. *Pobladors do resort to violence* to achieve their aims, and they *do die fighting the police* for home sites or defending land tentatively secured. The question is how to explain these facts, when most pobladors most of the time state a preference for alternative means.

Talton Ray has suggested that poblador violence is inversely related to the weight of *regime authority*.

The most obvious explanation for the lack of assertiveness is the barrio people's diffidence toward direct and unsanctioned political action, a characteristic which . . . is largely the consequence of their lack of confidence in themselves as political actors, distrust of their leaders, and insecurity in the ominous presence of "authority."[18]

This statement can be transformed into a null hypothesis explaining poblador passivity:

a. The less the feelings of political efficacy among pobladors,
b. the lower the legitimacy of grass-roots leaders;
c. the greater the authority of the regime,
d. the less the probability of violence.

Conversely, the proposition can be turned around to explain rampant land invasions. Reversing the equation:

a. The stronger the feelings of political efficacy among pobladors,
b. the greater the legitimacy of shantytown leaders;
c. the less the authority of the regime,
d. the greater the probability of violence.

It is impossible to test the full connotations of these hypotheses in the Chilean case, and it is not my intention to do so. Reliable data on the variables are incomplete, and a major exercise in model-building fully beyond the scope of this section would be necessary to confirm and refine Ray's contribution. However, the same indicators that he found most important in his study of Venezuelan barrios highlight some of the factors in play during this period of social mobilization in Chile. First, the trend in the dependent variable is clear: whereas at the

---

[17] Vanderschueren, p. 86.
[18] Talton Ray, *The Politics of the Barrios of Venezuela*, p. 152.

TABLE 14.   URBAN LAND INVASIONS IN CHILE, 1965–1970

Year	1965	1966	1967	1968	1969	1970
"Tomas"	1	1	14	8	21	215

SOURCES: 1965–67: Archivos Confidenciales de la Dirección General de Carabineros, reproduced in María Antonieta Avendaño E. and Justina Aguilera D., *Tomas de Terrenos: Estudio Descriptivo Exploratorio*, p. 4; 1968–70: Carabineros de Chile, "Ocupaciones Ilegales de Predios Urbanos e Inmuebles Ocurridas entre el 1/I/68 y el 15/VI/71." The latter document is partially reproduced in Equipo Poblacional del CIDU, "Campamentos de Santiago: Movilización Urbana," p. 8.

beginning of the Frei regime there were relatively few acts of poblador violence, these activities increased dramatically during the last year (see Table 14). The breaking point occurred toward the end of 1969; the number of tomas in 1970 was *ten times* as many as the year before, and over *two hundred times* as many as the first year of the regime.

Fortunately, some longitudinal data is available from the Goldrich, Portes, and CIDU studies which helps quantify political efficacy and local legitimacy. It is important to remember that the Goldrich survey was conducted early in the Frei presidency; the other questionnaires were administered just before the wave of takeovers in 1970. While the effective authority of the regime declined progressively from 1965 to 1970, feelings of political efficacy increased remarkably.[19] Goldrich's 1965 survey contained several questions to measure the strength of this latter variable; the Portes and CIDU results were very different. These questions and answers are reproduced in Table 15.

The reason for the rapid rise in feelings of efficacy can be partially attributed to the style and programs of the Frei regime, which attempted to facilitate organized access to government for the popular sectors of the society. CORHABIT sponsored a community development program called *Promoción Popular* that divided shantytown neighborhoods vertically into Juntas de Vecinos, Centros de Madres, and youth and cultural associations. Operation Sitio brought tremendous numbers of pobladors into direct contact with government for the first time, and apparently strengthened the image that the administration was disposed to act in function of their needs. These changing statistics

[19] The reader will recall that Chapter 1 used voting and inflation data as ways to illustrate declining legitimacy for and authority of the regime. See Figures 3 and 4. For one, Wayne A. Cornelius notes that the "authority" variable has been neglected in most studies of poblador political behavior. See his review article, "The Political Sociology of Cityward Migration in Latin America: Toward Empirical Theory."

TABLE 15. FEELINGS OF POLITICAL EFFICACY AMONG
POBLADORS IN SHANTYTOWNS, 1965 AND 1969 (*In percent*)

1965		
		Goldrich
Can have influence and make government help		36
Can only wait and accept government programs		61
Only if things change very much will I be able to affect what the government does		56

1969		
		Portes	*CIDU*
Do you think that pobladors could get the government to change its decision and help you?	yes	78	78
	no	20	16
	d.k.	2	6

SOURCE: Daniel Goldrich et al., "The Political Integration of Lower-Class Urban Settlements in Chile and Peru," p. 16: Franz Vanderschueren, "Significado Político de las Juntas de Vecinos en Poblaciones de Santiago," p. 86.

on political efficacy (36 to 78 percent) simply indicate that the Christian Democratic regime made considerable headway in one of its basic ambitions: to integrate the pobladors into the political system—ironically, to forestall violence.

If Talton Ray found widespread mistrust of local leadership in Venezuela, such crises in confidence are not so evident among the inhabitants of Chilean poblaciones, who appear to be ready "joiners." Even before Promoción Popular, there were large numbers of local organizations in Chilean shantytowns, most of them linked tangentially to political parties for particularistic payoffs. Pobladors have been conscious that organization is a prerequisite to winning government assistance and concessions. This positive attitude toward quasi-syndicalism is demonstrated in Table 16.

Unfortunately, the surveys did not specify to which kind of local organization the respondents were referring. The opposition parties did not let the Christian Democrats proselytize uncontested, and government-dominated Juntas de Vecinos were not the only political organizations in the poblaciones. First, the Communists and Socialists succeeded in gaining influence in many of the Juntas themselves. Second, they strengthened parallel structures called "*Comités de Pobladores sin Cusus*" (Committees of Pobladors without Houses), or simply, "Comités sin Casas." Prototypical Comités sin Casas existed as far back as

TABLE 16.   POBLADOR ATTITUDES TOWARD LOCAL ORGANIZATION
(*In percent*)

	1965	
		Goldrich
Extensive or substantial interest in what local organization does		49
Favorable evaluation of extent of help given by local association		58.5

	1969	
		Portes
Is there any person's opinion in this poblacion which you trust?	Leader of Communal organization	47
	Others	8
	None, d.k.	45
		CIDU
Do you participate in the local organization?	yes	62
	no	38

SOURCE: Goldrich, "The Political Integration," p. 8; Alejandro Portes, "The Urban Slum in Chile: Types and Correlates," p. 242; Franz Vanderschueren, "Significado Político," p. 80.

1947, when Communist organizers used them to spearhead invasions in La Ligua, Los Nogales, Recabarren, and San Miguel.[20] During the Frei period, the party again recognized that pobladors could be mobilized around housing more readily than any other ideological or political issue. These local organizations grew into active political forces in several municipalities experiencing the greatest urban growth over the previous twenty-five years, such as Barrancas, La Granja, San Miguel, and La Cisterna.[21] Eventually the Socialist party, the M.I.R., and even the Christian Democrats followed suit, organizing their own Comités sin Casas.[22]

Regardless of their political orientations, the families that were

[20] In 1957, the Communist leader Juan Costa miraculously coordinated the action of 3240 families (some 15,000 persons) in the invasion of La Feria in San Miguel. Jorge Giutsi, "La Formación de las 'Poblaciones' en Santiago: Aproximación al Problema de la Organización y Participación de los 'Pobladores.'"

[21] Closely associated with these Comités were the Communists Gladys Marín and Juan Araya Zuleta.

[22] Socialist organizers were Sergio Alvarez and Laura Allende Gossens, sister of the future president; for M.I.R., Victor Toro, who eventually ended up with three homesites in his own name; and for the Christian Democrats, Ramón Elizalde, Jorge Lavandero, Balbina Vera, and Renato Saintard.

prime targets for government housing programs were also attracted to
the Comités sin Casas, which offered an alternative route to a housing
solution should MINVU and CORHABIT falter. On the one hand, the
Comités claimed to be traditional interest groups representing the
pobladors' demands before the housing agencies. Their real success,
however, resulted from their ability to organize and execute land invasions as a means of pressuring the regime. The ultimate significance
of the Comités sin Casas came to light when they supplanted government in certain authority areas, such as the choice and distribution of
urban land. By the end of the period, the Comités and their followers
were responsible for an incredible outbreak of land invasions that
seemed to feed amazingly on its own momentum, placing government
helplessly on the defensive. The upper hierarchy of these groups became
accepted as the rightful arbiters of housing policy and were recognized
as authorities not only by the pobladors, but also by many housing
officials and carabineros.

Franz Vanderschueren has astutely stated that a violence-avoidance
mentality cannot be considered "an immutable characteristic of the
inhabitants of poblaciones." [23] Because of their lack of confidence in
the regime, tightly knit local organizations with a political affiliation
opposed to the party in power are more likely to instigate invasions,
irrespective of other structural or situational factors. Even if pobladors
gradually come to believe that they have direct access to governmental
decision-making, most are inclined to channel their demands through
nonviolent means. However, during moments of political indecision,
flux, or low support for the regime (such as when Frei was a lame-duck
president), feelings of high political efficacy and confidence in the
capabilities of local leadership are associated with land invasions carried out by pobladors of all ideological persuasions.[24]

POBLADORS, MINVU, AND CARABINEROS

There were very few persons in Chile in 1964 who lived in
tents, or regularly lacked some sort of roof over their heads. The families most in need of housing improvements were those in extremely
precarious circumstances—renters about to be evicted, residents of

[23] Vanderschueren, p. 87.
[24] Somewhat along the same lines, Albert O. Hirschman in *Exit, Voice, and
Loyalty,* p. 39, quotes Edward Banfield: "The effort an interested party makes to
put its case before the decision-makers will be in proportion to the advantages to
be gained from a favorable outcome multiplied by the probability of influencing
the decision." Also see Ted R. Gurr, *Why Men Rebel;* and Edward N. Muller,
"A Test of a Partial Theory of Potential for Political Violence."

condemned buildings in deteriorating neighborhoods, and people living in shacks along river banks or on public land such as garbage dumps. Another group was *"allegados"*—doubled-up with relatives or friends in houses that were overcrowded, but not necessarily of poor quality. These persons were either at an intermediate stage in the typical urbanization process (they had migrated from other locales and were staying temporarily with others until they found a job), or they were young married couples who had no choice but to continue living at home after they tied the knot. All of these families were affected by the country's "housing deficit," and were to be the primary beneficiaries of Frei's housing program.

The plan of the Christian Democratic Party called for the construction of 360 thousand houses from 1964 to 1970. MINVU abandoned this target when it realized that the ministry of Finance was not going to subsidize its budget adequately to eradicate the housing deficit through traditional means. In 1966 it redefined the goals of the plan in terms of "housing solutions" directed toward the lowest-income families living either in desperate circumstances or "allegados." These housing solutions, beginning with Operation Sitio, consisted of improving basic living conditions over a number of years through progressive steps: the provision of plots with some water and sewage facilities; construction of a provisional shelter (*mediagua*); the elaboration of community development facilities (schools, social centers, recreation areas); completing urban services (pavement and connection of water, sewer, and electric lines to each site); and the construction of a definitive house.[25]

In great measure, Operation Sitio was a way of preempting, through institutionalized rules and procedures, the motivations for poblados to resort to tomas as a means of improving their housing situation. MINVU opened enrollment for Operation Sitio in August 1965 to families proving a need for housing. In one phenomenal week, 62,739 families registered for the program (some 10 percent of the population of the Santiago metropolitan area), of which about 53,000 later proved to be completely eligible.[26]

Even though Operation Sitio was designed partly to release some of the pressure for homesites in the large *poblaciones marginales* (peripheral shantytowns), MINVU never considered that urbanized plots were to be free gifts to the poblados. The government had other goals either implicit or explicit in the distribution of this land. The first of these was the preservation of the social value of *private property*. The

[25] *Mensaje Presidencial sobre el Estado Político, Económico, Administrativo, y Financiero de la Nación*, May 21, 1969, p. 557.
[26] CORVI, *Operación Sitio*.

second was the advisability of transferring land totally through *legal procedures.* Third, the program was designed to inculcate the habits of *saving over time,* and encourage the concept of individual *self-help.* These assumptions were integral to MINVU's administration of Operation Sitio and underlay the standard reaction of the ministry of Interior to land invasions. The specific regulatory decrees of MINVU and the contingency tactics of the carabineros were the identifiable links between government policy and government philosophy.

MINVU Administration of Operation Sitio

In 1968 MINVU incorporated twenty-three distinct housing programs for low-income families into the *Plan Nacional de Ahorro Popular,* or Popular Savings Plan (PAP).[27] PAP No. 1 corresponded to Operation Sitio, a plot with minimal urbanization; No. 2, to an urbanized plot with home connections for water, sewage, and electricity; No. 3, to the completely urbanized plot, plus technical assistance and materials for a self-constructed house; No. 4, to a commercially built standardized home (*vivienda tipo racionalizada*), with floor space of 45m^2; and No. 5, a slightly larger standardized apartment dwelling.[28]

In order for a family to become the owners of a plot through PAP No. 1, it had to pass four major stages: (1) enrollment and receipt of a payment book (*libreta de cuenta de ahorro*); (2) accumulation of a minimum amount of savings; (3) assignment of a plot; and (4) payment of dividends on an installment basis for fifteen years. Enrollment entailed considerable red tape, such as presentation of an identity card (*carnet de identidad*), birth certificates for all family members, notarized proof of propertyless status, and documentation of a low salary level and the fulfillment of tax laws. Part 2 required the payment of 68 standardized quotas over two years, at the rate of approximately 8 per quarter. CORHABIT felt that the households would cancel their debt more faithfully later on if they had already had the experience of depositing money regularly against future assignment of the property.[29]

Once it had paid 68 quotas, the family became a "postulant" for the

---

[27] Charles A. Frankenhoff, *Hacia una Política Habitacional Popular: El Caso de Chile,* pp. 83–92.

[28] MINVU, "Plan de Vivienda Popular." For more details, see Antonio Labadía C., *"Operación Sitio:* A Housing Solution for Progressive Growth," in Guillermo Geisse and Jorge E. Hardoy (eds.), *Latin American Urban Research, Vol. II,* pp. 203–209. Also Diva Dinovitzer de Solar, "Operación Sitio: Una Estrategia Habitacional."

[29] Interview material. Also, savings were supposed to increase capitalization in the sector. See CORHABIT, Acuerdo No. 1909 (June 20, 1968) and modifications included in Acuerdo No. 2787 (Nov. 21, 1969).

homesite. The fact that there were always many more postulants than prepared plots meant that CORHABIT had to devise a complicated point system to assign them on a priority basis. The base number of points corresponded to the number of quarters that the family had been up-to-date in regular payment of its quotas. Housing officials added points to the base number according to need, self-help, and cooperative action. For example, the family's total was increased by 3 percent for each dependent, 10 percent if it belonged to Junta de Vecino or another neighborhood organization, 15 percent if it belonged to a cooperative (six-month minimum membership), and 20 percent if it belonged to a self-construction group. If the organized group bought its own land, the base was increased by 20 percent; if the group provided its own materials for urbanization, by 10 percent; and, if the group was ahead in its payments, by 10 percent for each additional quarter completed.[30]

Three other factors intervened in the assignment of homesites. First, if the cooperative was part of a *"población de erradicación,"* its arles (advance payment to bind a commercial transaction) were reduced from 68 to 20 quotas. Under this system, all the families in the shantytown abandoned their old homes and moved to newly urbanized sites. The buildings in the old población were razed, and the land was turned over to MINVU for another project. Second, if CORHABIT decided that the family was truly a hardship case, the number of quotas could be reduced indefinitely, just so the number of families benefiting did not comprise more than 5 percent of the postulants. Third, in special circumstances, MINVU could enter into direct contract negotiations with groups of pobladors in order to fix the conditions of the program.[31]

This point system was beyond the intellectual grasp of many pobladors governed by it. Nonetheless, most of them were satisfied that it was not being used as a smokescreen to distribute plots on a political basis.[32] They accepted the family name lists ranked by priority every quarter as binding and fair. The principal complaints revolved around the initial red tape for enrollment, the necessity of saving for two years with

[30] CORHABIT, Acuerdo No. 2787, pp. 8–10.

[31] The pobladors signed contracts with the "Commission for Operation Sitio," headed by the subsecretary of MINVU and including the vice-presidents of CORHABIT and CORVI, the intendant of Santiago, and CORHABIT's zonal delegate in the province. When the toma situation got out of hand in 1970, Frei retracted Decree No. 950 (1965) and had Decree No. 258 (May 14, 1970) written in such a way that the subsecretary reported directly to him, without passing through normal hierarchical channels.

[32] Indeed, the housing officials prided themselves on the fact that no housing solutions were assigned on the basis of political debts, favors, recommendations, or friends. Reportedly, Frei himself ran into a stone wall when he tried to get a house for his chauffeur.

nothing to show for it, and the long wait for a plot even after they had completed all of the pre-payments. The great majority of pobladors were willing to tolerate these inconveniences and wait for their home site. Others, however, led by Comités sin Casas or frustrated by the many requirements of the program, took part in land invasions.

What were the pobladors' motivations in participating in a toma? MINVU officials felt that the invaders, through a show of force, were trying to distort Operation Sitio to their own advantage. Rather than sacrificing to abide by its standards, they were trying to induce MINVU to twist its assumptions to meet their demands.[33] MINVU's program implied concepts of self-help and savings over time, added incentives for permanent social organization, and provided exceptions for unusual cases. Invaders could accomplish their goals if the housing officials subsumed their situation under a special category to which they were not entitled, or signed a contract with generous concessions as a direct result of their act of violence. The invaders were primarily interested in the third category, exceptions and concessions. For these possible gains they were willing to run the risk of encounters with the carabineros, forceful eviction, and weeks of pitiful living conditions under a state of semi-siege.

Urban Land Invasions

MINVU and the ministry of Interior cooperated to try to prevent tomas by anticipating them. CORHABIT officials, plugged into the grapevine of the poblaciones, learned quickly of impending invasions, which were not well-guarded secrets because of the number of persons who had to be organized. Once apprised of an impending toma, MINVU had the ministry of Interior station carabineros around the target land and intercept en route the trucks transporting the pobladors and their belongings. When an invading force circumvented these precautions, the ministry of Interior was concerned that the principle of private property was not violated and that the citizenry could not accuse the government of lacking resolve, faced with a blatantly illegal act. The authorities acted quickly. After ordering the pobladors to abandon the site, and receiving a negative reply, the carabineros' usual procedure was the destruction of the camp and forceful eviction of its in-

[33] Most housing officials ascribed to one or another hypothesis to explain land invasions. By frequency of mention, they can be ordered as: (a) an escape from deficient living conditions; (b) political agitation; (c) lack of respect for private property; (d) rising expectations, fed by Operation Sitio itself; (e) speculation. CORHABIT attributed the success of its program 20,000/70 (see Chapter 6) to the fact that it mobilized untapped resources and relieved frustration at the grassroots level, responding to (a) and (d) above.

habitants. According to the ministry of Interior, from 1955 to 1969 there were 74 tomas in Chilean urban areas, and the carabineros evicted the occupants on every occasion.[34]

If the police attack was not completely successful, the next step was to place the camp under military siege and deprive it of supplies until it capitulated. Initiation of a siege, however, was a turning point in the pobladors' favor, since the perimeters were difficult to seal off for long periods. As time progressed, repressive measures were less appropriate and the ministry of Interior tried to pass responsibility for the problem to MINVU.

The housing officials were interested in reducing the intensity of conflict, but not at the expense of disregarding the basic tenets of PAP: savings over time and self-help. They might promise a faster assignment of homesites, but only on condition that the occupants move to another plot of land and accept more onerous obligations for cancellation of the debt. If the invaders refused, the police made their resistance as painful as possible—continual supervision and harassment, no entry of building materials to strengthen the makeshift shelters, and no government services, until they left the land or negotiated a settlement. When conversations took place, MINVU always attempted to prevent the invaders from benefiting in any tangible way by their action. Quicker solutions would require a higher initial quota, a faster repayment of the debt, or a greater investment in labor or materials.

In a toma situation, both government officials and invading pobladors viewed a similar universe of factors that had to be maintained, or overcome, depending on the point of reference. These thresholds are laid out schematically in Figure 22. The pobladors pushed downward from numbers 1 to 10, trying to reach a final goal that implied a quick solution to their housing problem completely outside of the regular program. The government tried to hold the line from numbers 1 to 10; the ministry of Interior promoted the concept of private property and public order from 1 to 3, and MINVU tried to preserve the program goals of PAP from 6 to 9. Number 1, "anticipation and prevention of invasion," represented total defeat for the pobladors and total victory for the government. In contrast, number 10, "across-the-board concessions," signified a visible defeat for the government and a victory for the pobla-

[34] Speech by Edmundo Pérez Zújović to the Cámara de Diputados, Sesiones Ordinarias (No. 7, June 12, 1969), p. 444. Of 54 tomas in the Santiago area from 1964 to 1970, 40 were of public lands and 14 of private lands; 22 were motivated by poor living conditions, 2 in protest of MINVU red tape, 3 to prevent other pobladors from invading, and 27 for undetermined reasons. "Archivos Confidenciales de los Carabineros," cited in María Antonieta Avendaño E. and Justina Aguilera D., *Tomas de Terrenos: Estudio Descriptivo Exploratorio.*

dors. Generally, the power relationship between the pobladors and the government determined the level at which the toma situation was resolved.

URBAN LAND INVASIONS AND GOVERNMENT REACTION, 1965–1970

The changing configuration of four variables (violence, coercion, authority, and administration) in the housing sector can best be traced by examining a series of attempted invasions from 1965 to 1970. The longer an invading force succeeded in occupying the plot of land, the less valid the use of coercion to remove them and the greater the invaders' possibilities of winning some concessions from government. When feelings of political efficacy and the legitimacy of local leadership were high, yet the authority of the regime was low (all of

FIGURE 22.   POBLADOR AND GOVERNMENT STRATEGIES IN AN INVASION SITUATION

Event	Poblador Priorities and Tactics	Government Priorities and Tactics
1. Anticipation and prevention of invasion	First obstacle to overcome	First line of defense
2. Forceful eviction	Retreat but not disband	Protect concept of private property
3. Strangulation siege	Mobilize outside support	Make things very difficult
4. Truce: reduce conflict	First real hope	Transfer problem from Interior to MINVU
5. Promise solution if pobladors move to another location	Maintain skepticism	Distraction tactic
6. Savings over time and self-help (standard 68 quotas)	No solution	Fully preserve program assumptions
7. Faster solution but increased poblador sacrifice	Possible compromise	Partially preserve program assumptions
8. False classification as a registered social organization	First-level victory	First-level concession
9. False classification as población de erradicación (20 quotas)	Second-level victory	Second-level concession
10. Across-the-board concessions by direct contract	Final goal	Capitulation

which were evident in the last year of the presidential period), tomas
were more frequent. The later the date of the invasion, the more untenable a standard policy of eviction and the more distorted the administrative
response to the situation.

The first invasion treated, Santa Adriana (in the municipalities of La
Cisterna and San Miguel) in 1965, is a good example of rapid police
intervention and no government concessions to the occupants. The second, Hermida de la Victoria (Las Barrancas) in 1967, shows how almost heroic resistance by the occupants gained time and led to accommodation with government. The regime, however, was able to extract
a very high price for the pobladors' illegal action. Pampa Irigoin
(Puetro Montt), a 1969 invasion that resulted in the deaths of ten persons, marked a transitional point between two styles of government
reaction and two exchange rates for coercion and violence. On that occasion repression was tragically severe, but subsequent concessions to
the pobladors were generous. The condemnation of the government's
action on Pampa Irigoin discredited the use of raw force to evict invaders and preceded a tactical surrender by the housing officials to the
extraordinary pressures of 1970.

Santa Adriana (1965)

On July 27, 1965, a small group of families occupied 14
of 176 vacant CORVI houses in the municipality of La Cisterna. The
pobladors later attributed their move to a deep frustration at seeing perfectly good houses sitting empty while they were living "allegados."
The next day, carabineros evicted the 14 families, forcing them onto a
nearby section of the Pan-American Highway under construction. On
the 28th and 29th, 300 additional families joined the original group.
These late arrivals from the local Comité sin Casas hoped that direct
action would result in their obtaining a plot of land. On July 30, on
orders from the ministry of Interior, the carabineros told the group to
disperse. The pobladors refused and the police cordoned off the area.
They enforced the perimeter and refused to allow any supplies or persons to enter, including food, construction materials, and mothers who
had to breastfeed their children.[35]

At 6:30 a.m. on July 31, approximately 1000 carabineros stormed
the area, trampled tents, and forcefully evicted the pobladors. A five-
year-old child was accidently killed when a kettle of boiling water
spilled on her during the commotion. The municipality of San Mi-

[35] *El Siglo,* July 29, 1965, p. 5; July 31, 1965, p. 4.

guel issued an emergency resolution allowing the pobladors to settle in the Parque Subercaseaux, located in the middle of a busy thorough-fare directly in front of city hall, and 900 families (approximately 4500 people) took advantage of the offer, set up camp, and began the long wait for the government to resolve their housing problem.[36]

The response of the ministry of Interior to the pobladors was cate-gorical. The government would not tolerate land invasions in any way, shape, or form. The carabineros would be careful in evicting the in-vaders, but would act with absolute firmness. Those who left their homes to participate in the illegal occupation would have to return, or suffer the legal consequences. Carabineros reminded the pobladors that land usurpation was a felony and those who attacked police officers were subject to trial by military tribunal.[37]

Government leaders accused leftist deputies and senators supporting the pobladors of inciting the invasion to exploit the nation's housing deficit for political purposes. The minister of Interior repeatedly de-clared that the whole episode was artificially inspired, and pointed to the fact that pobladors held onto their plots in shifts, returning to their real homes at night. The regime stated that it would never let a wave of illegal occupations be used as a weapon to force assignment of a site or home. Both those families who were most impatient, and those who waited their turn, would receive houses with equal priority. In a meet-ing with representatives of the Comité sin Casas, the minister said, "If you wish, you can live there six years in the open air and have as many marches and demonstrations as you like. But if you are doing this in the hope of forcing a solution out of the government, you are wasting your time." [38]

The occupation collapsed after six weeks. The winter rains took a serious health toll among the children. The lack of latrines, the noisome-ness, and the destruction of the park roused the indignation of resi-dents living nearby, and the mayor of San Miguel had to rescind his original offer of help. Housing officials determined that 200 of the 900 families had been on the verge of being assigned a homesite before the invasion; these households were moved onto urbanized plots in the Parque Isabel Riquelme development. The rest of the families, com-pletely ignored by the authorities, were terribly demoralized and em-bittered by the experience. But after six weeks of struggle against nat-

[36] *El Siglo,* Aug. 1, 1965, p. 1; Aug. 3, 1965, p. 1.
[37] *El Mercurio,* July 31, 1965, p. 6; Aug. 3, 1965, p. 19.
[38] *El Mercurio,* Aug. 27, 1965, p. 30; *El Siglo,* Aug. 25, 1965, p. 4.
[39] *El Siglo,* Sept. 17, 1965, p. 1.

ural elements and man-made filth, they were in no mood to dispute the carabineros' orders to move out.[39] In Round One, the government was a clear winner.

Hermida de la Victoria (1967)

Approximately two years later, between 1 and 3 a.m. on March 16, 1967, a group of 5000 people affiliated with the Comité sin Casas of Barrancas occupied a plot of land belonging to the Instituto de Viviendas Popular–CARITAS, a nonprofit housing organization. At noon on the 17th, the invaders refused an order to disperse. The carabineros tore down their provisional shelters and drove them back to the edge of the property along the road. After the first charge, the police cordoned off the area and intercepted any supplies, including milk, bread, and water, heading for the probladors. The need for water to prepare baby formulas, however, induced the authorities to relax the prohibition of liquids. Soon afterward, persons with food were permitted to pass.[40]

Before the invasion, the Comité sin Casas had issued a five-part statement to the minister of Housing expressing the desires of its membership: (1) immediate provision of homesites with minimal urbanization; (2) provision of an emergency wooden shelter (mediagua) with no down payment or previous deposit with CORHABIT; (3) easy terms for canceling the 68 CORVI quotas, the first coming at the moment of taking possession of the site; (4) technical assistance, materials, and machinery to replace the mediaguas with self-constructed homes; and (5) the chance to demonstrate to the public-at-large that the Comité members were capable of improving their conditions through unity of action and hard work.[41]

Several days after the toma, a reporter from El Siglo, the Communist daily, sounded out the attitude of the government in an interview with the subsecretary of Interior.[42]

El Siglo reporter:	What has the government done to solve the situation of La Hermida de la Victoria?
Subsecretary of Interior:	The government hasn't done anything because it's not its job to solve the problem. The government cannot look for solutions to problems it didn't create.
Reporter:	But will there be some solution?
Interior:	None.

[40] El Mercurio, March 17, 1967, p. 23; El Siglo, March 18, 1967, p. 7.
[41] El Siglo, March 29, 1967, p. 7.
[42] El Siglo, March 21, 1967, p. 5.

R: Well, if it's not through the ministry of Interior, will it be through MINVU?

I: MINVU has its Operation Sitio.

R: But that program is insignificant if you take into consideration the enormous number of "pobladores sin casas."

I: Yes, we recognize the problem, but MINVU doesn't have more resources, and besides, it cannot go around making concessions to people who occupy land illegally. The ministry has a complete system of postulations, points, etc.

R: Yes, but many of the 1500 families of the Comité sin Casas of Barrancas have a CORVI payment book. Some of these date back nine years; many others are registered in Operation Sitio. Why aren't they given houses, then, instead of being strung along in red tape?

I: Those families will get houses.

R: When?

I: When they are due them.

R: Well, the congressmen from the Communist party have requested that you let these families stay where they are now.

I: We can't, because they are private lands.

R: What solution is there, then?

I: None. The people will have to leave this land and return to where they came from.

The ministry of Interior did agree to conduct a complete survey of the invaders. The results showed a universe of 1098 families, of which 601 had been "allegados" and 431 renters. Approximately 700 household heads had steady work, 241 were marginally employed, and 100 unemployed. Of those who answered questions on their economic status, 128 claimed to earn the minimum wage (*sueldo vital*), 448 earned more, and 355 earned less. As for participation in MINVU's PAP, 325 were registered for Operation Sitio and 317 for standardized housing units, and 366 were not enrolled. The great majority of the families (644) said they were prompted to participate in the invasion because of serious personality conflicts with their families or the owners of their previous residences. Another 169 wanted a separate house, and 72 were on the verge of being evicted.[43]

Eventually the ministry of Interior gave up its ambition of total victory over the pobladors and passed the problem to the housing authori-

[43] *El Siglo,* April 20, 1967, p. 4.

ties. As a peace-making offer, the minister of Interior even promised the pobladors 35,000 escudos to help them relocate on other property. A month after the original occupation, the minister of Housing met with leaders of the Comité to work out some sort of accommodation. This meeting was followed by two months of intermittent shadow-boxing and hard bargaining between the pobladors and the minister. Besides their five points, the Comité continually pressed for permission to bring building materials into the occupied area and spread their shelters over an additional six hectares of the property. The pobladors wanted to protect themselves from the humid weather, end the crowding of 5000 persons on a miniscule strip of land, and further consolidate their tentative hold on the spot.[44]

By late April, the pobladors felt that victory was in sight. But MINVU was determined to prevent gross violations of the basic tenets of PAP: self-help and savings over time. Symbolically, the invaders were meeting the first condition by living under difficult circumstances: many pobladors were paying for their persistence with their health. The winter cold and rain eventually required the evacuation and hospitalization of 188 children and 58 mothers. There were numerous cases of bronchial pneumonia, involuntary abortion, and infant deaths. Presumably, every day of the siege surrounded by mud and filth was equal to a month of normal effort under more humane conditions.[45]

The second condition of PAP was fulfilled by the onerous financial obligations that MINVU made the Comité accept. The ministry located a plot of land called Sucesión de la Hermana Cifuentes, costing 550,000 escudos, with a down payment of 100,000. The pobladors collectively had accumulated 45,000 escudos in deposits with CORHABIT; 35,000 escudos were committed by the ministry of Interior; and the minister of Housing was willing to contribute the remaining 20,000 if the rest of the bargain was accepted. MINVU was also disposed to lend the Comité an additional 1,200,000 escudos to cover the estimated cost of urbanizing the purchased land. But to qualify for the package, the pobladors had to agree to cancel the full amount of the debt in three years, regardless of any new obligations that they might incur by taking part in CORHABIT's self-construction program. The Comité sin Casas felt that each family could pay only 15 escudos a month; MINVU was demanding an average of 35 escudos. In late May, the ministry gave the pobladors forty-eight hours to accept or reject the offer.[46]

[44] *El Siglo,* April 11, 1967, p. 4; April 15, 1967, p. 7.
[45] *El Siglo,* April 26, 1967, p. 4; May 9, 1967, p. 5; May 19, 1967, p. 4.
[46] *El Siglo,* May 25, 1967, p. 5; May 27, 1967, p. 1.

Aware that they would have to sacrifice financially over the next few years, but feeling it was worth it, the pobladors voted overwhelmingly to accept. Though the invasion may have speeded their solution, the terms were much more onerous than those for other pobladors who went through normal channels. The minister even appointed a high-level commission to oversee the scheduled retirement of the debt and insure that the accounts of the Población Hermida de la Victoria were not misplaced or forgotten in the chaotic offices of CORHABIT. In the end, both parties were satisfied that they had won concessions.[47] MINVU, however, had successfully resisted the Comité's attempt to bypass the basic assumptions of Operation Sitio. The pobladors' "victory" required heavy sacrifices in their family budgets for several years. In Round Two, the government maintained the upper hand.

Pampa Irigoin (1969)

Puerto Montt is located one thousand kilometers south of Santiago. On March 7, 1969, on the north edge of town, 200 families set up their tents and provisional wooden shelters on a strip of land unsuitable for agriculture. Three factors motivated the invasion of "Pampa Irigoin." First, many of the families wanted to end their "allegado" status and establish a hold on their own piece of property. Second, the invaders wanted to reach this goal quickly and cheaply, without paying the 68 quotas over time to CORHABIT. The local Comité sin Casas, headed by Luis Espinoza, a Puerto Montt municipal councilman from the Socialist party, discouraged the pobladors from dealing with CORHABIT. Espinoza had recently been elected to Congress on a platform completely rejecting Operation Sitio, which he felt was a fraud inspired to protect the property of the dominating class. He personally had organized eight land invasions, including the one creating the población from which these families came. CORHABIT possessed a tract of land called Población Mirasol, on the other side of Puerto Montt, with 1255 urbanized sites. Of these, only 250 had been assigned, because of Espinoza's influence and the high rate of unemployment

---

[47] *El Siglo,* June 11, 1967, p. 30. This población is "Villa Oeste" in Portes' analysis. His survey of the residents led him to conclude that "the more protracted and difficult the initial invasion, the stronger and more durable the resulting social cohesiveness among participants and the higher their capabilities for collective action. . . . The most viable communities among the urban lower classes—those which integrate faster into the rest of urban society—are often the ones that society has attacked most violently. . . . The dialectics of the process often make official hostility and opposition against the invaders the necessary condition for the emergence of these dynamic traits." Portes, "Urban Slum in Chile," p. 243.

in the community, which reduced the number of potential postulants. And third, some families were interested in land speculation: they took part in the toma to obtain plots for resale or rent later on.[48]

To protect his rights, the owner of the property reported the invasion to the Intendancy (provincial arm of the ministry of Interior). Since the intendant was in transit to Santiago on business, his assistant made an emergency call on Saturday, March 8, to the subsecretary of Interior at his home in Santiago. Noting that the Intendancy had carried out numerous evictions in the province without serious incident, the subsecretary told the department official to evict if he deemed it advisable, and the ministry of Interior would back him up regardless of the outcome. The subsecretary made a quick call to the minister of Interior, Edmundo Pérez Zújović, to inform him of the situation, advising him that the toma was probably another maneuver by congressman-elect Luis Espinoza. As Talton Ray points out:

The government naturally tends to look much more favorably on the actions of one of its supporters than on those of its antagonists. An invasion carried out by independents or under the aegis of an opposing party would represent an open rejection of government authority and, were the action allowed to succeed, it would publicly expose the government's lack of control. To prevent that, officials would send out the police to protect the rights of property owners and remove the settlers from the land.[49]

On Saturday, March 8, an officer from the carabineros had visited the new settlement and reassured the occupants that the police were not going to interfere, contrary to usual policy. But early on the morning of the 9th, approximately 250 carabineros arrived at Pampa Irigoin and, apparently without warning, tear-gassed and stormed the camp. The pobladors retreated across the boundary line of their old población, but soon returned to contest the site with a force of some 1500 men armed with sticks, rocks, and iron bars. The carabineros attempted to repel this army with tear gas. When the gas ran out, hand-to-hand struggles ensued and several policemen fell injured. The carabineros then fired on the crowd, leaving ten dead and scores wounded.[50]

Even within the Christian Democratic party, the outrage over the deaths was enormous, and the government was shaken by the event. The leftist press began a salvo of attacks on the regime which lasted several weeks. During the funeral of the victims, several pobladors

[48] *La Nación,* March 20, 1969, p. 13; *El Mercurio,* March 10, 1969, p. 33.
[49] Ray, *Barrios of Venezuela,* p. 34.
[50] *El Siglo,* March 10, 1969, p. 1.

from the community astounded those present at the burial ceremony by proclaiming that the government had lied about the number of people killed in the incident. They then produced several cadavers found in the cemetery which they asserted were additional victims of Pampa Irigoin.[51] In the Chamber of Deputies, the Socialist and Communist parties began impeachment proceedings against the minister of Interior for abuse of power and possible premeditation of what came to be known as the "Massacre of Puerto Montt." [52]

The government gave MINVU the difficult task of recompensing the pobladors who had taken part in the original invasion. Instead of considering the pobladors as individuals (which required 68 quota payments), MINVU classified them as cooperative members from a "población de erradicación," which meant only 20 quotas. Furthermore, MINVU lowered the number of quotas from 20 to only 5, citing hardship cases, and granted an extraordinary sixty-day extension for the first installment.[53] Even though the government ascertained that seven of the dead had property in other poblaciones, all the affected families were given a CORVI house without rent. A law introduced in Congress eventually turned these houses over to the victims' survivors without cost, and ordered the expropriation of Pampa Irigoin for the original invaders.[54] Another law provided for free medical attention, and a pension at the rate of one "sueldo vital" as an indemnization to all of the invaders who had been totally, partially, or temporarily incapacitated during the incident.[55] Round Three was a pyrrhic victory for both sides:

[51] Dr. Salvador Allende, present at the funeral, agreed reluctantly to conduct an examination, which indicated that the corpses were unrelated to the incident on Pampa Irigoin. *La Nación,* March 11, 1969, p. 5.

[52] Cámara de Diputados, *Sesiones Ordinarias,* No. 1 (June 4, 1969), pp. 136–151; No. 71 (June 12, 1969), pp. 409–549. The measure was defeated by a vote of 78 to 54, with 3 abstentions. The minister resigned his post some time later and returned to his construction business. Despite his apparently remote responsibility for the Puerto Montt incident, the leftist press continually maligned Pérez Zújović, even after Allende assumed power. On June 7, 1971, three members of the extremist *Vanguardia Organizada del Pueblo* (V.O.P.) machine-gunned him to death as an "assassin of pobladors." Soon afterward, two of the vopistas died in shootouts with the police; and the third, after killing two detectives, committed suicide in front of the Dirección de Investigaciones by detonating dynamite sticks strapped around his waist. The last episode in this macabre sequence occurred on December 3, 1973, after the ouster of the Allende regime. A military brigade, which was transferring arrested Deputy Espinosa from one prison to another, was reportedly ambushed by a group of his followers. During the confusion, Espinosa was shot while "trying to escape."

[53] *El Siglo,* March 11, 1969, p. 7.

[54] Law No. 17,412 (*Diario Oficial,* March 3, 1971), Article 4.

[55] Law No. 17,563 (*Diario Oficial,* Nov. 19, 1971).

the pobladors earned their plots quickly, but with tragic loss of life; the government had taken a hard stand, but then succumbed to a policy of appeasement.

The Events of 1970

In 1970, the upcoming presidential election was the principal situational factor associated with the outbreak of tomas. All of the major actors gauged their behavior toward the September polls. The Christian Democrats distorted the fiscal budget. The opposition parties on the Left tried to embarrass the regime. The pobladors tried to further protect their interests in obtaining a housing solution. The presidential candidate of the Christian Democratic party, Radomiro Tomić, catering to a lower- and lower-middle-class electorate, played an indirect but important role in the confluence of events. Afraid that police repression in urban areas would sabotage his chances, he informed government leaders that if there were one death as a result of a land invasion, he would withdraw completely from the race, leaving the party without a standard-bearer.[56]

In 1970 the Christian Democratic regime, like others before it, programmed its capital budget in a way that terminated all projects with the greatest electoral impact. Since housing was an expendable item, Finance significantly reduced the budgetary allocations to MINVU. Although 42,000 postulants had completely met their initial 68 quotas for PAP No. 1, MINVU's budget could pay for only 16,000 homesites. The contraction of the supply coincided with a dramatic increase in demand, which expressed itself through the wave of tomas beginning in late 1969 (Table 14). The direct action of the pobladors eventually pressured Finance to supplement CORVI's and CORHABIT's budgets for Operation Sitio to 36,000 units. By the end of 1970, however, CORHABIT had assigned some 70,000 homesites, at least 34,000 of them to groups that had not deposited the minimum number of arles.[57] This massive redistribution of urban land was accomplished by complete distortion of MINVU's operating procedures.

As Figure 22 points out, in a toma situation the ministry of Interior's job was to help anticipate the invasion, evict the occupants, and, if necessary, enforce a siege. These defense mechanisms proved practically useless during much of 1970. It was impossible to anticipate tomas and intercept invaders before they arrived at their target area. Previously, when CORHABIT was aware of six or seven invasions in the planning

[56] Interview material.
[57] Interview material.

stage, it was conceivable for the carabineros to surround the lands and prevent the operation. But when twenty to fifty invasions were on the verge of execution, the carabineros could not possibly intervene with sufficient numbers to forestall the move. Second, high government officials feared that blanket repression of invasions was too risky a policy, given the possibilities of multiple deaths and a spasmodic popular revolt led by leftist elements.[58] Still reeling from the events of Puerto Montt, the ministry of Interior proceeded at a very cautious pace in handling the tomas.

The carabineros put aside their arms, and became sociological-survey interviewers and notary publics. They questioned all participants in the invasion to determine the number of families and dependents, salary levels, and enrollment in MINVU programs. They also officially informed the Housing ministry that a toma had taken place, and looked for excuses to justify the occupation on some legal grounds.

In order for Operation Sitio to be successful, MINVU had to perpetuate the impression that illegal land invasions did not result in any advantages over the normal bureaucratic channels. This policy, however, needed the energetic support of the carabineros to show that the government meant business and would not relent to illegal pressures. Because of the upcoming election, the events of Puerto Montt, and the generally low authority base of the regime, the ministry of Interior became very ambivalent on the issue of urban land invasions. On the one hand, it informed MINVU that tomas would not be accepted, and not to concede to violence. On the other hand, it vacillated at the very moment when a show of force was most appropriate. The carabineros no longer represented MINVU's dependable ally, protecting the integrity of its programs. The rupture of this coalition coincided with a deterioration in the personal relations between officials in MINVU and the ministry of Interior.

In mid-1970, for example, pobladors invaded MINVU offices, demanding that the government provide urban services to a tract of land that they had occupied illegally the day before. Following Interior's hard line, MINVU called the carabineros and asked them to evict the trespassers. During the mobilization of forces, hordes of onlookers gathered, reporters arrived in droves to ask questions and take pictures,

---

[58] Interview material. In 1964, few Christian Democrats would have predicted that their regime would witness so many bloody incidents between popular elements and the government. At the end of the period, historical-minded party members recalled that the 1938 massacre ot 57 young fascisti in the Social Security Service building had helped weaken public confidence in the incumbents and throw the election to the Popular Front led by Pedro Aguirre Cerda.

and the carabineros blocked off nearby streets, causing considerable traffic congestion. To the surprise of MINVU officials, the minister of Interior telephoned to announce that he was withdrawing the carabineros and suggested that they give in to the pobladors' demands, because the city could not afford to have traffic tied up during rush hour.

On another occasion, pobladors led by the M.I.R. occupied land belonging to the Agronomy department of the University of Chile. Although technicians had to attend to the agricultural experiments on a daily basis, the invaders would not allow anyone to enter, intent on staying if only to embarrass the government. Since the toma had taken place on university property, the ministry of Interior had a convenient excuse not to intervene: the tradition of "university autonomy" proscribed the use of police forces within the sanctity of the grounds. Interior turned the problem over to MINVU for solution. In a long informal meeting with the leaders of the toma, the opposing parties reached a compromise. MINVU had two alternative plots of land that were appropriately sized for the number of families taking part in the invasion. The housing officials offered the Miristas the plot which they preferred, on condition that they abandon the university property. The M.I.R. agreed to the conditions, and housing officials, pobladors, and Miristas sped off in MINVU trucks to examine the two sites.

When the minister of Interior discovered the terms of the bargain, he was outraged. He telephoned the subsecretary of Housing, asking him whether he thought that Chile was Bolivia or the Congo; how could he grant anarchists a choice of two excellent plots of land as a reward for their illegal action? Quite caustically, the MINVU official inquired why the minister was absent when the most appropriate response to the situation was forceful eviction of the invaders.

When the ministry of Interior ceased to play its assigned role in the affair, steps 1, 2, and 3 of Figure 22 were completely eliminated from the universe of factors viewed by both government and pobladors. MINVU tried vainly to protect the precepts of PAP (step 6), but no one believed that it was actually going to stick to any of the major goals of the program. For the pobladors, it was simply a question of how far they could push the housing officials on the path to capitulation. MINVU tried to preserve a semblance of legality in the process, but the pobladors overwhelmed its efforts with sheer pressure. The new reality transformed MINVU into a transaction agency. Violence was traded for homesites at a very favorable rate of exchange for the pobladors.

The situation became so confused that MINVU had no records of who received land, and even handed out more plots than the number of families actually taking part in invasions. The Comités sin Casas felt that they could extract more concessions by stressing their representativeness and implementing a modern system of cleruchy. For example, carabineros reported that 50 families had taken part in an invasion. By the time an official from CORHABIT arrived on the scene, the number had grown to 450 families. When negotiations began between the invaders and MINVU, the leaders of the toma could produce a list of 2500 heads of households who were not settled on the site, but whom they "represented." In the end, MINVU did not question the word of Comité leadership and handed out land with relative abandon. It was difficult for MINVU to take the time to determine a system of rightful distribution with hundreds of pobladors perpetually gathered outside their offices screaming and threatening to storm the building.

When pobladors refused to pay the 68 initial quotas to qualify for an urbanized plot, MINVU classified them as "poblaciones de erradicación," which required only 20 quotas. The Comité sin Casas pointed out that some of their members had already paid as many as 150 quotas to CORHABIT, while others had deposited only 1 quota, and demanded that an *average* of 20 quotas be accepted in place of the usual minimum of 20 for each family.[59] MINVU agreed. The housing officials were caught in a difficult emotional and administrative predicament. It was impossible for them to determine the percentage of invaders desperately poor and in need of a house, or those interested in speculation or motivated by political goals. Because the momentum was now with the pobladors, MINVU had little choice but to assume that they all were in need, and it treated them all generously even though in many cases the invasions were obviously speculative or electoral maneuvers.[60]

Toward the end, the situation was so topsy-turvy that owners of

[59] One of the first of these *convenios* or contracts was signed in late 1969, after 2000 families invaded land belonging to the bus terminal in Conchalí, giving birth to the Campamento Pablo Neruda. An intense argument on how to handle the situation ensued in MINVU, and the decision was reached in a cabinet meeting of all the ministers. Those in favor of appeasement prevailed, and the invaders were given urbanized sites in several poblaciones (Pincoya Cuatro, El Bosque, El Bosque II, Samur, and Rodríguez). Word of this convenio spread rapidly among the Comités sin Casas, which initiated a wave of occupations of MINVU and CORHABIT buildings both in Santiago and the provinces to pressure for similar convenios.

[60] The live-in maid of the director general of Planning and Budgeting obtained two sites, one for her ten-year-old son and another as insurance for herself. After the Allende government took power, many lower-level MINVU personnel took advantage of their access to keys and occupied vacant CORVI or Social Security Fund living units.

private land were encouraging pobladors to invade their land, and even ministry officials were organizing their own invasions, technically called "auto-tomas." Agricultural land on the fringes of urban areas was devoid of almost all economic value. It could not be farmed profitably, because residents of nearby poblaciones filched the produce before it could be harvested. The land was not salable for urban development, because of the low desirability of the surrounding neighborhoods. At the same time, the rise in taxes put the landowner in a tight squeeze. He could solve his problem by inducing a Comité sin Casas to invade his land. The ministry of Housing bought these invaded properties at inflated prices, paying a large percentage down and the rest within a year, and freed the property owner from accepting responsibility for the installation of urban services.[61]

During this frenetic jockeying for position in the pre-electoral period, two groups were left on the sidelines. One of these was the families who had completed the 68 initial payments of PAP No. 1, but were being displaced by pobladors using violence to take over urbanized plots. The other consisted of the Comités sin Casas affiliated with the Christian Democratic party, which had not participated in the tomas because they did not want to add to the government's headaches. These groups began to feel more and more betrayed when it became evident that their restraint placed them at a distinct disadvantage to those advocating direct action.

MINVU recognized that the first group was the most deserving of all pobladors agitating for a housing solution. In the third quarter of 1970, it corrected its previous neglect by working in their behalf. Housing officials located plots of ground that had not yet been invaded but were on the verge of falling. They established contact with the owners of the land and arranged for them to build a sturdy fence around that part of the property they wished to preserve for themselves. MINVU then assisted pobladors who had paid the full 68 quotas in a midnight invasion of the property, with the full cooperation of the owners, who had tied up their guard dogs. These families spent the pre-dawn hours choosing the best locations for themselves. The next day, hundreds of families who had been ready to pounce followed them onto the prop-

---

[61] Law 16, 741 (*Diario Oficial* of April 8, 1968), commonly known as the Ley de Loteo Irregulares or de Loteos Brujos, was designed to arrest land speculation by placing onerous responsibilities on those who subdivided plots for poblador occupation in return for payment or rent. Under the dictates of the law, owners of property who encouraged invasions and charged the pobladors a fee for the right to settle had to assume the full cost of urban infrastructure in water, sewers, and electricity. This provision also applied to local organizers who speculated in land invasions by charging pobladors for their services.

erty, and the invasion was complete. MINVU then purchased the land from the owner.

Christian Democratic party members realized that they were losing considerable amounts of poblador support to the Communists, Socialists, and Miristas who were carrying out invasions. Accordingly, they began to instigate their own takeovers to maintain their credibility. Despite the fact that these tomas enjoyed the *vista buena* of the government, their efforts were not as successful as those of the leftists in quantity of pobladors moved or number of camps established.[62] Their accomplishments were limited because they had started late, and their organizational ability did not compare with that of their adversaries who for years had mobilized the popular sectors around the housing issue.

By the end of the period, practically every one of the assumptions of Operation Sitio had been discarded. The dominating principles of the program were no longer savings over time and self-help. The institutionalization of grievances had given way to conflict resolution through direct action. The concept of gradual improvements of the homesite buckled as well. Operation Sitio transformed itself into *"Operación Tisa,"* meaning that MINVU simply staked off and assigned lots, and made no attempt to provide them with minimal urban services. Many MINVU officials could not quite believe the degree to which pobladors, through sheer audacity and excellent timing, had succeeded in altering normal government procedures. They shared mixed opinions, however, on the efficacy of violence as a way to receive preferential treatment.

It is conceivable that a group of local pobladors, by learning the intricacies of the ministry's schedules and rules, could time its petition and apply traditional types of pressure in order to get its program included in the yearly plan. That is, by handing in the demand in October, instead of January 15, it would have a good chance of including it in the budget stretching from January to December.

But the fact is that if enough pressure can be generated in January by another group, the October pobladors would be neglected in favor of the more bothersome and powerful group. The events of the last year showed that the most effective means of getting satisfaction is through direct, violent action.[63]

In contrast, another official was not quite so convinced.

[62] The party officially opposed these tomas, but could do nothing to stop many of its militants from organizing them. See Equipo Poblacional del CIDU, "Campamentos de Santiago: Movilización Urbana," p. 8; also, Joaquin Duque and Ernesto Pastrana, "La movilización reivindicativa urbana de los sectores populares en Chile: 1964–1972."

[63] Interview material.

I don't think that this type of violence is an efficient way of going about things. If the poblador waits and goes through regular channels, he will get better service. Many of the plots that were taken in the last year ended up without adequate water, only a little bit of electricity, and no drainage or sewer systems. Now with the recent rains these settlements are paying the price.

If they had waited perhaps a year and completed their PAP obligations in an orderly fashion, they would have gotten a site that was definitively urbanized and much cheaper to provide. Once they are taken by force, it is extremely expensive to continue work in them. Construction among playing children is not easy, and can result in two times the cost.

Violence is a bad solution. And I don't think that in the majority of cases the invaders had a real necessity. Once they saw what they were going to end up with, many just packed up and left the location. Of course, if the political leader did his job, he had their places filled by other pobladors soon afterwards.[64]

CONCLUSIONS

Violence has differential effects on at least three types of administrative units. First, it is little more than a nuisance factor for most government agencies, such as the birth certificate and post offices. Their activities do not normally engender violent responses, and rarely do their personnel have to change their administrative routines to adjust to it. At the other extreme, violent social protest is the raison d'être of the riot squad of the police department. Most of the agency's procedures are designed around violence, and elaborate techniques exist to handle it. Third, some agencies standardize their rules for application in a relatively tranquil, nonviolent task environment. However, their activities are either so controversial that they can arouse extreme opposition from disenchanted groups, or are directed toward clients who do not dismiss violence as a resource to achieve specific aims. Examples are the prison administration, the urban highway department working in a slum—or, in Chile, the housing corporations.

Especially when employed by persons with few other means of influencing government, violence is a highly dramatic social phenomenon.[65] It raises philosophical and moral questions that go beyond the mere issues sparking the outburst in the first place. Public officials usually interpret the act in terms of its *illegality,* and as a visible challenge to *regime authority.* As such, their normal reaction is to muster the forces of coercion to combat it. The government uses a show of force either to

[64] Interview material.
[65] See Michael Lipsky, "Protest as a Political Resource."

eliminate its adversaries physically, to dissuade them of the "wisdom" of their deviant behavior, or to reestablish its reputation among other relevant publics. If successful, one of the spin-off effects is to return the agency's task environment to a semblance of normality and allow it to continue implementing standardized rules with few alterations. Accordingly, the forces of coercion can be important allies to bureaucratic units that must face occasional incidents of violence while they carry out their normal functions. By intervening with physical force, the police or army assists the agency to preserve the integrity of its past procedures and maintain an upper hand when uncertainty rises above perilous levels.

The regime, however, must make a deliberate decision to use coercion. Sometimes it is reluctant to do so. Max Weber has written that the state monopolizes "the legitimate use of physical force" in society.[66] When he says "the legitimate use," Weber automatically assumes that the state, and the officials who represent it, are receiving legitimacy; that is, authority roles are accepted. This legitimacy, however, is a two-edged sword. On the one hand, a regime claiming pervasive support in society can achieve its goals relatively cheaply without resorting to coercion; when it does use force, broad sectors of public opinion uphold its action without really asking why. On the other hand, when regime legitimacy is in decline, the violence–authority–coercion paradigm imposes severe constraints. The achievement of administrative goals becomes more expensive, and the regime's recourse to coercion can engender a disastrous cobweb effect.[67] Violence becomes more prevalent, coercion rises, but the use of public force is no longer considered quite so justified. The fine line separating the authority of the system from the right of the regime to speak in the name of that system becomes obscure. The result can be a rise in the incidence of violence, to a point that brings about the collapse of the regime or even the rejection of the whole system of government.[68] Naturally, incumbent political leadership attempts to avoid

[66] Max Weber, "Politics as a Vocation," in H. H. Gerth and C. Wright Mills (eds.), *From Max Weber: Essays in Sociology*, pp. 77–128.

[67] Warren F. Ilchman and Norman T. Uphoff, *The Political Economy of Change*, pp. 70–86.

[68] Though his argument does not extend to the limits indicated below, Peter M. Blau suggests a multi-tiered explanation for this cycle. He begins with Leon Festinger's concept of cognitive dissonance (the mental discomfort incurred by having rejected an attractive alternative), which is resolved by inflating the value of the chosen and deflating the value of the rejected. (1) Compliance in a subordinate authority position, at first entered into after a cost-benefit calculation or by chance, is elevated in value for being the option "chosen." (2) Social processes transform the individual rationalization into a social norm. (3) This norm legitimates the superior's position as authority. (4) Even if objective costs equal objective benefits, the authority maintains a "credit" or margin of discretion vis-à-vis his subordinates. (5) For those touched or scandalized by coercion, the costs of

this eventuality. Because of the risks involved, it must sometimes disregard the use of coercion as a means of responding to antigovernmental or extralegal group violence.

When an agency's main reference group uses violence to influence bureaucracy, and this violence is not checked, the likely result is a change in the power relations between the administrative unit and the outside actors. Instead of bureaucracy imposing decisions on its clients, the clients distort administrative practices, substitute priorities, or simply foist new standards on bureaucray.[69] More specifically, violence can result in:

1. a relaxation of rules;
2. a compromise of standard principles;
3. a shift in fundamental organizational goals; and
4. an observable transfer of authority from inside to outside actors.

CORHABIT's rules and procedures for the administration of PAP No. 1 were predicated on the existence of a relatively stable task environment. When poblador violence destroyed the placidity of that environment, certain changes took place. MINVU's actions became oriented toward rapid answers, quick adjustment to new situations, and an effort *to reduce outside conflict effectively,* rather than *to solve housing problems efficiently and legally.* In the melee, the Comités sin Casas dismissed as irrelevant and antiquated the suppositions of savings over time and self-help, which the pobladors had never embraced wholeheartedly anyway. The leaders of the Comités penetrated the administration of the Housing ministry to such a point that they were deciding the location of projects, the families receiving lots, and the terms of the contracts. In some cases, such as M.I.R.'s "Campamento 26 de enero," toma leaders displaced governmental authority almost completely: even the carabineros did not dare challenge the armed guards patrolling inside.[70] The

---

compliance eventually become greater than the benefits of compliance plus the symbolic marginal value provenant from the dynamics of cognitive dissonance. (6) The legitimacy norm itself is subverted, and anti-regime or anti-system behavior (noncompliance) replaces rationalization as the means of resolving cognitive dissonance. Blau, *Exchange and Power in Social Life,* pp. 208–213, 133.

[69] The results are similar to the "turbulent field" environment described by F. E. Emery and E. L. Trist, "The Causal Texture of Organizational Environment," pp. 21–32. One might speculate that some of MINVU's behavior during this period stemmed from the fact that its environment passed from placid randomized, to placid clustered, disturbed reactive, and finally turbulent. See also Robert Biller, "Adaptation Capacity and Organizational Development," in Frank Marini (ed.), *Toward a New Public Administration,* pp. 93–121.

[70] *El Diario Ilustrado,* April 1, 1970, p. 3. Also, Joaquin Duque and Ernesto Pastrana, "La Mobilización Reinvindictiva Urbana." Another Mirista *campamento*

FIGURE 23. LEVEL OF CONCESSIONS WON BY POBLADORS IN FOUR
TOMA SITUATIONS, 1965–1970

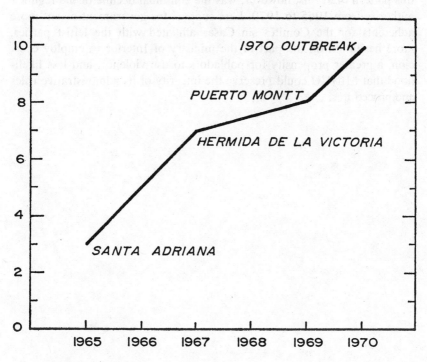

NOTE: Refer to Figure 22.

deterioration of the government's position is illustrated in Figure 23, which plots the progressive concessions won by pobladors through the four toma situations discussed in this chapter.

Several factors contributed to the spurious relationship between increasing poblador violence and the government's declining capacity to handle it. At the end of the period, the pobladors were much better organized and much more confident political actors than at the beginning. The Christian Democratic government was unwilling to add more deaths to the scores of civilian casualties in battles with students, workers, and pobladors which had troubled its rule over the previous five years. The opposition parties, to enhance their chances in the upcoming election, persistently tried to force the government to increase its level of repres-

was invaded by the police under the Allende regime in 1972, an episode that resulted in two deaths. The M.I.R.'s interpretation of the political significance of that event is contained in *Lo Hermida: La Cara Mas Fea del Reformismo.*

sion against the Comités sin Casas. The dominant factor underlying
this pattern of events, however, was the continual decline of the regime's
authority from 1965 to 1970. Less support for government meant more
adherents for the Comités sin Casas affiliated with the leftist parties,
more hesitation on the part of the ministry of Interior to employ coercion, a greater propensity for pobladors to use violence, and less likelihood that MINVU could preserve the integrity of its administrative rules
and procedures.

9

ADMINISTRATIVE THEORY
AND BUREAUCRATIC ACTION
FOR SOCIAL CHANGE

This research has been similar to others dealing in comparative public administration in its emphasis on dependent variables. Poor communication, corruption, goal displacement, indecisiveness, incrementalism, empire-building, nonenforcement, and other aspects of bureaucracy are very important matters of concern. Most observers would agree that a dynamic, communicative, public-oriented, efficient, and manageable bureaucracy is preferable to one that is particularistic, secretive, cynical, high-handed, prodigal, self-serving, and ineffective. For students of bureaucracy, the disagreements stem from the best way to explain these undesirable characteristics, and how to transform them into their more positive opposites.

In terms of independent variables, much of the literature on comparative administration is not very comparative at all. Some theoreticians argue that factors indigenous to low-income or non-Western countries are crucial in distinguishing bureaucratic practices. Students using this approach must squeeze their data into elaborate schemes of "traditional" and "progressive" values, pre-national and modern political structures, subsistence and industrialized economic systems, and open and closed social orders. The fact that bureaucracy tends to reflect similar patterns from country to country, despite the setting and level of gross national product, discredits the worth of many of these variables for predicting differences in kind.

POWER AND BUREAUCRACY

My research has employed concepts based on inherent features of bureaucracy to explain administrative behavior in Chile. In treating the budget, short-term planning, reform, coordination, and client relations, I have dealt with group interests rather than individual values. In focusing attention on policy formation and implementation, I have attempted to build links between theory and practice. Finally, in discussing the possibilities for administrative reform and social change, I have not assumed or expected a fundamental change in human nature.

Most bureaucratic action can be explained from two interlocking principles: agencies attempt to reach their goals, and they try to expand their resource base to enhance their capabilities in their task environments. These axioms can be extended theoretically by means of a series of definitions (D), premises or assumptions (A) and propositions (P), which, though somewhat simplified and not exhaustive, help summarize a number of my conclusions.

D. *Bureaucracy* is a major organizational depository for political and ecomonic resources devolved by society for public purposes.
A. These resources are differentially distributed within bureaucracy.
D. Resource stocks constitute the *structure* of bureaucracy.
A. Bureaucratic units are oriented toward the achievement of multiple organization goals.
A. Agencies are motivated to increase their access to resources to protect and further their goals.
D. Bureaucratic *politics* is the exchange of political resources among public institutions and clients in pursuit of their goals.

All organizations have at least three elements in common: resources (usually distributed according to a formal and informal hierarchy), goals, and environment. The public can channel resources to bureaucracy through formal mechanisms such as tax collection or informal ones such as political legitimacy and payoffs. Because resources are limited and goals are numerous, bureaucratic agents engage in competition to achieve their ends. The more frequent and regular the resource exchange among different institutions and groups (such as in the budgetary process, or in the servicing of traditional constituencies), the easier it is to observe and analyze bureaucratic politics, but the more difficult it is to alter the fundamental relationships over the short term. Attempts by institutions to increase their power base can be explained and *justified* on a number of grounds, such as efficiency, effectiveness, and better service to the public. Derogatory comments on bureaucracy's tendency to consolidate its power (e.g., empire-building, prestige-accrual) are value judgments to the extent that they are not examined in the context of the agency's need to increase its capacity for goal-oriented action.

Bureaucratic Power and Coalitions

P. The greater an agency's monopoly over a resource, and the greater the demand for that resource by other units, the more expensive that resource in an exchange situation.

P. The greater the fragmentation of power, and the greater the diversity of goals, the greater the incidence of bureaucratic politics.

D. Functional interdependence is the frequent exchange of valued resources between two or more actors, each attempting to reach individual goals.

P. The greater the functional interdependence between groups and bureaucratic units, the greater the likelihood of joint-payoff coalitions.

P. The greater the agency's or group's ability to form coalitions, the greater the possibilities for improving its bargaining position inside and outside of bureaucracy.

Agencies that monopolize finances, coercion, or information tend to exchange them sparingly and only when the transaction clearly serves their own interests. These resource advantages are important not only in the interaction between bureaucracy and society, and between different public organizations, but also in structured decision-making situations involving representatives of several agencies. Despite his informational base, the executive who controls coercion or finances will have considerable influence in determining final decisions; and if his power advantage is substantial, he may even be able to override the point of view of institutions with nearly perfect information at their disposal. Within bureaucracy, distorted information, poor communication, and faulty programming are partially the result of agencies trying to defend their best interests by hoarding information on their activities.

Bureaucratic competition is a function of power fragmentation and goal diversity. Political elites who believe that bureaucratic politics are counterproductive would do well to reduce the number of conflicting goals among agencies (or to choose ones that merit special attention) and to distribute power in a way that gives specific units a clear advantage over their competition.

Coalitions inside of bureaucracy, and between inside and outside actors, are extremely important in understanding the power balance among public institutions. These combinations in turn help predict the nature of bureaucratic output, since most decision-making and productivity trends depend on the political power of the participating actors and the nature of the goals they are sponsoring. Agencies that identify overlapping interests with client groups or other public organizations, and operationalize this congruence into a coalition, profit from additional leverage in important spheres of government activity. Functional interdependence is not the only foundation for coalition formation, but it results in the most resilient alliances. Short-term arrangements based on nepotism, social contacts, political pull (*cuña*), or bribery are less stable than those generated from functional interdependence except where social, economic, and political power are concentrated in a single, unified small group or class.

Bureaucratic Processes

P. The more an administrative process (planning, budgeting, coordination, reform) impinges on the goals of an organization or coalition, the greater the likelihood that the process will be an important arena for bureaucratic politics.

P. The wider the power base of the planning, budgeting, coordination, or reform agency, the greater its potential for successfully monitoring these functions in bureaucracy.

P. The more powerful an executing unit, the more capable it will be to ignore or override those agencies charged with planning, budgeting, coordinating, or reform.

Administrative processes would not exist if there were no need to control, regulate, or monitor bureaucratic units. The fact that these processes invariably restrict the freedom of action and counter the desires of some oganizations and groups means that those same elements will try to twist the procedures to their own advantage. As long as the planning, budgeting, coordination, and reform units operate from an inadequate power base or manage their resources poorly, the result will be fictitious planning, chaotic budgeting, redundant institutions, and successful resistance to reform.

Bureaucratic Environments

A. The environment is characterized by the multitude of goals and power capabilities of individuals, groups, and organizations which impinge more or less directly on the activities of the organization under study.

P. The greater the power advantage of bureaucracy in its task environment, the greater its ability to impose rules, gain compliance, and extract resources from its external clients and reference groups.

P. The greater the power advantage of elements in the task environment and the greater the discrepancy between goals, the greater the tendency of the relevant bureaucratic unit to relax its rules, shift the assumptions of its operating procedures, and transfer authority to outside actors.

The relative power balance is the most important consideration, as well as the most difficult to specify in measurable terms, in the relationship between an agency and elements in its task environment. Highhandedness, extensive formalism, cynicism, aloofness, and other types of bureaucratism are often a function of power relations favoring public officials over petitioners and clients. In these cases, the official's attitude may result from job insecurity, poor pay, overwork, and low morale which, in the internal bureaucratic context, are symptoms of agency weakness. But his pivotal role in providing necessary services translates into an element of strength compared with the reduced power base of the individual petitioner or client who has no means of protesting his treatment. The official is likely to provide better service to those groups (brokers, interest associations) that lessen his workload and boost his morale, or to those clients and petitioners who resort to tangential inducement mechanisms to improve his pay or threaten his job security. When organized interest groups with objectives countering the agency's organizational goals clearly predominate, the results typically are looseness of regulations, cooptation, nonenforcement, and even capitulation.

When the balance of power is uncertain for administrative units, they display signs of indecisiveness, withdrawal, cynicism, or, at best, incrementalism. This latter observation is especially pertinent for countries with social or economic systems requiring drastic overhaul. Fragmented or debilitated agencies are not apt to provide satisfactory service indiscriminantly to the public nor to *act on* society effectively in terms of economic development, social reform, or political mobilization. Although incrementalism may be appropriate for political systems with special historical evolutions, it is not a universal value. Nor can it be defended consistently as the most rational governing style on the basis of restricted information. If leadership has sufficient access to finances, legitimacy, authority, or even coercion, these resources can compensate for imperfect information and provide the political basis for much needed change.

SHIFTING COALITIONS FOR SOCIAL CHANGE

Is political activity a hindrance to goal-oriented bureaucracy? One of the initial assumptions of this research has been borne out by the empirical evidence: the question is practically irrelevant. For bureaucratic units to operate, they must exchange information, finances, and authority. Politics cannot be separated from administrative processes as long as conflicting policy choices exist and the public wealth is limited. Until organizations mutate into forms that are currently unknown, they will continue to use political resources for strategic ends. Enhanced possibilities for administrative output do not lie in removing power from administration but in the refinement of bureaucratic power for specific ends.

The perplexing question is: To what purposes should power be put? Public policy decisions cannot hide behind catch-all concepts such as "development administration" and "modernization." Deliberate choices must be made to enhance the power capabilities of specific administrative units and social groups. The preceding chapters examined individual cases of agency competition inside bureaucracy and the nature of the relationship between public organizations and society. Most readers probably sided with one or another of the participants in these encounters. Those favoring tight fiscal restraint and conservative monetary policies had heroes in the Finance ministry in the budgetary process, and the Restrictive Coalition in the Economic Committee. Others, in favor of administrative rationalization, may have identified with the Advisory Housing Commission, the Developmentalist Coalition, and MINVU's Planning and Budgeting agency. Those believing strongly in individual initiative and worried by the dangers of encrusted bureaucracy were probably heartened by the accomplishments of CORMU and the effective lobbying techniques of the CCC. Socially conscious or leftist-oriented readers probably sympathized most with the lower-level personnel in Sanitary Works trading off miserable salaries for the right of guaranteed employment, or the pobladors who lost their patience with the red tape of Operation Sitio and took matters into their own hands.

Whatever the reader's predilections, the record is not one of unmitigated success. Eventually, public agencies and private parties overwhelmed Finance and its allies with pressures for unprogrammed fiscal and monetary expansion. When its restrictive position began to erode, the regime had already missed its most promising opportunity to break inflation in Chile. Entrenched vested interests countered the aspirations of the Housing Advisory Commission, which saw its organizational reform badly mutilated by a coalition of motley forces, each looking out for its own particular concerns. On the whole, the housing corporations were able to resist unwanted interference from MINVU's planners. Subsequently, however, these same corporations were at the mercy of a turbulent task environment represented by leftist agitation and poblador violence. The prostitution of Operation Sitio temporarily ended the problem of "allegados" in Santiago, but the techniques used by pobladors, their leaders, the police, and housing officials hardly indicated progress toward more sophisticated relations between bureaucracy and society.

If bureaucratic politics are inevitable, the public interest requires that the respective actors eventually adopt roles that serve the general good. Charles Lindblom, Aaron Wildavsky, and others have argued that executives defending their own agencies (partial view of the public interest) eventually contribute to the general good when the goals of all parties are balanced off within the framework of a democratic system.[1] This judgment is based on the presumption that, although agencies vary in political power, they are conscious of their specific interests and tend to manage their resources efficiently in the pursuit of those interests. It also assumes that all groups in society have relatively equal access to the bureaucracy and are knowledgeable of ways to influence public policy. In Chile, neither of these fundamentals holds true. Nonetheless the argument is normatively attractive because it implies greater equality and productivity in society, *especially* among groups currently marginal to the system. At the same time it incorporates the realistic proposition that men are motivated more toward protecting and furthering their interests than toward sacrificing continually for altruistic ends. These seemingly contradictory ideas may be compatible in countries such as Chile if bureaucracy, leadership, and other claimants of authority increase their political skills, heighten their awareness of the responsibilities of public choice, and recognize the positive value of coalitions between administrative units and nonparticipant subgroups in the national community.

Agency Strategies for Aggrandizement

The first issue relates to the deliberate use of politics to achieve bureaucratic aims. My impression is that those groups that performed best in the described situations were unevenly aware of the political implications of their acts. *Those that were aware did much better* than those that were not. On the one hand, Finance, Public Works, CORMU, and the CCC did recognize that they were involved in a type of political struggle. This recognition was a prerequisite for the development of fairly elaborate strategies consolidating their positions and giving them structured access to political resources which were absolutely necessary to achieve their individual aims. The same cannot be said for the Restrictive Coalition in the Economic Committee, CORHABIT vis-

[1] David Braybrooke and Charles E. Lindblom, *A Strategy of Decision: Policy Evaluation as a Social Process*; Aaron Wildavsky, *The Politics of the Budgetary Process*.

à-vis MINVU, and the pobladors from late 1969 through 1970. They responded instinctively to certain elements in their environments without meditating long on their basic interests, the sources of their political power, or possible alternative strategies over the long term. They would not have achieved their final aims if they had not articulated them. Yet, by managing their resources poorly, they did not assure that their influence would have a lasting effect. The Economic Committee tried to seal itself off from the social forces around it, only to discover that outside support was crucial for the implementation of its preferences. COR-HABIT did its best to minimize the existence of MINVU—ignoring the fact that the planners were potentially its most faithful allies in the bureaucracy. The pobladors invested heavily in a one-year binge of euphoric land invasions, later to find that they were not much better off than before.

It cannot be denied that these groups at least had the satisfaction of coming out on top, however momentarily. Other units were perennial losers in these contests because they refused to believe that they were involved in political competition, or realized it at such a late date that they were helpless to regain lost ground. Because of its hegemony in the Economic Committee, the Restrictive Coalition could shunt the Developmentalists aside in the most important planning decisions of the Frei government. The Developmentalist Coalition did not realize the ultimate effects of this power imbalance until its adversaries had already dominated the president's attention. When the members of the Advisory Housing Commission locked horns with the parties interested in the preservation of the Public Works ministry, they were in a sad state of unpreparedness. They suffered the consequences when opponents to the reform snatched issues away, placing them irrevocably on the defensive. MINVU's decentralization program was a valiant effort to increase coordination in the housing sector. Unfortunately, the officials in the centralized portion of the ministry took several years to realize that coordination and policy-making were more a function of bureaucratic power than of a skillful planning methodology. If the pobladors had aided MINVU to expand Operation Sitio with Social Security monies in 1966 and 1967, both would have benefited. Instead of working together all through the regime, the pobladors were at MINVU's throat in the last year of the government. The final impression of the research, and of the Christian Democratic regime in general, was that violence, the crudest and most distasteful of all resources, was the most effective means for claimants to achieve gratification for their demands.

Interestingly enough, the bureaucratic units depending most on sophisticated administrative techniques fared most poorly in the competition. The data suggest that organizational methods and *technological breakthroughs are best employed as complements to bureaucratic politics,* and *not* as substitutes for it. Finance's program budget, the anti-inflation model developed in the Central Bank, the comprehensive housing reform based on the latest international models, and the planning methodology employed by MINVU all had extensive merits, but sooner or later broke down when challenged by the groups they were supposed to govern.

Even weak agencies wreaked havoc with the program budget by withholding or distorting the one resource easily at hand—information. For three years, the prestige of the president and the backing of the political party validated the short-term decision-rules of the Economic Committee; when that support vacillated, the Committee's efforts collapsed. The Housing advisors soon learned that expounding the inherent logic of their reform to important personages in Education, Health, and Public Works was wasted breath; political maneuvers were the key to progress. MINVU struggled for several years to carry its yearly plan past the formation stage, but the corporations did not cooperate. Most academics and detached observers would probably side with the planners in the belief that coordination implies greater efficiency and productivity. The planners' influence was neutralized, however, by the fact that practically everyone who mattered on the Chilean scene (Social Security Funds, contractors, ministry of Finance, Christian Democratic party) took the side of the corporations.

If successful budgeting, planning, and coordination are determined in great part by political variables, bureaucratic possessors of technology can put that capacity to good use by directing it toward those areas in which they suffer politically rather than trying to use it to refine purely administrative skills. The Housing Planning office used its computer to determine the per-unit costs of the houses in its annual operating plan; the fact that the corporations never implemented the plan meant that valuable computer time was used for exercises in futility. MINVU could better have used its technological capacity to monitor the corporations' multiple activities to avoid *faits accomplis* and enforce sectoral policy. The Budget Bureau encouraged the acceptance of program budgeting because of its presumed logic and its wide backing in international circles; it might have done better to admit unabashedly that PPBS has tremendous political connotations, and to design strategies for its implementation on the basis of political variables rather than technical advisability. Tactics might have included a series of coalitions with middle- and lower-level bureau functionaries, bypassing the upper reaches and solidified by an exchange of valued resources, including the accurate information needed for formulation and execution of the system.

An agency's productivity is a function of its management of political power. Success in bureaucratic politics requires access to a steady flow of political resources: authority, information, prestige, and finances. The surest clue to a need for political expertise is when ambition severely outruns capacity to implement.[2] In the Chilean case, this was the predicament of the Developmentalist Coalition, the Housing advisors, MINVU's planners, and the administrators of Operation Sitio in 1970. At the same time the weak unit carries out its routine functions, it must consolidate its resources to increase the importance of its operations. It is not enough for upper levels of different agencies to state their aims and hope to reach them through good intentions. Over the short term, they must convince the president to back them, Finance to subsidize them, clients to support them, and other public agencies to complement them. Sometimes they must induce the forces of public order to protect their operations in a volatile task environment, or look the other way when its agents skirt the margin of the law. The weak agency with grandiose plans can muster this persuasive power only by earning it. Goal-oriented bureaucracy cannot avoid politics; and the more ambitious the goals, the more the need for fervent and adroit political action.

Society and Bureaucracy

The "socialization" literature on administrative behavior discussed in Chapter 1 implies that the infiltration of bureaucracy by social groups is detrimental to the achievement of public goals. It argues that the mix of contradictory cultural values is incompatible with the operations of modern bureaucracy, and that the ability of dominating elites to control administration for their own self-interest subverts developmental goals. Both prevent government functionaries from making decisions and implementing programs by rational administrative criteria for the public interest. Following this line of analysis, the solution would be for bureaucracy to seal itself off from the forces around it and transform its diversified components into a homogeneous, unified, and disciplined machine for modernization. In their new role, public administrators would recognize the corrupting influence of society. They would act on their environment, not in association with it, and avoid any entanglements with individual client groups which might disrupt their rationalistic orientation.

At this point it is useful to recall the close relationship between the

---

[2] Albert Hirschman feels that mistakes occur when motivation to solve a problem outruns understanding of the problem. Since information is just one element of power, the phrase could be amended to read: Mistakes occur when motivation outruns capacity. Hirschman, *Journeys Toward Progress,* p. 236. I would admit that incremental changes are the best that can be hoped for in most policy-making situations. Nonetheless, political leadership should be sensitive to those moments when a great deal more can be accomplished in line with its political aims and ideology.

Public Works ministry and the Chilean Construction Chamber. The functional interdependence between the inside and outside groups gave ministry officials a broad range of resources that they could use for internal bureaucratic politicking. Likewise, the contractors were integrated into the decision-making of the ministry and thus played a role in government. Some observers may feel that this coziness undermined the public interest. If the contractors did indeed have too much influence on government, it was not because of the nature of their relationship with Public Works but because other, more change-oriented agencies did not have similar arrangements with powerful client groups who effectively challenged Public Works' definition of the general good. Over the long term such support must come from those elements in the society-at-large which back activities implying more equitable and productive relations among the nation's citizenry.

The answer to "bureaucratism" is not to destroy coalitions between clients and bureaucracy, but to enlarge the scope of such transactions to weak agencies and previously neglected sectors of society. Instead of viewing the petitioner as an enemy who exists to be mistreated, change-oriented agencies must utilize social pressures in their task environments for new strength in the administrative state. The strategy of turning to previously untapped resources can lead to increased responsiveness of bureaucracy to justified public claims, when accompanied by a higher level of shared decision-making and client intervention in the agency. Stable alliances between housing officials and *pobladors* (instead of housing contractors), agricultural officials and *campesinos* (instead of large landowners), medical officials and *poor citizens* (instead of the doctors' interest association) would totally transform the internal power relations in Chilean bureaucracy and its attention to the public. As coalitions between agencies and previously unmobilized social groups proliferate in bureaucracy, traditional alliances benefiting the few would decline in relative strength.

Choices for Leadership

The best way for organizations to reduce uncertainty in their internal procedures and external environments is to increase their access to political resources. This observation underlies the basic rationality of bureaucratic politics. Yet there are at least two ways in which organizational politics can lead to a generally irrational situation: (1) one unit's holding a decisive advantage over the others, to an extent that eliminates the possibility of enforcing acceptance of overall policy; and (2) all units' competing fervently on equal terms for the same resources, none gaining an advantage allowing it to consolidate its position and achieve its aims. In the first case, a power imbalance can lead to a situation of uncertainty for the whole if some agencies are able to elevate their interests above those of the collectivity. In the ministry of Housing and Urbanism, for example, the corporations' hegemony over MINVU during most of the period increased their own capabilities but probably reduced the productivity of the housing sector in general.

Similarly, a situation in which two or more agencies are competing equally for highly valued resources often results in a depressed exchange market in the interest of neither. Defensive maneuvers distract from purposeful action and result in relative stagnation, due to the permanently low resource base of each. Depending on the manner in which these ramifications are measured, the final outcome can be a generally undesirable situation of squander and mismanagement. Such allegations helped justify the creation of MINVU; this type of irrationality also characterized the modal budgetary pattern described in Chapter 2.

The president and his advisers must define rationality for the whole in terms of the regime's ultimate goals. They cannot delude themselves into believing that every unit of government can be satisfied simultaneously. Nor is it enough for bureaucracy to reach its own state of equilibrium, because those agencies that have predominated in the past will continue to do so, despite the stated aims of the regime. In an atmosphere of power fragmentation, the most likely result of a laissez-faire policy toward bureaucracy will be unprogrammed advances by certain units with little relation to the priorities of the regime.

All units of government cannot and should not have equal capacity to achieve perfect rationality in their operations. But it is worthless for outsiders to request politely that individual agencies limit their activities for the benefit of the whole. Leadership must enforce that restraint selectively, so that the power imbalance within an administration favors specific units, giving them advantages in the formal hierarchy, in finances and information. If leaders are serious about their intentions they must deliberately maintain that support, even though competing agencies continually contest their decisions. Generally, agencies with the highest immediate priority and those with a coordinating task in the service of overall governmental aims must have a more extensive power base and more skilled human resources, if leadership is to realize its goals.

PREPARATION AND ACTION
FOR COMPREHENSIVE CHANGE

This research has made an effort to ascertain the timeliness of certain political and administrative initiatives. The reform of the housing sector, the Capitalization Fund, MINVU's decentralization program, and the massive wave of land invasions by pobladors were all affected in one way or another by time. Time did not intervene directly in the events, but marked the current power status of the actors, reflected against the background of cyclical patterns in authority and other resource flows. The Capitalization Fund was convincingly crushed by overwhelming opposition, and the housing reform and decentralization program were diluted by the peculiar distribution of preferences pending at the time of their implementation. The pobladors were remarkably successful in achieving their immediate aims of land occupation because their activities coincided with low regime authority, constraints on the use of coercion, and situational factors conducive to direct action.

To appreciate the problems of the Christian Democratic regime from 1964 to 1970, it is useful to review the tables and figures on financial resources, voting, inflation, and violence in Chapters 1, 2, and 8, which show quite clearly the moments when comprehensive action was most appropriate and when programs arousing extensive controversy had little chance of succeeding. These indicators point to the fact that the most propitious period for a Chilean regime to implement the ideological aspects of its policy is during its first years of government. If the regime does not move swiftly in the initial months, the opposition usually sees to it that many of its programs never materialize.

A similar set of circumstances characterized the Allende regime, but the outcome obviously was different. His partisans did succeed in rearranging many social and economic relationships. But they refused to slow the pace of reform even after the opposition, by channeling the discontent of middle-class business and professional groups and winning over the armed forces, had built a decisive power advantage. The surprise was that Allende, the politician, did not reach a compromise with his opponents (as had his predecessors with theirs) in time to avert a total rejection of his policy accomplishments and the reigning political system.[3] He apparently chose to ignore the historical lessons indicating that, barring an unusual release of previously untapped resources, Chilean regimes in the latter part of their mandate have difficulty doing more than consolidating those changes initiated earlier.[4]

Comprehensive changes do not rest solely on infinite amounts of in-

[3] Another unexpected event was the virulence with which the armed forces and carabineros, which had the reputation of respectful moderation in their relations with civilians, then pursued, repressed and even physically eliminated large numbers of Allende's followers.

[4] The Communist party especialy had urged him to bring vanguard elements of the Unidad Popular into line, and soften some of the more controversial aspects of his economic policy.

formation, but they do require extensive preparation, a good sense of political timing, and the will to carry them to completion. Programs that drastically restructure basic relationships in society can be implemented incrementally, on the pretext that this approach reduces short-term transitional adjustments. But delay usually perpetuates injustices and attenuates the intentions of the change, and it can engender higher social costs by permitting an extended reign of pernicious elements of the status quo.

Extensive preparation for comprehensive change does not entail knowledge of every possible consequence and implication of the action. It means holding in reserve programs which reflect the regime's interpretation of the social reality, which alter that reality in ways that redress injustices and inefficiency, and lay the bases for new patterns of behavior. However, the basic program aims and the various steps for technical implementation do not represent the main parts of the contingency plans. More important are the political strategies used during the phase of rapid execution, and subsequent tactics either to consolidate the gains or to outflank the opposition if the first thrust falls short.

The importance of having these plans in reserve cannot be underestimated. The usual practice is for regimes to identify problems, prepare the specific programs to correct them, and then use a program's existence as the cue to implement it, after the most opportune moment for execution has already passed.[5] The ideal moment for implementation is rarely immediately after the outlines of the program have been elaborated, but when the political climate is most favorable. The regime, with the resources at its disposal, must be able to manage the combined resistance to its attempt to enact far-reaching social, administrative, or economic reforms.

The fact that structural reform has the greatest chance of being implanted when the influence of public authorities is at a peak is pertinent not just to Chile, and is an important program consideration in all attempts to use bureaucracy for purposeful ends.

---

[5] "There will be times, more favorable than others, when reform will forge ahead. With no more than a ready-prepared outline of systematic action, it should be possible to make full use of those fleeting moments, which are often wasted because programming is not begun until they are actually there. . . ." ECLA, "Administrative Planning for Economic and Social Development in Latin America," p. 179.

APPENDIX: FORMAL ASPECTS
OF THE CHILEAN BUDGETARY CYCLE

Three governmental units participate most actively in the formation of the budget: the *Budget Bureau* in the Finance ministry, the *Budget offices* in the sectoral ministries, and the individual *agencies* that execute programs. The central institution specifically charged with formulating the national budget each year is the *Dirección de Presupuestos* in the ministry of Finance, hereafter referred to as the Budget Bureau. The Budget Bureau's principal functions are to compute the total revenues available to the state over the coming year, allocate these revenues to agencies in the public sector, and control the orderly disbursement of funds during the execution of the budget. The bureau has four departments for these tasks: (1) *technical assistance,* which studies budgetary procedures and prepares manuals to train the budgeters at different levels; (2) *statistics,* which consolidates past and recent budgetary data, processes them mechanically, and establishes a flow of econometric information to the budget chief to keep him apprised of budgetary trends; (3) *programming and global statistics,* which estimates total revenues available to the state, coordinates fiscal policy, and rationalizes investment goals with the assistance of the National Planning Office (ODEPLAN); and (4) *operations,* which reviews budgetary requests from the different governmental units and is responsible for controlling the execution of the budget in its different categories.[1] The operations department is the largest section of the Budget Bureau, and is further subdivided into separate units that deal directly with ministerial Budget offices and sectoral agencies.

[1] Ministerio de Hacienda, "Descripción de las Funciones de los Departamentos y Divisiones de la Subdirección de Presupuestos."

The administration of the national budget is not completely centralized in the Budget Bureau. Each sector of government activity (e.g.,
Education, Public Works and Transport, Health, Housing) has a separate Budget office charged with estimating the ministry's spending needs
for the coming year and determining what portion of the total revenues
must be supplied by the National Treasury. In some sectors the budgetary and planning functions are combined in a single ministerial unit,
such as the Office for Agricultural Planning (ODEPA) in Agriculture
and the General Planning and Budgeting agency in MINVU. The general rule is that the various Budget offices summarize the budgetary
information for the sector and pass it on to Finance. In practice, however, many decentralized agencies and state enterprises negotiate directly with the national Budget Bureau for their allocations.

The individual agencies are at the bottom of the budgetary hierarchy.
Each agency has an accounting office that compiles departmental estimates and presents the agency's request to the ministerial Budget office
or directly to the Budget Bureau. Often the head of the agency is deeply
involved in preparing the allocation request. The accounting offices
within the agency are also responsible for controlling the flow of funds
that pass through the bureau during the course of the budget year, and
carry out various administrative duties such as submitting vouchers and
signing payroll checks. Frequently, sub-units of these budgetary accounting offices are established at very decentralized levels of the bureaucracy—such as the regional office (Concepcion) of a department
(Administration) of an autonomous corporation (the Agrarian Reform
Corporation, or CORA). Although individual agencies often work in
direct contact with officials in the national Budget Bureau, the intermediary of the ministerial Budget office cannot be totally ignored.
Eventually the Finance ministry must collaborate with the Budget office
to allocate the total sum that will be divided among all the agencies
within the sector.

According to the budget law of 1959 and standard practices developed in the Finance ministry, the procedure for formulating and
executing the budget is relatively clear and uncomplicated.[2] The budget
year corresponds to the calendar year, January 1 to December 31. The
budgetary cycle has four principal steps: formation, approval, execution, and evaluation. The national Budget Bureau in the Finance ministry, the sectoral Budget offices, and the agencies act sequentially within

---

[2] Ministerio de Hacienda, *Ley Orgánica de Presupuestos*; also *Manual para la
Ejecución de los Presupuestos en los Servicios de la Administración Pública Centralizada*.

their respective domains to formulate a budget document that is presented to Congress by September 1 preceding the year of its implementation. A summary of the different steps involved in the budgetary schedule is necessary for understanding the sequence of strategies of bureaucratic units to further their ends and protect their weaknesses during the cycle.

Year 1: Formation and Discussion

March	The department of programming and global statistics in the Budget Bureau makes a rough estimate of total revenues for the coming year.
April	After balancing the budget in preliminary fashion, the Budget Bureau sends a spending ceiling (*cifra tope*) for each agency, and the sector as a whole, to the ministerial Budget office. The ministerial Budget office transmits the respective ceilings to each agency within its jurisdiction.
May to June 30	The agencies formulate their budgets in line with the ceilings indicated by the Budget Bureau. Re the instructions of Finance, the agencies place additional expenses going above the imposed ceilings on a separate list to be discussed with the analysts in the department of operations of the Budget Bureau. This separate form is called the *Expansion List,* and usually represents a significant amount over the original ceiling.
July and August	The analysts in the national Budget Bureau thoroughly study the draft budgets of the different sectors. Special attention is paid to those items representing increases over the previous year and those expenses on the Expansion List. At this point the analysts examine the budgets of the decentralized agencies only in light of the total state subsidy they are requesting.

Meetings are held between the analyst and representatives of the sector. The analyst prepares a written report on the spending projections of the sector, which he discusses with the head of the Budget Bureau and the Finance minister. The Finance minister eventually approves final figures for the draft budget, and presents his conclusions to the Economic Committee, a permanent advisory body to the president made up of several ministers and top public officials concerned with the financial affairs of state. Later, the president's cabinet rubber-stamps the budget.

September 1 to December 31	The draft budget presented to Congress contains full budgetary information for the bureaus of the central ministries, and includes transfers to decentralized agencies and state enterprises. But it does not include a detailed breakdown of how these subsidies will be used by these latter units, nor are the budgets of these organizations, which account for approximately half the total state expenditures, ever reviewed by Congress. The budget is discussed first in the *Comisión Mixta* (Mixed Commission, made up of members of both houses of Congress), which is divided into small committees to deal with each sector. Representatives from the agencies, the ministerial Budget office, and the Budget Bureau are called upon to answer questions concerning the budget. Generally, however, the congressmen do not have enough information at their disposal to conduct an exhaustive analysis of the budget. According to the budget law, Congress cannot alter the revenue estimates submitted by the executive unless it provides for new tax sources. Nor can it autonomously add new projects without the president's agreement. In practice this clause means that the congressmen can "suggest" supplementary projects, tasks, and programs and add them to the budget. But the president invariably uses his item-veto to annul most of them. In general, Congress does not make substantial alterations of the document presented by the Finance minister, except in the category of Public Works.
Mid-December	The ministry of Finance issues an amendment to the projected law. This amendment, called the *oficio final,* is based on a last-minute estimate of the next year's revenues and a terminal evaluation of political and investment priorities. The oficio final often alters totals by several percentage points.
December 31	The budget must be passed by Congress. If not, the proposal submitted by the executive is automatically decreed.

Year 2: Execution

January	Before being published, the budget is trimmed of those items vetoed by the president on the advice of the Finance ministry. All of the ministries take a final look at their total allocation to determine the possibility of distributing the money in a better way to carry out their tasks. The itemized

budgets of the decentralized agencies and state industries are approved by the Budget Bureau and the president.

The Budget Bureau elaborates the annual payment schedule used by the National Treasury to distribute the funds to the agencies. In all items except remunerations, the practice is to issue 40 percent of the allocation during the first semester and divide the second semester into two periods, in each of which the maximum amount allowed is 30 percent of the total.

January through December Before the agency can spend its allocation, the Finance ministry must decree those amounts on which it is eligible to issue vouchers. There is no guarantee that the amounts decreed will reach the full budgetary allocation, although they usually do.

June through December The Finance ministry retains considerable leeway in manipulating the budget. If an agency has inaccurately estimated the requirements of one or another budgetary item, the Finance minister can effect a transfer (*traspaso*) in the second semester. He can transfer monies from one agency (*capítula*) to another, and even from one ministry (*partida*) to another. Only if the transfer is between the capital and current account must it be approved by special legislation.

More significant for the Finance minister's freedom of action is the fact that excess revenues collected during the year are usually classified in surplus (*excedible*) accounts. This term means that the Finance minister can transfer these surpluses directly to agencies running deficits without the necessity of consulting Congress.

Year 3: Evaluation

January At the end of the budget year, if decreed money has not been spent, these amounts (*saldos*) can be credited to the agency in its next year's budget. If the money has not been committed for ordered goods or services, however, it will most likely be reduced or absorbed by the National Treasury.

April The General Comptroller's office must publish the final figures for the budgets of the central government, in the *Memoria de la Contraloría General*.

BIBLIOGRAPHY

BOOKS, MONOGRAPHS (M), AND THESES (T)

Agor, Weston R. *The Chilean Senate: Internal Distribution of Influence.* Austin: University of Texas, 1971.

Agost G., Carlos. *Análisis y Descripción de la Labor Desarrollada por la Corporación de la Vivienda, 1959–1963.* Universidad Católica de Chile, 1964. (T)

Ahumada, Jorge. *En Vez de la Miseria.* Santiago: Pacífico, 1970.

Allison, Graham T. *Essence of Decision: Explaining the Cuban Missile Crisis.* Boston: Little, Brown, 1971.

Almeyda, Clodomiro. *Sociologismo Ideologismo en la Teoría Revolucionaria.* Santiago: Universitaria, 1971.

Altshuler, Alan A. (ed.). *The Politics of the Federal Bureaucracy.* New York: Dodd Mead, 1968.

Alvarez Suárez, Agustín. *La Transformación de las Razas en América.* Buenos Aires: Mauccio Hermanos, n.d.

Anderson, Charles W. *Politics and Economic Change in Latin America.* Princeton, N.J.: Van Nostrand, 1967.

Angell, Alan. *Politics and the Labour Movement in Chile.* New York: Oxford, 1972.

Apter, David. *The Politics of Modernization.* Chicago: University of Chicago, 1965.

Araneda Dörr, Hugo. *La Administración Financiera del Estado.* Santiago: Jurídica, 1966.

Aravena M., Tulio. *La Auto-Construcción en Chile.* Universidad Católica de Chile, 1969. (T)

Arriagada, Genaro. *La Oligarquía Patronal Chilena.* Santiago: Nueva Universidad, 1970.

Avendaño E., María Antonieta, and Justina Aguilera D. *Tomas de Terrenos: Estudio Descriptivo Exploratorio.* Escuela de Servicio Social, Universidad Católica de Chile, 1970. (T)

Banco Central. *Estudios Monetarios, I, II.* Santiago: Pacífico, 1968, 1970.

Banfield, Edward C. *Political Influence*. New York: Free Press, 1961.

Barnard, Chester I. *The Functions of the Executive*. Cambridge, Mass.: Harvard University, 1938.

Bascuñán Valdés, Aníbal. *Elementos de Ciencias de la Administración Pública*. Santiago: Jurídica, 1963.

Bassini Galli, Carlos. *Los Presupuestos por Programas en las Actividades Públicas: Su Aplicación a una Institución Estatal*. Santiago: Instituto de Administración, Universidad de Chile (INSORA), 1964. (M)

Behm Rosas, Hector. *El Problema de la Habitación Mínima*. Santiago: Le Blanc Stanley y Urzúa, 1939.

Benveniste, Guy. *Bureaucracy and National Planning: A Sociological Case Study of Mexico*. New York: Praeger, 1970.

Blau, Peter M. *Exchange and Power in Social Life*. New York: Wiley, 1967.

Bloomberg, Warner, Jr., and Henry J. Schmandt (eds.). *Power, Poverty, and Urban Policy (Urban Affairs Annual Review, Vol. II)*. Beverly Hills, Calif.: Sage, 1968.

Braibanti, Ralph (ed.). *Political and Administrative Development*. Durham, N.C.: Duke University, 1969.

Bravo H., Luís. *Chile: El Problema de la Vivienda a través de su Legislación, 1906–1959*. Santiago: Universitaria, 1959.

Braybrooke, David, and Charles E. Lindblom. *A Strategy of Decision: Policy Evaluation as a Social Process*. New York: Free Press, 1963.

Brazer, Harvey E. *City Expenditures in the United States*. Occasional Paper No. 66. New York: National Bureau of Economic Research, 1959. (M)

Bulnes A., Luís, and Diego Barros A. *El D.F.L. No. 2 y sus 105 Modificaciones*. Santiago: SOPECH, 1969.

Bunge, Carlos Octavio. *Nuestra América*, 7th ed. Madrid: Espasa-Calpe, 1926; first pub. 1903.

Bunster Correa, Pablo, et al. *Autoconstrucción*. Universidad Católica de Chile, 1969. (T)

Burnett, Ben G. *Political Groups in Chile*. Austin: University of Texas, 1970.

Caiden, Gerald. *Administrative Reform*. Chicago: Aldine, 1969.

Caiden, Naomi, and Aaron Wildavsky. *Planning and Budgeting in Poor Countries*. New York: Wiley, 1973.

Carvallo Hederra, Sergio. *Finanzas Públicas*. Santiago: Universitaria, 1971.

Castillo Velasco, Jaime. *Las Fuentes de la Democracia Cristiana*. Santiago: Pacífico, 1972.

Clark, Keith C., and Lawrence J. Legere (eds.). *The President and the Management of National Security*. New York: Praeger, 1969.

Cleaves, Peter S. *Developmental Processes in Chilean Local Government*. Berkeley, Calif.: Institute of International Studies, University of California, 1969. (M)

Contreras, Osvaldo. *Antecedentes y Perspectivas de la Planificación en Chile*. Santiago: Jurídica, 1969.

Crecine, John P. *Governmental Problem-Solving: A Computer Simulation of Municipal Budgeting*. Chicago: Rand McNally, 1969.

Crowther, Win. *Technological Change as Political Choice: The Civil Engineers and the Modernizers of the Chilean State Railroad.* University of California, Berkeley, 1973. (T)

————, and Gilberto Flores, *Problemas Latinoamericanos y Soluciones Estadounidenses en Administración Pública.* Santiago: INSORA, 1971. (M)

Crozier, Michel. *The Bureaucratic Phenomenon.* Chicago: University of Chicago, 1964.

Cruchaga, Miguel. *Estudio sobre la Organización Económica y la Hacienda Pública de Chile, 1612–1878.* Santiago: Los Tiempos, 1878.

Cruz-Coke Lassabe, Eduardo. *Discursos.* Santiago: Nascimento, 1946.

Curry, R. L., Jr., and L. L. Wade. *A Theory of Political Exchange: Economic Reasoning in Political Analysis.* Englewood Cliffs, N.J.: Prentice-Hall, 1968.

Cusack, David F. *The Politics of Chilean Private Enterprise under Christian Democracy.* University of Denver, 1971. (T)

Downs, Anthony. *Inside Bureaucracy.* Boston: Little, Brown, 1967.

Dror, Yehezkel. *Public Policymaking Reexamined.* San Francisco: Chandler, 1968.

Eaton, Joseph (ed.). *Institution Building and Development: From Concepts to Application.* Beverly Hills, Calif.: Sage, 1972.

Edwards Vives, Alberto. *La Organización Política de Chile.* Santiago: Pacífico, 1955.

Ehrmann, Henry W. *Politics in France.* Boston: Little, Brown, 1968.

Etzioni, Amitai. *The Active Society.* New York: Free Press, 1968.

————. *A Comparative Analysis of Complex Organizations.* New York: Free Press, 1961.

Facultad de Arquitectura. *Vida Familiar en Algunos Conjuntos CORVI de la Metrópoli.* Santiago: Universidad Católica de Chile, 1964. (M)

Fanon, Franz. *The Wretched of the Earth.* London: MacGibbon and Kee, 1965.

Fenno, Richard F., Jr. *The President's Cabinet.* Cambridge, Mass.: Harvard University, 1959.

Frankenoff, Charles A. *Hacia una Política Habitacional Popular: El Caso de Chile.* Santiago: CIDU, 1969.

Friedmann, John. *Venezuela, From Doctrine to Dialogue.* Syracuse, N.Y.: Syracuse University, 1965.

Gerth, H. H., and C. Wright Mills (eds.). *From Max Weber: Essays in Sociology.* New York: Oxford, 1946.

Gil, Federico G. *El Sistema Político de Chile.* Santiago: Andrés Bello, 1969.

Gilb, Corrine Lathrop. *Hidden Hierarchies: The Professions and Government.* New York: Harper and Row, 1966.

Godoy, Gastón, and Jaime Gúzman. *El Problema Habitacional y las Poblaciones de Erradicados.* Universidad Católica de Chile, 1963. (T)

Graham, Lawrence S. *Civil Service Reform in Brazil: Principles versus Practice.* Austin: University of Texas, 1968.

Greenberg, Martin H. *Bureaucracy and Development: A Mexican Case Study.* Lexington, Mass.: Heath, 1970.

Gurr, Ted R. *Why Men Rebel.* Princeton: Princeton University, 1970.

Halperin, Ernst. *Nationalism and Communism in Chile.* Cambridge, Mass.: M.I.T., 1965.

Heady, Ferrel, and Sybil L. Stokes (eds.). *Papers in Comparative Public Administration.* Ann Arbor, Mich.: Institute of Public Administration, University of Michigan, 1962.

Heaphey, James (ed.). *Spatial Dimensions of Development Administration.* Durham, N.C.: Duke University, 1969.

Herrick, Bruce H. *Urban Migration and Economic Development in Chile.* Cambridge, Mass.: M.I.T., 1965.

Hirschman, Albert O. *Development Projects Observed.* Washington: Brookings, 1967.

————. *Exit, Voice, and Loyalty.* Cambridge, Mass.: Harvard University, 1970.

————. *Journeys Toward Progress.* New York: Twentieth Century Fund, 1963.

Holtzman, Abraham. *Interest Groups and Lobbying.* London: Macmillan, 1966.

Honorato Cienfuegos, Marcelo. *Financiamiento de las Obras de Ingeniería Sanitaria de Chile.* Santiago: Casa Nacional del Niño, 1950. (M)

Huntington, Samuel P. *Political Order in Changing Societies.* New Haven: Yale University, 1968.

Ilchman, Warren F., and Norman T. Uphoff. *The Political Economy of Change.* Berkeley and Los Angeles: University of California, 1969.

Ingenieros, José. *Sociología Argentina.* Buenos Aires: Losada, 1946.

Instituto de Economía y Planificación. *La Economía Chilena en 1972.* Santiago: Facultad de Economía Política, Universidad de Chile, 1973. (M)

Jobet, Julio César. *El Partido Socialista de Chile.* 2 vols. Santiago: Prensa Latinoamericana, 1971.

Kaplan, Abraham. *The Conduct of Inquiry: Methodology for Behavioral Science.* Scranton, Pa.: Chandler, 1964.

Kaufman, Robert R. *The Politics of Land Reform in Chile, 1950–1970.* Cambridge, Mass.: Harvard University, 1972.

Keehn, Norman H. *The Politics of Fiscal and Monetary Stabilization.* University of Wisconsin, 1971. (T)

Kohán Fernández, Adriana. *Ministerio de Economía, Fomento y Reconstrucción.* Santiago: Instituto de Ciencias Políticas y Administrativas, 1969. (M)

Kriesberg, Martin (ed.). *Public Administration in Developing Countries.* Washington: Brookings, 1965.

Lagos E., Ricardo. *La Concentración del Poder Económico.* Santiago: Pacífico, 1965.

LaPalombara, Joseph. *Interest Groups in Italian Politics.* Princeton: Princeton University, 1964.

Lindblom, Charles E. *The Intelligence of Democracy: Decision-Making through Mutual Adjustment*. New York: Free Press, 1965.

Loma-Osorio Pérez, Cecilia, and Benjamín Moreno Ojeda. *Los Decretos*. Santiago: Universitaria, 1958.

López P., Rafael. *Algunos Aspectos de la Participación Política en Chile*. Santiago: INSORA, 1969. (M)

Loveman, Brian E. *Property, Politics and Rural Labor: Agrarian Reform in Chile, 1919–1972*. University of Indiana, 1973. (T)

Lüders, Rolf. *A Monetary History of Chile, 1925–1958*. University of Chicago, 1968. (T)

Lyden, Fremond J., and Ernest G. Miller. *Planning Programming Budgeting*. Chicago: Markham, 1967.

Maier, N. R. F. *Problem-Solving Discussions and Conferences: Leadership Methods and Skills*. San Francisco: McGraw-Hill, 1963.

Mamalakis, Marcos, and Clark W. Reynolds. *Essays on the Chilean Economy*. Homewood, Ill.: Irwin, 1965.

March, James G., and Herbert A. Simon. *Organizations*. New York: Wiley, 1958.

Marini, Frank (ed.). *Toward a New Public Administration: The Minnowbrook Perspective*. Scranton, Pa.: Chandler, 1971.

Marquezado O., Renato. *Génesis y Desarrollo de los Servicios de Hacienda*. Santiago: Contaloría General, 1940.

Martner García, Gonzalo. *Presupuestos Gubernamentales*. Santiago: Universitaria, 1962.

————. *Planificación y Presupuesto por Programas*. Mexico City: Siglo XXI, 1967.

———— (ed.). *El Pensamiento Económico del Gobierno de Allende*. Santiago: Universitaria, 1971.

Matus Benavente, Manuel. *Desniveles entre Presupuestos Iniciales y Presupuestos Realizados*. Santiago: Jurídica, 1957.

————. *Finanzas Públicas*. Santiago: Jurídica, 1969.

Matus Romero, Carlos. *Ensayos sobre Finanzas Públicas*. Santiago: Fernández-Roig, n.d.

Mercado Villas, Olga (ed.). *La Marginalidad Urbana*. 2 vols. Santiago: Centro para el Desarrollo Económico y Social de América Latina (DESAL), 1968–1969.

Merrill, Robert N. *Towards a Structural Housing Policy: An Analysis of Chile's Low-Income Housing Program*. Ithaca, N.Y.: Latin American Studies Program Dissertation Series, Cornell University, 1971. (M)

Meyer, Richard. *Debt Repayment Capacity of the Chilean Agrarian Reform Beneficiaries*. Ithaca, N.Y.: Latin American Studies Program Dissertation Series, Cornell University, 1970. (M)

Meyerson, Martin, and Edward C. Banfield. *Politics, Planning and the Public Interest*. Glencoe, Ill.: Free Press, 1955.

Molina S., Sergio. *El Proceso de Cambio en Chile*. Santiago: Universitaria, 1972.

Moore, Wilbert E. *Man, Time, and Society.* New York: Wiley, 1963.

Mott, Basil J. F. *Anatomy of a Coordinating Council: Implications for Planning.* Pittsburgh, Pa.: University of Pittsburgh, 1968.

Movimiento de la Izquierda Revolucionaria (M.I.R.). *La Hermido: La Cara Más Fea del Reformismo.* Santiago: Impresora Bío-Bío, 1972.

Neustadt, Richard E. *Presidential Power: The Politics of Leadership.* New York: Wiley, 1960.

Nevick, David (ed.). *Program Budgeting.* Cambridge, Mass.: Harvard University, 1965.

O'Donnell, Guillermo A. *Modernization and Bureaucratic-Authoritarianism.* Berkeley, Calif.: Institute of International Studies, University of California, 1973. (M)

Onafre Jarpa, Sergio, *Creo en Chile.* Santiago: Sociedad Impresora de Chile, 1973.

Orrego V., Claudio. *Empezar de Nuevo: Chile, después de la Unidad Popular.* Santiago: Pacífico, 1972.

Oszlak, Oscar. *Diagnóstico de la Administración Pública Uruguaya.* Montevideo: United Nations Development Program, July 1972. (M)

Perrow, Charles. *Organizational Analysis: A Sociological View.* London: Tavistock, 1970.

Petras, James. *Chilean Christian Democracy: Politics and Social Forces.* Berkeley, Calif.: Institute of International Studies, University of California, 1967. (M)

———. *Politics and Social Forces in Chilean Development.* Berkeley and Los Angeles: University of California, 1969.

———. *Politics and Social Structure in Latin America.* New York: Monthly Review, 1970.

Picón Cádiz, Manuel. *Habitaciones Obreras.* Santiago: Virginia, 1935.

Ponce Cumplida, Jaime. *La Desconcentración Administrativa.* Santiago: Jurídica, 1965.

Puga Borne, Federico, *La Administración Sanitaria en Chile.* Santiago: Cervantes, 1895.

Pye, Lucian W. *Politics, Personality, and Nation-building: Burma's Search for Identity.* New Haven: Yale University, 1962.

Rabinovitz, Francine F., and Felicity M. Trueblood (eds.). *Latin American Urban Research, Vol. I.* Beverly Hills, Calif.: Sage, 1970.

Ramos R., José. *Política de Remuneraciones en Inflaciones Persistentes: El Caso de Chile.* Santiago: Instituto de Economía y Planificación, Universidad de Chile, 1970. (M)

Ranney, Austin (ed.). *Political Science and Public Policy.* Chicago: Markham, 1968.

Ray, Talton. *The Politics of the Barrios of Venezuela.* Berkeley and Los Angeles: University of California, 1969.

Reyes Román, Gustavo. *Ministerio de Obras Públicas y Transporte.* 4 vols. Santiago: Instituto de Ciencias Jurídicas y Sociales, 1968. (M)

———, and Adriana Kohán F. *Política Habitacional y el Ministerio de la*

Vivienda y Urbanismo. Santiago: Instituto de Ciencias Políticas y Administrativas, 1967. (M)

Riggs, Fred. *Administration in Developing Countries: The Theory of Prismatic Society.* Boston: Houghton Mifflin, 1964.

Rodríguez G., Silvia, *Análisis del Financiamiento del MINVU.* Universidad de Chile, 1968. (T)

Rosemblüth, Guillermo. *Problemas Socio-Económico de la Marginalidad y la Integración Urbana.* Santiago: Universidad de Chile, 1963. (M)

Rourke, Francis E. *Politics, Bureaucracy, and Public Policy.* Boston: Little, Brown, 1969.

Rubat Rivera, Santiago. *Auto-Construcción de Alcantarillado en la Comuna de Barrancas.* Universidad Católica de Chile, 1957. (T)

Sáez S., Raúl. *Casas para Chile: Plan Frei.* Santiago: Pacífico, 1959.

Salce Molina, Hernán. *Estudio Comparativo de Costos en Viviendas Económicas.* Universidad Católica de Chile, 1969. (T)

Santa Cruz López, Manuel. *Pavimento de Carreteras y su Influencia en el Desarrollo Económico del País.* Universidad Católica de Chile, 1961. (T)

Santibáñez Muñoz, Luís. *Evaluación de la Inversión de los Excedentes de la Seguridad Social en Chile.* Santiago: INSORA, 1966. (M)

Schlesinger, Arthur M., Jr. *The Coming of the New Deal.* Boston: Houghton Mifflin, 1958.

Schmitter, Philippe C. *Interest Conflict and Political Change in Brazil.* Palo Alto, Calif.: Stanford University, 1971.

Seidman, Harold. *Politics, Position, and Power: The Dynamics of Federal Organization.* New York: Oxford, 1970.

Selznick, Philip. *TVA and the Grass Roots.* Berkeley and Los Angeles: University of California, 1949.

Shani, Moshe. *Administrative Considerations in a Planning-Programming-Budgeting System: The Case of the New York State Education Department.* Cornell University, 1970. (T)

Sharkansky, Ira. *The Politics of Taxes and Spending.* Indianapolis: Bobbs-Merrill, 1969.

Sierra, Enrique, Sergio Benavente C., and Juan Osorio B. *Tres Ensayos de Estabilización en Chile: Las Políticas Aplicadas en el Decenio 1956–1966.* Santiago: Universitaria, 1969.

Silvert, Kalman H. *Chile: Yesterday and Today.* New York: Holt, Rinehart and Winston, 1965.

Simon, Herbert A. *Administrative Behavior.* New York: Free Press, 1957.

Sinclair Ureta, Carlos. *Erradicaciones de Poblaciones Marginales.* Universidad Católica de Chile, 1967. (T)

Sinding, Steven W. *Political Participation, Public Expenditures, and Economic Growth in Chile.* University of North Carolina, 1970. (T)

Smithies, Arthur. *The Budgetary Process in the United States.* New York: McGraw-Hill, 1955.

Szulc, Tad. *The Winds of Revolution.* New York: Praeger, 1965.

Tagle Rodríguez, Enrique. *El Alcantarillado de las Casas, Instalaciones Sanitarias, Desagües, Agua Potable en los Edificios Privados y Colectivos.* Santiago: Universo, 1908.

Tapia Moore, Astolfo. *Legislación Urbanista de Chile, 1818–1959.* Universidad de Chile, 1961. (T)

Tapia-Videla, Jorge Iván. *Bureaucratic Power in a Developing Country: The Case of the Chilean Social Security Administration.* University of Texas, 1969. (T)

————, and Charles J. Parrish. *Clases Sociales y la Política de Seguridad Social en Chile.* Santiago: INSORA, 1970. (M)

Teitelboim, Volodia. *El Oficio Ciudadano.* Santiago: Nascimento, 1973.

Thompson, James D. *Organizations in Action: Social Science Bases of Administrative Theory.* New York: McGraw-Hill, 1967.

Tullock, Gordon. *The Politics of Bureaucracy.* Washington: Public Affairs, 1965.

Universidad Católica de Valparaíso, Escuela de Derecho. *Descentralización Administrativa y Desarrollo Regional.* Valparaíso: Instituto de Ciencias Sociales y Desarrollo, 1970. (M)

Universidad de Chile. *El Proceso de Toma de Decisiones en el Ministerio de la Vivienda y Urbanismo.* Santiago: INSORA, 1969. (M)

————. *El Proceso Presupuestario Fiscal Chileno.* Santiago: Instituto de Economía, 1958. (M)

Urzúa Valenzuela, Germán. *Prensa y Administración Pública Chilena.* Santiago: Instituto de Ciencias Políticas y Administrativas, 1968. (M)

————. *Evolución de la Administración Pública Chilena, 1818–1968.* Santiago: Jurídica, 1970.

————, and Ana María García Barzelarro. *Diagnóstico de la Burocracia Chilena, 1818–1969.* Santiago: Jurídica, 1971.

Valdivia Germain, Carlos. *El 5% CORVI.* Santiago: Jurídica, 1969.

Valenzuela, Arturo A. *Clientelistic Politics in Chile: An Analysis of Center-Local Linkages.* Columbia University, 1971. (T)

Valle, Ramón del. *Ingeniería Sanitaria: Agua Potable.* Santiago: Universitaria, 1959.

Violich, Francis. *Urban Planning in Latin America,* Department of City Planning, University of California, 1973 (M).

Waldo, Dwight (ed.). *Temporal Dimensions of Development Administration.* Durham, N.C.: Duke University, 1970.

Weidner, Edward W. (ed.). *Development Administration in Asia.* Durham, N.C.: Duke University, 1970.

Whyte, William F. *Organizational Behavior: Theory and Application.* Homewood, Ill.: Irwin and Dorsey, 1969.

Wildavsky, Aaron. *The Politics of the Budgetary Process.* Boston: Little, Brown, 1964.

Wilkie, James W. *The Mexican Revolution: Federal Expenditures and Social Change since 1910.* Berkeley and Los Angeles: University of California, 1967.

Wittfogel, Karl. *Oriental Despotism: A Comparative Study in Total Power.*
New Haven: Yale University, 1957.
Wynia, Gary W. *Politics and Planners: Economic Development Policy in
Central America.* Madison: University of Wisconsin, 1972. (T)
Zald, Mayer N. (ed.). *Power in Organizations.* Nashville, Tenn.: Vanderbilt
University, 1970.
Zegers Baeza, Luís. *El Presupuesto y su Legislación.* Santiago: Cervantes,
1918.
Zunini Zunini, Hugo. *Características del Sector Público Chileno.* Santiago:
INSORA, 1969. (M)

ARTICLES

Acharán Blau, Sonia. "Aguas Servidas del Gran Santiago: Problema de Geo-
grafía Médica," *Informaciones Geográficas* (Chile), 18:19 (1968–
1969), 143–157.
Achurra Larraín, Manuel. "La Experiencia de Planificación Regional en
Chile." ECLA (Economic Commission for Latin America), 1969,
mimeo.
Ahumada C., Jorge, et al. "Jornadas sobre Estabilidad Económica," *Em-
presa* (Chile), 10:50 (December 1964), 3–70.
Arbildúa, Beatríz, and Rolf Lüders. "Una Evaluación Comparada de Tres
Programas Anti-Inflacionarios en Chile, 1955–1966," *Cuadernos de
Economía* (Chile), 5:14 (April 1968), 25–105.
Armstrong, W. P., and T. G. McGee. "Revolutionary Change and the Third
World City: A Theory of Urban Involution," *Civilisations,* 18 (1968),
353–376.
Assael C., Héctor. "Planificación del Sector Público," *Economía* (Chile),
24:90 (1966), 26–46.
Ayres, Robert L. "Electoral Constraints and 'the Chilean Way' to Socialism,"
Studies in Comparative International Development, 8:2 (Summer
1973), 128–161.
Balán, Jorge. "Migrant-Native Socioeconomic Differences in Latin American
Cities: A Structural Analysis," *Latin American Research Review,* 4:1
(Spring 1969), 3–29.
Biller, Robert. "Adaption Capacity and Organizational Development," in
Frank Marini (ed.), *Toward a New Public Administration: The Min-
nowbrook Perspective* (Scranton, Pa.: Chandler, 1971), 93–121.
Browne, Enrique. "A propósito de un Dilema: Arquitectos y Planificadores,"
Revista Latinoamericana de Estudios Regionales (EURE), 1:2 (June
1971), 33–54.
———, and Guillermo Geisse. "¿Planificación para los Planificadores o para
el Cambio Social?" *EURE,* 1:3 (October 1971), 11–26.
Burke, T. Robert. "Law and Development: The Chilean Housing Program,
Part 1," *Lawyer of the Americas* (June 1970), 173–199.
Castells, Manuel, and Franz Vanderschueren. "Reivindicaciones Urbanas,

Estrategia Política, y Movimiento Social en los Campamentos de Pobladores de Santiago." CIDU, 1971, mimeo.

Cauas Lama, Jorge. "Stabilization Policy: The Chilean Case," *Journal of Political Economy*, 78:4 (July–August 1970), 815–825.

———. "Política Económica a Corto Plazo," in Banco Central, *Estudios Monetarios II* (Santiago: Pacífico, 1970), 9–24.

Cheetham, Rosemond. "El Sector Privado de la Construcción: Patrón de la Dominación," *EURE*, 1:3 (October 1971), 125–148.

Cisternas Pinto, Jaime. "Antecedentes sobre el Sector de la Construcción de Viviendas: Dinámica de la Concentración," Servicio de Cooperación Técnica, ODEPLAN, 1970, mimeo.

Coleman, James S. "Policy Research." Talk to the American Association for the Advancement of Science, Washington, D.C., January 1973.

Cornelius, Wayne A., Jr. "The Political Sociology of Cityward Migration in Latin America: Toward Empirical Theory," in Francine F. Rabinovitz and Felicity M. Trueblood (eds.), *Latin American Urban Research, Vol. I* (Beverly Hills, Calif.: Sage 1970), 95–147.

———. "Urbanization as an Agent in Latin American Political Instability: The Case of Mexico," *American Political Science Review*, 63:3 (September 1969), 833–857.

Cuellar, Oscar, et al. "Experiencias de Justicia Popular en Poblaciones," *Cuadernos de la Realidad Nacional* (Chile), 8 (June 1971), 153–172.

Davis, Otto A., M. A. H. Dempster, and Aaron Wildavsky. "A Theory of the Budgetary Process," *American Political Science Review*, 60:3 (September 1966), 529–547.

Davis, Otto A., and George H. Haines, Jr. "A Political Approach to a Theory of Public Expenditures: The Case of Municipalities," *National Tax Journal*, 19:3 (September 1966), 259–275.

Delgado, Carlos. "Three Proposals Regarding Accelerated Urbanization Problems in Metropolitan Areas: The Lima Case," *American Behavioral Scientist*, 12:2 (May–June 1969), 34–45.

Dinovitzer de Solar, Diva. "Operación Sitio: Una Estrategia Habitacional," October 1972, unpublished paper.

Dupré, J. Stefan, and W. Eric Gustafson. "Contracting for Defense: Private Firms and the Public Interest," *Political Science Quarterly*, 77:2 (June 1962), 161–177

Duque, Joaquin, and Ernesto Pastrana. "La Mobilización Reinvindicativa Urbana de los Sectores Populares en Chile, 1964–1972," *Revista Latinoamericana de Ciencias Sociales*, 4 (December 1972), 259–293.

ECLA (Economic Commission for Latin America), Public Administration Unit. "Administrative Planning for Economic and Social Development in Latin America," in *Administrative Aspects of Planning: Papers of a Seminar* (New York: United Nations, 1969), 171–225.

Emery, F. E., and E. L. Trist. "The Causal Texture of Organizational Environment," *Human Relations*, 18:1 (November 1965), 21–32.

Equipo Poblacional del CIDU. "Campamentos de Santiago: Mobilización Urbana." CIDU, Documento de Trabajo No. 46, 1971, mimeo.

Fisher, Glen W. "Interstate Variations in State and Local Expenditures," *National Tax Journal,* 17:1 (March 1964), 57–74.

Friedmann, John. "The Role of Cities in National Development," *American Behavioral Scientist,* 12:5 (May–June 1969), 13–21.

——. "Urban-Regional Policies for National Development in Chile," in Francine F. Rabinovitz and Felicity M. Trueblood (eds.), *Latin American Urban Research, Vol. 1* (Beverly Hills, Calif.: Sage, 1971), 217–246.

George, Alexander L. "The Case for Multiple Advocacy in Making Foreign Policy," *American Political Science Review,* 66:3 (September 1972), 751–785.

Giutsi, Jorge. "La Formación de las 'Poblaciones' en Santiago: Aproximación al Problema de la Organización y Participación de los 'Pobladores,'" *Revista Latinoamericana de Ciencia Política,* 2:2 (August 1971), 370–383.

Goldrich, Daniel, Raymond B. Pratt, and C. R. Schuller. "The Political Integration of Lower-Class Urban Settlements in Chile and Peru," *Studies in Comparative International Development,* 3:1 (1967–1968), 1–22.

Groves, Roderick T. "Administrative Reform and the Politics of Reform: The Case of Venezuela," *Public Administration Review,* 27:5 (December 1967), 436–445.

Gunnell, John G. "Development, Social Change, and Time," in Dwight Waldo (ed.), *Temporal Dimensions of Development Administration* (Durham, N.C.: Duke University, 1970), 47–89.

Horowitz, Irving L. "Electoral Politics, Urbanization, and Social Development in Latin America," *Urban Affairs Quarterly,* 2:3 (March 1967), 3–37.

Ilchman, Warren F. "Comparative Wisdom and Conventional Administration: The Comparative Administration Group and Its Contributions," *Sage Professional Papers in Comparative Politics,* 01–020, 2 (1971).

Jones, G. N. "Strategies and Tactics of Planned Organizational Change," *Philippine Journal of Public Administration,* 10:4 (1966), 320–342.

Jowitt, Kenneth. "Comment: The Relevance of Comparative Public Administration," in Frank Marini (ed.), *Toward a New Public Administration: The Minnowbrook Perspective* (Scranton, Pa.: Chandler, 1971), 250–260.

Kleingartner, Archie. "Collective Bargaining Between Salaried Professionals and Public Sector Management," *Administrative Science Quarterly,* 33:2 (March–April 1973), 165–172.

Labadía C., Antonio. "*Operación Sitio:* A Housing Solution for Progressive Growth," in Guillermo Geisse and Jorge E. Hardoy (eds.), *Latin American Urban Research, Vol. II* (Beverly Hills, Calif.: Sage, 1972), 203–209.

Lambert, Denis. "L'urbanisation acélérée de l'Amérique Latine et la Formation d'un Secteur Tertiaire Réfuge," *Civilisations*, 15:2,3,4 (1965), 158–174, 309–325, 477–492.

Lindblom, Charles E. "Economics and the Administration of National Planning," *Public Administration Review*, 25:3 (June 1965), 274–283.

————. "The Science of Muddling Through," *Public Administration Review*, 19 (Spring 1959), 114–120.

Lipsky, Michael. "Protest as a Political Resource," *American Political Science Review*, 62:4 (December 1968), 1144–1158.

Mangin, William P. "Latin American Squatter Settlements: A Problem and a Solution," *Latin American Research Review*, 2:3 (Summer 1967), 65–98.

Mechanic, David. "The Power to Resist Change among Low-Ranking Personnel," *Personnel Administration*, 26:4 (July–August 1963), 5–12.

Menges, Constantine C. "Public Policy and Organized Business in Chile: A Preliminary Analysis," *Journal of International Affairs*, 20:2 (1966), 343–365.

Mohr, Lawrence B. "The Concept of Organizational Goal," *American Political Science Review*, 67:2 (June 1973), 470–481.

Muller, Edward N. "A Test of a Partial Theory of Potential Violence," *American Political Science Review*, 66:3 (September 1972), 928–959.

Munizaga Vigeil, Gustavo, and Clinton Bowdon. "Sector Manuel Rodríguez: Estudio de un Sector Habitacional Popular en Santiago," *Cuadernos de Desarrollo Urbano* (Chile), 13 (August 1970), 2–56.

Nascimento, Kleber. "Reflections on Strategy of Administrative Reform: The Federal Experience of Brazil." ECLA Meeting of Experts on Administrative Capability for Development, Nov. 16–21, 1970, Santiago, Chile.

Neustadt, Richard E. "Approaches to Staffing the Presidency: Notes on FDR and JFK," *American Political Science Review*, 57:4 (December 1963), 855–863.

Parrish, Charles J. "Bureaucracy, Democracy, and Development: Some Considerations Based on the Chilean Case," *LADAC Occasional Papers* (Latin American Development Administration Committee, University of Texas), 2:1 (April 1970).

Perrow, Charles. "The Analysis of Goals in Complex Organizations," *American Sociological Review*, 26 (December 1961), 854–866.

Pfeffer, Jeffrey. "Size and Composition of Corporate Boards of Directors: The Organization and Its Environment," *Administrative Science Quarterly*, 17:2 (June 1972), 218–228.

Pinto Quesada, César. "Le Phénomène d'immigration dans l'agglomeration de Santiago du Chili," *Civilisations*, 18:3 (1967), 215–223.

Portes, Alejandro. "The Urban Slum in Chile: Types and Correlates," *Land Economics*, 47:3 (August 1971), 234–248.

Pumarino, Gabriel. "La Política de Vivienda como Instrumento de Desarrollo Urbano." CIDU, Documento de Trabajo No. 29, October 1970, mimeo.

Santos, Milton. "Le Rôle Moteur du Tertiaire Primitif dans les Villes du Tiers Monde," *Civilisations,* 18:2 (1968), 186–203.

Shoultz, Lars. "Urbanization and Political Change in Latin America," *Midwest Journal of Political Science* (August 1972), 367–387.

Simon, Herbert A. "On the Concept of Organizational Goal," *Administrative Science Quarterly,* 9 (June 1964), 1–22.

Snow, Peter G. "The Political Party Spectrum in Chile," in Robert D. Tomasek (ed.), *Latin American Politics* (Garden City, N.Y.: Doubleday, 1966), 399–412.

Stokes, Charles J. "A Theory of Slums," *Land Economics,* 37:3 (August 1962), 187–197.

Sunkel, Osvaldo. "Cambios Estructurales, Estrategias de Desarrollo y Planificación en Chile, 1938–1969," *Cuadernos de la Realidad Nacional* (Chile), 4 (June 1970), 31–49.

Tagle Yrarrázaval, Fernando. "Modernización en la Construcción, Un Estudio de Caso: Empresa Constructora de Vivienda," Servicio de Cooperación Técnica, ODEPLAN, 1970, mimeo.

Trist, Eric L. "Key Aspects of Environmental Relations," in *Administrative Capabilities for Development* (New York: United Nations, 1969).

Turner, John. "Uncontrolled Urban Settlement: Problems and Policies," *International Social Development Review,* 1 (1968), 107–130.

Vanderschueren, Franz. "Significado Político de las Juntas de Vecinos en Poblaciones de Santiago," *EURE,* 1:2 (June 1971), 67–90.

Warriner, Charles K. "The Problem of Organizational Purpose," *Sociological Quarterly,* 6 (Spring 1965), 139–146.

Weaver, Jerry L. "Bureaucracy during a Period of Social Change: The Guatemalan Case," *LADAC Occasional Papers* (Latin American Development Administration Committee, University of Texas), 2:2 (1971).

Wildavsky, Aaron, and Arthur Hammond. "Comprehensive versus Incremental Budgeting in the Department of Agriculture," *Administrative Science Quarterly,* 10:3 (December 1965), 321–346.

Wilson, James Q. "The Bureaucratic Problem," in Alan A. Altshuler (ed.), *The Politics of the Federal Bureaucracy* (New York: Dodd Mead, 1968), 26–32.

Zald, Mayer N., and Gary L. Wamsley. "The Political Economy of Public Organization," *Public Administration Review,* 33:1 (January–February 1973), 62–73.

DOCUMENTS

Allende Gossens, Salvador. "Incidentes Ocurridos en Puerto Montt: Respuesta a Discurso del Señor Ministro del Interior," *Diarios de Sesiones del Senado,* Legislatura Extraordinaria, 39a, March 20, 1969, apartado, 1–34.

Astica, Juan B. "La Dirección de Desarrollo Urbano y la Planificación Metropolitana." MINVU, 1966, mimeo.

Biblioteca del Congreso Nacional, Fichero de Artículos de Diarios. "Hechos de Sangre."

Cabello, Octavio. *Informe sobre Misión de Asistencia Técnica al Ministerio de la Vivienda y Urbanismo de Chile.* Santiago: MINVU, 1969.

Caja Central de Ahorros y Préstamos (CCAP). *Asociaciones de Ahorros y Préstamos: Disposiciones Legales que Rigen su Existencia y Funcionamiento.* Santiago: Jurídica, 1961.

Cámara Chilena de la Construcción (CCC). *Análisis de la Infraestructura del País.* 2 vols. Santiago: Pacífico, 1968.

————. "Informe Final: Conclusiones y Acuerdos de la 56a Reunión del Consejo Nacional de la Cámara Chilena de la Construcción." March 22–23, 1973.

————. "Plan Habitacional: Proyecto Entregado por la Cámara Chilena de la Construcción al Presidente Electo antes de su Asunción al Mando." *Revista de la Construcción,* 3:30 (November 1964), 33–69.

Carabineros de Chile, "Ocupaciones Ilegales de Predios Urbanos e Inmeubles Occuridas entre el 1/I/68 y el 15/VI/71." Report to the Chilean Senate, June 15, 1971, mimeo.

Casanueva del Canto, Ruperto. *Problema de las Aguas Servidas de la Ciudad de Santiago.* Santiago: Servicio Nacional de Salubridad, 1946.

Centro para el Desarrollo Económico y Social de América Latina. *Antecedentes y Criterios para una Reforma del Gobierno Municipal.* Santiago: DESAL, 1967.

Contraloría General de la República. *Memoria de la Contraloría General y Balance General de la Hacienda Pública.* Santiago: Sub-departamento de Coordinación e Información Jurídica, 1962–1973.

Corporación de la Reforma Agraria (CORA). *Balance Presupuestario del Año 1969.* Santiago: Departamento de Presupuesto y Control, 1970.

Corporación de la Vivienda (CORVI). *Operación Sitio.* Santiago: Oficina de Relaciónes Públicas, 1966.

Corporación de Servicios Habitacionales (CORHABIT). *Operación 20,000/70.* Santiago: Centro Chileno de Productividad en la Construcción, 1971.

Franz, John. *Organization for Housing Programs in Chile.* Santiago: CORVI, 1959.

Instituto de Ingenieros de Chile. *Estatutos.* Decreto 2926, Ministerio de Justicia, July 13, 1961.

Joint Economic Committee. *The Planning-Programming-Budgeting System: Progress and Potentials.* Hearings before the Subcommittee on Economy in Government, 90th Congress, First Session. Washington: U.S. Government Printing Office, 1967.

Manteola, José (ed.). *Guía de la Administración Pública de Chile y de los Principales Organismos del Sector Privado.* Santiago: Guía, 1968.

Ministerio de Defensa Nacional. *Reglamento de Inversión de Fondos Fiscales e Internos*. Santiago: Instituto Geográfico Militar, 1971.

Ministerio de Hacienda. *Balance Consolidado del Sector Público de Chile, 1964–1967*. Santiago: Dirección de Presupuestos, 1968.

———. *Bases Metodológicas de la Reforma Presupuestaria*. Santiago: Dirección de Presupuestos, 1968.

———. "Descripción de las Funciones de los Departamentos y Divisiones de la Subdirección de Presupuestos." Santiago: Dirección de Presupuestos, 1970, mimeo.

———. *Exposición sobre el Estado de la Hacienda Pública*. Santiago: Dirección de Presupuestos, 1961–1972.

———. *Ley de Presupuesto de la Nación*. Santiago: Dirección de Presupuestos, 1960–1973.

———. *Ley Orgánica de Presupuestos*. Diario Oficial, No. 47 (Dec. 4, 1959).

———. *Manual de Organización del Gobierno de Chile*. Santiago: Gutenberg, 1960.

———. *Manual Descriptivo de las Cuentas Extrapresupuestarias*. Santiago: Dirección de Presupuestos, 1967.

———. *Manual para la Ejecución de los Presupuestos en los Servicios de la Administración Pública Centralizada*. Santiago: Dirección de Presupuestos, 1970.

———. *Plan Operativo Fiscal para el Año 1971*. Santiago: Dirección de Presupuestos, 1971.

———. "Proyecto de Reorganización de la Dirección de Presupuestos, Descripción de las Funciones de los Departamentos y Divisiones de la Subdirección de Presupuestos." Santiago: Dirección de Presupuestos, 1970, mimeo.

Ministerio de Obras Públicas. *Memoria*. Santiago: Departamento de Estadísticas y Control, 1963–1971.

———. *Plan Decenal de Agua Potable y Alcantarillado, 1961–1970*. Santiago: Dirección de Obras Sanitarias, 1962.

Ministerio de la Vivienda y Urbanismo (MINVU). *El Ministerio de la Vivienda y Urbanismo: Instrumento de la Política Habitacional*. Santiago: Secretaría Técnica y de Coordinación, 1967.

———. *Estadística de la Edificación No-Habitacional, 1965–1967*. Santiago: Departamento de Publicaciones y Documentación, 1969.

———. *Estadística Habitacional, 1960–1967, Nivel Comunal*. Santiago: Departamento de Publicidad y Documentos, 1968.

———. "Plan de Vivienda Popular." Santiago: CORHABIT, September, 1967, mimeo.

———. *Política Habitacional del Gobierno Popular: Programa 72*. Santiago: Universitaria, 1972.

———. *Viviendas Iniciadas por el Sector Pública entre los Años 1960–1968*. Santiago: Departamento de Publicaciones y Documentación, 1970.

Ministerio del Interior. *II Censo Vivienda*. Santiago: Dirección de Estadísticas y Censos, 1960.

———. *XIV Censo Nacional de Población y III de Vivienda, Gran Santiago*. Santiago: Instituto de Estadísticas, 1971.

Movimiento de la Izquierda Revolucionaria. *El M.I.R.* Santiago: Manuel Rodríguez, 1972.

Obras Civiles, Sección Sanitaria. *La Ingeniería Sanitaria en el País y su Enseñanza*. Santiago: Universidad de Chile, 1968.

Oficina de Planificación Nacional (ODEPLAN). *Evolución de Gran Santiago hasta 1970*. Santiago: Departamento de Planificación Regional, 1970.

Organization of American States. Consejo Interamericano Económico y Social. *El Esfuerzo Interno y las Necesidades de Financiamiento Externo para el Desarrollo de Chile*. Washington, D.C.: Pan-American Union, 1966.

Partido Demócrata Cristiano, Departamento Técnico Nacional, Consejo Ejecutivo. "Acuerdo del Departamento Técnico Nacional del Partido Demócrata Cristiano en relación con la creación del MINVU." July 29, 1965, mimeo.

———. "Memorandum sobre el Artículo 5 del Proyecto de Ley sobre el Ministerio de la Vivienda y Urbanismo." September 22, 1965, mimeo.

———. "Antecedentes sobre la Creación del MINVU." N.d. (approximately October 1, 1965), mimeo.

Pavez B., Darío. "Alcances sobre el Desarrollo de las Técnicas Presupuestarias." Santiago: Dirección de Presupuestos, 1970, mimeo.

Presidencia de la República. *Mensaje Presidencial sobre el Estado Político, Económico, Admistrativo, y Financiero de la Nación*. Santiago: Oficina de Información y Difusión, 1969.

Santa Ana, Gustavo G. "El Sistema Mecanizado para el Control de la Ejecución del Presupuesto por Programas del Sector Fiscal." Santiago: Dirección de Presupuestos, 1970, mimeo.

Segunda Convención de las Provincias de Chile. *En Marcha hacia la Decentralización*. Valparaiso: Universo, 1948.

Senado. *Boletín No. 21,776*. August 30, 1965.

———. "Estudio Sobre los Presupuestos de Gastos de la Nación desde 1950 a 1971." *Boletín de Información Económica*. No. 204. Santiago: Oficina de Informaciones del Senado, 10-12-1970.

Servicio de Cooperación Técnica, ODEPLAN. *El Mercado de la Vivienda en Chile*. Santiago: Caja Central de Ahorros y Préstamos, 1970.

United Nations. *A Manual for Program and Performance Budgeting*. New York: Department for Economic and Social Affairs, 1965.

———. *La Participación de las Poblaciones Marginales en el Crecimiento Urbano*. Santiago: Consejo Económico y Social, 1965.

INDEX

SAM N/M54MM
00
Cleaves